CHILDREN OF ABRAHAM

ALSO BY MARC DAVID BAER

The Ottomans: Khans, Caesars and Caliphs

CHILDREN OF ABRAHAM

THE STORY OF JEWISH–MUSLIM RELATIONS

MARC DAVID BAER

Profile Books

First published in Great Britain in 2026 by
Profile Books Ltd
29 Cloth Fair
London
EC1A 7JQ
www.profilebooks.com

Copyright © Marc David Baer, 2026

1 3 5 7 9 10 8 6 4 2

Typeset in Garamond by MacGuru Ltd
Printed and bound in Great Britain by
CPI Group (UK) Ltd, Croydon CR0 4YY

The moral right of the author has been asserted.

All rights reserved. Without limiting the rights under copyright reserved above, no part of this publication may be reproduced, stored or introduced into a retrieval system, or transmitted, in any form or by any means (electronic, mechanical, photocopying, recording or otherwise), without the prior written permission of both the copyright owner and the publisher of this book.

Profile Books takes seriously the responsibility of defending our authors' copyright. No part of this book may be used or reproduced in any manner for the purpose of training artificial intelligence technologies or systems (including but not limited to machine learning models and large language models (LLMs)). In accordance with Article 4(3) of the DSM Directive 2019/790, Profile Books expressly reserves this work from the text and data mining exception.

A CIP catalogue record for this book is available from the British Library.

Our product safety representative in the EU is BGC Sustainability & Compliance, 7 avenue du Général Leclerc, Paris, 75014, France https://baldwinglobalconsulting.com

ISBN 978 1 80522 361 0
eISBN 978 1 80522 363 4

To Ayşe, Azize, and Firuze

CONTENTS

Introduction: Interfaith Utopias or Antagonistic Histories? 1

Part I: Pre-Modern Times
1. Judeo-Islamic Religious Symbiosis and Pacts of Alliance and Protection, Seventh–Thirteenth centuries 15
2. The Secular Symbiosis and Jews Ruling over Muslims: The Turkish Jewish Khazar Kingdom, Eighth–Tenth Centuries 46
3. Jewish–Muslim Symbiosis and Alliance: Al-Andalus, Eighth–Seventeenth Centuries 74
4. Muslim Saviours: Jews and Muslims in the Ottoman Empire and Morocco, Fifteenth–Nineteenth Centuries 112

Part II: Modern Times
5. Severed Symbiosis and New Saviours: Colonialism and New Alliances in the Long Nineteenth Century, 1789–1914 157
6. Enemies and Allies, Persecutors and Protectors: Jews, Muslims, and Nazism in Europe and the Middle East, 1933–45 193
7. Transforming Jewish–Muslim Relations: Jewish Nationalism and the Establishment of Israel 249

8. The Arab Jew in the Middle East and Europe after 1948	302
9. Duelling Myths, Divided Histories, and Promoting Symbiosis Today	350
Conclusion: Abraham's Inheritance: Ishmael and Isaac, Hagar and Sarah Today	377
Notes	384
Index	454
Picture Credits	487
Acknowledgements	488

INTRODUCTION

INTERFAITH UTOPIAS OR ANTAGONISTIC HISTORIES?

For the past ten years I have taught a seminar at the London School of Economics and Political Science entitled 'Muslim–Jewish Relations: History and Memory in the Middle East and Europe'. Many of the students are young Jewish or Muslim men and women from London, who grew up amongst the other group and have a desire to learn more about them. The week the topic is 'Judeo-Muslim Religious Symbiosis' I pass out two dozen notecards with handwritten phrases on them at the start of class. I divide the students into groups of two. Their assignment is to show the card to the class and tell us whether the phrase on the card refers to Judaism or Islam. As many times as not, the answer is both:

> Holy Script written right to left (both).
> Fast until you can distinguish between a dark and a light thread (both).
> Pray towards Jerusalem (Islam at first; Judaism).
> Jerusalem is a holy city (both).
> God is One (both).
> Graven images are forbidden (both).
> Dietary restrictions: no pork! (both).
> Prostration as form of prayer (both: one day a year in Judaism; Islam).

Children of Abraham

There is no god except God (both, Islamic formulation).
The Lord is our God, the Lord is one (both, Jewish formulation).
Moses is a prophet (both; for Judaism he is the greatest prophet).
Any man sound of mind can lead public prayers (both).
You must pray with intention (both).
Daily prayer (both – three times in Judaism, five times in Sunni Islam).
Purification before prayer (both).
Ritual purity with water (both).
Circumcise your sons (both).
God cannot beget nor can God be begotten (both, Islamic formulation).
Pharaohs are the symbol for evil tyrants (both).
Fasting (both; sundown to sundown in Judaism, sunup to sundown in Islam).
The Way or Path is a body of law to guide daily life (both).
Abraham is the first believer (both).
Celebrate Abraham's sacrifice or re-enact it each year by sacrificing animals (Islam).
Abraham is our father, we are the children of Abraham (both – through Sarah and Isaac in Judaism, through Hagar and Ishmael in Islam).

How many know about such similarity, the intimate rivalry and cooperation? With this knowledge, is it right to depict these relations in a negative way? Is the last century of conflict between Israelis and Palestinians representative of the past?

This book tells the true story of the relationship of Jews and Muslims from the seventh century to the twenty-first century.

Interfaith Utopias or Antagonistic Histories?

It covers 1,415 years from around 610, when Muslims say that Muhammad started to preach, to today, in the Middle East and in Europe, focusing mainly on those lands located around the Mediterranean. The book tells this history of their relations within the context of power relations. There are four moments across this history when Jews are either more powerful than Muslims or hold power over Muslims. For the rest of this history, Muslims hold power over Jews. At times, Christians, who also claim to be the Children of Abraham, yet only in a spiritual sense, hold power over both, favouring one group or the other, usually the Jews.[1] Whenever Christians enter the scene, relations between Jews and Muslims worsen.

The reader should not have the impression that Jews and Muslims (and Christians) are homogeneous groups, for there is a wide-ranging diversity within each. The poor and the wealthy, women and men have had different interests and different experiences living with people from other groups. Often the only voices captured in the historical record are those of the male elite. Yet there is no question that the Jews and Muslims whose stories I tell in this book would have described themselves as Jews or Muslims and would have been considered so and treated as such by the other group. These were not only religious categories, but ethno-religious and legal categories as well, determining what laws they lived by, whom they could marry or have sexual relations with, what professions they could practise, their social status, the taxes they paid, the foods they ate, and the clothes they wore.[2] Yet at the same time, often the only thing distinguishing people was religion, as they shared language and most aspects of culture. I do not presume that all these people were religious, especially as I tell the story of Jewish and Muslim nationalists, secularists, or communists, but Jews and Muslims were almost always closer and had better relations with each other than with Christians until modern times.

Readers may find it disconcerting that the Christian–Jewish or Christian–Muslim relationship does not take centre stage, or that European Christians are not at the centre of this story. They may not like that unchristian people, such as French colonialists or Nazis, are referred to as Christians. Yet they are the offspring of the earlier European Christian culture carrying its views of Jews and Muslims that produced the Reconquista and the Crusades, historical events that pushed Jews and Muslims further into each other's arms against a common enemy. Jews and Muslims, whether in pre-modern or modern times, whether religious or secular, had and have deep and enduring bonds.

Over the centuries we see the same themes repeating, all of which arise in the context of the power relations between Jews and Muslims: the Jew as ally of the Muslim; the Muslim as the saviour of the Jew; Jewish–Muslim religious and secular symbiosis; the rise of elite Jews to positions of wealth and influence, and their subsequent fall as Muslims perceive a violation of the dhimma pact (pact of protection); the triangular relation with Christians which worsens Jewish–Muslim relations; and the political use of myth and counter-myth obscuring that history. Telling the history of Jewish–Muslim relations through these themes is a way of arguing against two dominant myths: that the history of the Jewish–Muslim relationship is one of interfaith utopia, or that it is one of Jewish–Muslim enmity or antagonistic rivalries of violence and persecution by the powerful group.

The myth of golden ages and interfaith utopias is the story of Jewish–Muslim harmony, where the two groups get on so well that it seems that nothing can get between them. This myth is drawing on an exaggeration of historical experience. Jews themselves, from very early on in their relation with Muslims, write about Muslims to other Jews, praising them for allowing them to be Jews, especially when Christians do not.

The second myth also has its moments in history. It is based upon the idea that Jews and Muslims are at loggerheads, that Jews and Muslims are committing violence against each other, that the Muslim or the Jewish ruler over the other group is persecuting them. It's also grounded in fact but exaggerated. This myth of perpetual, perennial enmity from time immemorial, from the very first contact, is a more recent story.

Both myths have especially been articulated since the creation of the Jewish state of Israel in 1948. Those who are opposed to the existence of a Jewish state of Israel argue that Jewish–Muslim relations were always harmonious, and that it was Zionism, Jewish nationalism, which ruined those relations.

Those who support Israel as a place of redemption for persecuted Jews – not just those persecuted by Christian Europe, culminating in the Holocaust during the Second World War, but also the Jews of Muslim-majority societies – have argued that Israel needed to come into being to save all Jews. Because according to this claim, Jews were always persecuted. That same protection pact, the dhimma pact, kept them humiliated and second-class citizens, and they needed Israel to which they could migrate and leave those lands. Israel, not the Muslim ruler, is the saviour of the Jews.

Part of the reason for the difficulty of comprehending the ebb and flow of Jewish–Muslim relations today is that neither Jew nor Muslim knows their history of interaction. When asked what relations between Jews and Muslims are like, most people respond with the myth of interfaith utopia. Before the modern age, it is claimed, Jews lived at peace in Muslim-ruled societies. They were allowed to live freely as Jews without fear of persecution, or forced conversion, because they were accepted and tolerated. Tolerated, they experienced golden ages, whether in Spain, Morocco, or the Ottoman Empire, as they could reach the heights of cultural, intellectual, and religious expression while even serving in government and as commanders of armies. Islamic tolerance is contrasted with Christian intolerance expressed in the horrors of massacres, expulsions, and forced conversion of Jews in the medieval period and pogroms and the Holocaust in modern Europe. Adherents of the interfaith utopia myth are proud that Islamic societies never produced the extremes of intolerance of Christian societies, such as Crusaders leading anti-Jewish pogroms, Inquisitors burning Jews at the stake, or Nazis gassing Jews in death camps.

They point out how the Jews persecuted in Spain and Portugal took refuge in Muslim-ruled Morocco and then the Ottoman Empire after their expulsions. For over 500 years, Jews in Muslim societies have been among the main proponents of this myth of peaceful coexistence. It begins when Jews praise the Ottoman sultan for allowing them refuge from their Catholic Spanish oppressors. It continues today, where in Turkey, Jews have been promoting '500 Years of Peace and Brotherhood' between Jews and Muslims since 1992, the anniversary of the 1492 expulsion from Spain and the arrival of Iberian Jewry, the Sephardim, in the Ottoman Empire.[3]

According to this myth, while Jews in Muslim-ruled societies 'on the whole enjoyed peace and relative freedom, the Jews of Christendom stood upon volcanic soil, "every moment threatening to swallow them up"'.[4] Whereas Western civilisation was at variance with Judaism, Islam 'is of the very flesh and bone of Judaism', which 'can draw freely and copiously from Muslim civilisation and, at the same time preserve its independence and integrity'.[5] The ancient Greeks and modern Germans compelled the Jews to assimilate to join their culture, but the Muslims did not force them to convert as baptism 'was the entrance ticket to European culture'.[6]

Since the emergence of the Israeli–Palestinian struggle in the twentieth century, the interfaith utopia idea has been used for other purposes, just as a second myth has been used for contemporary ends. Those who promote the Palestinian cause deploy the interfaith utopia myth to romanticise the past and criticise Zionism as spoiling once harmonious relations between Muslims and Jews.

In many of these accounts, tolerance – which in the pre-modern era simply means to bear, to put up with, to allow to live – is confused with coexistence, and even equality and egalitarianism, which existed nowhere. Today, we equate tolerance with pluralism, a live-and-let-live attitude in a free society where all are equal, and all views and religions are equally respected. What we overlook in romanticising pre-modern Jewish–Muslim relations is that no modern person would wish to return to a social and legal structure based on discrimination, hierarchy, differentiation, and subordination. In pre-modern Muslim-majority societies, there is tolerance of religious difference, as the dhimma, the pact of protection granted to Jews (and Christians, but even Hindus and Zoroastrians) was conditioned on the acceptance of legal and social restrictions in return for payment of a yearly poll tax, the jizya. As hard as it is for moderns to imagine, discrimination and hierarchy went together with tolerance. Islam was promoted as the superior religion and other accepted religions were considered false but were tolerated.

Those who support Israel, borrowing a page from Jewish historians who take an antagonistic approach to the history of relations between Jews and Christians, refer to another myth that claims that Jews in Muslim-majority societies were always persecuted and had to flee anti-Semitism, taking refuge in

Israel. They use the myth of a persistently grim past to justify the reason for the existence of a state for Jews. It portrays ceaseless Muslim persecution of Jews. Muslim Arabs are compared to Nazis. If Jews were always treated badly, then Israel serves as their redeemer.

In contrast, 'if life was as grim', as the antagonistic thesis would have us believe, a Sephardic Jewish American scholar asks, 'how was it possible for thousands of books to be written, for artisans to continue producing a wide array of beautiful objects, or for Jews to attain positions of wealth and power in every Arab country they lived in right up until the dissolution of those communities in the 1940s and 1950s?'[7]

Despite the different history of Jews in Muslim-majority and Christian-majority societies, the single Jewish experience is supposed to be universal victimisation and persecution. Since the Islamist terror attacks of 11 September 2001 in the US, additional voices, especially on the right, including the Zionist Christian right, promote the myth of a Judeo-Christian culture and depict Muslims as the perpetual persecutors and enemies of Jews. Where in pre-modern times Christians viewed Jews as the internal, spiritual enemy, and Muslims as the external, political enemy, and Jews as allies of the Muslims, since 1945 and the defeat of Nazism when the full extent of the Shoah became known, Europeans and North Americans promoted the concept of Judeo-Christian civilisation, as Christian theologians sought to atone for the sins of the Nazis and were ashamed of the 2,000 years of persecution to which they subjected Jews, culminating in the Holocaust. From the 1950s, Jews were offered inclusion in society like never before. But inclusion of some means exclusion of others. Further terrorist attacks by Muslims in the UK, France, and Germany has led in more recent years to right- and far-right politicians in North America and Europe attacking

Muslims as anti-Semites to legitimise criticism of immigrants and their society's tolerance, while supporting Israel.

Jews and Christians are seen as Western and Muslims as foreign, even where they have been living in Europe and North America for generations. Both anti-Semitism and Islamophobia scapegoat minorities from a constructed 'We'. Islamophobia is the 'strange, secret sharer of Western anti-Semitism' and 'the Islamic branch' of anti-Semitism.[8] Transferring 'popular anti-Semitic animus from a Jewish to an Arab target was made smoothly', because 'the figure was essentially the same'.[9] Yet the battle against anti-Semitism and Islamophobia differs. Whereas European states such as France and Germany are committed to commemorating the Holocaust and combatting anti-Semitism, and supporting the Jewish state of Israel, they simultaneously wage a war on terror, which mainly targets Muslims rather than the far right, while paying lip service to fighting against all forms of racism, including Islamophobia.[10] Following colonialism, where France and Britain favoured the Jews over Muslims, and following the Second World War, Jews and Muslims/Arabs have become uncoupled in the European mind: only the latter remain Semites and Orientals.[11] It is now the Judeo-Christian West (and Israel) versus the Islamic East (and Palestine).[12] Relations worsen when Muslims express anti-Semitism, and Jews Islamophobia.

As an American Jewish historian of medieval relations between Muslims and Jews notes, the visions of an interfaith utopia and a persecutory hell are 'two antithetical, biased' interpretations that distort history.[13] Whether Zionism is blamed for ruining relations, or it is claimed that relations between Muslims and Jews have always been dreadful since the rise of Islam in the seventh century, both sides agree that relations today are horrible, and see no way of improving them. That facts do not always correspond with political bias is overlooked.[14]

The influential British Jewish historian Bernard Lewis, whose classic book *The Jews of Islam* (1984) first sparked my interest in this topic when I was an undergraduate in the 1980s, supported neither the antagonistic myth of persecution, nor the utopian myth of perpetual interfaith harmony. He argued Muslims were not fanatical oppressors comparable to Nazis, nor were Muslim-majority societies interreligious utopias comparable, perhaps, to the USA.[15] He noted that 'there is nothing like Auschwitz in Islamic history', nor a Muslim Hitler.[16] The restrictions on Jews were 'more often disregarded than strictly enforced'.[17] Jews were subjected to measures that reminded them of their social and legal inferior status vis-à-vis Muslims. Persecution was rare and atypical. Jews 'were allowed to practice their religion, pursue their avocations, and live their own lives, so long as they were willing to abide by the rules'. It was only during the nineteenth and twentieth centuries, when the '*dhimmi* were no longer prepared to accept or respect the rules, that the most violent and bloody clashes have occurred'.[18]

It is a human trait to be complex. But what we see in so many accounts of Jewish and Muslim relations are cardboard cutouts of bloodthirsty Muslim persecutors and faceless mobs, or happy Jewish subjects who are so grateful they are allowed to pray in their synagogues they wish for nothing better, such as equal rights. The long, complex history of Jewish–Muslim relations cannot be explained by a single myth, historical character, or event; none can prove peaceful coexistence or serve as prooftext of persecution. Entire societies or civilisations cannot be deemed tolerant or intolerant based on a collection of positive or negative examples.

Without intending to downplay any of the blood shedding or anguish caused by recent violence, as a Jewish scholar who has devoted his career to researching Muslim and Jewish relations,

Interfaith Utopias or Antagonistic Histories?

I cannot help but recall how Muslims and Jews saw each other in Palestine in other eras. In 638, shortly after the death of the Prophet Muhammad, Arabs besieged the walled Byzantine town of Hebron. Hebron is sacred for Jews as the location of the Cave of Machpelah, the burial place of the Jewish patriarchs and matriarchs Abraham, Isaac, Jacob, Sarah, Rebecca and Leah. It is also sacred for Muslims, who recognise the men as prophets. According to a medieval chronicle, some Jews in Hebron approached the Arab Muslims besieging the Byzantine town. The Jews asked that in exchange for being allowed to build a synagogue at the entrance to the cave, which the Christians forbade, they would show the Arab Muslims where they could make a gateway to enter the city. They agreed, and the Jews helped them conquer Hebron.[19]

What happened in Hebron is a repeat of what occurred two years earlier in Homs, Syria, where Jews aided the Muslim armies against the Byzantines. When the Muslims were victorious, they 'opened the gates ... and sent out a festive welcome with music'.[20] The same story was repeated the following century in Spain. When Arab and Berber armies conquered Córdoba, Granada, and other towns, they 'gather the Jews in each town and set them as a garrison over the municipality', as the Muslim army marched on to further conquests.[21] Again in 1324, local Jews helped the Ottomans conquer Bursa from their oppressors, the Byzantines, and were rewarded by Sultan Orhan (r. 1324–62) with permission to build the Etz ha-Haim synagogue.[22] Tripoli, Caesarea, Istanbul – Jews aiding Muslims to conquer cities from Christian rulers became a topos in Islamic history writing that cemented the Jews' place in society.[23]

The Jews as allies of Muslims in the Middle East (Palestine, Syria, Turkey) and Europe (Spain) against Christian oppressors is not the usual image we have of Jewish and Muslim relations.

Children of Abraham

What this historical example shows is that Muslims and Jews have engaged one another, sometimes for better, sometimes as partners, for over 1,400 years. But because of the Israeli–Palestinian conflict, which fills our screens daily, most discussions of Jewish–Muslim relations in history are stuck focusing on the worst aspects of relations today. We do not have to close our eyes or deny what is occurring there. Nor must we be beholden to either the myth of interfaith utopia or an antagonistic view of relentless violence and persecution. Just as at the beginning when Muhammad first met Jewish Arabs in Arabia in the seventh century, Jewish and Muslim relations span the spectrum of human interaction from love and friendship to hate and violence.

What is needed is a book telling the unknown, forgotten, or purposely buried story of the connected histories of Jews and Muslims in the Middle East and Europe from their earliest relations in Arabia to relations in the Middle East and Europe today. What is needed is a retelling of their relations without myth and counter-myth. This is that book.

PART I

PRE-MODERN TIMES

1

JUDEO-ISLAMIC RELIGIOUS SYMBIOSIS AND PACTS OF ALLIANCE AND PROTECTION, SEVENTH–THIRTEENTH CENTURIES

Relations between Jews and Muslims began in seventh-century Arabia. Jews were present to witness the birth of Islam. The simplified view of Jew versus Arab is a creation of later historians and nation states. Jew and Arab are not opposites. The first is an ethno-religious category, the second a linguistic one. Until modern times, a Jew was someone who practised Judaism, the religion of their mother. An Arab was a speaker of Arabic, of whatever religion, a person who was immersed in Arab culture. One could not distinguish Jews from Arabs based on language. Different groups lived together and became allies based on common interest. Nomads settled and converted to Judaism. One could be a Jew, and an Arab, and a Bedouin all at the same time.[1] Social groups in urban areas, along with tribes in the desert, were made up of Jewish and non-Jewish clans and subgroups.

Arab Jews in seventh-century Arabia and Yemen were merchants, farmers, nomads, poets, artisans, and warriors. They lived in castles, oases, mud houses in towns, and tents in the desert. They spoke Arabic, Aramaic, and Judeo-Arabic, the latter written in Hebrew characters.[2] Most had Arabic, not

Hebrew names. They read the Torah in Hebrew and discussed it in Arabic. Arabic assimilated Jewish Aramaic and Hebrew terms including *qurban* (animal sacrifice), *salat* (prayer), *sadaka* (charity), and *nabi* (prophet).[3] Arabian and Yemeni Jews maintained ties to Jews in ancient Israel and in Babylon.

The first Jews to encounter Muslims were these Arabs. Islam emerged in the Hijaz, a region at the commercial crossroads situated between two competing, proselytising monotheist poles, a Jewish Yemeni political epicentre to the south and a Christian Syrian one to the north. Himyar in Yemen was ruled by Jewish kings from the fourth to the first half of the sixth century, just prior to the rise of Islam, and its influence extended to the Najd in central Arabia.[4] Jews were a powerful presence in the land in which Islam emerged. They lived as Arab kings, as warriors; they were wealthy. They fought against Christians.

Jews relate how at the age of forty, Moses, the most famous Egyptian Jew, who was saved by Pharoah's daughter and raised in the palace, was called to God, and led the Israelites out of Egypt to Israel, as celebrated every year at the Passover Seder. Muslims tell how also at the age of forty, Muhammad was called by God, and began preaching monotheism in the pilgrimage and market town of Mecca.[5] It is estimated the year was 610.

Muslims believe the Qur'an, or Recitation, is the recording of the revelations Muhammad received from God through the angel Gabriel, the same angel that came to Mary, mother of Jesus. The Qur'an can be read as preaching to Christians, Jews, and others well versed in biblical stories.

Muhammad expected the Jews of Arabia and Yemen to believe in his prophecy. He argued that prophetic messages are identical and universal, and emanate from the same divine source, a hidden book.[6] Muhammad preached to the Jews, 'Have you considered? What if it is from God and you disbelieve in it?' (46:10). The Qur'an narrates how 'before it was the Book of Moses, a model and a mercy. And this [Qur'an] is a confirming Book, in the Arabic language, to warn those who do wrong – and good news for the doers of good ... a Scripture, sent down after Moses, confirming what came before it' (46:12, 30). Muhammad told of his mysterious night journey, where he was whisked to the Jewish Temple in Jerusalem and introduced to all the prophets who came before him, including Moses. He referred to Abraham as 'my father'.[7]

In this we see symbiosis, as the nascent Muslim community, the Believers, adopted Jewish beliefs and practices. Muhammad told his followers to pray in the direction of Jerusalem, like the Jews (2:142). Muhammad considered blowing a shofar (ram's horn) like the Jews to call the faithful to prayer.[8] At first, the Believers fasted on the tenth (*'ashura* in Aramaised Arabic) of the Hebrew month of Tishri (which is Yom Kippur), prayed in the middle of the day like Jews, were permitted to eat kosher food and marry Jewish women, were not allowed to eat pork or animal blood, dressed as Jews, and let their hair flow loose like Jews and did not part it like pagans.[9] Some Jews converted, such as Abdullah ibn Salam, who declared that Muhammad 'is the brother of Moses and follows his religion, being sent with the same mission'.[10]

Jews asked Muhammad, if he recognised the prophets and the Torah as a holy book, why did he not believe in Judaism? How could the revelations he received oppose what is written in the Torah? If he was not Jewish, what was he?[11]

Muhammad responded, 'The religion of Abraham.' They replied, 'But Abraham was a Jew.' The response is recorded in the Qur'an: 'Abraham was neither a Jew nor a Christian, but he was a Muslim *hanif* [monotheist]'.[12] At the same time, the term *muslim* (one who submits to God) is used interchangeably for Christians, Jews, and those we today call Muslims.[13] Most

Jews did not accept Muhammad's message because Muhammad asserted that he was a prophet receiving revelations from God's angel. The Jews said Moses was the last prophet, there was no other – 'whom the Lord knew, face to face' (Deuteronomy 34:10) – so there were disputes, but the disputes were more about power. Jews did not accept him.

Muhammad told them it was better to follow Abraham than Judaism or Christianity, echoing Paul who declared Abraham 'was the father of us all' (Romans 4:16), the 'father of all them that believe, though they be not circumcised' (Romans 4:11–12).

In the Torah (Genesis 17:19–21) we read:

> God said, 'Indeed, your wife Sarah will bear you a son, and you shall name him Isaac, and I will establish My covenant with him as an everlasting covenant for his seed after him. And regarding Ishmael, I have heard you; behold I have blessed him, and I will make him fruitful, and I will multiply him exceedingly; he will beget twelve princes, and I will make him into a great nation. But my Covenant I will establish with Isaac, whom Sarah will bear to you at this time next year.'

In contrast, in the Qur'an (2:135–6) we read:

> The Jews and Christians each say, 'Follow our faith to be guided.' Say, 'No! We follow the faith of Abraham, the upright – who was not a polytheist.' Say, 'We believe in God and what has been revealed to us; and what was revealed to Abraham, Ishmael, Isaac, Jacob, and his descendants; and what was given to Moses, Jesus, and other prophets from their Lord. We make no distinction between any of them. And to God we all submit.'

Judeo-Islamic Religious Symbiosis

Persecuted by his own Qurayshi tribe at Mecca, and wishing to establish his own dominion, Muhammad fled with his followers to Yathrib, over 200 miles north of Mecca, in 622. Muslims refer to the event as the *hijrah* (migration). His followers are called *muhajirun* (migrants) and *mu'minun* (Believers).[14] The town was later renamed Madinat al-Nabi (City of the Prophet), shortened to Medina, by Muslims. Like the Jewish story of David fleeing King Saul, Muhammad was saved from his pursuers by a spider that spun a web over the entrance to the cave in which he was hiding.[15]

This is one of the four moments when Jews have had more power than Muslims. When the Believers migrated from Mecca to Medina, they found there were five Jewish tribes living there. Three of them were powerful. They had palm groves, castles, and weapons; they were wealthy. Jews in Arabia at the time were economically powerful and Muhammad knew he needed to co-opt them. Jewish women travelled in camel caravans hundreds of animals long, 'decked out in litters wearing silk, brocade, velvet and fine red and green silk'.[16] Three of the tribes, presumably descendants of migrants from ancient Israel, were the Banu ('Children of') al-Nadir, the Banu Qaynuqa, and the Banu Qurayza. They possessed lucrative palm groves. They lived in fortified castles. The Banu Qaynuqa were largely made up of craftsmen, especially goldsmiths, with 700 soldiers at the ready, 400 of them in armour.[17] The two smaller Jewish tribes included the Banu 'Awf, a subgroup of the Banu 'Aws. Other polytheist tribes, which would become Believers, included judaised Arabs, including the Banu Khazraj. The Banu Khazraj's path to Islam was prepared for them by the fact that they 'lived side by side with the Jews who were people of the scripture'.[18]

A rupture emerged between Muhammad and these Jewish tribes. It was not caused merely by their rejection of Islam. They did not pose a great threat to Muslims, either. The greatest threat was posed by the group the Believers called *munafiqun* (hypocrites, false converts), those who converted to Islam out of convenience, but did not support Muhammad as they pledged. They threatened Muhammad's power. Muhammad needed to consolidate political control, and to ensure living space, homes, and financial resources for his followers. Expelling or killing the hypocrites' allies, the Jews, would increase his power at the expense of the much stronger hypocrites.[19] The three Jewish tribes possessed the best lands and crops, strongholds, weapons, and suits of armour, and even a market.

To obtain Jewish cooperation from his Meccan enemies, Muhammad drew up what became known as the Pact or, anachronistically, as the Constitution of Medina. While Muslims interpret it as a magnanimous act of goodwill, he made the pact because he and his fledgling community needed to survive. It was an alliance made between the stronger Jews and weaker Muslims. They needed to be allies against their pagan Meccan enemies. The very first pact between Muslims and Jews was formulated at Medina between Muhammad and the Believers and these Jewish tribes. These Jewish tribes were Arabic-speaking. They were Arabs. They had been there a long time.

The first written text of the Pact appeared in the biography of Muhammad written by Muhammad Ibn Ishaq and was incorporated into the biography written by Ibn Hisham a century and a half after it was supposedly drafted. The three powerful Jewish tribes of the Banu al-Nadir, Banu Qaynuqa, and Banu Qurayza were not named in it. The three tribes were likely party to the original Pact, but their names were probably erased in the light of subsequent historical events.[20] The smaller Banu 'Awf, however, were proclaimed part of the *ummah*, or community: 'the Jews of the Banu 'Awf are an *ummah* (community) with *al-Mu'minun* (the Believers)'.²¹ Many of them subsequently became Muslims.

The Pact is a non-belligerence treaty, a declaration of loyalty and mutual aid in return for security and religious freedom. It is a 'friendly agreement' based on mutual financial and military obligations.²² In it, immediately after the first sentence cited above about the Banu 'Awf, we read that 'the Jews have their religion, and the Muslims have theirs'.²³ This means that the community was a multireligious one. The Jews of the Banu 'Aws were also included with the same standing as the Banu 'Awf. The agreement expresses both a desire for unity as allies against their common enemies, and religious pluralism. They formed an *ummah*, a community, which had two religions.

During times of war, Jews and Believers were required to aid the other against the enemy: 'If an outsider attacks Jews, Muslims must come to their defence,' and vice versa. Jews were considered allies of Muslims at the outset of their first encounter. Yet Muhammad established himself as the political and religious leader of the community, acting in the name of God: 'Whenever you differ about a matter, it must be referred to God, and to Muhammad.'²⁴ At the time of the agreement, the three Jewish tribes were the dominant military and economic powers in Yathrib. To establish himself in the town, Muhammad needed to conclude non-belligerence treaties with the Jewish tribes, not as a matter of tolerance but of practicality.²⁵ He needed the Jews to survive.

Amid wars with the Meccans, as Muhammad and the Muslims' power increased, three Jewish tribes of Medina were accused of engaging in treachery and violating this pact of mutual assistance.

The Banu Qaynuqa were sent into exile following the Muslims' victory over the Meccans at the Battle of Badr in 624.

Members of the Banu Qaynuqa were accused of harassing a Muslim woman in the market. They lifted her skirt to expose her genitals. A Jew and then a Muslim were killed in retaliation. There was no arbitration, or payment of blood money, as was expected.[26] They withdrew to their castles. The Muslims besieged them. After two weeks they surrendered and agreed to go into exile.

A year later, the Banu al-Nadir were expelled following the Muslims' defeat at the Battle of Uhud. The Banu al-Nadir were alleged to have plotted to assassinate Muhammad, who Muslims relate was forewarned of the plan by the angel Gabriel, and not harmed.[27] Muhammad took the property, date palm plantations, and weapons they left behind and divided them among his followers. Some of the expelled Jews migrated to the oasis of Khaybar, about 100 miles north of Medina, others to Syria, Palestine, or Yemen. Those expelled from Medina supported the Meccans in the Battle of the Trench in 627.[28]

The Banu Qurayza remained neutral during the battle but were treated with unprecedented brutality afterwards. Muhammad besieged their castles for twenty-five days, after which they were given three choices. The first was to accept him as a prophet and become Muslim to save their lives and property and that of their families. They refused. The second choice was that the Jews of the Banu Qurayza kill their own wives and children and fight Muhammad and his army to see who the victor would be. The logic was that if they lost, their families would not be treated as spoil. If they won, they would make wives of those of their enemies slain in battle. They also refused to accept this option. The fateful final choice was to profane Shabbat and battle Muhammad that evening, which they also refused to do.[29]

Muhammad had one of the tribe's allies, Sa'd ibn Mu'adh of the Banu 'Aws, as the Banu Qurayza were their clients, pass judgment on them, as he lay mortally wounded from the battle.³⁰ Earlier, Muhammad had one of the Banu Khazraj pass judgment on the Banu Qaynuqa. Sa'd gave the judgement that 'the men should be killed, the property divided, and the women and children taken as captives'.³¹ The Banu Qurayza surrendered. Muhammad

> went out to the market of Medina (which is its market today) and dug trenches in it. Then he sent for them and struck off their heads in those trenches as they were brought out to him in batches ... There were 600 or 700 in all, though some put the figure as high as 800 or 900 ... This went on until the Apostle made an end of them.³²

A woman from the Banu Qurayza tribe was also beheaded. She had killed one of the attackers with a millstone.³³ Muhammad divided their property, wives, and children among the Muslims, or sold the women for horses and weapons. He chose a Banu Qurayza woman for himself. She was named Rayhana, and at first refused to veil, marry him, or abandon Judaism. She later changed her mind.

Muhammad wrote to the Jews of the Khaybar oasis referring to himself as 'brother of Moses who confirms what Moses brought' so that it was time they accepted his prophethood.³⁴ They refused. In 628, Muhammad besieged the Jewish castles of Khaybar, conquering them one by one, distributing captive women among the Muslims. He took a Jewish woman widowed in the fighting named Safiya for himself.³⁵ When he asked her why she had a black eye, she told him her husband, slain in the recent battle, had hit her when she told him she dreamed that the moon would fall into her lap, which he interpreted to mean she desired the Prophet.³⁶

After Muslim victory over the last forts, Muhammad allowed the Jews to remain, so long as they handed over half their produce to him every year.[37] Jews in other oases made similar agreements.[38] Arab Jews remained in Arabia for several centuries.

In 628 a Muslim army occupied Himyar. The Persian governor converted to Islam, as did all the Persians ruling Yemen along with some Yemeni tribes. Most Yemenis converted, except Christians and Jews. By 632, following two rebellions, most Yemenis converted to Islam. A few Christians and Jews converted. Ka'b al-Ahbar is the most famous. He was one of the most important sources for the *Isra'iliyyat*, a corpus of legendary, popular stories, traditions, and teachings of ancient Jews that Muslims used to write about the past and Judaism.[39] The Arab Jewish convert to Islam Wahb ibn Munabbih assembled the first collection of this material.

In that era, some Jews believed that Muhammad was the Messiah. A Jewish convert, Abdallah ibn Saba al-Himyari, provoked upheaval among Muslims by proclaiming in the decade following Muhammad's death in 632 that Muhammad was the Messiah and that he would reveal himself a second time. He also affirmed that until then, Muhammad's cousin and son-in-law Ali was to assume the regency. This caused some Muslims to label him seditious, the originator of the Shi'i schism, as Shi'is believe Ali should have been the rightful leader of the Muslims after Muhammad.[40]

The Jews of Yemen were treated differently from the Jews of Arabia, who faced expulsion and massacre. A Jewish community existed in Najran, located on the border between Arabia and Yemen, until 1949, when it migrated to Israel.[41] Nevertheless, the status of Jews suffered a great diminution, from ruling as kings, to becoming protected subjects of the Muslim ruler,

Judeo-Islamic Religious Symbiosis

compelled to pay a poll tax already in 631. The situation for Yemeni Jews worsened over time as Muslim rulers held firm rule, while beyond their authority in the tribal areas Jews did not face discriminatory laws and carried weapons, sometimes even joining Muslims in combat against their common enemies.[42]

Muhammad's relations with Jews were mixed. Allies and enemies, friends and betrayers, wives and detractors, converts and steadfast in remaining in their own religion, Jews were treated as members of Muhammad's community and were expelled from it. Those promoting the myth of interfaith utopia cite the Pact of Medina, by which Jews were allowed to be Jews and were allied with Muslims, as evidence. Those promoting the antagonistic myth mention the perhaps exaggerated number of Jewish men of the Banu Qurayza executed by Muhammad in the market to prove their point.

More important was what happened next. Relations between Jews and Muslims after the death of Muhammad followed the model established by the Prophet with the Pact of Medina.

Despite the exile of the Banu Nadir and Banu Qaynuqa and the massacre of the men (and one woman) of the Banu Qurayza, as Muhammad's armies conquered Palestine and Syria, local Jews assisted them, seeing the Muslims as their saviours from Byzantine Christian oppression. Persia conquered Jerusalem from the Byzantines in 614, and allowed Jews, banned by the Christians, to return to the city and pray on the Temple Mount, site of the ancient Israelite Temple, the second of which was destroyed by the Romans in 70 CE. But the Armenian-origin Byzantine Emperor Heraclius (r. 610–41), who was hostile to Jews, recovered it in 625, massacring Jews in Jerusalem and the Galilee in 630.[43] Jews welcomed the arrival of the Muslims later that decade.[44]

Many of the Banu Nadir settled in Adhri'at (today Dar'a, Syria) and Nawa in Persian-ruled Syria. Despite being expelled from Arabia by the Muslims, the Banu Nadir were more antagonised by the anti-Jewish policies of Heraclius than by their treatment by Muhammad. They were a disaffected group living in the critical towns close to major Byzantine–Muslim battles including that of Jabiya-Yarmuk in 636.[45]

In 638, when the army of Muslims

> came to Hebron, they marvelled at the strong and beautiful construction of its walls and that there was no opening by which they could enter it. Meanwhile, some Jews, who had remained under the Greeks [Byzantines] in that region, came over to them and said: 'Grant us security so that we would have a similar status amongst you, and may we be conceded the right to build a synagogue ... If you will do this, we will show you where you should make a gateway.' And it was done.'[46]

A Jewish apocalyptic account, *The Secrets of Rabbi Shimon Bar Yochai*, composed in the eighth century or later,[47] proclaimed that God made the Muslims the saviours of the Jews. God 'established the kingdom of Ishmael [Muslims] for the sole purpose of redeeming you from the wicked kingdom of the Romans [Byzantines]' as Muhammad 'conquered Palestine, and the Muslims will return it to Israel with glory'.[48]

Likewise, the conquest of Egypt – a land which plays a large role in Jewish history as a place of refuge since the biblical Joseph arrived and rose to be vizier of the Pharaoh – by Amr ibn al-As in 641 gave Jews relief from Byzantine Christian oppression. In North Africa it was a different story.

Jews have lived in North Africa since antiquity. There are two competing myths about their origins.[49] Most believe that the ancient Hebrews arrived by sea along with the Phoenicians, making Jews the first non-Berber people who came to the Maghreb and who continue to live there today.[50] Some argue instead that the Jews of North Africa do not originate in ancient Israel, but are Berber in origin. Berbers converted to Judaism, making Jewish proselytes the main origin of the Jewish presence. The chiefs of nomadic tribes converted their clans to monotheism, and forced vanquished tribes to convert as well, facilitating Judaism's diffusion in sub-Saharan and North Africa.[51]

The twelfth-century geographer al-Idrisi mentions the presence of groups of Jews in Sudan who, contrary to the Torah, tattooed their faces, and nomad Jews living in the Djerid at the arrival of the Arabs. The Tunisian historian Ibn Khaldun, scion of an Arab family from Seville, notes that 'some Berbers professed Judaism, which they took from the Children of Israel when their might had increased, because of the proximity of Syria [Palestine] and its power'.[52] Oral history in southern Morocco refers to lands controlled by a king of the Jews, the Jewish kingdom of Tamghrut.[53] A group of Jewish Berbers reportedly constituted a small kingdom in Touat (Morocco) which survived the advent of Islam and persisted until the fifteenth century.[54] There was another small Jewish kingdom in the region of Oujda (Morocco).

Maghrebi Judaism emerged in the west, in the provinces of Tunisia, and in the east, in Libya. The two met thanks to the nomadism which assured African Judaism the greatest circulation. Fleeing Byzantine persecution, Jews of Roman Africa joined the tribes of the interior, where conversion to Judaism progressed via their active proselytisation.[55]

Arab historians attest to Judeo-Berber resistance to the Muslim conquest.[56] When the Muslim Arabs arrived in the seventh century, they found Berber tribes that were animist, Jewish, Zoroastrian, or Christian. The Zénata, who came from

Egypt and Libya in the wake of the Arab conquest, participated in the conquest of Al-Andalus, converted to Islam over the centuries, while preserving numerous branches practising Judaism.[57]

The Muslims rapidly took the coastal cities from the Byzantines, but encountered fierce resistance from the Jewish Berber tribes. Among the nomadic Jewish tribes were the Djerawa. Their leader was the kahina (diviner, soothsayer), the Jewish Berber queen and prophetess of the Aurés mountains (Algeria).[58] After defeating Umayyad General Hassan ibn al-Nu'man al-Ghassani at the Battle of Oued Nini in 698, she reigned for almost five years in a North African territory where Jewish monotheism was a factor in uniting Berber society.[59] She was ultimately defeated in battle by the invading Arabs.

Although already in the ninth century Arab historians mentioned the Berber kahina, it was not until 1377 that Ibn Khaldun attributed Jewish origins to this emblematic figure within the context of depicting the Berbers as a heroic nation.[60] To this day Jewish North Africans, especially Tunisians, celebrate her alleged Jewishness.[61] The kahina, African hero and Berber warrior of Jewish faith, is considered the 'Berber Deborah', the only female charismatic military leader (judge) among the ancient Israelites.[62]

What makes the kahina exceptional, as a symbol, is that it is shared by many groups. Claimed by the Jews of North Africa and their diaspora, it is also an important Berber symbol, as well as for the Arabs.[63] She has even been called a Christian belonging to a judaised tribe which had converted to Christianity, and the last Christian Berber ally of the Byzantines.[64] What all agree on is that she offered local resistance against the invading Muslim armies. The kahina gave Jews political importance in history and integrated them in the history of North Africa. It is a metaphorical way of reinforcing the process of belonging specific to the Jews of this region.[65] André Chouraqui, historian and Algerian-born Israeli deputy mayor of Jerusalem (1965–73), claimed, 'The last battles of the Jewish people before the modern age thus date not to the struggle against Rome in the first century CE in Palestine', but 'to the seventh century, against the Arabs, on African soil'.[66] For the Berbers, she was not Jewish, but pagan. There is a giant statue of the kahina, called by her Amazigh name, Dihya, in Khenchela, Algeria. For Arabs she is considered first a Muslim anti-hero, but then a pagan who adopted Islam, symbolising the merger of Berbers and Arabs as co-religionists. For French colonialists, her heroism symbolised the superiority of Berbers and Jews to Arabs and Muslims. In the twentieth century, Berber nationalists denied the Arab dimension of their heroine, just as Arab Islamists will not concede her being Berber.[67]

In Berber regions one found monolingual Amazigh-speaking Jews, but most often Jews were bilingual in Arabic and Amazigh.[68] They lived in the Moroccan Atlas, in the valley of Dadès and Todgha and in the Draâ, earning their livelihood from agriculture, livestock, and itinerant trade. On the Algerian–Tunisian border at the beginning of the twentieth century one still found the 'tent Jews' belonging to judaised tribes whose members were formidable warriors on horseback.[69] Urban Jews, who were mainly craftsmen and traders, spoke Arabic, reserving Hebrew for liturgy, though they had versions of sacred texts in Arabic, such as a translation of the Torah, and one even finds an Amazigh-language Passover Haggadah from the region of Tinghir in the Todgha valley in central Morocco, although Amazigh was not a Jewish literary language.[70]

While distinctions were drawn, based on their belonging to a separate religion, and intermarriage remained taboo, Jews were part of the local population, using the same Amazigh or

Arabic language, reserving Hebrew for worship, wearing the same clothing, sharing the same artistic and literary creations, music and poetry, the same festive ceremonies, the same cults of the saints, with the pilgrimages to tombs venerated by Jews and Muslims, such as Sidi Ayache in the eastern High Atlas mountains, in the foothills of the town of Midelt. Jews and Muslims engaged 'in the same practices and acts, making the same offerings, using the same invocations, the same formulas of prayer'.[71]

Over time Jews became native and referred to themselves in this way. After the advent of Islam, ancient communities of judaised tribes of Berbers continued their existence alongside Muslims. Jews dominated in the Draâ and their kingdom of Tamghrut lost its importance in the seventh and eighth centuries with the establishment by the Muslims of Sijilmassa in 757. In this prosperous, royal entrepot of gold and salt connected to Niger in the south and Egypt and India in the East, Jews played a leading role: the city produced famous rabbis in the tenth century. Idris II (r. 803–29) brought Jews to the new city of Fez, founded by Idris I in 789, which became an important commercial and religious centre for Muslims and Jews alike, where the latter were tolerated.[72]

The Pact of Medina formed the blueprint of the system of tolerance subsequently developed in Islamic law and realised in Islamic societies. It includes the so-called Pact of Umar, named after the Muslim Caliph Umar I (r. 634–44), in which Christians and Jews in lands conquered by Muslim armies proclaimed their loyalty to their Muslim rulers in exchange for protection. The protégé pact is known as dhimma, those subject to it are the dhimmi, and the poll tax is the jizya. The Pact of Umar was a conquest treaty to protect the Muslim minority in the regions the Believers conquered, establishing rules that would allow their number to expand, and Jewish and Christian communities to be preserved, but stagnate.

The oldest written version is from the ninth century. The most often-cited version was recorded three centuries later by the jurist Abu Bakr Muhammad al-Turtushi in Spain, yet concerns the surrender of Christians in Syria to Muslim rule in the era of Caliph Umar I. These are the prohibitions to which Christians, and by extension, Jews, agreed to, in order to be allowed to live among Muslims:

> We shall not build, in our cities or in their neighbourhood, new monasteries, churches, convents, or monks' cells, nor shall we repair, by day or by night, such of them as fall in ruins or are situated in the quarters of the Muslims.
> We shall not give shelter in our churches or in our dwellings to any spy, nor hide him from the Muslims.
> We shall not teach the Qur'an to our children.
> We shall not manifest our religion publicly nor convert anyone to it.
> We shall not prevent any of our kin from entering Islam if they wish it.
> We shall show respect toward the Muslims, and we shall rise from our seats when they wish to sit.
> We shall not seek to resemble the Muslims by imitating any of their garments, the headgear, the turban, footwear, or the parting of the hair.
> We shall not speak as they do, nor shall we adopt their honorific names.
> We shall not mount on saddles, nor shall we gird swords nor bear any kind of arms nor carry them on our persons.
> We shall not sell fermented drinks.

> We shall not display our crosses or our books in the roads or markets of the Muslims.
> We shall only use clappers in our churches very softly.
> We shall not raise our voices in our church services or in the presence of Muslims, nor shall we raise our voices when following our dead ... We shall not bury our dead near the Muslims.
> We shall not take slaves who have been allotted to the Muslims.
> We shall not build houses overtopping the houses of the Muslims.
> We accept these conditions for ourselves and for the people of our community, and in return we receive safe-conduct.
> If we in any way violate these undertakings for which we ourselves stand surety, we forfeit our dhimma (pact), and we become liable to the penalties for disobedience and sedition.[73]

Both the Pact of Medina and the Pact of Umar reflect a Qur'anic verse (9:29): 'Fight against those [Jews and Christians] who do not believe in God or the Last Day, who do not forbid that which God and His Messenger have forbidden, and do not follow the Religion of Truth, until they pay the jizya (poll tax) with willing submission, being humbled.' In a letter to a governor, Umar I decreed, 'If you take the poll tax from them you have no claim on them or right over them ... Do not let the Muslims oppress them, harm them, or consume their property except as permitted.'[74] When a Muslim ruler was not capable of protecting Christians and Jews, he was not allowed to levy the poll tax. The Prophet Muhammad did not collect the jizya from every Christian, Jewish, or pagan tribe that submitted to him.

Judeo-Islamic Religious Symbiosis

Umar I allowed some Arab Christians to pay zakat (almsgiving) rather than jizya, which they found degrading.[75]

The dhimma pact is not an alliance like the Pact of Medina, but a different assurance of power relations which was formulated after Muhammad died, as the Muslims conquered territory in what we now call the Middle East. If Jews (and Christians) were loyal and paid their tax, they were allowed communal autonomy and much freedom in religion throughout pre-modern times in places where the Muslims were more powerful, and it was the Jews who needed them for protection.

Jews were treated better in medieval Islam than during the Prophet's era, and much better than in medieval Christendom, giving rise to the myth of the interfaith utopia. One cause was theological and demographic. Christendom's primacy of religious exclusivity, based upon an innate religious antagonism, where Christianity declares itself as the 'new Judaism', or the 'new Israel', is absent in Islam. Jews were tolerated in Christendom only to serve as living witnesses of the punishment God imposed on them because they continued to reject Jesus as Christ, according to Augustine. No theology of calumny emerged in Islam as in Christianity where Jews were called Christ killers and child murderers and whose alleged evil deeds were made into an iconographic tradition. One can still worship in England today in front of medieval rood screens depicting Jews draining the blood from a Christian boy to use in the baking of matzah. Muhammad died a natural death, and did not proclaim himself the Messiah, or divine, unlike Jesus. Hostility to Jews where it existed in Islamdom was non-theological.[76] References to God transforming Jews into apes and pigs in the Qur'an (5:60) were not as severe as the charge of deicide in the gospel (Matthew 25:27).

Whereas Christians at first engaged in a struggle to establish themselves among a Jewish majority, Muslims quickly grew in a region that had many religions (except for Northwest Africa, the Maghreb), Judaism was only one among them. Islam is depicted as restoring the pure monotheism of Abraham rather than being the divine fulfilment of Judaism, as allegedly is Christianity.[77] They are fellow Children of Abraham, who accept their siblings' claims to the same paternity.

Unlike in Christendom, Muslim-ruled societies tolerated human diversity as normal, supported by Qur'anic verses: 'O humankind, God has created you from male and female and made you into diverse nations and tribes so that you may come to know each other' (49:13, repeated in 11:118–19). Such a view promotes pluralism and an acceptance of religious difference.[78] While asserting that Islam is the truth, and that Muhammad is the final messenger, in whose recitation people are urged to believe (5:48), Islam accepts that:

> To each of you We have prescribed a Law and a Way. If God had willed, He would have made you a single *ummah* (community). But God's purpose is to test you in what He has given each of you, so strive in the pursuit of virtue, and know that you will all return to God [in the afterlife], and He will resolve all the matters in which you differ.

Another Qur'anic verse (5:69), which is repeated elsewhere in the Qur'an verbatim and repeated in content almost ten times, accepts that Jews and Christians may attain salvation while remaining faithful to their own religion: 'Those who believe, Jews ... Christians ... and any who believe in God and the Final Day, and do good, will not come to fear or grief.'[79] These passages occur in the same sura which tells Muslims not to take Jews and Christians as allies, which is a political claim that does not supersede religious tolerance, for it is not a 'blanket condemnation' of Judaism (or Christianity).[80] In Christendom the ethnic pluralism of the early Christian world was replaced by the eleventh century with religious exclusivity and a crusading spirit: the former was rare in pre-modern Islamic history.

Jews were excluded from most areas of the economy in Christendom and compelled to be moneylenders for monarchs; as such they became scapegoats for unpopular rulers. When the king needed them, they were safe. When he needed their assets, he expelled them, and claimed what was owed them as his own. Jews were allowed to contribute to the economy in Islamdom, which was more open to commerce and the accumulation of wealth and did not restrict them to certain professions. Muhammad was a merchant, and there was no stigma attached to trade, although there was also the prohibition of usury.

Other reasons for Jews' better treatment in Muslim-majority pre-modern societies than in contemporary Christendom were legal and socio-economic. Jews had a confirmed legal status as protected people, in the social hierarchy in Islamic society, as opposed to arbitrary special law and status in Christendom, as Christians marginalised, excluded, and expelled them from society.[81] Social exclusion was much more severe in Christian societies, where Jews had no social rank, occupied no rung in the hierarchy. In Islamic society Jews were also discriminated against, faced the banning of interfaith marriages where the male partner was Jewish, and clothing distinctions, and had a subordinate position in the social hierarchy, but that was still superior to Christendom, where most kingdoms excluded them.[82] Jews in Muslim-ruled societies where Arabic was the predominant language adopted Arabic as their native tongue, which eased integration, leading to an intellectual meeting of minds with Muslims scientists, physicians, and philosophers.

The bond between Judaism and Islam is one of the reasons

Muhammad expected Jews to accept his call. Muhammad declared himself to be the son of Abraham, the brother of Moses confirming the message that Moses delivered. To both Jews and Muslims, radical monotheists, God is the King (or Lord) of the Universe to whom praise is due.[83] Both religions repeatedly describe God as being merciful and compassionate. In both religions the basic credo proclaims the unity of God. For Jews it is, 'Hear o Israel, the Lord is our God, the Lord is one' (*Shema*). For Muslims it is, 'There is no God except God, and Muhammad is God's messenger' (*Shahadah*). Both Muslims and Jews 'magnify' God (*Allahu akbar*, 'God is most great', and *warabbuka fakabbir*, 'And magnify your Lord', Arabic; in the *Kaddish*, *yitgaddal ... shemey rabbah*, 'magnified is God's great name', Hebrew). [84] Both religions proscribe graven images. Jews look to the figure of Abraham as the first Jew. For Muslims, he is the first *muslim* (believer). The first Believers are open to all like-minded monotheists.

The integration of Jews has been labelled a Judeo-Islamic symbiosis, a concept invented by the German-Israeli historian Shelomo Dov Goitein.[85] He argued: 'Never has Judaism encountered such a close and fructuous symbiosis as that with the medieval civilisation of Arab Islam.'[86] It was in *Jews and Arabs: Their Contacts through the Ages* (1955), based partly on his ethnography of Yemeni Jews in Israel, that he presented this theory.[87] Ironically, despite the book's title, he made the case for Jews *being* Arabs. It was proven by his belief that the Jews of Yemen, whom he interviewed in Israel from the 1920s to the 1950s, were 'the most Jewish and the most Arab of all Jews'.[88]

Goitein defined 'creative symbiosis' as mutual and beneficial for Muslims and Jews. In his view, by the year 1300, 'Muslim religion ... took form under Jewish impact' and 'traditional Judaism received its final shape under Muslim-Arab influence'.[89] From 700 to 1000 Judaism as we have it today was formulated, including the synagogue service, the prayer book, law, ritual, theology, and Hebrew grammar and vocabulary, under Islamic influence, as up to 90 per cent of Jews in the world lived in Muslim-ruled societies.[90]

Beyond mere borrowing and influence, symbiosis occurs as one group accommodates itself to the existence of the other in a process of self-definition that is characterised by 'genuine mutuality and authentic benefit'.[91] The term was popularised by Bernard Lewis in his synthesis *The Jews of Islam* (1984) as 'the Judaeo-Islamic tradition'.

Goitein identified belief, rituals and practices, mysticism, sectarianism, the law, sacred space and territory, and prophetic history as the elements of that centuries-long cooperative relationship. The Muslim rise to power made Muslim and Jew look to the other to understand themselves. This is because of 'the sibling resemblance' of the 'form and content of Judaism and Islam'.[92] Muslims felt the need to claim a connection to Judaism, yet also to clarify the difference between Muslims and Jews. Because Muslims were too much like Jews, they were compelled to articulate what made the Jews their other. Too similar as their brother, they had to determine who they were through a process of self-construction in opposition to their intimate other.[93]

When we compare Judaism and Islam side by side, we see how similar they are. In Judaism's holy book, the Torah, Abraham's wife Sarah gave birth to Isaac (Genesis 21:1–7). God commanded Abraham to sacrifice his son (Genesis 22:1–19). Circumcision, which replaced the attempted sacrifice, ritual purity, intention, a concentrated devotional frame of mind while praying, fasting, ritual slaughter of animals, dietary laws including prohibiting pork, praying towards Jerusalem, the holy city, are all important practices. In Islam's holy book, the Qur'an, it is Ismail (Ishmael), the son of Abraham and his concubine Hagar, banished to the desert by a jealous Sarah (Genesis 21:8–21), who was to be sacrificed (Qur'an 37:100–12). Abraham and Ishmael allegedly built the Ka'ba in Mecca (Qur'an 2:125–7). Muhammad was supposed to be confirmed as a prophet by all previous prophets. Circumcision, along with ritual sacrifice of animals, ritual purity, intention, a concentrated, devotional frame of mind while praying, fasting, initially for one day (Ashura, the tenth of Muharram) but then extended to one month rather than twenty-five hours as in Judaism, ritual slaughter of animals, dietary laws including avoiding pork, praying first towards Jerusalem, and then Mecca, and pilgrimage to tombs of holy men are all important practices.

The letters of the Hebrew alphabet are given numerical values, used in the mystical quest for ontological meaning. The letters of the Arabic alphabet are given numerical values, used in the mystical quest for ontological meaning. Vows of poverty and abandonment to meditative prayer are practices of the Jewish holy man (kabbalist, *tzaddik*), to whose tomb believers make pilgrimage. Vows of poverty and abandonment to meditative prayer are practices of the Muslim holy man (Sufi, *marabout*), to whose tomb believers make pilgrimage.

Judaism is based on the Torah, the written law, and the Mishnah, the oral law, allegedly given to Moses at Mount Sinai. The Mishnah along with the Talmud (divided into Palestinian and Babylonian schools, or collections of scholars linked in a chain of authority) together form the path (*halakhah*) to live a Jewish life. Islam is based on the Qur'an, the written tradition, and the *hadith*, the oral tradition, the sayings attributed to Muhammad categorised by chain of authority. Schools of thought which are largely geographical interpret these, and together they form the way (*Shariah*) to live a Muslim life. In Judaism, a custom may be treated as a law. The law is studied in academies (*beyt midrash* or yeshiva). A bestowal of authority is given at the end of study allowing a graduate to transmit that knowledge. A question and its response allow for further interpretation of the law by learned authorities. A judge applies the law. Rabbis are teachers and leaders, not connected to the state. They are normal men, and not priests. In Islam, a custom may be treated as a law. The law is studied in a college (madrasah). A bestowal of authority is given at the end of study allowing a graduate to transmit that knowledge. A question and response (fatwa) allow for further interpretation of the law by learned authorities (*mufti*). A judge (*qadi*) applies the law. Imams are teachers and leaders, not connected to the state. They are normal men, and not priests.

Jews split into the sectarian groups of rabbinic Jews and Karaites (who do not accept the Talmud) in southern Iraq in the eighth century, which is also where Jewish pietists first emerged. Muslims split into the sectarian groups of Sunnis, Shi'i, and Kharijites (scriptural literalists who resemble Karaites) in southern Iraq in the seventh century, which is where the first Sufis or mystics emerged in contact with their Jewish counterparts. For Jews, Hebron is a holy city because 'Abraham buried his wife Sarah in the cave of the field of Machpelah, facing Mamre – now Hebron – in the land of Canaan' (Genesis 23:19). Abraham was buried in the same cave, as were the rest of the Patriarchs and Matriarchs, his son Isaac, Isaac's wife Rebecca, his grandson Jacob and Jacob's wife Leah (Genesis 49: 29–32; 50:13). For Muslims, Hebron is a holy city because Abraham and the Patriarchs and Matriarchs, who are viewed as pious women, were buried there. For Jews, Jerusalem is a holy city because it contains the Temple Mount. Jews believe it is that site where Noah's ark landed after the Flood and the spot where Abraham was to sacrifice Isaac. The two Temples stood there. It was the site of the Holy of Holies, the presence of God, to which Jews sacrificed animals. What remains of the Second Temple (destroyed in 70 CE) is the Western or retaining wall. For Muslims, Jerusalem is a holy city because it contains the Noble Sanctuary (Haram al-Sharif). Muhammad allegedly touched that site, the furthest point (*al-aqsa*) he reached during his night journey, from which he ascended to the heavens and met all previous prophets who confirmed his prophecy. The Dome of the Rock and Al-Aqsa Mosque were built on the spot.

The Dome of the Rock was completed in 691–2 by the Umayyad Caliph Abd al-Malik ibn Marwan (r. 685–705) as an octagonal shrine, akin to an ancient martyrium, or a victory monument. It was not built as a mosque.[94] The construction of this building, commemorating the permanent establishment of Islam in the city holy to Christians and Jews, decorated by Byzantine mosaic artists and craftsmen, was the moment when Islam distinguished itself from Christianity. It had already been separated from Judaism in Medina. There the first Believers started calling themselves Muslims, stopped praying towards Jerusalem and prayed towards Mecca, cut their hair in a fashion different than Jews, extended the one-day Jewish Yom Kippur fast to the one-month Ramadan fast, and prohibited the consumption of wine for ritual purposes. At Jerusalem Muslims decorated the Dome of the Rock with anti-Christian Qur'anic passages, ridiculing the idea that God could have a son, promoting the unity of God and refuting the Trinity, echoing Jewish critiques of Christianity.[95] On the inner face of the arcade we read that God 'has no partner', and that 'Jesus son of Mary was only the apostle of God ... do not say "three" ... God is one deity only, He is above having a son.'[96] On the outer face of the arcade it is written repeatedly, 'There is no deity except God alone, He has no partner,' and 'God did not beget nor was He begotten, and there is no equal to Him.'[97]

Regarding Judaism, because the Dome of the Rock was built on the raised platform of the Temple Mount, the site of the First and Second Jewish Temples, destroyed in 586 BCE and 70 CE respectively, and was identified with Mount Moriah, where Abraham bound his son for sacrifice, Muslims announced an explicit connection to the preceding monotheistic expression of God's will. The fact that its builder, Abd al-Malik ibn Marwan, ordered the slaughter of all pigs in Syria and Mesopotamia is evidence for the Jewish connection.[98]

Despite the respect given to Judaism in the Qu'ranic verses revealed to Muhammad in Mecca, there is hostility expressed towards the Jews in the verses reported in Medina. 'You will find that the most implacable of men in their enmity to the faithful are the Jews' (5:82). Jews make fun of Islam (5:57), believe in neither God, nor His Revelation, nor Muhammad (5:81). They incite war (5:64) and even betray Muhammad: 'You will ever find them deceitful, except for a few of them' (5:13). Elsewhere, it is 'many of them' (5:81). God tells Muhammad to forgive them nevertheless (5:13). It is not that all Jews are condemned, but only some or many of them. Judaism is not rejected, either: 'God made a covenant with the Israelites' (5:12) and 'Whoever believes in God and the Last Day and does what is right – shall have nothing to fear or regret' (5:69).

The main criticism of the Jews in the Qur'an is the accusation of *tahrif* (distortion, alteration), that Jews changed the Revelation, and do not follow it. Muhammad's mission is to 'come to reveal to you much of what you have hidden of the Scriptures, and to set aside much' that they allegedly added to it (5:15).

Those who 'make war against God and His apostle and spread disorder in the land' (5:33) deserve to be killed or banished, justifying Muhammad's actions against the three powerful Jewish tribes at Medina. The warning 'Do not take the Jews and Christians as allies. They are allies of each other, and he amongst you who becomes their ally is one of them' (5:51) is political, and not social, and has hardly ever been observed in history.

Muslims are permitted to dine with Jews, and Muslim men are permitted to marry Jewish women (5:5). Anti-Jewish hostility 'is attributable to circumstantial historical situation', coexisting with a conciliatory attitude, 'both theological (recognition of the Jewish covenant, salvation for the Jews) and social (conviviality and marriage)'.[99]

Jews were so immersed in the Islamic culture that when writing in Arabic, they used the terms Allah for God, imam for rabbi, and al-Qur'an for the Torah, and Islamic terms and concepts made their way into some of the most famous Jewish works.[100] Chapters of the Torah were called sura; oral law, *sunna*; Jerusalem was referred to as Dar al-Salaam (Abode of Peace); Abraham as Khalil Allah (Friend of God); Moses as Rasul Allah (God's Messenger) like Muhammad; the direction of prayer to the East the *qibla*; *jama'a* for *minyan*, the quorum of ten men required for Jewish prayers; *qadi* for judge, and fatwa for rabbinic responsa. Jews even combined Hebrew and Arabic in such formulations as *Salat al-Shaharit* (morning prayers, using the Arabic word for prayers and Hebrew for morning), or *laylat al-Pesah* (Passover Eve, eve being the Arabic word).[101]

A Yemeni Jewish convert to Islam, Abdallah ibn Saba', is credited with being the first to proclaim that Muhammad, then Ali, was the Mahdi, the redeemer, the rightly guided one who will arrive at the end of time to reign in a world of justice.[102] Concepts of the Mahdi were taken from the *Isra'iliyyat*, the collection of stories and traditions from the pre-Islamic world recorded largely by Yemeni Jewish converts to Islam.[103] The first

Shi'i or pro-Ali group emerged in Kufa, Iraq from the activities of Abdallah ibn Saba', and his followers, the Saba'iyya.[104] They were accused of judaising by Sunnis.[105] Jewish uprisings occurred, and sectarian groups emerged at the same time and in the same region as the first Shi'i groups formed.

The Jewish sects were the 'Isawiyya, which lasted a couple of centuries before all its adherents converted to Islam, and the Karaites, who still exist.[106] Abu 'Isa al-Isfahani (Arabic, Father of Jesus) or Eved Elohim (Hebrew, Servant of God) was an illiterate tailor and eighth-century leader of the 'Isawiyya, who modelled himself as a servant of God, messenger, and prophet, which is similar to Muhammad, and a missionary, like Ali.[107] He prescribed ten daily prayers, and forbade meat and wine, while proclaiming that Jesus and Muhammad were prophets, but only for their own communities.[108] Abu 'Isa rallied his supporters, and led them on horseback, fighting against the Muslims in a massive armed rebellion.[109] It was a Jewish militant reaction to Islamification in Iraq and Iran and expressed long-standing messianic hopes. It was like contemporary extremist Shi'i movements.[110] The uprising was suppressed by the caliph's army. Nevertheless, he left a mark on Muslims. In the Islamic tradition, the Dajjal, or Anti-Messiah, who is a Jew who will oppose the Messiah, 'will emerge from Isfahan followed by 70,000 Jews wearing Persian shawls'.[111] The Jewish Dajjal will be defeated by the Muslim Mahdi.[112]

One finds religious symbiosis between early Shi'is and Jews, especially Isma'ilis, the second largest branch of Shi'i Islam, and Jews. Shi'i–Jewish connections were considered so extensive that Sunni Muslims cited them to defame their Muslim rivals.[113] Sunnis claimed, 'the Shi'is are the Jews of our community'.[114] From the tenth century, Sunni polemicists compiled lists of parallels between Shi'is and Jews which formed a threat to Muslims from within. Sunnis claimed that the Shi'i patterned their leadership structure (the imamate) after the Jewish one (the exilarchate, see below) as succession in leadership was based on hereditary descent: the imams from the house of Ali, the exilarchs from the line of David. They asserted that the Jew Abdallah ibn Saba' first deified Ali, and another Jew, Maymun ibn Qaddah, established the Isma'ilis.[115] In his fourteenth-century *Minhaj al-Sunna*, the Sunni theologian Ibn Taymiyya blamed the two Jews mentioned above for establishing Shi'ism 'out of hatred of the Muslims'.[116] His list of shared doctrine and practices included such parallels as both Jews and Shi'is falsifying the holy book, praying only three times per day, and 'their outward expression being the opposite of what they really do, out of enmity'.[117]

Mysticism is an integral part of Judaism and Islam and further evidence for religious symbiosis. Jewish kabbalists and Muslim Sufis emerged and developed in tandem. The Jewish *hasidim* (pietists) and early Sufi ascetics in Basra, Iraq were very similar and in contact with one another. Both promoted a practice where the love of God is the centre and goal of human life. Muslims and Jews made pilgrimage to the tombs of the same saints or holy men to ask for intercession, especially in Morocco and Egypt. Jews and Muslims offered common prayers for rain in times of drought, or the ending of disease in times of plague. They believed in the power of spirits, or magic, and holy men inserted their written blessings into charms and amulets they wore on the body. As an example of this religious symbiosis, Muslims adapted the chief of the angels, Metatron, from post-biblical Judaism for use in magic spells and cosmologies for popular and elite classes alike.[118]

The estate of a medieval Jewish coppersmith who emigrated from Spain to Egypt included Hebrew-language prayer books from Iraq and Morocco, as well as a book of poetry in Arabic.[119] His possessions are evidence that in addition to converging

Judeo-Islamic Religious Symbiosis

religious cultures, Jews and Muslims had a shared secular culture. The pre-modern secular symbiosis was evident in language and literature, science and philosophy, poetry and music, and trade and commerce, especially in eighth- to tenth-century Baghdad, ninth- to twelfth-century Al-Andalus, and across the medieval Mediterranean centred on Old Cairo from the tenth through to the thirteenth centuries.[120]

2

THE SECULAR SYMBIOSIS AND JEWS RULING OVER MUSLIMS: THE TURKISH JEWISH KHAZAR KINGDOM, EIGHTH–TENTH CENTURIES

What Jews and Muslims had when they lived together was intimacy, similarity, trust, translatability, proximity, shared language, rhythm of daily life, music, and food. What they had was 'a common Jewish–Muslim culture' cultivated by Jews who 'spoke Arabic and were deeply influenced, not only by some spheres of Islamic civilization, such as Muslim philosophy, but by Islam as a religion'.[1]

At the end of the tenth century, a conservative Spanish Muslim named Abu Umar Ahmad ibn Muhammad ibn-Sadi visited Baghdad, where he reported his shock at what he witnessed at meetings of rational theologians. He attended them twice but vowed never to return.

What he objected to was something we today applaud. Individuals of different faiths and no faith met together in friendship and respect, engaging in dialogue about controversial subjects, obeying the basic rule that they meet as equals on the plane of ideas and methods of argumentation, where one can only appeal to reason and not faith to prove their points, where no one can claim superiority based on the asserted supremacy or correctness of their religion. They respected others who possessed knowledge, whatever their religion, and created a space where merit and talent were appreciated and friendships develop.[2] A 'society that recognised the religious Other, and where different religious groups intermingled and exchanged ideas' was 'the embodiment of something extraordinary for its time'.[3] One such example was Abbasid Baghdad.

Babylonian Judaism, established in 586 BCE when Babylonian King Nebuchadnezzar II conquered Jerusalem, destroyed the First Jewish Temple, and exiled most Jews to Babylon, flourished under Islamic rule and the establishment in Baghdad of the Abbasid dynasty (750–1258).

In Abbasid Baghdad, the Jewish exilarchs (leaders of the exile), modelled on the caliphs, became the civil, communal leaders of all the Jewish communities, and were until the eleventh century lay leaders responsible for collecting taxes among Jews on behalf of the caliphs, overseeing the markets, and nominating heads of Talmudic academies, judges, and rabbinic judges, while serving as a rabbinic judge of high rank.[4] The wealthy exilarch, claiming descent from King David, who in his dress and processions with many retainers appeared as if a king, boasted a Great Synagogue of the Exilarch, 'built of marble columns in every imaginable colour, covered with gold and silver. Written on these columns in gold letters are various passages from the Psalms. At the front of the ark are about ten marble steps, with the Exilarch seated on the top one,' according to the visitor Benjamin of Tudela in 1170.[5] Along with the exilarch, in the tenth century powerful and wealthy families were also established in Baghdad, as well as the Talmudic academies (yeshivot) of Sura and Pumbedita (near what is Fallujah, Iraq today). The *geonim* (singular: *gaon*), heads of the yeshivot, teaching thousands of students, became spiritual leaders, as they issued responsa to questions about Jewish life, homogenising rabbinic Judaism.[6] The *geonim* were like the ulema who delivered legal opinions (fatwa), as they gave responsa.

With the exilarch and *geonim* ensconced in the capital, the Abbasid caliphate ushered in what is considered the first golden age of Jews living under Muslim rule.[7] The Arab conquests led to the creation of a new civilisation bringing together the cultures, lands, and commerce from the Atlantic to China, which collected, resurrected, developed, and transformed the heritage of the ancient world. And almost all the Jews of the world were encompassed within this new empire.

Founded in 762, Baghdad became the new centre of this world as the Abbasid Empire was the most powerful, wealthy, and cultured empire at its time. From the beginning, Jews were involved. Caliph Al-Mansur (r. 754–75) appointed a Jewish physician and astrologer, Mashallah, to plan Baghdad and determine the auspicious day for its ground-breaking.[8] Officially named Madinat al-Salam (City of Peace) but popularly known by the pre-Islamic Persian phrase 'given by God', Baghdad was a round city. It served as the caliph's royal residence and government complex, with three concentric walls, four equal quarters housing his retinue, and four main roads leading from within to the rest of the empire. The most legendary reign was that of Haroun al-Rashid (786–809), in whose epoch the fabled *Thousand and One Nights* is set.

Caliph Al-Mansur brought about stability among contending Jews, leading to an era of creativity.[9] He moved the exilarch to his new capital of Baghdad. Al-Mansur sided with one faction of geonim, leading to Anan ben David's breaking from rabbinic Judaism by rejecting the Talmud and establishing the Karaite sect. The Karaites adopted some Muslim ideas, allegedly when Anan ben David shared a jail cell with the influential Muslim

The Secular Symbiosis and Jews ruling over Muslims

jurist Abu Hanifa, whose rulings concerning Jews (and Christians) were more lenient than the other leading Sunni jurists.[10]

The caliph Al-Ma'mun (r. 813–33) founded an academy, *Beyt al-Hikma* (House of Wisdom), to translate ancient Greek philosophy and science into Arabic, and showed an interest in Chinese wisdom as well. Linguistics and grammar, history, geography, mathematics, astronomy, medicine, chemistry, physics – this dynasty was open to collecting and expanding upon all human knowledge. Al-Ma'mun was a rationalist, a Mu'tazilite, who declared that the Qur'an was created and not coeternal with God, since God had no separable parts. He put scholars on trial who did not conform to this state-imposed view, the only inquisition in pre-modern Islamic-ruled societies.[11]

Jews did not compete with Muslims in the economy: they filled roles concentrating in professions disdained by Muslims or where they had skills Muslims lacked, or did not want to undertake, such as those involving interest. The Jews of Abbasid Iraq were divided by class. At the top were long-distance traders, goldsmiths and minters of coins, physicians, ambassadors, astrologers, architects, and viziers.[12] The mass of Jews made up an underclass of poor cloth makers, tanners, weavers, and dyers, along with the very worst jobs, such as jailers and executioners.[13] In the cities commerce and artisanal work provided the main livelihood for Jews. From the beginning of the tenth century wealthy Jewish traders served as court bankers to the Abbasid caliphs. They accumulated fortunes thanks to the sums entrusted to them by prosperous Jewish merchants in exchange for part of the profits from the loans.

A significant part of the Jewish trade took place beyond the caliphate, to Western Europe and East Asia. Thanks to their family networks, common language, mutual trust, and recourse to similar laws they ensured the link between the Muslim empire in the East and Christian Europe. Jews also specialised in professions related to gold working and silver working, medicine, astronomy, and translation. Among the urban middle class, there was an atmosphere that was relatively tolerant and open between the Jews and their Muslim neighbours that included social and intellectual links, economic cooperation, and friendships. It was not equality, 'but collaboration in a climate of tolerance and a certain respect with regard to the heirs and transmitters of older cultures'.[14]

Jewish political and spiritual leaders came into close contact with the intellectual currents of the early Islamic world, as the superior education offered in the two yeshivot was diffused to Jewish communities in the Muslim world and beyond, and Babylonian scholars' authority and their Talmud shape rabbinic Judaism until today.

The main factor in the Judeo-Islamic symbiosis was the Jewish adoption of Arabic. Compared with the other diaspora languages, Yiddish and Ladino, Arabic 'has had the longest recorded history' and 'the widest geographical diffusion'.[15] Jews spoke Arabic more than any other language because most Jews lived in Arabic-speaking regions from the seventh through to the seventeenth century. It was in this language that Jews formulated key elements of Judaism.

According to Yehudah ibn Tibbon, translator of Arabic works into Hebrew, a statue of whom stands today in his birthplace of Granada, Spain – one of the only marks of the once flourishing Jewish presence in the city – Arabic is a 'rich language for every subject and for every need, for every speaker and every author; its expression is direct, lucid and capable of saying just what is wanted much better than can be done in Hebrew ... it is simply impossible to express the thoughts of our hearts succinctly and adequately in Hebrew, as we can in Arabic'.[16] Whether they expressed themselves in Arabic or Hebrew, the Jewish thinkers of the age were imbued with the spirit of the Muslim world.

Jews in Muslim-majority lands mostly dropped Aramaic (except for Kurds) and adopted Arabic. Adopting Arabic names for themselves, they used it to translate and comment on the Torah and the law, producing theological as well as philosophical treatises in the language. They used Muslim methods of approaching Arabic and the Qur'an to study Hebrew grammar, the Torah and its language, all the while writing in Arabic and using Arabic terminology, even for the systematic study of Hebrew pronunciation, grammar, and vocabulary. Giving rise to comparative linguistics, they discovered that Arabic and Hebrew are related languages, with common origins, with the same tri-consonantal root structure, similar grammar, and much shared vocabulary. *Salaam* and *shalom* are the most obvious examples. It is easy for a speaker of either language to learn the other. Jews created varieties of Judeo-Arabic – Arabic spoken dialect transcribed in Hebrew letters – along with Judeo-Persian. It is this commonality of languages that led European race scientists in modern times to imagine Jews and Arabs as members of a mythical Semitic race.

The linguistic connection also enabled intellectual movements between Jews and Muslims. One example is philosophy. Both Jewish and Islamic philosophy developed at the same time, building on the translation of ancient Greek texts in Baghdad at first by Christian Arabs into the Syriac dialect of Aramaic and then into Arabic between the eighth and tenth centuries in the Abbasid caliphate.[17] A new corpus of Greco-Arabic thought emerged. Arabic-writing Jewish doctors, mathematicians, astronomers, and philosophers learned Greek science and methods of thought from these Arabic translations and commentaries.

Both Jewish and Islamic philosophers played important roles because they recovered, preserved, clarified, interpreted, translated, corrected, and improved the works of Greek philosophers and scientists. They also used their knowledge of logic, philosophy, and science to attain the truth concerning God, creation, prophecy, divine law, and free will.[18] They were innovative and moved beyond the original texts. Their writings were translated from Arabic into Latin in Spain from the ninth to the twelfth centuries, and sparked the thirteenth- and fourteenth-century Renaissance in Christian Europe.

Jews and Muslims engaged in public interreligious disputes in Abbasid Baghdad where the exilarch represented Jews and the caliph or the imam the Muslims.[19] Another kind of interconfessional engagement occurred in the late ninth and early tenth century at private disputations among friends, in the homes of like-minded critical thinkers. They shared an intimacy, frequenting the same philosophical and social circles, but were labelled deviant by their respective religious authorities for their view that all monotheistic religions are different expressions of the same divine truth.[20] They are credited with being the first to engage in comparative religion, criticising the singularity of revelation and the scriptural traditions of Islam and Judaism. Contending with each other in private, their attacks on apparent logical inconsistencies in the holy scriptures caused Jews such as Sa'adia Gaon – a Hebrew grammarian, theologian, and philosopher, who wrote the first translation of the Torah into Arabic – and Muslims alike to defend their traditions with allegorical interpretations, sharpening the contours of their own religions, and to articulate what makes them different from the other.[21]

Dunash ben Labrat, a tenth-century native of Fez with

a Berber name, journeyed to Baghdad to study with Sa'adia Gaon.[22] Ben Labrat introduced quantitative metres, verse forms, themes, and genres from Arabic into Hebrew secular and liturgical poetry.[23] His work became the source and model of subsequent poetry. Around 960 he went back west, lured by Hasdai ibn Shaprut to the court of Abd al-Rahman III (commander of the faithful, 912–29; caliph, 929–61) at Córdoba, Spain. His hymn *D'ror Yiqra* ('Freedom shall He proclaim') is sung on Shabbat to this day.[24]

After the Arab conquest Iraqi Jews settled in the main Egyptian cities.[25] They maintained their connections with the great Jewish academies (yeshivot) in Iraq. Palestinian and Syrian Jews settled in Egypt as well and maintained their connections to the great academies there. Eventually the authority of the *geonim* of Palestine and Iraq was transmitted to local community leaders in Egypt.

The Karaites also established themselves in Egypt in Fustat (today part of Cairo), and the *harat al-yahud al-qara'in* (neighbourhood of the Karaite Jews) was next to the *harat al-yahud* (neighbourhood of the Jews). The Karaites became prosperous and influential. The term Karaite comes from the Hebrew *kara'im* or *bene mikra* (readers of the scripture) because of the scriptural basis of their faith.

Karaite theology was influenced by the Muslim Mu'tazilite movement in the tenth and eleventh centuries, so much so that Muslims called Karaites the Mu'tazilites of the Jews.[26] The Mu'tazilites believed in divine unity and divine justice, rewarding the good and punishing the bad in the afterlife, and that people have free will to choose between right and wrong, and will be judged for their actions. Writing in Judeo-Arabic, the Karaites rejected the oral law (Talmud and Mishnah) and interpreted the Torah with new methods, including the rational approach (*'aql*), for which logic and grammar are vital, taking a literal approach.[27]

In Egypt Jews practised unique symbiotic customs. Hebrew liturgical poems were sung to local tunes, then translated into Arabic during the *Laylat al-Tawhid* ('Unity of the Divine', a ceremony held on the first day of the month of Nisan, two weeks before Passover). The Arabic text recited at midnight contained many Islamic phrases beginning with *Bismillahirahim* (In the name of the merciful, the compassionate), the ninety-nine names of God, and the Qur'anic names of Torah figures such as Al-Khalil for Abraham, Al-Imam for Aaron, and Rasul Allah for Moses.[28]

The Shi'i Fatimid dynasty (909–1171) which built Cairo in 969 was tolerant towards Jews (and Christians) except for Caliph Al-Hakim bi-Amr Allah (r. 996–1021), who imposed the regulations of the dhimma, made Jews wear a distinctive yellow badge, and destroyed synagogues, compelling many Jews to convert to Islam or flee his kingdom. After his disappearance, his decrees were revoked, converts returned to Judaism, and synagogues were rebuilt.[29]

Muslim rulers appointed a single leader of Egyptian Jewry (*rais al-Yahud* in Arabic, *nagid* in Hebrew).[30] He both played a religious role within the Jewish community and served as an intermediary and representative of Jews before the Muslim authorities, defending their interests and ensuring their autonomy. Most of the leaders of the community and prominent scholars were émigrés from around the Mediterranean and the Middle East.[31]

Life for Jews and Muslims in Egypt and other societies in the Mediterranean and Middle East from the tenth to the thirteenth centuries was marked by economic interdependence. In Old Cairo houses and shops were held in partnership by members of

The Secular Symbiosis and Jews ruling over Muslims

different religious communities. Muslims and Jews engaged in relations based on trust, as when one would furnish the capital or goods and the other would carry out the business transaction. Jews served as agents of commerce for Muslims and vice versa.[32] In the Fatimid era Jews were involved in the textile, cotton, and silk industries, the manufacture of glass and pottery, the import–export trade with North Africa, the export of indigo dye, spices, and sugar, and the importation of copper, lead, olives and olive oil, soap, and wax. They included merchants who migrated from Tunisia and Palestine and played a vital role in the India trade, encouraged by the Fatimids, who granted autonomy to merchants. Jewish physicians in large cities also became members of the entourages of Fatimid caliphs, Ayyubid sultans (1171–1250), viziers, viceroys, governors, and generals.[33]

These Jews were privileged specialists who were often the heads of the community.[34] They interceded and obtained concessions on its behalf when needed. Prominence in the government and at court led to opposition, as voiced in this poem: 'The Jews of our era have obtained their goal – honours are theirs and riches as well. Viziers and kings are chosen from among them. Egyptians! I advise you to become Jews, because heaven itself has become Jewish.' Yet the mint remained in the hands of Jews in the Fatimid, Ayyubid, and Mamluk (1250–1517) eras.[35] The government relied on the Jews because it knew that as the most vulnerable group, they were the most loyal. Jews were also entrusted to manage taxes collected on silk, as customs collectors at the port in Old Cairo, and as tax farmers in Egyptian markets.

The Fatimids accelerated the immigration of Jews to Egypt, as they saw them as loyal allies.[36] Ya'kub ibn Killis was another Jew who rose at the Fatimid court. He was a Baghdadi Jewish merchant and financial expert who had converted to Islam. In

979 he was appointed 'most illustrious vizier'. He held a weekly salon at court, where Muslims and Jews debated theology, but sided with Muslims, using Sa'adia Gaon's Arabic-language prayer book, *Book of Beliefs and Opinions*, and translation of the Torah to ridicule Jewish ritual.[37] Some of the harshest critics of Judaism were such converts.

The dhimmi laws were more strictly applied under the Sunni Mamluks, a regime of converted slave soldiers of Turkish and then of Circassian origin, who welcomed the surviving members of the Abbasid caliphate after Baghdad was destroyed by the Mongols in 1258, and drove the last Crusaders out of Acre, Palestine in 1291. Jews had to wear a yellow fabric on their turbans.[38] The Mamluk regime was encouraged to discriminate against Jews by a Jewish convert to Islam, Sayyid ibn Hasan, and the Sunni theologian Ibn Taymiyya. Violent riots shook Cairo in 1301 and 1354 accompanying the imposition of sartorial decrees.[39] The Jews of Egypt suffered less than the Christians. A Christian man and Muslim woman were stoned to death in 1417 for having had sex.[40]

The economic situation of the Jews deteriorated as the Mamluks imposed a monopoly system favouring their own mainly Muslim trading cartel – decreasing trade with India – and turned to rural Muslim landowners who were their loyal allies.[41] In 1448, the sultan issued a decree forbidding Jewish and Christian physicians from treating Muslim patients. Jewish physicians continued to serve eminent Muslim theologians and sultans alike despite the decree.[42]

Above all it was in economic relations that we see the secular symbiosis in medieval Egypt and the Mediterranean. In the twentieth century, anthropologists observed how Jewish–Muslim relations on the Tunisian island of Djerba experienced 'elements of friendship and hostility, confidence and suspicion,

The Secular Symbiosis and Jews ruling over Muslims

collaboration and competition'. What governed their relations in daily life and in the market was the concept of 'the honesty of the Jews'. Jews and Muslims invoked it equally: 'concluding a discussion with the invocation' was 'equivalent to giving an oath'. The Jewish merchant put his reliability, integrity, and honesty on the line, and that of his profession. It was a reference to respect for the law. The idea was that since Jews 'are people of the law, one can deal with them'.[43] They patronised only Jewish jewellers because they knew their work was of the highest quality and they were honest. What was true in twentieth-century Djerba was true in tenth-century Cairo and across the Middle East and wherever Jews and Muslims traded.

Jews and Muslims lived next to one another in the same neighbourhoods in Egypt, Tunisia, Syria, and Palestine. Muslims and Jews worked in the same workshops and formed commercial partnerships stretching across North Africa, Southern Europe, and South Asia. They called their business partners 'brothers' despite their being from different religions.[44] 'Should a caravan set out in which trustworthy Muslims, who have given you sureties, will travel, let the merchandise of my brothers be sent with them as if it was yours,' states an eleventh-century letter.[45] A medieval Jewish merchant, in a caravan from Palestine back to Libya, mentioned that most of the travellers were Muslims from his homeland who promised to be considerate regarding his keeping of Shabbat.[46]

Informal commercial partnerships in the pre-modern period were built on mutual trust, honesty, good reputation, and friendship, which lasted a lifetime, even generations.[47] How much more trust mattered in an age when merchant voyages lasted months. In the eleventh, twelfth, and thirteenth centuries, when communications took many months, international trade was largely dependent on personal relationships. When one shipped goods across the seas, one waited a long time before learning whether they arrived safely and for what price they sold. The merchant had to rely on his friends in the country of destination for the handling of his trade.[48] Although his friends were often from his own religious community, his business partners were 'interdenominational and international'.[49] Large Jewish businesses employed a Muslim, in case a boat carrying shipments for them arrived on Shabbat. A slave was expected to observe Shabbat like his master, so could not execute such tasks.[50]

Jews and Muslims entered into commercial arrangements employing slaves as well, often Hindus, as their business agents, as they traded spices (pepper, cloves, ginger, cinnamon, cardamom, nutmeg), perfumes (musk, ambergris), textiles, dyeing and silk work (robes made of fine silks lined with fur), precious metals, ironware, bronzeware, and glassware between the west coast of India and Aden and Cairo–Fustat, just as they traded between Egypt and Tunisia, Sicily, and Spain.[51] Because so many of these Jews were druggists and perfumers, most of their overseas trade involved costly medicinal plants, spices, and perfumes.[52] Persian Jews in Yemen served as superintendents of its port, and built boats for the Aden–Sri Lanka trade route and shipped huge quantities of goods to Cairo.[53] Other twelfth-century Jews from Morocco served as legal representatives in Fustat, and a Spanish Jew in al-Mahdiyya, Tunisia, served as a representative of merchants.[54] One of the most important of the merchants was the Jewish Egyptian Abraham ben Yiju of al-Mahdiyya, who spent two decades in India and many years in Yemen.[55]

We know the details of intimate economic relations of trust between Muslims and Jews in the medieval period because of a discovery, aided by colonialism. The synagogue of Ben Ezra in Fustat, known as the synagogue of the Palestinians or Levantines, named for the Jerusalemite Abraham ben Ezra, was supposedly built on the spot where the Pharaoh's daughter found Moses among the bullrushes. Built next to a Coptic church, it has a basilica plan, recognisable from its ground-floor colonnades, and an upper floor made of Roman arches. Its decorations come from Islamic art.[56] It was rebuilt on an earlier foundation in 1025. That synagogue was the place of worship of North African Jews involved in international trade. The synagogue also boasted Maimonides (Musa ibn Maimun, or Rambam), the greatest medieval Jewish thinker. While its original design was in keeping with its early Islamic context, such as the geometric patterns displayed on its walnut Torah ark doors, its nineteenth-century version reflects Mamluk and Ottoman style, with polished marble and a gilded interior with soaring arches in alternating black and white bands and Torah ark in an intricate Arabesque, mother-of-pearl design containing Stars of David.[57] The interior is in stark contrast to its plain exterior, several neighbouring ancient Coptic churches with their crosses, and the rubbish-strewn ground succumbing to the rising groundwater on the eastern bank of the Nile.

Rather than throw away old paper documents, to prevent the accidental desecration of God's name, which may have appeared even on bills of sale, Jews deposited them in a two-and-a-half-storey chamber connected to the synagogue known as the geniza, whose contents at other such synagogue storehouses were regularly removed and buried in a solemn ceremony. But the Ben Ezra geniza was never cleared out. For 800 years, several hundred thousand scraps of papers and book manuscripts accumulated. They provide evidence of relations between Muslims and Jews marked by a familiarity that lacks animosity or barriers.

Evidence of religious and secular symbiosis emerges from these parchments. One fragment from twelfth- or thirteenth-century Egypt contains the first and second suras of the

Qur'an, the Fatiha, written in Hebrew letters. It is entitled: *fatih el-kitab, 7 ayet* (opening of the Book, seven verses):

> In the name of God, the infinitely Compassionate and Merciful. Praise be to God, Lord of all the worlds. The Compassionate, the Merciful. Ruler on the Day of Reckoning. You alone do we worship, and You alone do we ask for help. Guide us on the straight path, the path of those who have received your grace; not the path of those who have brought down wrath, nor of those who wander astray.[58]

Nothing in these verses is objectionable to a religious Jew. The Fatiha is followed by the second sura and then a version of a prayer for travellers. The writing was composed for a Jew, as it was written in Hebrew letters, who folded the parchment in an amulet and took it with them on their journey to ward off dangers.

Another eleventh-century text from Egypt did the reverse: it is a series of Torah verses written in Arabic script, but with Hebrew vowel signs.[59]

Even more remarkable was a Turkish Jewish kingdom, now long forgotten, that rose on the shores of the Caspian Sea. Rather than inscribe coins in Arabic, *la ilaha illa Allah wa Muhammad rasul Allah* (There is no God save God and Muhammad is the Messenger of God), they chose *la ilaha illa Allah wa Musa rasul Allah* (There is no God save God and Moses is the Messenger of God). It is the Muslim credo, made Jewish, minted in Ard al-Khazar, the Land of the Khazars in the ninth century.[60]

The history of Jews and Muslims does not only encompass Arabs, nor does it take place only in the Middle East. Jews had lived in Eastern Europe, the Caucasus, along the northern

The Secular Symbiosis and Jews ruling over Muslims

shores of the Black Sea, and in Crimea since Roman times. Greek-speaking, they made jewellery and pottery, and traded in grains, fish, and slaves. Southern Russia became a refuge for Jews persecuted in the Byzantine Empire. Over the centuries, Byzantine emperors decreed that Jews must convert to Christianity and these decrees were accompanied by destruction of synagogues and killing of Jews.[61]

Shortly after the first Muslim communities emerged in Arabia, Palestine, and Egypt, the Khazar kingdom was established by a Turkic nomadic tribe by 650, in what is today southern Russia (Dagestan) on the western shore of the Caspian Sea between the Volga River in the north and the city of Derbend, at the gateway between the Caucasus mountains and the Caspian Sea, in the south. They later moved their capital north to Atil/Itil (Volga), in the delta where the river of the same name flows into the Caspian. No trace of it has ever been found. Khazaria was situated between the Caspian (also called the Khazar Sea) and the Black Seas, and stretched across the Ukrainian steppe to what became Kyiv and to the borders of what are now Kazakhstan and Uzbekistan. From Itil, the Khazars controlled access to the Black and Caspian Seas, and their commercial network reached much of Eurasia. Dozens of pagan, Christian, and Muslim peoples were their tributaries. During the ninth and first half of the tenth century trade flourished on the Eurasian steppe and in Rus' (Viking) towns, and trading posts sprang up along the rivers. The land route to China was open, and Jewish merchants from the West used it to trade goods, moving through Itil en route.

The Khazars were victorious in battle and feared by their neighbours, especially the hated 'wicked' emperor Romanus of 'the uncircumcised' Byzantines and Russians.[62] The Khazars ruled a mighty kingdom on the periphery of the Byzantine and

Persian empires, waging successful military campaigns from Albania in the west to Georgia and Armenia in the east. In 730 the Khazars invaded Muslim-ruled territory, taking Ardabil in Kurdistan, and attacking Mosul and Diyarbakir. There they began to rule over Kurdish Jews.

Jews had arrived in Kurdistan in the eighth century BCE when the Assyrian kings Tiglath-Pileser III and then Shalmanaser and Sargon II exiled the Jews from northern Palestine.[63] According to 2 Kings 17:6: 'The King of Assyria captured Samaria and deported the Israelites away to Assyria. He settled them in Halah [Nineveh], in Gozan [Tell-Halaf, Syria] on the Habor [Habur] River [Kurdistan].' These Jews gave up Hebrew for Aramaic, the language of the Assyrians. According to Isaiah 27:13, the Israelites were 'lost' in Assyria. In the first-century CE Kurdish kingdom in Erbil of Adiabene, the Parthian pagan queen and crown prince, Helen and Izates, converted to Judaism, built a palace and tombs in Jerusalem, and sent troops and supplies – the only diaspora Jews to do so – when the Jews launched their fateful rebellion against the Romans in 66 CE.[64] The Khazars alternately fought against or allied with other Turkic and Iranian nomadic and pastoral peoples, and some members of these tribes became Jewish.[65]

Three Arab–Khazar wars in the seventh and eighth century stopped the Muslim advance into Eastern Europe and the Caucasus. The leader of the Khazars was so respected by the Byzantine emperor that he considered the Khazar ruler to be a peer, an honour bestowed only also on the Emperor of the Franks and the Caliph of Baghdad. Byzantine Emperor Leo III (r. 717–41) married off his son, Constantine, the future Constantine V (r. 741–75), to the Khazar Princess Çiçek in 732, and their son, Leo IV (r. 775–80), is known as 'Leo the Khazar.'[66] Seven years after another Khazar victory over the Arabs, in 737,

The Secular Symbiosis and Jews ruling over Muslims

Marwan, the future Marwan II (last Umayyad caliph, 744–50), invaded the kingdom and took its leader captive, allegedly compelling him to convert to Islam.[67] He later returned to paganism. In 760 Khazars established marital ties with the Abbasid caliphate. The year 798 witnessed the last Khazar attack on Muslim territory, ending in a peace agreement with the Abbasids that changed their relations: the Khazars now served as a defensive shield protecting Muslim-ruled regions to the south, thus facilitating international commerce. Over a century and a half later the Khazar ruler Joseph proclaimed that he 'did not allow the Rus' [Vikings] who come in ships to come by sea to attack the Ishmaelites [Muslims] … I war with them. If I left them in peace for one hour, they would destroy the whole country of the Ishmaelites [Muslims] up to Baghdad.'[68] It was after these wars against the Arabs as allies of the Byzantines that the Khazar ruling elite took their most surprising decision.

Around 800, under Bulan I, the royalty and nobility of the Turkish Khazar kingdom converted to Judaism. Over the next century many of the Khazar commoners converted as well. According to the early tenth-century Abbasid Muslim traveller Ahmad ibn Fadlan, 'The Khazars and their king are all Jews.'[69] The majority of the Khazar subjects were not Jews. The Khazar kingdom incorporated Jews, Christians, Muslims, and pagans. Although they adopted Hebrew, the Khazars maintained the runic Khazar language and Turkic tribal symbols. Khazar officials read and wrote both runes and Hebrew, the latter with square rather than round letters. Tombstones on the Crimean peninsula and in the Ukrainian tributary state have both Jewish symbols and Turkic runes.

Hasdai ibn Shaprut, Jewish vizier at the court of Caliph Abd al-Rahman III (r. 929–61) in Córdoba, sent an emissary in 960 to the Byzantines to correspond with the leader of the Khazars,

Joseph son of Aaron.[70] In 1896 Solomon Schechter discovered a Hebrew-language letter in the Cairo geniza. It is an account by a Khazar Jew of the Khazars' conversion and history. It tells how Jews had arrived in Khazaria, as migrants from Armenia, but no longer practised Judaism other than circumcising their sons and in some cases observing Shabbat, and they intermarried with the local pagan Turkic population. Jews served as soldiers defending the land, and when during one battle a Jew proved himself exceptionally heroic on account of his swordplay, the Khazars appointed him their general.[71] The ruler, who was married to a Jewish woman named Sarah, converted to Judaism and was circumcised, which upset the rulers of Christendom and Islamdom.[72] The leader invited Christians, Jews, and Muslims to send envoys to explain their religions. The Christians presented their religion, and the Muslims and Jews contradicted them. The Muslims made a presentation, and the Christians and Jews contradicted what they had said. The Jews narrated the history of the world from Creation to the Exodus, which the Christians and Muslims confirmed. The ruler asked them all to explain the ancient books that he had stored in a cave. They were Torahs, and the Jews read from them as they had earlier narrated. The king and the Khazars were most pleased with the Jews and converted to their religion, and Jews from the Abbasid caliphate immigrated to the empire.[73] Jews continued to proselytise within the kingdom. When the Byzantines sent Christian emissaries, they were told by the ruler that people believed in one God, not the Trinity.

Before converting to Jewish monotheism, these Turks practised shamanism. They turned to the east to pray, worshipped animals, and considered trees as sacred. Formerly pagans who worshipped animals, spirits, and the sky, using trance-entering shamans as mediators with *Tangri*, the Sky God, *Umay*, the

The Secular Symbiosis and Jews ruling over Muslims

mother Goddess, *Erlik-Khan*, the God of Death, and *Ku'ar*, the Thunder God, offering sacrifices to trees, the Khazars became monotheistic Jews. They prayed to one God and adopted the rituals and practices of Judaism including circumcision, observance of the Shabbat, study of the law, prayer, dietary laws, and worshipping in synagogues. It is likely that the Radhaniya played a role in their Judaisation. These Arabic-, Persian-, Greek-, Spanish-, and Slavic-speaking Jewish merchants, who exported eunuchs, slaves, furs, brocades, and weaponry to the East and imported cinnamon and other spices, musk, and camphor to the West, travelled from Morocco to China and back, crossing Khazar territory and trading in its capital and other cities.[74] One such town was 'Samkarsh, the city of the Jews' (Taman, the town on the eastern shore of the Kerch Strait, connecting the Black Sea and the Sea of Azov, separating Crimea from Russia).[75] Their empire became a refuge for persecuted Jews fleeing the Byzantines, ironically their ally against their Muslim enemies.

Khazar leaders chose Judaism to preserve the political independence of Khazaria from Christian and Muslim kingdoms, rather than to represent a demographic fact after mass conversion. The Khazar Empire became a powerful kingdom at the periphery of the Byzantine and Abbasid empires and one which was in constant war with the Vikings. The history of the Jewish Khazar kingdom is fleeting, but significant for it is the longest period Jews ruled over Muslims in history. Contemporary Muslim diplomats, geographers, and historians commented on this inversion of normal relations and gave us our best description of the Khazars, whose alphabet scholars have not been able to decipher.[76]

The geographer and historian Ibn Rusta, a native of Isfahan, Iran, writing in the first two decades of the tenth century, tells us that the Khazar 'supreme authority is Jewish, and so is the military and political leader and those commanding officers and important men who support him'. The rest followed the Turks' religion, paganism.[77] Every year the military led an expedition against the Pečenegs (a semi-nomadic, pagan Turkic people whose territory was east of the Volga River). According to Ibn Rusta, 'they present a handsome spectacle ... fully armed, with banners, lances and strong coats of mail ... [their leader] with 10,000 horsemen ... a sort of disk, like a drum, is carried in front of him. A horseman bears it before him and he follows leading the army, who can see the light reflected from the disk.'

Writing a decade later, an Abbasid envoy of Caliph Al-Muqtadir (r. 908–32), Ahmad ibn Fadlan, offered extensive information on the Turkic Jewish kingdom and its political system. He described a system of two sovereigns, a doubled kingship. One ruler was the religious authority known as the kagan.[78] He was like a Muslim caliph. His secular 'lieutenant is known as *kagan beg*'. Like a Muslim sultan, the beg 'leads the armies, directs the affairs of the kingdom, appears in public and receives the allegiance of neighbouring kings'. The beg was the only person allowed to see the kagan in person. Every day, he entered his presence humbly, barefoot. The kagan never gave public audience and never spoke to his subjects.

According to Istakhri, of ancient Persepolis, writing in the middle of the tenth century, the kagan 'is held in great respect and anyone who comes into his presence must make a full prostration'.

> No one but an elite group, such as the king [beg] and those of his standing, can approach him. The king [beg] only enters his presence on special occasions; when he does,

The Secular Symbiosis and Jews ruling over Muslims

he rolls in the dust, prostrating himself, then stands at a distance until given permission to approach. The kagan is brought out only if some calamity occurs. The Turks and the unbelievers dare not look upon him; they turn away ... out of reverence for him. When he dies and is buried, everyone who passes his tomb dismounts and prostrates himself. A man remounts only when some distance from his tomb. Their obedience to their king [kagan] reaches such a pitch that when one of their important men is condemned to death, the king does not have him publicly executed. He orders him to kill himself and he goes to his dwelling and kills himself.

Finally:

The kaganate is confined to a well-known clan, which possesses neither political power nor wealth. When it is the turn of one of them to rule, he is appointed irrespective of his condition. I was told by someone I trust that he saw a young man selling bread in the market and they said that when the kagan died, he was the worthiest to succeed to the kaganate. He was, however, a Muslim, and only a man who professes Judaism can become kagan.[79]

Al-Mas'udi narrates how:

The king [kagan], his court and all those of the Khazar people practise Judaism, to which the king of the Khazars was converted during the reign of Harun al-Rashid [786–809]. Many Jews from Muslim and Byzantine cities came to settle among the Khazars, particularly since Romanus I [r. 920–44], the king of the Byzantines in our own time

[943], forced the Jews in his kingdom to convert to Christianity ... A great number of Jews fled from the land of the Byzantines and sought refuge with the Khazars.[80]

He mentions that the Jewish kagan and beg have many pagan subjects, 'among which are the Saqaliba [Slavs] and the Rus' [Viking traders], who live in one of the two parts of the city'.

The Khazars employed a kind of pact of protection that the Muslims also used with Jews. Muslims had their law courts in the Turkish Jewish Khazar kingdom, just as Jews had their law courts in Muslim-ruled lands. Muslims had their mosques, just as Jews had their synagogues in Muslim-ruled lands. The difference was that in this kingdom, unlike in many pre-modern Islamic-ruled societies where Jews (and Christians) were not allowed to bear arms, Muslim soldiers made up the Arsiyya, the elite segment of the military.

Ibn Fadlan tells us about Jewish–Muslim relations in the kingdom. In an inverse of the way it was in Muslim-ruled societies, the Muslims were the dhimmi. In Itil, 'The Muslims live on one bank [the eastern bank] and the king and his followers on the other [the western side]. The head of the Muslim community is one of the king's officers ... and he is a Muslim.'[81] All legal decisions concerning Muslims living in the land of the Khazars or visiting the country on business were referred to this Muslim officer. He was the only person with the authority to examine their affairs or judge their quarrels.[82] The Muslims in this town had a congregational mosque where they performed the Friday prayers. It had a tall minaret and muezzins. Ibn Rusta confirmed that 'they have mosques, imams, muezzins and Qur'an schools'.[83] Istakhri mentions another Khazar city called Samandar, located between Itil and Bab al-Abwab (Derbend), which had Muslim inhabitants, whose homes and mosques were domed, made of wood, and woven together. 'Their king is a Jew, related to the king of the Khazars.'[84]

The kagan was as a caliph who represented and acted on the behalf of all Jews. When in 922 the kagan learned that Muslims had destroyed the synagogue that was in Dar al-Babunaj (the House of Chamomile, in Derbend), he ordered the minaret of the mosque in Itil to be destroyed and the muezzins put to death.[85] 'If I did not fear that not a synagogue would be left standing throughout the lands of Islam,' he said, 'I would have destroyed the mosque.'

Al-Mas'udi notes how it is a custom in the Khazar capital that there were 'seven judges, two for the Muslims, two for the Khazars, who make their decisions in accordance with the Torah, two for the Christians, who make theirs according to the Gospels, and one for the Saqaliba [Slavs], Rus' [Vikings] and other pagans. This last judge follows pagan law, which is the product of natural reason.'[86] Istakhri confirmed how, like the dhimma legal system, 'If a lawsuit arises among the people, they make a judgement on it. The litigants do not go to the king himself, they go to these judges.'[87]

The Rus' and the Saqaliba, who were pagans, 'served as mercenaries and slaves of the king'. Istakhri mentions how 'the slaves of the Khazars are idol worshippers, who allow their children to be sold and enslave each other'. Yet 'the Jews and Christians who live among them, like the Muslims, are not permitted by their religion to enslave one another'.[88] Besides the Arsiyya,

> There are also a certain number of Muslim merchants and artisans, who have emigrated to this country because of the justice and security with which the king rules. In addition to the congregational mosque, whose minaret towers over the king's palace, there are many other mosques to which

are attached schools where the Qur'an is taught to children. If the Muslims and the Christians united, the king would have no power over them.[89]

Istakhri tells us that they have 'many Muslim residents; it is said there are more than 10,000 Muslims. They have about thirty mosques.'[90] Their king 'is a Jew and it is said that his entourage numbers some 4,000 men. The Khazars are Muslims and Christians and Jews, and among them are idol worshippers. The smallest number are Jews and the largest Muslims and Christians, but the king and his entourage are Jews.'[91] Nevertheless, they retained their pagan customs: 'The greater part of their manners and customs are those of the idol worshippers. A man prostrates himself before another to show respect. Their legal rulings are peculiar to themselves, following ancient usages that conflict with those of the Muslim, Jewish and Christian religions.'

The dynasty was destroyed when the Rus' under pagan Svyatoslav of Kyiv invaded the Khazar kingdom and conquered Itil in 965 and the rest of the kingdom in the succeeding years. Ironically, trade was the downfall of the kingdom, for unlike other Turkic pastoralist nomads, the Khazars settled, built cities, tilled fields, and engaged in agriculture and trade. They invited the pagan Vikings to peaceably sell their amber, furs, honey, beeswax, slaves, and timber from the north, in exchange for Abbasid silver dirhams obtained from the south. Ibn Fadlan describes these Vikings as having bodies 'like palm trees. They are fair and ruddy. They wear neither coats nor caftans, but a garment which covers one side of the body and leaves one hand free. Each of them carries an axe, a sword and a knife and is never parted from any of the arms we have mentioned.'[92] Unlike the people of the steppe, including the Khazars, the Vikings fought not from horseback, but from boats. Describing a Viking raid on the Caspian in 913, in which 500 ships carried 100 warriors each, Al-Mas'udi notes 'The Rus' spilled rivers of blood, seized women and children and property, raided and everywhere destroyed and burned. The people who lived on these shores were in turmoil, for they had never been attacked by an enemy from the sea, and their shores had only been visited by the ships of merchants and fishermen.'[93]

The fair-haired river kings turned from long-distance traders to raiders. They looted and pillaged Khazar towns from the river and the sea with their light and strong boats capable of unprecedented reach and speed.[94]

The Vikings left behind 'cities of carrion and widows, husk-and-stump cities where the Northmen's fires still burned'.[95] Ibn Hawqal noted that 'in the year 969, or thereabouts, I asked a man about the vineyards, and he said: "There is not enough left of a vineyard or garden worth giving to a beggar. If a leaf were left on a branch, one of the Rus' would carry it off. Not a grape, not a raisin remains in that country."'[96] The Vikings, who facilitated the trade of furs and slaves for silver between the steppe and the Islamic world, became Slavic-speaking Orthodox Christian Russians, their trading posts developing into the fortified towns of Kyiv and Novgorod.[97]

What became of these Jewish Turks? According to a popular but discredited theory, after the collapse of the Khazar Empire the Jews migrated north and west to Poland where they became the progenitors of Eastern European Jewry, the ancestors of today's Ashkenazi Jews.[98] If this were true, it would mean most Jews in the world today are descended from converted Turks, not from the German Jews who migrated to Poland in medieval times, who in turn were descended from the Jews of the Roman Empire, which conquered and ruled ancient Israel. This theory, in turn, is used to discredit modern Jewish claims to establishing a Jewish state in Israel based on ancestral claims to the land. If the Ashkenazi Jews who created the Zionist movement and settled the land which eventually became a Jewish state were really Turks, Palestine could not be theirs.

The truth may be simpler. Perhaps some Khazar Jews migrated to the Byzantine Empire, or Spain, or elsewhere in Europe. Some Khazar Jews may have remained in place. Al-Muqaddasi gives a more convincing account. Writing between 985 and 990, he offered a sobering description of the land of the Khazars following the fall of the Jewish kingdom, a region which was 'a grim, forbidding place, full of herd animals, honey and Jews'. The capital city, Itil, 'is surrounded by trees, which grow even within the [walls]'.

> Muslims are numerous here. Their king used to be Jewish, and made laws and appointed judges [from the communities of] Muslims, Jews, Christians and idol-worshippers ... I heard that an army of the Byzantines, called Rus', invaded them [along with their Oghuz allies] and conquered their lands. The city [Itil] is walled, and the houses are scattered about within ... Their [the current inhabitants, Oghuz Turks] dwellings are tents of wood and felt, and large [yurts].[99]

Itil 'is a poor, infertile place, bereft of [agricultural?] prosperity and without fruit'.

After mentioning the other towns and their Muslim and Christian inhabitants in Khazaria, he describes the town of Khazar's inhabitants as 'formerly Jewish, [but] they have become Muslims'.[100] Rather than retain their Jewishness, migrate to the West, and form the Ashkenazi community, they converted to

The Secular Symbiosis and Jews ruling over Muslims

Islam and blended into the population, while German Jewry moved from West to East, establishing the Ashkenazim of Poland.

The most comprehensive study to date of the human genome supports the view that Ashkenazi Jews do not descend from the Khazars. Population geneticists found that 'Ashkenazi Jews derive their ancestry primarily from populations of the Middle East and Europe, that they possess considerable shared ancestry with other Jewish populations, and that there is no indication of a significant genetic contribution either from within or from north of the Caucasus region', the former Khazar kingdom.[101] Ashkenazim are closest to other Jews, Italian, Middle Eastern, North African, and Sephardi, in their genetic ancestry.[102]

Long after the fall of the Khazar kingdom, a Spanish Jewish poet, Judah Halevi, composed *Kitab al-Khazari* (Book of the Khazar), a fictive dialogue between a rabbi and a pagan Khazar king. The Khazar king rejected Aristotelian philosophy, Islam, and Christianity and chose rabbinic Judaism. Judah Halevi penned this work to criticise philosophers for claiming to arrive at truths that only revelation offers.[103] Jews in Spain, immersed in Arabic Islamic culture, found a way to remain Jewish while engaging with the world around them. Like the Khazar Jews, they too would face the choice of conversion or exile when a non-Muslim people rose to power.

3

JEWISH–MUSLIM SYMBIOSIS AND ALLIANCE: AL-ANDALUS, EIGHTH– SEVENTEENTH CENTURIES

Jewish–Muslim relations in medieval Europe were more long-lasting than on the Eurasian steppe. Al-Andalus, Muslim Spain, emerged in the eighth century. The Berber (Amazigh) Muslim general Tariq ibn Ziyad crossed the Strait of Gibraltar (an English corruption of the Arabic *jabal tariq*, Tariq's Mountain) and conquered southern Spain from the Christian Visigoths in 711. Having been persecuted by the Visigoths, Jews tell how they welcomed the Muslims as liberators. Muslims report that Jews were recruited from among the local population to serve as soldiers in the conquering army. Arab chroniclers related how after the Muslim army conquered Granada, they entrusted it to a garrison composed of Jews and Muslims, as they did in every place where Jews resided, including Seville. Tariq ibn Ziyad gathered the Jews in Toledo and left them in charge of the newly conquered city. Christians blamed the loss of their kingdom on the Jews' treason.[1]

By 732 Al-Andalus was established, and Christians and Jews would live as dhimmi. Later the Umayyad prince Abd al-Rahman fled to the Iberian peninsula as a refugee from Syria, defeated his rivals, and founded a new Umayyad dynasty based in Córdoba in 756. There he constructed the famous mosque with its most distinctive feature, the endless rows of ornamental arches with alternating red and white stripes inside the house of prayer. Its *mihrab* (prayer niche) was designed and decorated by Byzantine Christian mosaic artisans, like the floral-patterned golden mosaics within the Dome of the Rock in Jerusalem. His descendants are credited with establishing idealised inter-faith relations referred to as *convivencia*.

The notion of *convivencia* was promoted by the Spanish historian Américo Castro, who declared in 1948 that the Spanish people emerged from the fusion of Muslims, Christians, and Jews living together in the peninsula thanks to Muslim tolerance.[2] His romanticised view of interfaith coexistence in medieval Muslim Spain became a key component of the myth of interfaith utopia.[3] Between 929, when Abd al-Rahman III established the Umayyad caliphate in Córdoba, uniting Al-Andalus and making it the wealthiest kingdom in Europe, proclaiming himself the protector of Christians and Jews, and 1140, when the Berber Almohad dynasty based in Marrakesh rose to power in Spain, abolished the dhimma pact, compelled Jews to convert to Islam, and destroyed synagogues, 'no other medieval Jewish community had so many high-ranking personalities' in politics and the economy.[4] For two centuries a courtier-rabbi culture flourished like no other. Modern Jewish scholars tell of how no other kingdom 'produced a literary culture of such breadth', based on a shared Jewish–Muslim intellectual life. What was unique was Spanish Jews' 'extraordinary cultural vitality ... combined with material prosperity, their participation in public affairs', in government administration as viziers (ministers), at half a dozen courts, and as leaders of Jewish communities.

Scholars have called this a golden age, for 'nowhere else was the concentration of eminent Jewish personalities in the cultural, scientific, professional, and political realms as high as it was in Al-Andalus between the tenth and twelfth centuries.'[5] When the Umayyad caliphate in Córdoba collapsed in 1031, rule in Al-Andalus splintered, and as 'books were like treasure chests and knowledge was like gold', every court wanted the greatest minds of the age to join it.[6] At least half a dozen courtier-rabbis served as viziers to Muslim sovereigns.[7] For this reason, Al-Andalus has long been written about nostalgically by those promoting the myth of Jewish–Muslim harmony and Muslim tolerance as opposed to Christian persecution of Jews.

In the twelfth century, Abraham ibn Daud declared that Jewish poets 'began to chirp' in the days of Hasdai ibn Shaprut, 'and in the days of Samuel ibn Naghrela ha-Nagid, they sang aloud'.[8] *Nagid* is the Hebrew title for the designated leader of the Jews, similar to the exilarch in the Abbasid Empire. He was the privileged interlocutor of the sultan, viziers, and provincial governors, and was invested with the power to levy taxes and to execute the decisions of the rabbinic courts over which he presided. The *nagid* offered counsel to the sultan, serving as ambassador on his behalf and army leader. Ibn Shaprut was credited for being 'the preeminent Jewish dignitary of tenth century Al-Andalus' who 'set in motion the Hebrew Golden Age'.[9] He was the trusted personal physician and statesman of Caliph Abd al-Rahman III and his son, Al-Hakam II (r. 961–76) and a living manifestation of the cultural *convivencia*. Known by Muslims as Abu Yusuf, fluent in Arabic and Hebrew, and with knowledge of Latin, a rare skill for a Jew, he was a translator of ancient medical treatises, working with those who knew Greek, and a trusted diplomat, conducting negotiations with the Byzantines, Holy Roman Empire, and Andalusi Christian kings, as well as corresponding with the Khazars. At the same time, he was the *nasi* (prince, descendant of King David) or head of the Jewish community, and utilising his immense wealth gained while chief customs officer, was patron of Jewish letters, head of a Talmudic academy, philosopher, and writer of secular poetry who catalysed Hebrew-language literary achievements of the age.[10]

Samuel ibn Naghrela ha-Nagid of Córdoba (known as Abu Ibrahim Isma'il to Muslims) was the model courtier-rabbi, 'the most powerful Jew of the Middle Ages'.[11] Master of Arabic and the Qur'an, speaker of Amazigh, at Granada he was commander-in-chief of Muslim armies battling Muslim foes, vizier at the court of the Berber Muslim Zirid rulers Sultan Habbus ibn Maksan (r. 1020–38) and then Badis ibn Habbus (r. 1038–73).[12] With his prowess in Hebrew and Jewish law, Samuel ibn Naghrela was also rabbi and first *nagid*, leader of Andalusi Jewry, esteemed Jewish scholar and 'a poet who seemed as at home in singing a thanksgiving hymn to God as in extolling the fetching beauty of the *saki* [young boy who poured wine], describing the exuberant anticipation of the wine goblet on his rounds, or in excoriating the incompetence of talmudic lawyers in a Granadan study-house'.[13] This courtier legitimised having feet in two worlds by comparing his military victories in the service of Muslim Granada over the Muslim kings in Seville and Almería to King David defeating the Amalekites, the Israelites' worse enemies.[14] His eldest son Joseph also served as vizier, and was given even more power by Sultan Badis than Sultan Habbus had allowed his father.

The most perfect expression of Jewish–Muslim symbiosis occurred in cities such as Granada and Córdoba. It was found not in the Arabic literature of the Jews, but in the secular and religious Hebrew poetry and musical melodies created in medieval Muslim societies including Al-Andalus. Religious poetry composed by Solomon ibn Gabirol, Abraham ibn Ezra, and his friend Judah Halevi used the metres, motifs, and genres of Arabic poetry in the synagogue as part of the worship service. Secular Hebrew poetry about wine, women, young boys, and song was shared at mixed soirées.[15] Consider the verse by Moses ibn Ezra about wine and young boys: 'It kisses and bites, nauseates and remedies. People delight in its vicissitudes! The greatest of them have been "knocked off" by Bacchus's boy – but not by homicide!'[16]

Jewish thought from that period is 'justly considered the most fruitful and creative in Jewry's long history'. Between 950 and 1150 an entire class of courtier-rabbis embraced Arab culture to the extent that they composed 'bacchic Hebrew wine songs' and 'more remarkably, lyrical songs of love for beloved "gazelles", male as well as female'.[17] The same writers composed many more sacred liturgical poems.[18] These pious scholars, community leaders, and literati recited poetry and drank wine until dawn, then attended the morning prayer service. Yet later in life some repudiated their sinful younger selves for the obscene verse they had written.[19] The Jews absorbed Islamic and Arabic culture from the elite Muslims of Spain, and also learned how to live with the contrast between 'piety and worldliness, spirituality and pleasure, prayer and poetry', cultivating both *din* (religion, or the afterlife) and *dunya* (this material world).[20]

The Jewish and Muslim elite of Al-Andalus shared a common education and a common culture. It was for this reason that a Muslim could praise a Jew for his 'great erudition', for his mastery of Arabic and poetry, mathematics, astronomy, and music theory, and for having 'a perfect knowledge of logic and of the practice of research and observation', mastering the natural sciences and the work of Aristotle, concluding by adding that 'If he lives long enough, and if his zeal is sustained', he 'will soon know philosophy to perfection ... And yet he is still only a very young man. But God is the Highest, who is omnipotent, grants his blessings to whomever he pleases.'[21] Even a Jew.

This is not to overlook the fact that these were exceptional spaces for exceptional men, living in a society that was hierarchical and discriminatory, not an idyllic coexistence. Yet even Muslim polemicists, such as Ibn Hazm, famous for his book on love, *The Neckring of the Dove*, who also wrote a work refuting Judaism, entitled *Radd ala ibn al-Nagrila* (*Refutation of Ibn Naghrela*), debated and engaged with Jews, and, as he attested, socialised with Jewish friends even as he attacked Judaism.[22] That Jews could also criticise the Qur'an, a Holy Book to which the dhimma pact prohibited their access, and read and refuted the works of Muslim scholars they knew personally, attests to a level of tolerance unusual in the pre-modern world.[23] Yet that tolerance was limited: Ibn Hazm was so infuriated by the pamphlet criticising the Qur'an attributed to Samuel ibn Naghrela, whom he knew from the caliph's court in Córdoba, that he called for him to be humiliated and made to suffer along with the ruler who befriended him.[24]

Moses ibn Ezra, in his *Kitab al-Muhadara wa'l-Mudhakara* (*Conversations and Recollections*, translated into Hebrew as *Shirat Yisrael*), explained the benefits of learning in the wake of the Arab Muslim conquests:

> They obliterated the borders but filled their cities and towns with wisdom and knowledge. They translated all the sciences, ancient and modern, assembled them all, and added to them their own clarifications and commentaries. Everything that had been compiled and translated in all areas of knowledge, they compiled and translated into Arabic, since God gave the Arabs the gift of a rich, poetically superior language.[25]

Moses ibn Ezra was prominent at the court of Granada. He is an example of the 'compunctious poet', for he had an ambivalent attitude to the poetry he wrote and the life he led.[26] He renounced his life's work yet never escaped composing in its forms. He repented but continued writing.

His student Judah Halevi was a famous poet. Whereas his master had personal misgivings, yet defended his work, Halevi after a career as the darling of Jewish courtly society attempted to turn his back on the culture and society that nourished him, and migrated to Palestine. Despite his desire for renunciation, he found that he could not escape that society, and he composed more than fifty secular poems in Andalusi style about the pleasures of this world for notables in Egypt.

Judah Halevi has long been promoted as a proto-Zionist, in part for his poem composed while in Spain before setting out for Palestine in 1140, which begins

> My heart is in the East and I am at the edge of the West.
> How can I savour what I eat, how find it sweet?
> How can I fulfil my vows and pledges while
> Zion is in Christendom's fetter, and I am in Islam's shackle?[27]

Few recall that the poet was also known as Abu al-Hassan. He wrote his most famous work, the *Kitab Al-Khazari*, in Arabic. Most of his poetry was steeped in Islamic culture. The financial insurance behind his pilgrimage was a silk turban.[28]

Jews in medieval Spain were especially influenced by pre-Islamic and Islamic Arabic-language poetry. They include the ancient form of the long, single-rhymed, single-metred *qasida*, and the strophic *muwashshah*, and the rhymed prose and rhymed poetry of the *maqama* introduced in the tenth century. The *muwashshah*, set to music, was used for drinking songs and love poetry as well as for liturgical poetry, a convergence between the secular and religious, Arabic and Hebrew.[29] The Hebrew love poetry expressed the same themes of pre-Islamic and Muslim poets of 'the yearning for a beloved woman who is off wandering; the suitor prisoner to her love; the cruel beloved, who coats her lips with her lovers' blood and whose eyes launch arrows that pierce the heart of any man who desires her; lovesickness; the fire of love; the beauty of young ladies, which surpasses the brilliance of the sun and moon'.[30]

The poetry was connected to music. Jews studied it and performed it together with Muslims. They shared the same melodies. Jews imported the melodies and rhyme schemes of profane Arabic poetry sung and accompanied by musical instruments directly into their synagogue services.[31]

The music, a merger of Iberian and Arab musical and poetic traditions, emerged in Islamic Spain in the ninth century. The legend about its origin is that in 822 the famous musician Abu al-Hasan Ali ibn Nafi, known as Ziryab (blackbird or lark), who first gained fame in Baghdad, travelled from Kairouan (Tunisia) to Córdoba at the invitation of Al-Hakam II. But when he crossed the Strait of Gibraltar, he was told by a messenger that he had passed away, yet the new ruler, Abd al-Rahman II (r. 822–52) would welcome him. It is fitting that that messenger was a Jew, Abu al-Nasr al-Mansur Abu al-Buhlul, head musician of the court and personal envoy of the emir. Ziryab is credited with inventing Andalusi music, although it is unlikely, as the music is based in a new type of poetry, the *muwashshah*, invented after his death.[32] The final verses of the poems were bilingual, composed in Romance (popular spoken Latin) and Andalusian colloquial Arabic. What was original was how the same poem used many different rhymes and each verse ended in a rhyme, and how the main rhyme repeated each time with different words.[33]

Jews appreciated the new poetic style, composing at first poems in Arabic, then in Hebrew. Hebrew *muwashshah* 'became one of the signature genres of the florescence of secular Hebrew poetry in medieval Islamic Spain'.[34]

Although the love poetry was mainly about beauty and not sex, it was as common to employ erotic and homoerotic poetic conventions for Muslim as for Jewish writers, despite each religion's prohibition of such relations.[35]

For these poets, what made the good life were

> Five things there are that fill the hearts of men with joy,
>   And put my grief to flight:
> A pretty girl, a garden, wine, the water's rush
>   In a canal, and song.[36]

Reading this poetry may cause us to think, 'the world must have seemed one great wine party held in the enormous, lush garden of Spain' and that the courtier-rabbis were 'themselves a uniquely gifted generation'.[37] Yet what did Spanish Jews themselves say about the period? Did they present their lives as either an idyllic interfaith utopia, or marked by constant persecution? Andalusi Jews, unlike their modern historians, did not ask: was it good for the Jews, or where was it better? Rather, some Jewish writers of the time were critical of those principles we moderns hold dear, such as openness, acceptance, and the fluidity of social boundaries. They realised these lead to lax observance of religion, fraternisation, intimate relations, and conversion.[38] Jews displayed ambivalence, distance, and relativism. They were not committed to staying. When persecuted in one kingdom, move to the other! Jews wrote of Muslims as sometimes savants, mentors, promoting meritocracy to protégés, but usually they did not mention Muslims at all in their writings.

Jewish–Muslim Symbiosis and Alliance

Muslims wrote of Jews as elites, dignitaries, advisors, who were useful and admired for their skill and expertise, but who were ignorant of religious truth, Islam. Worse, Jews were described as cunning and deceitful, appearing knowledgeable, but dangerous. Jews were empowered by their knowledge, expertise, and usefulness, but empowerment was seen by Muslims as going against the natural order, as manifested in the dhimma pact, which favoured Muslims. Their place in society was more ambivalent than is remembered today, disdained and socially subordinated; they were supposed to know their place, yet were accepted and protected subjects, who could in fact rise to great heights.[39]

Some of the most important writers, smarting in the wake of persecution, wrote negatively about Muslims, predicting their downfall as revenge for daring to harm God's Chosen People. Judah Halevi offered a dream-fantasy of Muslims as dhimmi, 'humbled and low':

Tell Hagar's sons, 'Let down your haughty hand
    From Sarah's son, the rival you have scorned,
For I have seen you in my dream, a ruin:
    Perhaps in life you really are undone.
Perhaps this year, eleven-hundred thirty
    Will see your pride thrown down, your thinking thwarted.'[40]

Abraham ibn Daud recounted the rise and fall of the ibn Naghrelas in his *Sefer ha-Kabbalah* (*Book of Tradition*, 1160–1). He praised Samuel ibn Naghrela ha-Nagid for having lived a long life and 'died after having earned four crowns: the crown of Torah, the crown of power, the crown of a Levite [the priestly class], and towering over them all, by dint of good deeds in each of these domains, the crown of a good name'.[41] But as for his son, Joseph, 'of all the fine qualities which his father [Samuel] possessed he [Joseph] lacked but one', which cost him his life. It was humility. The dhimma pact insisted on the humbling of Jews: 'he grew haughty – to his destruction', as the Muslims were so jealous of him that they killed him 'along with the [Jewish] community of Granada'.

The Berber Zirid Sultan Abd Allah ibn Buluggin (r. 1073–90) penned a memoir, *Tibyan* (1095), in which he discussed both ibn Naghrela viziers, which provides evidence of the precariousness of the public prominence of elite Jews, who were seen as useful and potentially dangerous by the Muslim rulers whom they served. Ibn Buluggin referred to Joseph as 'the Jew' and 'swine', a malicious man who poisoned his father, Buluggin ibn Badis, prince and governor of Málaga, in 1064.[42] Ironically, the murder was only conceivable because of *convivencia*, the intimate, trusting friendship between the Muslim and the Jew, as the governor often drank with Joseph and visited him in his palace.[43] Ibn Buluggin accused Joseph of spiking his father's drink, killing him, which was one of the reasons, along with alleged treason – purportedly he connived to open the gates of Granada to the soldiers of a rival Muslim kingdom, who would eliminate the Zirids and make Joseph ruler – for his own assassination on 30 December 1066: 'The Jew turned and fled for his life inside the palace pursued by the populace, who finally ran him down and did him to death. They then turned their swords on every Jew in the city [Granada] and seized vast quantities of their goods and property.'[44]

Abu Ishaq was *qadi* (Islamic judge) of Granada under Sultan Badis ibn Habbus, who preceded Abd Allah ibn Buluggin. At some point Joseph ibn Naghrela convinced the sultan to dismiss him from his post and send him into exile.[45] His poem attacking

Joseph and the Jews of the city is a scathing diatribe, angered as he was by the rise of Jews above their assumed dhimmi status. Sultan Badis 'has made a mistake' because

> He has chosen an infidel as his secretary
> when he could, had he wished, have chosen a Believer.
> Through him [Joseph ibn Naghrela], the Jews have become great and proud
> and arrogant – they, who were among the most abject
> And have gained their desires and attained the utmost
> and this happened suddenly, before they even realised it.
> And how many a worthy Muslim humbly obeys
> the vilest ape among these miscreants.[46]

Abu Ishaq wanted Badis to

> Put them back where they belong
> and reduce them to the lowest of the low,
> Roaming amongst us, with their little bags,
> with contempt, degradation and scorn as their lot,
> Scrabbling in the dunghills for coloured rags
> to shroud their dead for burial.

He asked Badis directly why he was a Jew lover, a lover of 'this bastard brood'. Joseph was 'a villain', 'evil company', a member of 'the society of the wicked'.[47] He did not understand why, if in other kingdoms 'the Jews are outcast dogs', he should bring them close to him when in other lands they were kept at a distance. About Jews in Granada, he wrote that rather than being humbled, they were the revenue collectors, dressed in the finest clothes, and were entrusted with state secrets.

Referring to Samuel ibn Naghrela ha-Nagid's writings, he

attacked the boldness of Jews in Granada, who were not hindered from criticising Islam, instead enveloping Muslims with the sound of their prayers, controlling the meat markets and selling Muslims their offal. Then he incited the murder of Joseph ibn Naghrela, and all the Jews of Granada, for the inversion of the dhimma pact where Muslims were on top and Jews on the bottom:

> Hasten to slaughter him as an offering,
> sacrifice him, for he is a fat ram
> And do not spare his people
> for they have amassed every precious thing.
> Break loose their grip and take their money
> for you have a better right to what they collect.[48]

Abu Ishaq affirmed that because they did not keep to their humble status, their blood was licit:

> Do not consider it a breach of faith to kill them
> the breach of faith would be to let them carry on.
> They have violated our covenant [dhimma pact] with them
> so how can you be held guilty against violators?

Jews were massacred by mobs in Granada in 1066. The caliphate of Córdoba fell at the beginning of the same century.

Those who depict Jewish life in Muslim-ruled societies as an interfaith utopia point to Samuel ibn Naghrela as their main evidence. *Convivencia* has been popularised in books and films. The flap of María Menocal's *The Ornament of the World: How Muslims, Jews, and Christians Created a Culture of Tolerance in Medieval Spain* exalts 'the vibrant civilisation of medieval Spain where tolerance was often the rule, and literature, science, and art flourished in a climate of cultural openness'.⁴⁹ The book begins, 'Once upon a time', as if it was a fairy tale.

Those who paint a darker picture of Jewish–Muslim relations point to the murder of Samuel's son Joseph ibn Naghrela and the massacre in Granada, and the verse of Muslim poet Abu Ishaq who castigated the ruler for violating the dhimma pact. Others point to the forced conversion and massacres of Jews by the intolerant Almohads in 1146 and 1147, which spurred Maimonides of Córdoba, who called himself 'Moses the Sephardi' in exile, and many other Jews to flee to Christian Spanish territories, or to other Muslim lands, such as Egypt, taking Andalusi culture and knowledge with them. The fact is that court Jews were 'simultaneously empowered and vulnerable'. Lacking any other basis of political power, they owed their positions to the sultan, and they walked the tightrope of trying to maintain the sultan's favour without being seen as having too much power and influence, which could lead to their personal downfall and violence against all Jews.⁵⁰

Jews and Muslims engaged in interfaith intellectual and social exchanges, gathering for discussions using only human reason, where scriptural proofs were disallowed. They demonstrated mutual respect for others who possessed knowledge, whatever their religion, creating a space allowing for an appreciation of merit and talent and real friendship. Among teams of translators, Jews normally dominated. In this intellectually intimate environment, seniority was not automatically given to the Muslim, attesting to the overcoming of rigid ideas governing interfaith social contact.⁵¹ These men were equal members of the same textual communities, despite their religious differences.

Medieval philosophers were divided into Aristotelians and neo-Platonists. What mattered to philosophers was not whether one's faith was Judaism or Islam, but where one stood in the debate between the two camps. One of the disputes concerned Creation. Aristotelians believed the world always existed, whereas neo-Platonists argued God created the world out of material that had always existed with God.

Moses ibn Ezra justified his writing of love poetry by claiming the themes were found in the Bible, in the Song of Songs. He argued that Arabic love poetry was suitable for the synagogue as well because it had so much in common with the Song of Songs, which is devoted to the beloved, a metaphor for God.[52] More novel was his defence of such frivolity with a reference to the neo-Platonist belief that spiritual love, alluded to in his poems, was noble, whereas carnal love was not. This argument was based on the philosophers known as the *mutakallimun*. *Kalam* was defence apologetics, or the science of discourse. The *mutakallimun* were distinguished by their concern to engage in disputation and argument to defend Islam or Judaism against heretics. They were inspired by respect for reason in the defence of religious tenets, the concern to purge the notion of God of multiplicity and anthropomorphism, and the desire to proclaim and justify absolute divine perfection. Ibn Ezra also argued that love poetry was not necessarily based on experience, referring to an Aristotelian argument that imagination was sanctioned because lies such as these were not really lies.[53]

Jewish philosophers were influenced by Muslim philosophers, as individuals used reason to defend revelation. The Torah in their view contained truths validated by reason in the form of logical inferences. One stream of thought was influenced by Aristotle's empiricism, his logic, physics, and metaphysics, as well as Plato's *Republic* and *Laws*. Al-Farabi in Baghdad, Avicenna, Ibn Bajja, and Ibn Rushd (known as Averroes in Western Europe) in Al-Andalus were the greatest of these Muslim thinkers. They influenced their Jewish counterparts, such as Abraham ibn Da'ud, who composed the first book of Jewish Aristotelianism, *Ha-Emunah ha-Ramah* (*Exalted Faith*), which aimed to harmonise Judaism and Aristotelian philosophy and science, and Maimonides in Al-Andalus, the greatest of the Jewish Aristotelians.[54] Medieval Muslim and Jewish scholars demonstrated innovation, through original contributions and engaging in rationalist thought that was novel within Abrahamic religious culture, for they used reason to examine sacred texts. The engagement with translated thought altered the philosophical culture of medieval Muslim and Jewish scholars and resulted in a synthesis that attracted Christian minds.

Circles of intellectual affinity emerged. Arabic-speaking Jewish and Muslim philosophers who supported themselves as physicians gathered in each other's homes in a *majlis* (gathering) with a teacher to learn and to debate philosophical concepts.

Ibn Bajja established the Spanish school of Aristotelian philosophy. He argued that union with the divine or Active Intellect, which is the last in the series of ten separate Intellects, is possible and the aim of man. Abraham ibn Da'ud of Córdoba was a fellow traveller. An Aristotelian, he believed science was built on the principles of religion, and that physics and philosophy and revealed religion are the same. His chronicle, *Sefer ha-Kabbalah*, is significant because it defends rabbinic Judaism against Karaism, and defends the nobility and legitimacy of the courtier-rabbis after Judah Halevi defected. Ibn Da'ud defended Andalusi Jewry and its philosophy as a means of redemption. He linked the rabbis to revelation and the tradition which defended it. He argued that a new cycle of messianism was about to begin and prophecies had not yet been fulfilled. He also argued that Islam was the fourth world empire. Spain was the land in which the third world empire, Rome, and fourth kingdoms were waging war.

He posited a messianic function for the Andalusi courtier-rabbis: since they lived on the stage where history would change, they would play a momentous role. The messenger of the new redemption would spring from it. Their Hebrew compositions cried out for redemption which gave hope to the Jews. Ibn Da'ud placed the struggle between Muslims and Christians over Andalusia and the role of the courtier-rabbis in reviving Hebrew through poetry in a messianic context. Redemption would take place in Spain after the eschatological struggle was resolved. He fled from his native Córdoba to Christian Toledo, in central Spain, which after the fall of the caliphate of Córdoba became the centre for translating from Hebrew and Arabic the studies of Ibn Rushd, Maimonides, and other Jewish and Muslim scholars into Latin, and disseminating it to Western Europe, planting the seeds for the European Renaissance. For the translation movement was much more than an 'autopilot transmission from East to West', as 'the two-century-long Muslim effort to understand and adapt the Hellenistic intellectual universe reintegrated the vital worldview of the classical world back into a living culture', at a time when the Greek body of knowledge 'had become fossilized' and may have been lost had it not been revitalised through Arabic translations.[55]

Ibn Rushd or Averroes became royal physician and *qadi* (judge) of Córdoba. His philosophy was later disavowed by his patrons, and he was exiled to Marrakesh, where he ended his days. He was one of the most influential of Aristotelians. He believed that man's ultimate destiny was the contemplative life, and he reconciled reason and revelation in a perfect faith which embraces rational knowledge.

As Ibn Rushd was the greatest Muslim Aristotelian, his Jewish counterpart was Maimonides, the pre-eminent Jewish philosopher of the medieval period, author of many influential works, including *Mishneh Torah* (1180) and *The Guide of the Perplexed* (in Arabic, *Dalalat al-Harin*, 1190). In his magnum opus, *Mishneh Torah*, his fourteen-volume code of Jewish law, Maimonides integrated a rationalist philosophical approach into his religious thought. He articulated the bases of Jewish faith and argued that the laws of religion are essential for social order and the people must observe them without necessarily understanding them. He encouraged his readers to fulfil the commandments for peace in this world and bliss in the hereafter. A rationalist, he put philosophy and science in the service of theology. He presented a metaphysical system with traces of Aristotelianism, utilised astronomical calculations to establish the calendar, discussed the doctrine of the Messiah and refuted Islam and its founder. This work is the most complete corpus of *halakhah* in Jewish literature. It is the single post-Talmudic work detailing all Jewish celebrations – one of the greatest Jewish works of the medieval period. Written not in Talmudic Aramaic but in Hebrew, it is a compendium of all Jewish law, written (Torah) and oral (Talmud), a simplified code of law. It is said that a Jew who masters the Torah and the *Mishneh Torah* has no need for any other book.[56]

Maimonides, a child of Andalusia, initiated from an early age into classical Arab culture and Judaic spirituality, was able, in a few years' residence in Fez, to assimilate into Judeo-Moroccan culture to the point of becoming its guide.[57] In five years in Morocco he wrote *Treatise on Logic*, a didactic work inspired by the Muslim philosopher Al-Farabi, and his commentary on the Mishnah. In *Treatise on Logic* he shares with Averroes the concern to reconcile divine revelation and science, and the explanation of the mystery of human understanding through astral influence. The celestial and the terrestrial are synthesised by the secret interconnections of physics and metaphysics, of the visible and the invisible, of the sayable and the unspeakable.

In *The Guide of the Perplexed* Maimonides' audience was those who already fulfilled the commandments, but whose study of philosophy caused doubts of reconciliation between the two. It is a meeting ground for both religions, and was read in Arabic by Jews and Muslims.[58] In it, Maimonides argues that the goal for which it is worthwhile to live is pure, abstract thinking; the book determined the course of Jewish philosophy from the thirteenth century onwards. With roots in Greek philosophy and Muslim interpretation it is a perfection of thought, not merely because it was written in Arabic by an original Jewish thinker and was studied by Muslims, but because it develops and conveys to large sections of the Jewish people ideas which had so long occupied Muslims.[59]

Ibn Rushd, in his *Tahafut al-Tahafut* (*The Incoherence of the Incoherence*, 1180), and Maimonides attacked *kalam*, Karaites and the Mu'tazilites for not offering reasoning that would lead to certainty, and not allowing the scientific person to bring scripture and philosophy together in a satisfying way.[60] Much of the first volume of Maimonides' *The Guide of the Perplexed* is devoted to refuting the *mutakallimun*, while agreeing with them on the temporal creation of the world.[61] Ibn Rushd and Maimonides developed a political philosophy with a scientific understanding of the place of religion and philosophy in society, viewing a prophet as founder of a political community possessing laws to ensure its continuity, and asserting the place of the philosopher in public life.[62]

Chased out of Córdoba and then Fez by the Almohads, Maimonides wrote his greatest works in refuge in Fustat after 1166. Because Maimonides was renowned for his responsa to legal questions, an Egyptian Jew in Yemen posed questions to him on behalf of Yemeni Jews, who, like Spanish and Moroccan Jews under the Almohads, were faced with forced conversion by the ruler. The result was *The Epistle on Yemen/Epistle on Martyrdom* (Arabic, *Al-Risala al-Yemeniyya*, written *c*.1173). Maimonides composed it in Arabic, as he wrote all his philosophical works, as an analysis of oppression.[63] He argued that violence loses its omnipotence in the face of peaceful resistance because it can tame neither consciences infused with truth nor intelligences loving freedom. It is a strategy of civil disobedience. During forced Islamisation, imposed on the Jews by the Almohads, he advocated feigned conversion to escape martyrdom. Maimonides argued that the convert was absolved by the scriptures when he applied the Ten Commandments in his private life.

Regarding forced conversion to Islam, Maimonides argued that someone who is compelled to make a false oath, such as declaring that Muhammad is God's messenger, is also not culpable, echoing the Muslim practice of *taqiyya*, dissimulating one's true beliefs to avoid persecution.[64] Stating the Islamic credo is not a terrible sin. Reciting the *Shahadah* is mere speech, and not action. A Jew is 'to suffer martyrdom only when it is demanded of him to perform a deed, or something that he is forbidden to do'.[65] Maimonides urged persecuted Jews to 'leave these places and go to where he can practice religion and fulfil the Law without compulsion or fear', and told them not to be depressed by the persecutions, by the rise of the enemy, or the weakness of Jews, but to see them as tests of faith, so that only the pious will remain to observe Judaism.[66]

After Maimonides' death in 1204, his son, Abraham, took over from him as community leader. Abraham was a rabbinic authority, head of the Cairo Jewish community and leader of a Jewish pietist movement influenced by Islamic Sufism. He promoted elements that came from Sufism, including spiritual fellowship, guidance under a spiritual leader or shaykh, rituals of meditation and fasting, and wearing of distinctive dress, along with Sufi religious vocabulary and ideas.[67]

This followed a trend whereby, rather than reject all religion, as did some philosophers, certain mystics (Sufis, kabbalists) appeared to embrace them all. In Al-Andalus, Jews so absorbed neo-Platonism, the philosophical idea including the myth of the descent of the soul into the body and its yearning for restoration by returning to God, causing them to focus more on the individual soul, which was reinforced by Sufi ascetism, that they changed their prayer service to focus more on the individual's inner religious experience. The innovation was expressed by adding poetry for the first time to the readings intended for private prayer, making redemption and purification more personal, individual, and inward than communal, focusing on the soul.[68] Whereas before this development Jews at synagogue spoke in the collective, their prayers representing the congregation as a whole, in Al-Andalus the individual voice emerged in the service through this religious poetry.[69]

The author of *The Fountain of Life*, Solomon ibn Gabirol, was a philosopher who also composed secular and liturgical poetry. Ibn Gabirol's *Fountain of Life* is a neo-Platonist guide on how to use human reason to develop one's intelligence or soul so as to return and gain union with the Intellect which created it and of which it is a part.[70] He converted an Arabic maxim, 'The heart and tongue are the whole of man,' into the core verse of a poem still recited in synagogues today, 'What is there that man's mind [or heart] and mouth / Can make? What power is there in the body's breath?', as mind/heart (*lev*) and mouth (*lashon*) alliterate in Hebrew, but not in Arabic (*qalb* and *lisan*).[71] Other of his liturgical poems incorporated the Sufi idea that God resides in the human heart and neo-Platonist ideas about the soul. Judah Halevi translated a secular Arabic love poem about accepting suffering and self-denial into Hebrew and converted it for synagogue use by the addition of a single line referencing God's love for the Jews.[72] Immersed in Arabic Islamic culture, the Jewish poet and philosopher modified ancient traditions. Maimonides' son took this transformation even further.

Abraham was so inspired by Islamic spirituality that he sought to incorporate its innovations into the synagogue to make Jewish religious life more pious. He added prostration, kneeling, and lining worshippers in orderly rows, as performed at the mosque during prayers. He wanted to remove the pillows from the synagogues and spread prayer mats and carpets on the floor as in mosques.[73] He was attacked by Jews for introducing *bida'*, innovations, imitating Islam. Jews had already been practising polygamy only in Muslim-majority societies, so the adoption of Muslim traditions was not out of place. But what was unique was Abraham Maimonides' defence of their introduction by claiming, in a way of thinking familiar to Muslims, that they were not innovations, but ancient Jewish obligations forgotten over the centuries.[74] He was reappropriating from the Muslims what the Muslims had taken from original Jewish practices. Maimonides argued that the Muslims' unwavering monotheism helped Jews preserve their own monotheism, unlike Jews in Christian-majority societies, who erred like Christians.[75] At the same time, he argued that whatever is commendable about Islamic faith is of Jewish origin. He urged Jews to model their spiritual renewal on Muslims, who imitate Jews in their glorification of the single, incorporeal divine.[76]

A similar process went in the other direction. We see the reappropriation of the ancient Jewish Temple in Jerusalem by Islam in the writings of the Muslim Sufi Jalal al-Din Rumi. In a poem, he stated that the Al-Aqsa Mosque is the Temple of Solomon. Speaking to David, God told him, 'The Farther Mosque will not be built by your toil / and strength: it is your son who will build it; his act / is your act; man of wisdom, know that the / faithful are bound in union everlasting.'[77] The poem refers to the Qur'anic verse (17:1) 'Glory be to the One Who took His servant by night from the Sacred Mosque to the Farthest Mosque whose surroundings We have blessed, so that We may show him some of Our signs.' Rumi was inspired by Muhammad's night journey, visiting not merely the Temple Mount, where the Jewish Temple had once stood, but the Temple itself.

Ibn Arabi understood the limits of rational understanding, preferring instead the union of reason, spirituality or mysticism, and revelation. Born in Murcia, Valencia, he studied in Al-Andalus and North Africa, went on the hajj, then remained in the Middle East, travelling through Iraq, Anatolia, and Syria, ending his days in Damascus. The author of *The Meccan Openings* and *Fusus al-Hikam* (*The Bezels of Wisdom*), he is the most important Muslim theoretical and practical narrator of the Sufi path.

Ibn Arabi's Jewish counterpart was Moses de León, the author of the *Zohar* (*Book of Splendour*, 1250), the central work of Andalusi Jewish Kabbalah (mysticism). He was anti-Aristotelian and anti-Maimonides. To understand his work, we must bear in mind the Jewish philosopher Bahya ibn Paquda of Zaragoza, Spain, who was a neo-Platonist. Ibn Paquda believed in the emanation of superior beings. His book of pietism called the faithful to their inner experience, and was influenced by a neo-Platonist Muslim group, the Brethren of Purity (*Ikhwan al-Safa'*). To Ibn Paquda, unity of God was central. His late eleventh-century Judeo-Arabic *Guidebook to the Duties of the Heart* (*al-Hidaya ila fara'id al-qulub*), translated by Yehudah ibn Tibbon into Hebrew in 1161, was the most important ethical treatise with a kabbalistic tendency. The *Guidebook* explains his perspective that the heart and mind are united, in narrating the ten duties of the heart, principles of spiritual action. The first is affirming the unity of God. This is followed by contemplating the works of Creation, obeying God, surrendering to God, purifying intention to serve God, and praising God. The final steps in the journey are repentance, self-examination, asceticism, and finally, everything culminates in loving God.[78]

More important, the book is popular among Jews to this day in its Hebrew translation. What most Jews do not know is that the text is indebted to Islamic thought and Sufism. What was original was the integration of philosophical rationalism and mystical piety. Influenced by Sa'adia Gaon, Ibn Paquda in turn would influence Jewish thinkers ranging from Judah Halevi and Maimonides to Maimonides' son Abraham, to later pietist movements, which quote the work today.

In the *Zohar* the ninth sphere is *tzaddik* or *yesod* (pillar, foundation), the one which bears the entire world, the pillar of the cosmos, which is a concept like Ibn Arabi's *kutb* (pole), the saintly person who also stands at the centre of the cosmos where four directions meet and is the reason for the sustaining of the world. The world which Muslims and Jews shared, however, was shrinking.

Muslims remained powerful on the Iberian peninsula at the end of the eleventh century, although the once-unified land was fractured with the dissolution of the Umayyad caliphate in 1031 into numerous small kingdoms, as Christian power, especially in Castile and León, grew. In 1236 Córdoba, once the very spirit of Al-Andalus, fell to the Christians, who would drive a massive cathedral into the heart of the Mesquita and add a statue behind the altar depicting Christians slaying Muslims. The largest city in Al-Andalus and the Almohad's second capital, Seville, fell in

1248. Its grand mosque was converted into the cathedral, which took two and a half centuries to finish, and would include the tomb of Christopher Columbus, hero of global Christian conquest. Towering over the centre of the city, the mosque's seventy-seven-metre square minaret, modelled on that of the largest mosque in Marrakesh, the twelfth-century Kutubiyya (Booksellers' Mosque), became the Giralda bell tower, which in the sixteenth century was given an additional thirty-metre Renaissance tower. It is Seville's proud symbol today, a magnet for tourists, as are its oranges, including those in the cathedral courtyard, brought to Spain by the Arabs. What was once likely a synagogue in the Jewish neighbourhood is now a shop selling products made from Seville oranges, although two pillars inscribed in Hebrew are still visible at the entrance. No other Jewish trace remains in the city.

The Almohad kingdom collapsed in 1269. Only the region of Granada on the southern tip of the peninsula surrounded by the snow-capped Sierra Nevada mountains remained in Muslim hands, those of the last Muslim dynasty of Al-Andalus, the Nasrids (1232–1492). The Nasrids, whose monotheistic motto was *wa la ghalib ilallah* (There is no victor but God), took in Jews and Muslims as refugees from Seville and other regions. Despite their humble motto, on a hill overlooking Granada they built the Alhambra, the greatest architectural wonder of Muslim Spain, a palatine city, garden fortress, and royal court delighting the senses. Its marble walls inscribed in poetry praise God and the ruler, and the exuberant stucco and multi-coloured geometric tilework and stalactite prisms fill with light to dazzle the eye. The palace is an intricate maze leading to courtyards decorated with gurgling, playing fountains, its paths leading to green reflecting pools lined with myrtle, mingled with the heady scents of orange blossom, jasmine, and rosemary. The most distinctive feature of the Nasrid palace is Sultan Muhammad V's (r. 1354–9, 1362–91) Palace of the Lions, at whose centre is the Lion Court, which contains an alabaster basin supported by twelve symmetrically arranged white marble lions, each with distinct manes, heads, and tails, whose jaws spout water. It is likely, and alluded to in Abu Ishaq's poem, that the lions represent the twelve tribes of Israel and were chiselled by a Jewish artist for the Ibn Naghrelas' Red Palace (al-Hamra') in the eleventh century, over whose ruins the Alhambra was built.[79]

The Christian kingdoms accepted Jews at first in their society, benefiting from the skills and knowledge they offered. Alfonso X El Sabio (the Learned, r. 1252–84), ruler of the largest Christian kingdom, Castile and León, enjoyed Arabic poetry, learning, and culture, and translated many Andalusi works into Latin. He issued the *Siete partidas*, a law code that mirrors the dhimma pact. The legal status of Muslims and Jews in Christian Spain has great similarities to the Pact of Umar, the surrender agreement whereby Christians and Jews agreed to pay a tax and abide by a series of restrictions on their religious lives in exchange for communal autonomy and security. Like the way the Pact of Umar treated non-Muslims, Alfonso X's law code admonished Jews to be humble among Christians and quietly practise their own religion. They were not to be compelled by force to become Christian. Should they convert, 'no one shall dare reproach them or their descendants, by way of insult, with having been Jews' and 'they can hold all offices and dignities which other Christians do'. The law code ordered them not to insult Christianity, and to avoid preaching to or converting Christians to Judaism, lest they be put to death and lose all their property. A Christian who became a Jew would be put to death. Jews were not allowed to build new synagogues, but could repair demolished ones, so long as they did not rebuild them any larger than they previously were. In disputes between Jews and Christians, cases were to be adjudicated at the Christian court. Jews were not to keep Christian servants, or bathe with Christians.[80] Jewish men who had sexual intercourse with Christian women were to be put to death. Jews had to wear a distinguishing mark so that Christians could recognise them as Jews. If we exchange 'Christian' for 'Muslim', we see how these prohibitions were the law in pre-modern Muslim-ruled lands as well.

Unlike the Pact of Umar, this Christian law code was violent in its imagination and threats to Jews. It ordered Jews to remain at home during Good Friday, and if they should be outside and happen to be assaulted, they would not receive reparations. Likewise, appealing to an ancient anti-Jewish canard, should they kidnap and crucify Christian children, they would be 'put to death in a disgraceful manner'.[81]

Jews and Muslims, it seems, had a place in Christian Spain. But as Spanish Christians gained in strength, they sought to purify their kingdom and humiliate the Jews and Muslims amongst them. As Muslim rule receded in the peninsula, Muslims and Jews found themselves as equals for one of the only times in the pre-modern era, and under Christian rule. In the Crown of Aragon, Jews and Muslims 'engaged in open competition and conflict'.[82] In Spain, Jewish–Muslim relations did not operate in a vacuum, instead becoming a triangular relationship between Jews, Christians, and Muslims, a new dynamic of power.[83]

Muslims and Jews competed over economic power, for civic prestige, for sexual access to women, and for converts, and this sometimes led to intercommunal violence in Christian Aragon.[84] That most Muslims were rural vassals of lords whereas Jews were urbanites dependent on the king led to further tension.[85] Although Muslims also lent at interest as moneylenders, and the

Jewish–Muslim Symbiosis and Alliance

Crown depended on taxation of Jewish profits, Jews were associated with usury. The Crown usually supported Jews, because the tax collected on a few wealthy moneylenders could be as much as that collected from all the *aljama*, the Muslim councils.[86] Usurers exploited Muslims, who were not protected by the same rules regarding interest rates as were Christians.[87] The *aljama* frequently sought to obtain debt relief, especially when the lenders were Jews.[88] Jews made up only 5 per cent of the population of the kingdom of Aragon in the thirteenth century, yet contributed 22 per cent of royal taxes. When Muslims sought to evade paying their debts to Jewish creditors, royal decision was usually made in the Jewish lenders' favour, although Christian officials and Muslim debtors alike colluded to avoid implementing court orders.[89] Sometimes orders authorising Jews to impound goods of Muslims debtors led to violence in towns such as Zaragoza.[90]

Civic processions were another arena of conflict. Muslims and Jews saw the occasions of parades celebrating military victories or births of princes or deaths of royals as excuses for intercommunal mayhem.[91] We see this in Daroca in 1290, when Muslims attacked Jews.[92] Sometimes what precipitated the violence was disagreement over which community could take precedence in the march honouring the Christian king. Should Muslims march first because they served in the royal military? Should Jews march first because their religion was more ancient?[93] Which group held more status and prestige in the eyes of the ruling Christians?

Muslim and Jewish men also fought over women from their community who committed adultery with a member of another religion, which was considered by both as unforgivable. Muslim slaves were owned by Jews, and this led to interreligious sex. Yet there were no rules on Jewish–Muslim relations. Muslim and

Jewish men were prohibited on pain of death from sexual relations with Christian women, yet Muslim and Jewish prostitutes were licensed and permitted.[94] In Murcia, in 1298 the Jewish man Abulfacem lived with his Muslim concubine Axona, and was arrested for it, but the Christian judge ruled they were innocent of any crime and permitted them to live together, as there were no rules forbidding it.[95] Muslims sought to prevent such situations, which were common. The Jewish communities encouraged these men to marry their Muslim concubines. What Muslims feared was that these concubines would convert to Judaism, as they did.

Muslims lobbied for Muslim conversion to Judaism to be banned and penalised by death, just as was Christian conversion to Judaism.[96] Jews also demanded the death penalty for Jews who converted to Islam, and in this they had more success than the Muslims in having the Crown enforce their wish.[97] In 1280 and 1284 Jews from Zaragoza were executed for having converted to Islam at the insistence of a Jewish courtier, Jucef Ravaya, the king's treasurer.[98]

In intercommunal disputes both communities adopted Christian prejudices to gain an advantage over the other and strengthen their own position in society.[99] Muslims promoted themselves over Jews by the fact that Islam accepts Jesus as prophet and Judaism does not. Tensions erupted into violence, as at Muslim participation in Holy Week riots against Jews. By stoning Jews during Easter, such as at Pina in 1285 where Christians and Muslims attacked the synagogue and stole the Torah, and in Daroca in 1319, Muslims asserted their bond with the rulers, targeting those who rejected Jesus.[100] These eruptions of violence, with Muslims aligning with Christians, reveal how Christian favouring of one group led to worsened Jewish–Muslim relations.[101]

Jewish–Muslim Symbiosis and Alliance

In the fourteenth century, Spanish Christians sought scapegoats and fixed their ire on Jews, leading to massacres and marking a turn for the worse in Jewish fortunes on the peninsula. In 1391, Christian pogroms led to mass forced conversion of Jews. The new converts became full members of society, as opposed to marginalised second-class subjects, which many Christians resented. They labelled them New Christians, Conversos, and assumed they continued to practise Judaism in secret. In 1479 the Christian kingdoms of Aragon, Castile and León – which by now covered almost all of Spain – were ruled by the same couple, Ferdinand II of Aragon and Isabella of Castile, the so-called 'Catholic Kings'. They turned on the Jews and Muslims. The Crown established the Inquisition to root out 'judaising' heresy amongst the baptised Jews. The first tribunal was established in Seville in 1481. The monarchs' eyes then turned south to the last remaining Muslim dynasty in Iberia, the Nasrids of Granada, to whose kingdom forcibly baptised Jews fled so they could return to Judaism. The Catholic rulers found in Abu Abd Allah Muhammad (Boabdil, r. 1482–3, 1487–92), eldest son of the sultan, and a rebel, an ally of Castile against his Muslim family.

In 1492, after being given the keys of the Alhambra by Boabdil, Ferdinand II and Isabella issued the Edict of Expulsion of all Jews in their Spanish Catholic kingdom. The estimated 120,000 Jews were given the choice to either convert to Catholicism and remain or leave. Most fled to Portugal, where the same choice was offered in 1497. Portuguese King Manuel I (r. 1495–1521) accepted the demand of the Catholic Kings to expel the Jews as a condition for him to marry their widowed eldest daughter, Isabella. The Jews had to convert to Catholicism to remain. Only Conversos remained in Spain and Portugal. The era of tolerance was over. The Jewish refugees fled to Fez,

Tlemcen in Algeria, Tunisia, Sicily, and Italy. A near contemporary Jewish witness explained how 'a part of the exiled Spaniards went overseas to Turkey [the Ottoman Empire]. Some of them were thrown into the sea and drowned, but those who arrived there the King of Turkey [the Ottoman Sultan] received kindly, as they were artisans.'[102]

In the wake of Muslim uprisings against Christian rule in Granada beginning in 1499, as the new rulers violated the terms of the capitulations, forcibly converted Muslims to Christianity, and burned Arabic-language books in a public bonfire, the Catholic Kings issued an edict offering the choice between baptism or expulsion to Muslims in Granada and the Crown of Castile in 1502 (the Crown of Aragon followed in 1526), modelled on the edict expelling Jews a decade earlier, linking the fight against Muslims to their spiritual struggle against Jews. Muslims, like Jews before them, were perceived as a spiritual danger to Christians old and new.[103] Just as the 'greatest cause of subversion of many Christians was their interaction and communication with the Jews, there is similarly much danger in the interaction of said Muslims in our realms with the newly converted, which can cause the newly converted to be tempted or induced to leave our faith and return to their original errors'.[104] For a second time, the principal cause of temptation had to be removed. The Christians were so insecure, and Christianity was so fragile, requiring constant surveillance, that the king and queen decreed 'that none of the captive Muslims or Muslim women or any other person dare to say anything or speak to the new converts to our holy Catholic faith that may attract them to leave our faith'. Muslims, like Jews before them, were ordered to 'never come back' 'forever and ever' upon penalty of death.[105]

Convivencia and symbiosis from the ninth through to the twelfth centuries was replaced by forced conversion of the Jews

Jewish–Muslim Symbiosis and Alliance

between 1391 and 1492 and of the Muslims from 1492 to 1609. Spanish society was divided between New Christians – the converted Jews (Conversos) and Muslims (Moriscos) – and Old Christians in the fourteenth and fifteenth centuries. Because every Converso was seen as a potential 'judaiser', or practitioner of the 'Law of Moses', New Christians were discriminated against and persecuted by the Inquisition. Heretics were burned alive. Conversos, who were more urban and integrated into Christian culture, were seen as a spiritual danger, while Moriscos, who were more rural and isolated in their own villages, were feared as a territorial and political danger. Those New Christians who wished to secretly maintain the daily rituals of their former religion had to rely on women, because public expressions of Judaism and Islam, the responsibility of men, were prohibited. Conversos and Moriscos intent on preserving their beliefs had to do so within the home, the domain of women, because synagogues, mosques, and other faith institutions including schools for studying the holy scriptures were closed.[106] For it was Conversas who were responsible for ensuring the commandments such as keeping the household kosher, observing the Sabbath, and maintaining dietary prohibitions during festivals such as Passover.

Unlike their converted Jewish counterparts, Moriscas joined in armed rebellions as women warriors alongside Moriscos against their Christian oppressors.[107] Moriscas participated with Moriscos in revolts, such as in the Alpujarra mountains south of Granada from 1568 to 1570, and the insurrection in Granada in 1580. The female warrior Zarçamodonia became famous.[108] A final rebellion led to the decision to expel these baptised Muslims in 1609, when Philip III (r. 1598–1621) decreed the expulsion of more than 300,000 Moriscos, a task that took five years to complete. Expulsion was decided upon after counterproposals of enslaving or killing all former Muslims were rejected. Morisco children were forced to remain, separated from their deported parents, to be raised as Christians by Old Christians. Yet some Morisco families, slaves, wives, and vassals to wealthy nobles were allowed to stay.[109]

Muslims were again saviours of Jews; Jews were allies of Muslims. Moriscos boarded ships into exile, most to North Africa and the Ottoman Empire, where they returned to practising Islam just as Jews and former Jews expelled from Iberia returned to the open practice of Judaism in the Muslim-ruled empire. Diasporas of Moriscos and Conversos coalesced in Morocco, Algeria, Tunisia, and the Ottoman Empire. In the port cities of Salé, Tunis, and Tétouan, Moriscos and Conversos 'coexisted and shared their Iberian culture, their "foreignness" in the societies that received them, their involvement in redeeming captives, their relations with corsair activity, and their posts as interpreters and diplomats'.[110]

Spanish Muslims settled in the same neighbourhood in Istanbul, Galata, where Spanish Jews had arrived after their expulsion. Galata was home to foreign ambassadors, Christian missions, merchants, Greeks, Jews, Armenians, and Muslims. The Moriscos settled near what became known as the Arab Mosque, a converted Catholic church.

Some Moriscos plotted the defeat of the Spanish kingdom and to re-establish the Nasrid kingdom of Granada, or fight so that Al-Andalus was under Ottoman suzerainty, and engaged in military campaigns toward those ends.[111] Whether promoting war or peace, they found Spanish Jewish allies. Moriscos formed guerrilla units organised and financed by Conversos and Jews. They compelled Muslim rulers to send arms to rebels, to launch war against Spain, to go against their common enemy as allies.[112]

Jewish–Muslim Symbiosis and Alliance

*

In Morocco, from the mid-fifteenth to the eighteenth century, Jews served the sovereign as royal merchants, interpreters, ambassadors, or counsellors, as go-betweens between Western Europe and the North African kingdom. The monarch's pragmatism 'prevailed over the most restrictive principles concerning the granting of power to non-Muslims and thus allowed Jewish notables to access avenues which were theoretically forbidden to them', because of the social and legal position of the dhimmi.[113] A new social and cultural elite emerged among the Jews, made up of the expelled Spanish and Portuguese Jews and Conversos who were welcomed into the kingdom, where they played the main role in international commercial and diplomatic relations on behalf of the sultan.[114]

In the seventeenth and eighteenth centuries, at Rabat, Salé and Tétouan, Jews armed vessels that Moriscos, after their expulsion from Spain, launched to attack the Christian navies in the Mediterranean, the North Atlantic, and as far as the New World.[115] Andalusi Jews and Muslims took refuge in Tétouan after their expulsion, and the Jews nicknamed it 'Pequeña Jerusalem' (Little Jerusalem); its Jewish quarter was called *la judería*, like that at Córdoba, and its cemetery was 'Castilla'. Situated close to the Strait of Gibraltar, it became a diplomatic capital with a large port in the seventeenth and eighteenth centuries.[116]

The rise of Jews in Morocco coincided with the period when Western Europeans appointed ambassadors to encourage trade, and when Portugal established itself in several ports on the Atlantic coast of Morocco, and Spain occupied Ceuta and Melilla, where the Spanish Christians called upon the services of the very people they had expelled to serve as translators and to tap into the Mediterranean Jewish trade network. Abraham ben Zamiro, interpreter for Portuguese King Manuel

I (r. 1495–1521), reported to the Christian king on local developments and provided him with strategic advice, 'whilst maintaining contacts between the rebellious Berber tribes and the Portuguese occupiers'.[117]

The Sa'adian sultans (1509–1659) allied with the Ottomans and the Dutch against Spain and Portugal, 'equipping their troops and their ships with armies and munitions negotiated and purchased in the Netherlands, with whom they shared a strong Hispanophobia'.[118] Moroccan Jews had contacts with Jews and Conversos in Spain, Portugal, the Netherlands, and the Ottoman Empire, and their trade networks exported sugar and wheat to Southern Europe and imported weapons to Morocco from Northern Europe. The same Sephardic families in Morocco had served at Catholic courts in Spain, and were fluent in Castilian Spanish, which was Morocco's language of diplomacy in the sixteenth and seventeenth centuries.

Samuel Pallache of Fez is an example of a Sephardic Moroccan Jew entrusted by a Moroccan ruler to serve as mediator with Christian European powers. He was granted privileged relations both with the Sa'adian Sultan Ahmad al-Mansur and his son and successor Moulay Zaidan at Marrakesh and with Maurice of Nassau, Prince of Orange, at Amsterdam. Fez boasted a thriving Jewish population, made up in part by Iberian Jewish refugees, as well as of Conversos who passed back into Judaism in the city after having arrived from Iberia as New Christians in Portuguese coastal garrison towns such as Tangier, Ceuta, and Azemmour.[119] In 1603 Pallache was sent to Madrid by Sultan Ahmad al-Mansur on a commercial mission to buy precious jewels.[120] Pallache fostered ties with the rich and powerful by trading in goods, information, and personal favours.[121] He was not allowed to continue to Lisbon, for fear that this practising Jew would cause the Conversos there to 'judaise'. He offered the

Jewish–Muslim Symbiosis and Alliance

Spanish Crown his service as an informer about the Moroccan political situation, as well as Moriscos hatching plots in Morocco to undermine Spain, which was accepted. He decided to return his family to the ancestral home and to do so, he ostensibly converted to Catholicism to be allowed to remain, the path taken by a number of Fez Jews in that era.[122] But in 1607 the family decided to flee Spain for southern France as the Inquisition began to take an interest in these New Christians.[123] In 1608 Pallache moved to Amsterdam, home to a Converso and Jewish community, led by Moroccan or Ottoman rabbis, as well as a Morisco community, some of whose members attempted to convert to Judaism.[124] Pallache travelled there by way of Saint-Jean-de-Luz, France, centre of licit and illicit trade networks of Jews, Conversos, and Moriscos. Conversos and Jews helped Moriscos smuggle wealth out of Spain.[125] Pallache obtained two warships for Morocco in 1609.[126]

From 1609 to 1614 he served as a Moroccan political and commercial diplomat in the Netherlands, as the interpreter for Morocco's ambassador, negotiating commercial and military treaties with the Dutch against Spain, which mentioned the Moriscos as an ally and asset.[127] In 1610 Pallache encouraged Morocco to use the ships acquired from the Dutch to launch thousands of Morisco harquebusiers to raid the Spanish coast at Málaga. Alliances between Jews or Conversos and Moriscos only rarely occurred in Spain, but 'united by mutual interests, by their knowledge of Iberia, and, no doubt, by a shared feeling of embittered resentment of it, the Jews and the Moriscos found themselves in a position where they could try to take advantage of their common backgrounds'.[128]

When Pallache passed away in The Hague in 1616, Maurice of Orange accompanied his funeral procession part of the way to the new Jewish cemetery at Ouderkerk aan de Amstel near

Amsterdam.[129] Rembrandt, or one of his school, painted his portrait, labelling it 'Man in Oriental Costume' (c.1635). He did not label it 'Oriental Man', reflecting Pallache's belonging to East and West. The sitter wears a magnificent, multi-coloured turban, crowned with a jewelled aigrette, and a fur-lined cloak clasped with a gold chain: a man of success.[130]

Along with serving Moroccan royals, Jews also worked for Sufi shaykhs or brotherhoods, some of whom engaged in warfare and international diplomacy, such as Muhammad al-Ayyashi, who in the 1630s ruled northern Morocco. He employed a Portuguese Jew, Benjamin Cohen of Salé, who had a brother in the Netherlands, and managed the shaykh's relations with the Dutch Republic along with another Spanish Jew. They succeeded in obtaining gunpowder for their master.[131]

Jews such as Samuel Pallache were in close contact with Moriscos employed by Moroccan sultans as interpreters, foreign agents, diplomats, corsairs, and soldiers in the service of the sultan in the battle against Spain. Said ibn Faraj al-Dugali of Granada settled in Tétouan, living as a corsair. In 1563 he was tasked with creating an all-Morisco elite artillery corps which in 1571 attacked the Canary Islands and occupied and sacked the island of Lanzarote. In 1573 it was the turn of a town in Granada province, whose entire population his men carried back to Morocco as hostages.[132]

Medieval and pre-modern Christians associated Jews with Muslims, as Jews did. This association was also connected with Christian anti-Judaism: beginning with the Crusades, Christians perceived Jews as 'agents of the dangerous foreign Islamic conspiracy', even 'Islamic fifth columnists in Christian territory'.[133] Jews and Muslims appeared similar, in that both are pure monotheists, practise circumcision, claim descent from Abraham, and speak similar languages.[134] For this reason, when the Crusaders

Jewish–Muslim Symbiosis and Alliance

took Jerusalem in 1099, after massacring Jews in Europe, they massacred Jews and Muslims and banned them both from residing in Jerusalem. They made Jews and Muslims into legal inferiors and prohibited sexual relations between European Christians and indigenous peoples. Throughout Europe, in literature and law, Jews were classified together with Muslims, considered infidels or blasphemers who undermined the unity of Christian faith and territory, treated as socially inferior, prohibited by law from gaining power over Christians. Marriage and sexual relations between Christians and Muslims or Jews were banned. Christians even believed that Jews worshipped Muhammad in their synagogues.[135]

Because in Christian Europe the Jewish question was related to the Muslim question, Muslims were seen as a threat, with the Jew as their ally. The greatest threat was the powerful Ottoman Empire, where Jews thrived.

4

MUSLIM SAVIOURS: JEWS AND MUSLIMS IN THE OTTOMAN EMPIRE AND MOROCCO, FIFTEENTH–NINETEENTH CENTURIES

History comes full circle. At the end of Muslim rule in Spain, much of Spanish Jewry took refuge in the Ottoman Empire, whose ruling dynasty's ancestors had settled among the ruins of the Jewish Khazar kingdom. Writing nearly two centuries after the Khazar kingdom's downfall, Abu Hamid al-Andalusi al-Gharnati ('the Granadan', d. 1170) visited the former Khazar capital of Itil, which had been renamed Saqsin. He described a city full of mosques, and mentioned that it was occupied by forty tribes of Oghuz Turks, each of whose leaders set up giant felt tents housing 100 or more men.[1] The Oghuz were the shamanist, nomadic ancestors of the Ottoman dynasty, which ruled much of the Middle East and Europe from c.1288 to 1922.

In the story of the Ottoman Empire the Jew was ally of the Muslim. In 1324 local Jews helped the Ottomans conquer Bursa from their oppressors, the Byzantines, and were rewarded by Sultan Orhan (r. 1324–62) with permission to build the Etz ha-Haim synagogue[2] – just as Jews helped Arabs and Berbers take the cities of Al-Andalus from the Visigoths, and were rewarded by being appointed to garrisons to guard them, and

Muslim Saviours

just as Jews helped Arab Muslims take Hebron from the Byzantines in 638.

The Conversos and Sephardim migrated to the Ottoman Empire and rose to elite positions. Most Conversos settled in Salonica (modern Thessaloniki, Greece), which became the third most populous city in the Ottoman Empire, and the largest one with a Jewish majority. After conquering the city in 1430, the Ottomans allowed Jews to settle within its walls, but not Greek Christians. Jews were seen as the Ottomans' trustworthy allies. Although all of Salonica's Greek Jews were subsequently deported to Constantinople to repopulate the city and make it flourish after the Ottoman conquest of 1453, Sephardic Jews re-established their lives in Salonica after 1492, making it a centre of Jewish learning and Kabbalah, as well as headquarters of the empire's woollen cloth and textile industries: they received a monopoly to furnish uniforms for the elite troops of the sultan, the Janissaries.[3]

To the detriment and damage of the Christian-ruled lands from which they fled, Conversos and Sephardic Jews gave much in return: among them were skilled physicians offering the latest advances in medicine, scholars introducing the printing press, quartermasters with knowledge of the latest weapons technology (artillery, harquebuses, gunpowder, and other munitions), translators speaking European languages, and merchants with connections to international trade in textiles and woollens. The Ottomans trusted the Sephardic elite as physicians to the sultan, diplomats, translators, farmers of taxes, customs and mint custodians, and quartermasters to the Janissaries.

They spoke *judezmo*, a Jewish Spanish, mainly Castilian. They established synagogues named after their homelands including Ispanya, Çeçilyan (Sicilian), Maghrebi, Lizbon, Talyan (Italian), Otranto, Aragon, Katalan, Pulya, and Evora Portukal. They maintained family names that revealed their origins: Navarro, Cuenca, Algava. They dressed as Iberians. They ate *pan d'Espanya* (almond sponge cake), *rodanchas* (pumpkin pastries), *pastel de kwezo* (cheese pie with sesame seeds), *fijones kon karne* (beef and bean stew), and *keftikes de poyo* (chicken croquettes), and offered their house guests *dulce de muez verde* (green walnut preserve).[4] They formed a Spanish and Portuguese island at the northwest corner of the Aegean Sea and called it 'the Mother of Israel'.[5]

Chief Rabbi Samuel Medina, scion of a Castilian family, was lenient towards Conversos. He regarded them as offspring of Jewish parents. He did not subject them to ritual conversion as Jewish law requires. He had them take Hebrew names, although he allowed those for whom it was important for their businesses to retain their Christian names and Portuguese inheritance rights. Like the opinion of Maimonides, according to an early sixteenth-century responsa from Ottoman Istanbul Rabbi Joseph Shalom:

> This is how it is with these *Conversos* (*ha-yehudim ha-'anusim*, forced converts): They derive from the hope of Israel [i.e. Jewish roots], despite the fact that they have been immersed among the idolaters [Christians]. Their hope and righteousness endure forever – [the hope] that they will come to a city that is a haven for them in the lands of the Turk's [Ottomans] righteous rule, may God raise him up.

When they arrived, they were circumcised, but not immersed in the ritual bath like converts 'who were never part of the Jewish people'. They were not given the status of converts, for they were considered Jews.[6]

The Sephardic elite became the Ottoman dynasty's trusted allies. The Portuguese Conversa and international merchant

Muslim Saviours

Doña Gracia Nasi (Mendes) returned to Judaism in Ferrara, Italy, and migrated to Istanbul in the 1550s. She continued her economic success in the empire. Her nephew, João Migues, having worked as her agent and representative in Western Europe, migrated to Istanbul and returned to Judaism, becoming known as Don Joseph Nasi.[7] Joseph Nasi entered royal circles, specifically that of Prince Selim, who became Selim II upon Suleiman I's death in 1566. During Selim II's reign (1566–74), Joseph Nasi, whose commercial agents in Western Europe proved useful for gathering intelligence for the Ottomans, quickly rose at court, as advisor and diplomat. Throughout the 1560s, he negotiated treaties with Poland, the Habsburgs, and France, and promoted rebellions by Protestants in the Netherlands and by Moriscos in Spain. He allegedly convinced the sultan to launch the successful conquest of Venetian Cyprus in 1571. He dissuaded the sultan from deporting Palestinian Jews to the island to make it flourish. He was named Duke of Naxos and the rest of the Cyclades, a group of recently annexed former Venetian islands in the Aegean Sea. His wife, Gracia Jr, was named the Duchess of Naxos.[8] Nasi was granted extensive tax farms, as well as the monopoly on the regional wine trade.

Like Conversos and Moriscos in Morocco, Joseph Nasi promoted anti-Catholic foreign policy, against Venice and Spain. Like their courtier counterparts in Al-Andalus, Joseph and Gracia served the Jewish community as wealthy philanthropists. They established synagogues, yeshivas, and libraries in Istanbul, Salonica, and Tiberias, Palestine, and promoted the textile industry and the Jewish community in Safed, Palestine. A relative of theirs, Don Alvaro Mendes (Salomon ibn Yaesh), served as counsellor to Sultan Murad III (r. 1574–95) and promoted the first relations between the Ottomans and England, to counter Phillip II of Spain.[9]

Jewish culture flourished in this environment. In Ottoman Palestine, in Jerusalem and Safed, primarily Sephardic Jews produced works that are influential in Judaism today. They composed hymns still sung or recited in synagogues and in homes, including the Salonica-born Shlomo ha-Levi Alkabetz's 'Lekha Dodi' ('Come My Beloved'), which welcomes Shabbat. Jewish scholars produced legal works Jews still use today, including Toledo-born Joseph Caro's *Shulkhan Aruch* (*The Set Table*). Kabbalah reached new heights in the sixteenth century, as we see in the spiritual works of Moses Cordovero, who was born in Safed, and Isaac ben Solomon Luria, who was born in Germany, educated in Cairo, and lived in Jerusalem and Safed. In messianic expectation, Doña Gracia Nasi settled former Conversos returned to Judaism in Palestine. She paid for the construction of public works, housing, and a synagogue in the holy city of Tiberias. She had mulberry trees planted to jumpstart the silk industry and imported merino sheep to be raised for their high-quality wool. Gracia Nasi planned to move to Tiberias, close to the main kabbalist centre of Safed, due to feverish expectations about the onset of the messianic era, but passed away in 1569 before doing so.[10]

Sultan Suleiman I served as a saviour of Jews, intervening on behalf of Conversos in Ancona, Italy, who had been sentenced to burn to death in 1556 for 'judaising'. Multiple times from the sixteenth to the nineteenth century Ottoman sultans issued writs condemning and ordering the punishment of their subjects who accused Jews of the blood libel.

Jews in the Ottoman Empire did all the things that were forbidden by the dhimma pact, despite the most prominent Muslim religious authorities in the empire declaring that the dhimmis should be prevented from 'building high and ornamented houses, riding horses in the city, dressing themselves in sumptuous and costly garments, wearing kaftans with collars and fine muslin and furs and turbans', and 'belittl[ing] Muslims and exalt[ing] themselves'.[11] From the fifteenth century Sephardic Jews rose to similar heights as court Jews in Al-Andalus. Joseph and Moses Hamon and others mentioned above served as courtiers, diplomats, royal physicians, or wealthy merchants, just as Jewish women such as Esther Kira served as intermediators between Ottoman royal women and the outside world. Through the historical record we can also witness their fall when Muslims were keen to put them back in their dhimmi place.

This story has been distorted by exaggerated myths, deploying the story of *convivencia* at the eastern end of the Mediterranean. Typical is a recent painting labelled *The Embrace of Freedom* by Mevlut Akyıldız, which depicts a galleon overcrowded with Spanish Jewish refugees being welcomed by the sultan and his viziers in Istanbul. In a shocking anachronism, Sultan Bayezid II reaches out to shake the hand of a rabbi who has arrived with the ship.[12] The rabbi would have been made to prostrate himself before the Ottoman ruler and kiss his foot, like other subjects.

The story told about the Jews of the Ottoman Empire and Turkey 'is so rife with myths that it is tempting to wonder whether they emerged to provide palliatives to the gloomy "lachrymose" episodes in Jewish history'.[13] Since the 1970s, 'playing their part in international arenas, Jews regularly proclaim Turkey's eternal hospitality and tolerance'.[14] The story serves as counterpoint to outside criticisms of Turkey's abysmal human rights record today and historical crimes including the genocide of Armenians in 1915.[15]

When compared with their contemporaries, the Ottomans were more tolerant of Jews, who took refuge and thrived in the Ottoman realm.[16] The problem is that Ottoman treatment of Jews expressed a power relation: it was not coexistence.

Coexistence implies equality between groups. But in the Ottoman Empire women, Christians and Jews, and commoners were legally subordinated to men, Muslims, and the military class. Tolerance is a useful concept when we include a notion of power, for tolerance is an expression of a power relation that can be wielded as a threat against a tolerated, vulnerable group. Tolerance 'is based on a state of inequality in which the most powerful party (such as the ruler) decides whether a less powerful group can exist or not and to what extent members of that group are allowed to manifest their difference. A regime can discriminate against certain groups while tolerating their being different.'[17] Tolerance was an imperial means 'to organize the different communities, to establish peace and order'.[18] Toleration was 'a means of rule, of extending, consolidating, and enforcing state power' and is not to be confused with equality or multiculturalism.[19]

The first expression of the myth of Turks as saviours of the Jews came from Itzhak Tzarfati, a French Jew, born in Germany, who settled in the Ottoman Empire and was the pre-eminent rabbi of Edirne (Adrianople), the Ottoman capital prior to Istanbul.[20] Either collaborating with or instigated by Ottoman authorities, Tzarfati composed his account shortly after the Ottoman conquest of Constantinople in 1453. It is propaganda.[21] He contrasts the horror experienced by Jews in Christian-majority lands with an interreligious utopia in the Ottoman Empire: 'I proclaim to you that Turkey is a land wherein nothing is lacking, and where, if you will, all shall yet be well with you. The way to the Holy Land lies open to you through Turkey. Is it not better for you to live under Muslims than under Christians?'[22]

By asking, 'Is it not better for you to live under Muslims than under Christians?' Tzarfati seems to endorse the myth of the interfaith utopia. Yet buried within the text is the key line that allows us to understand his mentality: 'The way to the Holy Land lies open to you through Turkey.' With the questions 'Where was it good for the Jews' and 'Where was it better?' in mind, we tend to focus on Tzarfati's comparison of the torments suffered by Jews in Christian Europe with the Ottoman paradise he describes. But what motivated pre-modern Jews was an effort to understand the working of God's plan in human life. Jews were less concerned with the actions of humans in history than with how human actions are signs of God's plan for the Jews.[23] When will God's kingdom on earth be established? When will the Jews return to Jerusalem to witness the rebuilding of the Temple and the End Time? Tzarfati makes no comment on the Turks' character. The Turks have no agency, God does. The Jews are hapless creatures subject to God's mercy.

The sultan who vanquished the Byzantine Empire, Mehmed II (r. 1444–6, 1451–81), brought Jews from throughout his domains to Istanbul, and allowed them to build new synagogues, contrary to the dhimma pact. Sultan Bayezid II (r. 1481–1512) ordered his governors to allow migrating Iberian Jews to settle in his kingdom. Turkish Jews invented the ridiculous myth, repeated to this day, that Bayezid II sent ships to Spain to pick them up. How could he do so, when the Ottomans and Spanish Habsburgs were at war? The fifteenth-century Ahrida synagogue in Balat, Istanbul, nevertheless features a wooden prayer pulpit in the shape of a prow of a ship, representing the Ottoman boats that Bayezid II allegedly sent to save their ancestors.[24] The same Ahrida synagogue, bedecked in Ottoman flags, was the site of prayers offered for the victory of the Ottoman army against Russia in 1877, attended by Grand Vizier Ibrahim Edhem Pasha. Fifteen years later, Ottoman Jewish leaders celebrated the four hundredth anniversary of the arrival of the Sephardim in the empire in their synagogues. It was a second celebration of the special relationship between Muslims and Jews in the empire, presenting the Ottoman Muslim rulers as their kind hosts and Jews as loyal Ottoman subjects.[25]

More influential than Tzarfati's letter is the 1523 chronicle of the Greek Rabbi Elijah ben Elkanah Capsali, whose ecstatic sentiment, exuberant messianism, and exaggerated claims dominated Jewish history writing for five centuries.[26] Capsali promoted the view that the Ottoman dynasty was given a role by God to allow Jews to smite their Christian enemies and resettle in the Holy Land. Capsali introduced four claims that have figured prominently in myths regarding Ottoman treatment of Jews: that Mehmed II invited and did not force Jews to settle in Istanbul; that Mehmed II established the chief rabbinate, and that Capsali's uncle, Moses, was the first holder of the position; and that Bayezid II invited the Iberian Jews to settle in his empire.

Capsali was a native of Candia (Heraklion), on Venetian Crete, and a member of a wealthy and learned Greek Jewish family.[27] His great-uncle Moses Capsali was a confidant of Ottoman Sultan Mehmed II.[28] Rabbi Elijah Capsali's famous chronicle *Seder Eliyahu zuta: Toldot ha-'Ot'omanim u-Venitsi'ah ve korot 'am Yisrael be-mamlekhot Turki'yah, Sefarad u-Venitsi'ah* (*Minor Order of Elijah: History of the Ottomans and Venice and the People of Israel in Turkey, Spain, and Venice*) mainly focuses on the reigns of Mehmed II, Bayezid II, Selim I, and Suleiman I.[29] Capsali deployed the ancient Jewish tropes of the link between destruction and redemption; the idea that what occurred in earlier ages explained what was transpiring in his own day; the tradition that four world-empires would precede the messianic age, as predicted in the Book of Daniel, placing the newest empire into that final slot; and that the final conflict between two world powers, Gog and Magog, would come before the advent of the Messiah.³⁰ He cast the Ottoman sultan as the Persian monarch Cyrus the Great, who conquered Babylon and restored the captive Jews to Israel, where they rebuilt the Temple in Jerusalem.³¹

Capsali comforted Jews, proclaiming that although Jews thought the expulsion from Iberia 'was a great evil, in fact, "God designed it for good" [Genesis 50:20] [to keep the Jewish population alive], [Job 38:7] for the Gatherer of the Dispersed of Israel has gathered us together to be ready for the ingathering of the exiles ... a sign of the coming of the Redeemer'.³² The Ottoman sultans gathered together the Jews not because of an inherent humanitarianism, but because they were tools of God's plan.

Also in the sixteenth century, Converso writers such as the Portuguese Samuel Usque, who wrote *Consolação ás tribulações de Israel* (*The Consolation of the Tribulations of Israel* [1553]), and Joseph ben Joshua ha-Kohen, who was born in France, the son of expelled Castilian Spanish Jews, who wrote *Sefer divre ha-yamim le-malkhey Tzarefat u-malkhey beyt Ottoman ha-Togar* (*History of the Kings of France and the Kings of the Dynasty of Othman, the Turk* [1554–77]), made similar arguments. Europe was 'hell on earth', so God made the Ottoman sultans the saviours of Iberian Jewry, 'scourge and breaker of the uncircumcised'.³³ In their empire, 'the gates of liberty are always wide open for you that you may fully practice your Judaism,'³⁴ the portent for Redemption and the messianic age when all Conversos returned to Judaism.³⁵

Suleiman I did rebuild the walls of the Old City of Jerusalem. The walls include Jaffa and Damascus Gates, as well as the sealed Golden Gate, or Gate of Mercy, located on the eastern side of the Temple Mount. According to Jews, this is the door through which the Messiah will come.³⁶

Capsali and the other writers told Ottoman history to reveal God's plan in the world, which ends with the messianic age of redemption. They did not treat the Ottoman sultans 'as political and historical figures but as messianic figures according to a Jewish messianic interpretation'.[37] These historians were not expressing gratitude for benevolent treatment by the Turks or the Ottoman dynasty; rather, they believed that the Ottoman sultans were the instruments of God's will.[38]

In the early seventeenth century, a fifth myth was added to the enduring Sephardic narrative of the legendary Ottoman reception of the Jews. The Spanish Converso Immanuel Aboab, who returned to Judaism in Italy and died in Jerusalem, invented the apocryphal claim that Bayezid II, upon hearing of the expulsion of Iberian Jewry, said of the Spanish King Ferdinand, 'Can you call such a king wise and intelligent? He is impoverishing his country and enriching my kingdom!'[39] The quotation is prominently displayed in Istanbul's Jewish Museum.

Despite what Jewish chroniclers wrote, and what their modern historians have proclaimed, when Ottoman Muslim historians from the fifteenth to the eighteenth century selected Jewish figures, they almost always did so to offer the same theme. The figures chosen by these authors provided examples where Jews rose above their subordinate dhimmi status and caused harm to Muslims in some way, and were ridiculed, humbled, converted, or put to death for it. The first prototype in Ottoman-language histories from that period is the Jewish tax farmer, convert vizier, lady-in-waiting in the harem, or court physician who is useful, but his or her possessing power and authority over Muslims violates the social hierarchy based on the dhimma pact. Being in a position of influence, he or she inevitably harms Muslims, causing their moral corruption, so the Jew is rightfully humbled: converted, executed, or lynched. Of especial concern is the powerful lady-in-waiting in the harem. The second Jewish prototype is the Jewish man who causes social disruption and disturbs the peace in an even more galling manner, breaking the law and violating taboos, by having sexual relations with Muslim women or (sexually) abusing Muslim children. These Jews were put to death.

These typologies originated in the literature of earlier Muslim-ruled societies. The Jewish figures in Ottoman history writing served as edifying cautionary tales for Muslim readers as to what happened when Jews gained power or influence over Muslims, and the necessary fate of these Jewish men and women who overturned the gendered religious hierarchy established by the dhimma pact that privileged men and Muslims over women and Christians and Jews.[40]

As in earlier Islamic societies, the privileged tolerated but disdained those with an inferior legal-political, religious, and social status. When members of the theoretically inferior classes became more influential, powerful, or wealthy than those of the normatively superior classes, especially without having converted, violent opposition to the subversion of distinctions occurred. To assuage this anger, the offenders of majority sensitivities were disposed of as convenient scapegoats, and the stories of their rise and downfall served as cautionary moral tales worthy of being retold for centuries.

Anti-Jewish sentiment expressed in the chronicles which reflected elite Muslim ideological visions is at odds with the favourable Ottoman treatment of Jews in general and the Jewish elite in particular. Their authors projected a version of the desired situation of the time they lived. The historical works were intended for religious purposes, moral edification, entertainment, or political ends. They were best read to gain 'insight into how elite men and women at that time shaped, formed, and articulated their understanding of the moment in which they lived'.[41] The works, the bestsellers of their day, were written by the most significant Muslim authors, who lived through the ruptures which were the milestones in the history of their interaction.

The first Jews in Ottoman chronicles are greedy, ill-omened corrupters of morals.

Tensions over the formation of the Ottoman state, especially following the conquest of Constantinople in 1453, centred on the rise of a Christian convert-administrative class, the appointment of Christians and Jews to positions of authority, the allocation of revenues and landholdings to them, and the decreased power of born Muslims, especially Sufis, nomads, frontier warriors, and the religious class, the latter infuriated by Mehmed II's abolishment of endowments that funded religious institutions.[42] As a result, viziers of Christian and Jewish origin and Jewish tax farmers were vilified in historical accounts. It is in this context that we can understand the first mention of Jews in an Ottoman chronicle, which appears in the *Tevārīḫ-i Āl-i ʿOsmān*, written by Aşıkpaşazade at the behest of Sultan Bayezid II, remembered in Jewish chronicles and modern Jewish scholarship for his warm embrace of Iberian Jews.[43]

Aşıkpaşazade, whose writing best represents the interests of the Sufis and frontier warriors whose power and privilege was limited by Sultan Mehmed II, expressed resentment of the financial favours given to Greeks settled by Mehmed II in Constantinople, as a result of which some Christians or converted Christians rose to positions of wealth and power.[44] Aşıkpaşazade also cast his aspersion on Jews, focusing on Mehmed II's converted Jewish physician and vizier, Giacomo of Gaeta (Italy), whose Muslim name after conversion was Hekim Yakub Pasha. Aşıkpaşazade remarks that 'Prior to Hekim Yakub, they never assigned public office to Jews because they are considered corrupters of morals. But thanks to Hekim Yakub when he became vizier, however many greedy and ill-omened Jews there are, they all meddled in the sultan's business.'[45] Even after converting to Islam, Hekim Yakub was referred to as a Jew, whose appointment to government office opened the floodgate for other Jews to interfere in imperial politics. According to Aşıkpaşazade, Jews are invariably sources of moral corruption. In one recension of the text Aşıkpaşazade, referring to the Jewish tax farmer Yakub son of Israel, executed in 1472, wrote: 'Until he came, financial administrators were not hanged.'[46]

Ottoman Muslims were silent about the arrival of the Andalusi Jews. Ottoman and other Mediterranean Jewish authors wrote ecstatically about Mehmed II bringing Jews to Istanbul and allegedly establishing the position of chief rabbinate, honouring its first holder, and Bayezid II's welcoming of the Iberian Jews, an immigrant population that may have exceeded 100,000 people. Although the influx is attested to in Ottoman archival sources, the most significant Ottoman Muslim chronicles were written by men closest to these two sultans, including eyewitnesses to the conquest of Constantinople and its repopulating and rebuilding – Mehmed Neşri, Tursun Bey, Idris Bitlisi, Ruhi, and Kemalpaşazade – and chronicles from later centuries are silent about the welcome.[47] Elite men writing for posterity about the greatness and munificence of their sultanic patrons did not deem it significant to mention the acceptance of mass numbers of Jews, as evidence of sultanic virtue, or the rise to influence of court Jews, as a sign of sultanic tolerance. No treatises written within the genre of advice to kings specified that Jews are the most useful and loyal group whose immigration should be encouraged. Rather than mentioning the influx of *Jews* expelled from Spain, as in Jewish writing, some referred to the *Muslims* who took refuge in the empire.[48]

All these Muslim authors tell of the conquest of a Christian city and the erection of a Muslim city in its place, ignoring the appearance of Jews (and Christians) between 1453 and 1600. They could have commented on the wisdom of deporting Jews to the city to make it flourish, or welcomed Jews expelled from other lands, or listed the benefits of having Jews in government service. But they never mentioned individual Jews, such as Mehmed II's confidant Moses Capsali, purportedly the first Ottoman chief rabbi according to Jews, nor did they mention Jews as a group present in Byzantine Constantinople when it was conquered. Bayezid II was depicted by his chronicler as the refuge of Muslims, not of Jews. In the Ottoman mind, 'Spain is a major antagonist, and the Ottomans make little distinction between the plight of the Andalusi Muslims and that of the Jews when both communities are threatened by Spain and both appeal for Ottoman aid and protection.'[49] It would be correct to say that in the historical consciousness of Ottoman Muslims a distinction *was* made. The arrival of Muslims was significant. That of Jews did not deserve mention. Rather than being evidence of a negative attitude, Ottoman chroniclers' silence about the massive inflow of the Sephardim is further evidence that history writers singled out individual Jews when they could be used to represent alleged Jewish moral corruption and financial malpractice.

The most significant Jewish character in Ottoman Muslim chronicles is a lynched dame.

Tensions over the increased power of royal women and the institution of the harem led to the creation of new scapegoats by the end of the sixteenth century, the targets of the wrath of those who opposed the role of women, especially the queen mother. It was in this context that the *kira* (Greek: dame), the lady-in-waiting, entered Ottoman literature, serving as the sign of an inverted order in which women exercised power at the expense of men. This led to rebellion, which only ended when established hierarchies were restored. It mattered that the *kira* was both a woman, and Jewish.

Jewish women served as *kira* to the harem throughout the fifteenth and sixteenth centuries. They functioned as mediators between the harem and the outside world, exchanging gems, jewellery, and other valuables, and 'because they won the trust of the sultanas, were entrusted with important (political) missions', namely, exchanging communications with representatives of foreign powers.[50] According to Ottoman chronicles, they also served as go-betweens, passing bribes between ambitious men and the harem. Rather than discussing the rise to power and influence of male court Jews, as in pre-modern Jewish texts and modern Jewish history writing, one of the most frequently repeated Ottoman Muslim narratives illustrating how to put Jews in their rightful place is that of the lynching of the *kira* to Safiye Sultan, favourite of Murad III (r. 1574–95) and mother of Mehmed III (r. 1595–1603).[51]

We learn about the unfolding of events regarding the *kira* from her contemporary Selaniki Mustafa Efendi, who was most likely an eyewitness, since he was responsible for overseeing the distribution of salaries to troops returning from campaign and entrusted with special duties by the grand vizier and the Shaykh al-Islam, the leading Muslim jurisconsult and head of the religious hierarchy.[52] At the time he was writing, Selaniki was an elder statesman, having served a long career in Ottoman government, especially in financial administration, and was given access to confidential information due to his employment as secretary in the Imperial Divan. He was known as a sharp critic of what he perceived to be the corruption that seemed to mark his age – he highlights maladministration of the public treasury, the selling of public office to the highest bidder, excessive expenditure and bribery, inflation and debasement of the coinage, and the rise of tax farmers and the influence of the women of the harem.[53] All of these issues came together in the incident of the *kira*, which he used to illustrate these interrelated weaknesses in the state as he perceived them.

On a Friday at the end of March 1600, when the grand vizier, Ibrahim Pasha, returned from campaign, thousands of outraged *sipahi* (cavalry troops) stormed his palace in Istanbul demanding lucrative tax allocations, which they claimed were owed them, instead of the less valuable ones that they received.[54] 'Were they distributed to the women and eunuchs in the palace?' they asked, and they also complained that the coins with which they were paid were worthless.[55] They rushed to the Shaykh al-Islam, Sunullah Efendi, and demanded: 'Is the food that we purchase with [the] worthless silver coins given to us as our salary halal [i.e. ritually approved]?' 'It is not,' he responded. 'The Jewish hag *kira* farms the custom revenue [has been given the right to collect revenue on customs]. She is the one who gives us these counterfeit coins; they belong to her. We will kill her,' the *sipahi* declared, and requested a fatwa approving her execution.

'Sharia does not permit the killing of the non-Muslim woman, but she may be expelled from the city,' the Shaykh al-Islam told the *sipahi*.[56] His response enraged them further. His telling them to record their wishes in a petition, which he would then pass on to the sultan, who would issue an imperial decree on the matter, failed to calm them. Accordingly, 'on Saturday at the crack of dawn, a great throng went to the gate of Halil Pasha's palace' (since he stood in for the grand vizier in his absence) demanding the '*kira* hag' who possessed the register of posts that they claimed were rightly theirs.

When 'the *kira* hag' was found in her home in the Jewish

quarter and brought out, she was 'mounted on a packhorse and brought to the gate of the Pasha's palace. No sooner had she alighted from the horse at the foot of the stairs than the impatient *sipahi* drew their daggers and cut her to pieces. They tied a rope to one foot and dragged the carcass to the Hippodrome, where they left it.' There they took an oath on the Qur'an, agreeing, 'Tomorrow let us do the same to all her children and family members.' And the next day, 'The big crowd as before went to the gate of the Pasha's palace saying, "Unless that Jewish hag's children and other relatives are brought forth without fail, we cannot be held responsible for what happens next."' So saying, they 'found her older son and brought him out. Showing no mercy, they drew their daggers and hacked him from limb to limb. They tied a rope around one foot and dragged the carcass to the Hippodrome, placing it next to his mother's carcass.'[57] They accepted her younger son's conversion to Islam, thus sparing his life, on condition that he promised to pay the state treasury the revenues held by his mother as tax farms.

Because 'the disgusting carcasses of the accursed ones were prey to the dogs for many days on the Hippodrome, creating an abominable stench, which annoyed Muslims', they were cremated.[58] Recoiling from the 'shameful' way a woman so closely connected to the dynasty was killed, the horrified mother of the sultan declared, 'If her execution was necessary, did it have to be carried out like this? She could have been thrown into the sea.'[59] Islam and Judaism view cremation as an abomination. The treatment of the *kira* and her son was shocking to Muslims and Jews alike.

Her horrible end 'served as a cautionary tale'.[60] As reported by Selaniki, immediately after these events the sultan issued a decree imposing sumptuary and employment restrictions on Jews.[61] Confirming that what upset the Ottoman gendered religious order of things the most was the rise to power and influence of a Jewish woman, after that the sultan commanded that 'henceforth Jews may not wear fine garments, but wear a red cap; and not be permitted to become involved in tax farming'.[62] In this way, it was hoped, Jews would not become rich and lord it over Muslims. Wearing a distinguishing, coloured cap, they would always be identifiable as Jews.[63]

The story of the fall of the *kira* reappeared in other seventeenth-century chronicles, including that of Shaykh al-Islam Karaçelebizade Abdül Aziz Efendi, who presented his *Ravzatü'l-ebrâr fi'l Tarih* (*The Gardens of Fruit*) to Mehmed IV in 1649.[64] Karaçelebizade blamed Jews for the interrelated issues of dishonest viziers, bribery, and frequent turnover in public office, the state treasury suffering from a decline in revenues and an increase in expenditures, devalued coinage, and rebellion, since 'Jews of the rejected religion are the destroyers of the treasury' (referred to as the 'Muslims' treasury').[65] He complained of corrupt viziers 'who borrow counterfeit coins from opportunist Jews of the rejected religion and other traitors to the dynasty and religion', saying, 'May God curse those who give and take bribes!'[66] Solakzâde Mehmed Hemdemî Çelebi, a palace-educated boon companion of Murad IV (r. 1623–40), dedicated his history to Sultan Mehmed IV (r. 1648–87).[67] Solakzâde named the *kira* Esther, as would the Ottoman Jewish educator Moïse Franco, the author of the first French-language monograph on Jews in the Ottoman Empire in 1897.[68] Even if this particular *kira* was not named Esther, it is an important literary allusion for Jews and Muslims alike.[69]

For Jews, Esther is a heroine, the Jewish queen in a non-Jewish kingdom who saved the lives of her co-religionists. The Book of Esther in the Bible, which Jews recite every year during the festival of Purim, is a surprising tale of reversals, as the secret Jew

Muslim Saviours

(Esther) reveals herself as a Jew, and the Jews kill their enemies rather than become victims. Esther is the beautiful Jewish wife of the Zoroastrian Achaemenid Persian King Ahasueras (Xerxes I, r. 486–463 BCE). Her uncle, Mordecai, as vizier, prevented a plot to murder the king, but his heroism was never rewarded. Years later, the grand vizier, Haman, angered by Mordecai, who refuses to bow down to him, plots to kill all the Jews of the kingdom and confiscate their property. But the night before the appointed day for the massacre, a sleepless king has an attendant read him the imperial chronicles, where he discovers that Mordecai was never rewarded for saving his life. Now siding with Mordecai, rather than Haman, the next day, when Esther reveals herself to him as a Jewess, the king is convinced to hang Haman instead of Mordecai, saving the Jews of Persia, who are permitted to slay their enemies and confiscate their wealth. Many non-Jews were impelled to convert to Judaism to spare their lives and property.

Reading the Ottoman narrative of a non-fictional Esther intertextually with the Jewish biblical account, we find similarities. Here, too, a Jewish woman enters palace service in a non-Jewish kingdom and is linked with the figure of the queen (being a confidante of the queen mother), gaining power and influence over the rightful rulers. However, this Esther is not beautiful, but a hag; she is not a heroine, but a villain; unlike the biblical story, Esther is slain, along with her sons, who may figuratively represent all Jews; rather than non-Jews converting to Judaism, her youngest son becomes a Muslim; rather than the Jews obtaining wealth at the expense of their enemies, the wealthy Jewess's immense fortune is seized by the (Muslim) state treasury. Esther may not be mentioned in the Qur'an, but Haman appears as the vizier of the Pharaoh at the time of Moses. That Pharaoh had decreed that all male children born to

Jews in Egypt were to be killed. In this Ottoman narrative the male children of the Jews (as represented by the *kira*'s older son) were indeed slain.

The story of the *kira* murdered in 1600 had resonance over half a century later, when another queen mother played a significant role as regent. This time, however, her supporters used the tale as a foil to praise a royal woman who knew 'how to put Jews in their place'. Despite her close personal relations with the *kira*, Safiye Sultan was responsible for expelling Jews from Eminönü, the Jewish quarter of the city, to begin construction of a royal mosque in 1598.[70] After Safiye Sultan's mosque was completed by a successor, Hatice Turhan, in 1665, Mustafa, known as the Kurdish preacher – who served as the Friday imam of Sultan Mehmed IV – devoted a panegyric to the latter queen mother.[71] Mustafa returned to the narrative of the *kira*'s lynching, but countered it with the example of another Jew, the Sephardic Jewish physician Moses son of Raphael Abravanel – descendant of a family, members of which had served as financiers and tax collectors to King Ferdinand II of Spain – who was humbled, not by murder, but by conversion to Islam. He became Hayatizade Mustafa Fevzi Efendi in 1669.[72]

In the middle of his history of the Valide Sultan Mosque, Mustafa juxtaposes two stories about Jews in palace service, prototypes of what should happen to the Jew who rose above his or her station. After discussing Safiye Sultan's first attempts to build the complex in the late sixteenth century, he launches into a tirade against the lynched *kira*: 'Strangers and foreigners meddled greatly in the state of the deceased queen mother and stirred rebellion. One of them was an accursed Jewish hag known as *kira*. Those taking refuge at the gate of this malicious one's home were too numerous to count.'[73] She 'incited affairs' by manipulating palace correspondence 'concerning appointments to official duties and unjustly caused many innocent people to be oppressed and transgressed [against]'.[74] Mustafa does not narrate her brutal end, which it is assumed his readers already know. Instead, following this riff on the danger of Jews in palace service, Mustafa segues into a moral tale about how the dynasty should treat such servants.

To illustrate the piety of Hatice Turhan, the queen mother who completed the mosque in his day, Mustafa explains that she did not permit Moses son of Raphael Abravanel, another Jew in palace service, to remain as physician to the sultan until he became a Muslim.[75] Although Hayatizade (i.e. the converted Jew Moses) 'was renowned for his high degree of skilfulness in medicine, because he had not become ennobled and graced by the honour of Islam, and was not exempt from and absolved of the filth of infidelity, she was not pleased that he should take the noble pulse and diagnose his excellency's maladies'. In fact, 'treatment of the sovereign was not permitted to Hayatizade as long as he did not ennoble himself with the teaching of Islam and distinguish himself from among the Jews with the banner of Islam'.[76]

After contrasting the (end of the) *kira*, the once useful Jew who rose to power over Muslims and encouraged immorality (and whom readers knew was killed for it), with that of Hayatizade, the useful Jew who was humbled by conversion, Mustafa returns to narrate the glorious completion of the mosque in an area cleared of Jews.[77]

The consequences of the sultanate of women, when palace women were most influential from the end of the sixteenth century to the mid-seventeenth century, were still being debated at the beginning of the eighteenth century, and the narrative of the *kira*'s downfall was recounted in a popular Ottoman chronicle, the *Tarih-i Naima* or *Ravdat-ül-Hüseyn fi Hülâsâ-i*

Ahbâr-il-Hâfikayn (*Garden of al-Huseyin, or, Choicest News of East and West*; c.1697–1704), by the official chronicler Mustafa Naima. This work 'maintained its prestige' down to the twentieth century, representing 'the thoughts and the feelings of his time'.[78] Naima offers the most brutal account of the killing of the *kira*, claiming that both her sons were murdered: as the *kira* and her sons were being brought before the vizier, ascending the steps of the audience hall,

> the *sipahi* could not be held back and thrust their curved daggers into the shrew and her sons, cutting the three of them to pieces, and then dumped their wicked carcasses on the public square. They cut off the accursed one's hand, which was the appendage of bribery, and cut out her vulva, [and cut them to pieces], nailing them to the doors of those conceited ones who obtained their posts by means of that accursed woman.[79]

Naima condemned the lynching. He recognised that in every age there will be people who obtain their posts though bribery. However, 'It is necessary to strive to hinder the buying and selling of office with wise and reasonable measures, rather than inciting a lynch mob and arousing disorder which disgraces the honour of the dynasty.'[80] The gruesome end of the *kira* served to illustrate his cautionary tale.

Jews continued to appear as corrupters of morals in seventeenth- and eighteenth-century Ottoman Muslim chronicles. Evliya Çelebi, a Muslim Turkish Istanbulite educated in the palace and a companion of Sultan Murad IV, narrates how when the future Sultan Selim I (r. 1512–20) was governor of Trabzon, 'two boys, an older and younger brother, disappeared. Despite the efforts of the magistrates and the populace, they were unable to find them and gave up the search.' Years later a Sufi discovered a message that read: 'You who wish to learn of our condition should know that we have been held captive underground for the past twenty years by Jewish tanners. Rescue us, for God's sake and for the sake of God's messenger.' The Sufi alerted Prince Selim, who sent soldiers, 'armed to the teeth', to raid the Jewish tanneries, where they 'found the brothers inside the cave that was mentioned'. The backs of the boys were flayed, the brothers attached back to back and set to tanning:

> When one stood up to work, the other was left helpless loaded onto his back. When the first one finished his job, they were reversed, and the other one was set to work. They were suffering terribly. Also, several hundred other young boys named Muhammad had either been killed or else were being held captive and used as apprentices and servants.

Outraged, the Muslims of Trabzon 'massacred all the Jews in the city, including women and swaddled babies in their cradles. From that time on they have had imperial edicts permitting them to kill any Jews whom they may see. This is the reason why there are no Jews in Trabzon; and if someone suggests to a Jew that he go to Trabzon, the Jew tells him to go to Hell.'[81]

Although the serio-comic way he narrates this 'strange tale' implies that the author did not believe it, he did not criticise the libel involving Jewish ritual murder, slavery, and abuse of Muslim boys, which echoes libels against Jews long attributed to Christians. Evliya 'can serve as the typical (archetypal?) Ottoman', Muslim member of the Ottoman Turkish Istanbul elite. His *Seyahatname* (*Book of Travels*), in which this story appears, covers the wanderings of the famed raconteur between 1640 and 1680 and has been popular since the seventeenth century. It 'provides the materials for getting at Ottoman perceptions of the world'.[82] As we see in this story and elsewhere in his work, Evliya imagined that Jews were driven by an evil desire, since 'all their deeds are calculated to treachery and the killing of Muslims, especially anyone named Muhammad'.[83] As proof he related that in the mid-sixteenth century a Jewish physician in Ottoman Budapest confessed, 'I have poisoned forty men named Muhammad,' including a vizier, by lacing a fruit drink with deadly poison.[84]

Muslim authors after Evliya Çelebi continued to use Jewish figures in their chronicles as symbols of moral corruption. The messianic movement of Shabbatai Tzevi offered Ottoman Muslim chroniclers another opportunity to describe the humbling of a bad Jew. Born to a Romaniote (Greek Jewish) family in Ottoman Izmir in 1626, Shabbatai Tzevi was a charismatic preacher by the age of eighteen and began to lead his own students of Kabbalah. His erratic behaviour may be a sign that he experienced bipolar disorder. His followers believed he possessed magical powers, and he became the spiritual guide to Jewish men and especially women. Jews believed the Messiah would appear in 1648. In that year Shabbatai Tzevi pronounced the holy name of God, which Jews are forbidden from saying, and engaged in other scandalous practices, including prohibited sexual relations. The rabbis banned him. Shabbatai Tzevi wandered the Ottoman Empire, gaining followers attracted to his antinomian preaching, including Salonica, from which he was also banned. He ended up in Istanbul in 1658 where his blasphemy, offences against tradition, strange acts, and elevation of sexual sin to a holy act compelled him to flee the rabbis. He also attracted the following of Sufis. In the early 1660s he preached in Jerusalem, Cairo, and Gaza. While in Egypt in 1664 he married Sara, a convert and former prostitute.[85]

Muslim Saviours

Natan of Gaza, a well-known kabbalist and supposed miracle worker, propagated Shabbatai Tzevi's message. Shabbatai Tzevi smashed through the doors of the Portuguese synagogue in Izmir with an axe in 1665, proclaimed himself the Messiah, and allowed women to read from the Torah. Jews in Europe and the Middle East believed in his claim. Alerted by his Jewish opponents, Ottoman authorities arrested him in Istanbul, imprisoning him for upsetting the peace. Called to appear before Sultan Mehmed IV in 1666, Shabbatai Tzevi was given the choice of either performing a miracle by surviving a volley of flaming arrows fired by the sultan's bowmen or converting to Islam. The Messiah turned Muslim. Yet until his death in Albanian exile in 1683, Shabbatai Tzevi, renamed Aziz (Saint) Mehmed Efendi, acted like a Converso, one who publicly is compelled to follow one religion, but secretly follows another. He continued to preach his messianic faith.

Hundreds of his Jewish followers followed him into Islam, where they, too, secretly practised the faith and rituals their Messiah taught them while ostensibly following the requirements of Islam, including fasting at Ramadan, as if they, too, were Conversos.[86]

Since the forced conversions of Jews in Iberia made it normal for Jews to pretend to be one faith in public, whilst practising another in secret, Jewish Messiahs arose who emphasised their intentions and not their acts, including religious conversion. Many prophets of and followers of Shabbatai Tzevi around the Mediterranean including in Morocco were in fact Spanish or Portuguese Conversos, for whom messianism and the emergence of a Converso Messiah were important.[87]

Gazan Rabbi Jacob Najara reported in 1671 about the lack of Muslim concern with Shabbatai Tzevi's synthesis of Judaism and Islam. After converting to Islam, Shabbatai Tzevi read the entirety of the Torah portion and afterward feasted in great joy. Throughout all this the windows and doors were closed. At the time of the afternoon prayer, he opened all the doors and all the windows, and, although several [Muslims] were watching through the windows and doors, not one of them made any protest. When he came to the *Aleynu* prayer, he told the turban-wearers [Shabbatai Tzevi's followers who converted to Islam] to recite the prayer in a loud voice along with the Jews, facing eastward as they did so, and to pay no attention to the [Muslims] who watched them ... That night, at the close of the [Jewish] Sabbath, he recited the evening prayer in a most melodious fashion, and with great joy. Once the Sabbath was done, he went riding on a horse, taking with him some thirty of the Faithful Ones who wore the turban [i.e. his converted followers] ... He went about the city, through the marketplaces and the streets, and all the dignitaries of the [Ottoman] empire saw him going about with his troop of followers ... Not one made any protest.[88]

Their descendants perpetuated Shabbatian messianism underground in Ottoman Salonica. They created a new religion that is a symbiosis of Jewish and Muslim beliefs and practices, while living ostensibly as Muslims. They called themselves Believers (*Ma'aminim*, Hebrew), like the first followers of Muhammad, whereas Muslims called them Converts (*Dönmeler*, Turkish).[89]

Sultan Mehmed IV's chronicler Abd al-Rahman Abdi Pasha wrote an Ottoman account of Shabbatai Tzevi's movement and his conversion to Islam. Not able to tolerate the reverse, he deployed the theme of the Muslim as saviour of the Jews. The Ottoman authorities would not have bothered to intervene had it not been for the 'mischief-making, disorder, and moral depravity' caused by Shabbatai Tzevi's fanatical followers.[90] Before the sultan and his council, Shabbatai Tzevi 'denied all the nonsense said about him' by his followers, and 'they proposed that he embrace Islam'. When the council concluded by saying, 'After this council there is no possibility for escape: either come to the faith, or you will be immediately put to death. Become a Muslim at last, and we will intercede for you with our gracious emperor,' he converted. To Abdi Pasha there was no contradiction in writing that a Jew who was forced to become a Muslim was a sincere believer. In his *Tarih-i Râşid*, the eighteenth-century official historian Mehmed Raşid Efendi questioned this, writing: 'Because he knew that his execution was certain [if he did not do so], he showed an inclination to become Muslim.'[91]

Shabbatai Tzevi converted to Islam along with most palace physicians during the second half of the seventeenth century, just as the dynasty and men of state compelled the Islamisation of the main Jewish neighbourhood in Istanbul.[92] By the end of the seventeenth century, there were very few Jews in influential positions, and elite Jews in the empire never recovered their privileged economic and political position.[93]

Reflecting the fact that Jews were no longer visible in sensitive positions, and that the tensions of the sultanate of women had been resolved – as palace women no longer exerted political authority – with the exception of Naima, writing at the very beginning of the century, eighteenth-century chroniclers found the account of the downfall of the *kira* no longer the best example of the moral danger Jews posed. They presented instead the execution of another Jewish figure who violated the dhimma pact, a man who was condemned for fornication with a Muslim woman.

They declared his punishment to be unjust, as his guilt was

unproven, although they did not criticise the legal regime based on the principle that Muslims are superior to Jews. A Jewish figure was accused of causing such egregious moral disorder that he and his partner in moral crime had to be executed. He was also converted to Islam to atone for his enjoying the forbidden privilege of a Muslim man by fornicating with a Muslim woman. These punishments were meant to enforce the dhimma pact.

At noon on Friday 28 June 1680, hundreds of thousands of people crowded into the Hippodrome to stone to death a Muslim woman and a Jewish merchant who was alleged to be her lover.[94] Neighbours who raided her home claimed to have found the couple having intercourse, which was doubly illicit: she was married, and sexual relations between Jewish men and Muslim women were forbidden by law. The accused denied any wrongdoing, but a mob dragged the two before the chief justice of the empire's European provinces, who had previously been the main judge in Istanbul's Islamic law court. He accepted the testimony of the witnesses, denied the accused pair a trial, and condemned them to death. Grand Vizier Kara Mustafa Pasha reported his decision to Mehmed IV, who confirmed the sentence. The sultan attended the double execution in person and offered the man conversion to Islam, permitting him to die swiftly and with dignity by decapitation.

Eyewitness Silahdar Fındıklılı Mehmed Agha, a member of Mehmed IV's palace guard during the stoning of the woman, depicted the sultan as eager to punish the innocent pair.[95] 'Let me see [their execution] in person,' he had the sultan say, and accordingly, 'he arrived from Üsküdar [on the Asian side of the Bosporus] at noon and established himself in the mansion of Ibrahim Pasha overlooking the Hippodrome', the same mansion where the *kira* was lynched nearly a century earlier. When the sultan took up his position overlooking the plaza, 'they brought the woman and the Jew to the place of execution. Being told, "Become a Muslim, you will be redeemed, you will go to Paradise," the Jew was honoured by the glory of Islam and then decapitated at the base of a bronze dragon,' the serpent column, near the Egyptian obelisk.⁹⁶ 'Wailing and lamenting, she cried, "They have slandered me. I am innocent and have committed no sin. For the sake of the princes, do not kill me, release me!" But they did not let her go.'

The episode casts doubt on the claim that violent episodes directed against Jews were always to be blamed on the populace and the religious class; here it was the highest representative of the governing elite and the sultan himself who were responsible. More significant for the history of Ottoman Jewry is the role Ottoman historians ascribe to the sultan in allowing an injustice to be perpetuated against his Jewish subject. Their depiction of Mehmed IV presiding over a public execution of a Jew who should not have been punished counters the prevailing consensus that Ottoman sultans were always the saviour of the Jew.

A striking aspect of the Ottoman chronicles from the fifteenth to the eighteenth centuries is how they generally remain silent about the individuals that Jewish chroniclers and historians boast about, those who served as physicians, advisors, bankers, and diplomats. The service of useful and politically reliable men and women was used to illustrate the Ottoman Jewish–Muslim symbiosis of the fifteenth and sixteenth centuries, an essential pillar in the edifice of the 'Judaeo-Islamic tradition'.⁹⁷

Jewish men and women were entrusted with an intimate advisory role and with sensitive diplomatic missions, which demonstrates how sultans and sultanas and members of the elite placed their trust in them. But this is not what the Ottoman chroniclers – usually patronised by the sultan – chose to remember about Ottoman Jews. Jewish usefulness and loyalty go unmentioned in their chronicles, whose authors preferred to present an image of untrustworthy Jews, expressing relief when those in prominent positions were replaced by Muslims. Nev'izade 'Ata'i criticised Moses ben Joseph Hamon's rise to prominence, celebrating instead how upon the privy physician's death, 'the sultan's court was purified of the filth of his existence'.[98] Depicted as a source of danger, because he transgressed the social order spelled out in the dhimma pact, the Jewish physician is the only Jew mentioned in the biographical entries devoted to Sufis.[99] Eighteenth-century Ottoman historian Silahdar wrote that Hayatizade – used as a foil in a seventeenth-century chronicle to illustrate how Jews should be treated – died alone in prison, his downfall engineered by Muslim physicians who convinced the Shaykh al-Islam that he was a Converso, a convert secretly practising Judaism.[100]

Ottoman Muslim history writing from the fifteenth to the eighteenth century contains anti-Jewish sentiment. Writers had an arsenal of anti-Jewish stereotypes, among them that Jews are greedy, cunning, and deceitful, and obtain their wealth through corrupt financial practices. For centuries, Ottoman Muslim chroniclers labelled Jews as disturbers of the peace, mischief-makers, intriguers, corrupters, and seditious, implying evil, malicious intent. Rather than focusing on the positive role of Jewish figures, their attention was drawn to troublemakers such as a *kira* who betrayed their trust. Her life proved to the authors that Jews could not and should not be trusted, and her lynching reflected discomfort with the reality that Jews rose above dhimmi status.

The Ottoman Empire gets the plaudits, but Moroccan Jews, contrary to a common view that, like the Jews of Iran, their position 'was substantially worse', were as successful and influential as their Ottoman counterparts.[101] As we saw in Chapter 3, the Jews in Morocco flourished under Islamic rule, but much like their co-religionists in the Ottoman Empire, they also faced episodes of persecution. The first mellah was established in Fez in 1438. The word, subsequently applied to Jewish neighbourhoods throughout the Maghreb, comes from the Arabic and Hebrew word for salt, as it was built on the site of a salt deposit, whose concession was held by Jews (just as the first ghetto, established in 1516 in Venice, may have been named, as it was built near a foundry, *giotto*).

Most Jews preferred to live among themselves, but many others in the Maghreb lived side by side with Muslims, as there were few differences between them.[102] The *mimuna*, celebrated the evening after Pesach has ended, is the festival of good fortune, shared with Muslims, where gifts and food that are symbols of abundance are shared. It is acclaimed by Muslims and Jews alike as a perfect example of Jewish–Muslim brotherhood in that country, as Jews, after having marked their difference from Muslims by refraining from eating any flour products for eight days in commemoration of the Exodus from Egypt, mark their return to a normal diet by breaking bread with Muslims in the mellah.[103]

The first mellah at Fez was constructed not in the medina (old town) but next to the Merinid royal palace in New Fez (Fez Jdid), under the protection of the sovereign following a massacre of Jews. Jews held the highest posts in the Merinid court and had been attributed a share of responsibility for the unpopular tax measures and the suppression of the privileges of groups that believed they were entitled to them. The dynasty wanted to spare the Jews from the violence that could turn against it and protect its interests tied to elite Jews who served the sultan.[104] Some of these Jews converted to Islam rather than give up their homes and businesses and move to the new Jewish quarter. Within Fez's Muslim society they became one of the essential components of its economic elite at the Qissarya, heart of the fabric trade, and the Qarawiyine, home of the learned elite. The *nagid* (Hebrew) or *shaykh al-yahud* (Arabic) was at the centre of the regulation of Jewish communal life, as well as representing Jews to the Muslim authorities and Muslim magistrates, the one person guiding relations between the mellah and the medina.

The privileged few, mainly of Andalusian background, who accumulated great wealth and influence were, as Jews, vulnerable to being stripped of their property, imprisoned for ransom, and even executed by order of the rulers.[105] Perceived violations of the dhimma pact led to outbreaks of anti-Jewish violence. In Fez in 1642 the followers of the marabout of Dila, a Sufi leader, Mohamed el-Haj, destroyed synagogues. The Jews aided Sultan Moulay Rashid in entering their neighbourhood and seizing New Fez, and subsequently defeating and impaling Mohamed el-Haj.[106] Sultan Moulay Rashid later asked his Jewish goldsmith, counsellor, and banker, Aaron Carsinet, to establish commercial relations with the French.[107] The other episode of violence against Jews in Fez occurred during the brief and bloody reign of Sultan Moulay Yazid (1790–2), who proclaimed himself the Mahdi and massacred many Muslim opponents. He believed that during the reign of his father Sidi Mohamed ben Abdallah (1757–90) Jews had refused to give the funds he needed; he tortured and executed prominent Jewish courtiers such as Jacob Attal in Tétouan, yet employed other Jews in the palace.[108] He suddenly disappeared in Marrakesh. The event was celebrated in a Purim play, Jews renaming Moulay Yazid as *mezid* (deliberate sinner).[109] His successor, Moulay Sulayman (r. 1792–1822), annulled his restrictions and ordered the destruction of the mosque erected by his predecessor in the mellah.

Muslim Saviours

As Morocco had more than one capital city and royal residence, the second mellah, also built next to a royal palace, was established at Marrakesh. It was built in response to a demand of the wealthy Jews who had a monopoly on sugar production and its trade with England and the Netherlands, and wanted to be protected.[110] As important, Moulay Ahmed al-Mansur (r. 1578–1603) saw the value of establishing the mellah in the 'Red City', seat of the Sa'adian dynasty. He aimed to have his own Jewish neighbourhood to display his wealth and power in competition with the rival dynastic seat at Fez. Marrakesh's light orange and pink walls wrap the medina in their embrace. Palace, merchants, tanners, tinsmiths, and the Jewish quarter were safely within.

The mellah's synagogues include la-Azama (Synagogue of the Deportees), established by Rabbi Yitzhak Daloya and other Spanish Jews arriving in 1492. It is one of three synagogues still open for worship today of the thirty that were once active. The Jewish stores, artisanal workshops, courtyard homes, and schools within the mellah's narrow alleyways, painted the same light pink as the city walls, were safely ensconced on one side by the opulent El Badi Palace. The palace, in ruins today, which once boasted several hundred rooms sumptuously decorated in Italian marble, Sudanese gold leaf, and Indian onyx, featuring courtyards with sunken gardens and reflecting pools, was financed by reparations paid by Portugal following their defeat at the Battle of the Three Kings, when Sultan Mulay Abd al-Malik defeated Portuguese King Don Sebastian on 4 August 1578 at Al-Ksar Kebir (Alcazarquivir): an event celebrated every year as the Purim de los Cristianos by the Jews of Tangier, Tétouan, and Fez.[111]

On the other side of the mellah is the Jewish cemetery, laid out in 1537, the largest in Morocco with more than 20,000 tombs, including those of 600 holy men. The cylindrical casket-like raised tombs of the Jewish dead, walled within a salmon-coloured city, are the same cylindrical shape and sugar-cube white as the tombs of the Muslim kings in the dynastic tomb at the mosque of the palace, but lacking the exquisite latticework.

Al-Mansur followed the lead of the founder of the dynasty, Moulay Mohammed, who employed two Portuguese refugees, Abraham and Isaac Cabessa, as his bankers and advisors.[112] The Sa'adian era, but especially the next epoch under the 'Alawi dynasty (1659 to today), descendants of Muhammad through his daughter, Fatima, has been marked by the rise of a record number of Jewish men to positions at court overseeing trade and diplomacy with Christian Europe.[113]

The mellah at Meknes was erected by Moulay Ismail (r. 1672–1727), of the 'Alawi dynasty. Ismail made Meknes his capital and dynastic seat. He needed to meet the needs of his treasury and a large army by taking advantage of maritime trade and like previous dynasties he built a mellah to legitimise his power, encouraging wealthy Jewish merchants, especially his silversmiths. Among them was the trader Abraham Maimran, counsellor to the ruler, and the *nagid* or *shaykh al-yahud*.[114] Meknes would become known as 'little Jerusalem', boasting the illustrious rabbinic families Berdugo, Toledano, Maimran, and Messas.

The mellahs of Rabat, Salé, Essaouira, and Tétouan were built at the beginning of the nineteenth century, between 1806 and 1811 during the reign of Moulay Slimane (r. 1792–1822), nicknamed 'the pious' by his Jewish subjects. These new mellahs functioned more like ghettos, to keep Jews apart from Muslims, than the earlier mellahs had done, reflecting a new streak of fundamentalist Islam. But this sovereign's personal physician was a Jew, Eliahu Outmezguine, and he named Jews to important posts in the financial and customs administrations, as well as

Muslim Saviours

Jews such as Meir Mecnin (Meyer Ouaknine) and Judah Benoliel to be ambassadors or consuls in London and Gibraltar, centres of global and Mediterranean trade.

Until the mid-eighteenth century, when the Spanish and the Portuguese occupied the Atlantic and Mediterranean coasts of Morocco, most external trade was with sub-Saharan Africa and the Middle East. Under the Merinids and the Sa'adians, these relations extended to Spain, England, and the Netherlands. The sovereigns of these two dynasties relied on Jewish merchants for the export of grains and sugar cane. From the English taking of Gibraltar in 1704 to the end of that century, the successors of Moulay Ismail sent Jewish agents to England for commercial and political reasons. Jacob ben Idder was appointed vice-consul of Tangier in 1769, then was appointed the sultan's representative to the Court of St James's.[115]

In the eighteenth century the 'Alawi sultans Sidi Mohamed ben Abdallah (r. 1757–90) and Moulay Abderrahmane (r. 1822–59) encouraged maritime commerce to increase the treasury. Sidi Mohamed ben Abdallah agreed to the suggestion of an influential Jew at court, Samuel Sumbal, to select ten wealthy Jewish families from around Morocco and have them each send one representative to set up business in the new port of Essaouira on the Atlantic coast as Morocco's principal seaport for European trade.[116] Many of them were Sephardim, such as the Corcos family.[117] They were given royal monopolies on trade with England, Sweden, Denmark, France, Spain, and the United States.[118] Jewish traders mobilised in this way contributed to the increase in treasury revenues and benefited from it.[119] Advisors to the sultan, such as Mordechai Shriqui, Eliaho Levy, Jacob Attal (a Tunisian), and Samuel Sumbal, negotiated treaties with the Danes and Swedes, including their payment of a tribute to the sultan in exchange for security from Moroccan corsairs. These wealthy merchants ate refined dishes, played the best music, dressed in the finest cloth, contrary to the dhimma pact, clothed their women in silk, and adorned them with gold and pearls, rubies and emeralds.[120] Wealthy merchants collected the customs duties at Tangier, Tétouan, and Essaouira, and ran the port of Safi.

An 1858 decree declared, 'The two merchants Abraham and Jacob, the sons of Solomon Corcos, are our Jews, and their father was our Jew. Among the Jews they are the cream of the crop [the fruit], and very few [Jews] are equal to them in yielding profits. So protect them and look after their well-being.'[121] They supplied luxury goods, including silk, linen, English furniture, and chocolate, to the palace, and imported fabrics for army uniforms, making them wealthy and influential; Abraham was appointed US vice-consul in the city.[122] The Elmaleh family and its patriarch Joseph gained even greater influence as they also included rabbis along with merchants and dominated the Jewish community for nearly a century.[123] While the Corcos were dependent on the sultan, and the Elmaleh led the Jewish community and were intermediaries for French and British Jewish organisations, the Afriats had the most foreign investments, rising to become merchant bankers to London and Marseille, settling abroad in England or France, or gaining foreign protégé status, enjoying continued prosperity to the end of the nineteenth century.[124] Most of the Jewish merchants obtained foreign protection; those in Morocco dependent on their ties with the sultan remained dhimmis.

They were dependent on the palace and their loyalty was assured. As merchants, however, they could exert local influence since the prosperity of the town depended on their businesses.[125] Equipped with foreign languages and international connections, to Livorno, London, Marseille, and Amsterdam, as well as the Jewish network inland across North Africa, these Judeo-Arabic-speaking court Jews served as diplomats as well, as in Al-Andalus and the Ottoman Empire.[126] A special personal relationship between Jew and ruler tied them together, as both were 'separated from the rest of society' as the Jew was 'a member of a religious minority', and the ruler was 'a relatively inaccessible sovereign of holy lineage'.[127]

Moulay Abd al-Rahman followed the strategy of Sidi Mohamed to relaunch the monopolies and tried to reinvigorate maritime trade. To meet his aim, he mobilised the most prominent merchants. The rulers preferred these loyal *tujjar sultan* (sultan's merchants) to be Jews rather than Muslims. They were given a near-total monopoly of the import–export trade by the ruler.[128] They were required to make an annual visit to pay their liege to the sultan in Marrakesh.[129] The sultan's merchants made large profits, yet they depended on the official recognition and patronage of the palace. The foreign and Jewish merchants were given houses in separate quarters in the *casbah*, the fortified centre of the city.[130]

These royal merchants were similar to the *Hofjuden* (court Jews), who came to prominence in Europe. *Hofjuden* provisioned and paid armies. They also provided intelligence, and were expert jewellers, such as the Oppenheimers, but were not used as diplomats, as were Moroccan and Ottoman Jews.[131] In both cases, elite Jews were economic instruments of the rulers. One of the best examples is Meir Macnin.

Meir Macnin ('Goldfinch' in Moroccan Arabic) was born into a Marrakesh Jewish merchant family that settled in Essaouira in the 1770s. The most active merchants in the town were Moroccan Jews, who had trade relations in the interior of Morocco, and whose family members located abroad facilitated international trade, which also was a reason for appointing them to diplomatic missions.[132] The Macnin family accumulated wealth in Essaouira by the 1790s, as the pre-eminent merchants for the government, because of trade and marital relations with other wealthy Jewish trading families, lucrative commerce within Morocco and overseas, and ownership of urban real estate.[133] Despite their elite status and wealth, as late as the 1840s the Macnins and other wealthy Jewish families were liable to the legal subordination of the dhimma pact, and had to pay the jizya; as late as the 1820s they had to dress like other dhimmi.[134]

Spanish- and Arabic-speaking Meir Macnin, referred to by Sultan Moulay Sulayman as 'our Jew', became the sultan of Morocco's Jewish agent to Europe.[135] He moved to London in 1800 and rose to prominence, with a near-monopoly in the trade between Morocco and Britain, securing arms, ships, and munitions for Morocco, and gifting Moroccan lions to England's king.[136] Unlike much of the rest of Christian Europe, in England Jews faced few restrictions, and many began to acculturate into society, some converting to the Church of England to remove all remaining disabilities, or marrying out of the faith.[137]

As a sign of his ascendancy to the pinnacle of the Sephardic elite of London, in 1815 Macnin served as *presidente* of the board of Bevis Marks, the Sephardic synagogue in the City, founded a century earlier, modelled on the Sephardic synagogue of Amsterdam.[138] It was the successor of the first synagogue at Creechurch Lane permitted following the readmission of the Jews in 1656, under the Commonwealth: Oliver Cromwell had been convinced to do so by Menasseh ben Israel.

Menasseh ben Israel was born to Converso parents in Lisbon. He was rabbi of the Portuguese and Spanish synagogue in Amsterdam, and founder of the first Jewish printing press in the Netherlands. He believed that the Messiah would come if Jews lived in every part of the world. To accelerate this process,

Muslim Saviours

he promoted Jewish settlement schemes in Latin America and Western Europe. He corresponded with English Puritans, who believed the Ten Lost Tribes of Israel were to be found among the indigenous people of the Americas. He published a Latin translation of his Portuguese work, *Esperança de Israel* (*Hope of Israel*), about the Ten Lost Tribes being found in South America, and dedicated it to the English Parliament, where millenarian feeling was strong among the Puritans and radical Christian sectarians. In 1655 Menasseh travelled to London to deliver a petition to Oliver Cromwell, ruler of England since the execution of King Charles I in 1649, asking for the readmission of the Jews. London merchants opposed access to their markets by men of the Portuguese nation. Cromwell was in favour, and a conference at Whitehall of judges, clergy, and merchants agreed. In 1656 Jews leased a home at Creechurch Lane in the City of London and converted it into a synagogue.

That first post-readmission house of worship was replaced by a purpose-built synagogue, modelled on the Portuguese and Spanish synagogue in Amsterdam. Bevis Marks was opened in 1701 and is the only synagogue in the City of London. Its rabbis included Jacob ben Sasportas of Oran, Algeria, rabbi in Tlemcen, who moved to Amsterdam in 1651 and travelled with Menasseh ben Israel to England in 1655. He served as rabbi in London until 1666 when he moved to Hamburg, becoming famous for his multi-volume denunciation of Shabbatai Tzevi.[139]

The first Jews to live in England after readmission were Sephardim. At the end of the eighteenth century, many Sephardic Jews in London were Moroccan. They reached England by way of Gibraltar and pursued trade in London, which replaced Amsterdam as financial capital of the world after the Napoleonic Wars.[140] In the mid-eighteenth century, as many as one-third of Gibraltar's population were Jews, mostly of Moroccan origin.[141]

A large number arrived in London in 1781 after the French siege of Gibraltar. They settled in the City of London and rose to prosperity and elite status, part of the Sephardi world trade network, considering themselves 'the Portuguese nation', even if their ancestors were not Portuguese or Spanish, but Moroccan. At the time synagogue records were kept in Portuguese and children were taught in Spanish and Portuguese.[142] The Moroccan Jews rose from being stockholders in the Bank of England, merchants, and contractors for the king, to being at the centre of England's foreign trade and banking industries, hobnobbing at the City's coffeehouses.[143] Bevis Marks, located in the financial district, boasted members of the leading Moroccan Jewish families, the Abitbol, Afriat, Pinto, Coriat, Guedalla, and Sebag, among others.[144]

As an expression of symbiosis, when the Moroccan sultan sent Muslim merchants to London they lived at the homes of these Moroccan Jewish merchants because of their shared culture. Although they were Muslims, they told British authorities that their address was the Spanish and Portuguese synagogue.[145] Al-Haj Abd al-Salam Buhillal of Tangier resided with the Jew Abraham Benjamin next to the Bevis Marks synagogue.[146] It was the same relationship built on trust that we have seen in earlier centuries, for in economic relations, Muslims and Jews formed partnerships, not rivalries.

Macnin – who, along with his role in London high life, maintained ties to the sultan and his firm in Essaouira, which kept its records in Judeo-Arabic – returned to Marrakesh, city of his birth, in 1822. The next year he was appointed the new sultan's Jew, granted control of most of Morocco's foreign trade, with financial control of its seaports, and ambassador-at-large to all Christian nations.[147] Hardly any Jew (except Samuel ibn Naghrela) had ever amassed so much power in a Muslim-ruled land.

Muslim Saviours

There is no other known case in which so many responsibilities involving foreign trade and diplomacy were concentrated in the hands of a single Jew.[148] Despite the dhimma pact, Sultan Abd al-Rahman entrusted Macnin to purchase muskets from the US consulate and also gifted him two horses to ride. In 1824 the sultan presented Macnin with the opulent home of a Muslim who could not pay his debts to the ruler. Moroccan sultans could only imagine Jews as their resident representatives in Christian Europe, where these wealthy merchants served as bankers for the government. Just as the Moroccan Jew Judah Benoliel served as the sultan's consul-general in Gibraltar, Macnin was put in charge of customs at Tangier, where the foreign consulates were located, to the foreigners' dismay. In 1826, still referred to as a dhimmi, he was appointed ambassador to the Court of St James's.[149] By the 1830s, Moroccan Jewish merchants in London had adopted English, integrated into English society, and obtained peerages.[150]

Alongside male Moroccan success stories, there is also the teenage saint Sol Hatchuel (also known as Lalla Suleika), beheaded in the main square of Fez at the age of seventeen for the crime of apostasy in 1834.[151] Her last words were, '*Hebrea naci y Hebrea quero morir*' ('Born a Jew, I want to die a Jew').[152] Little could Jews realise her death was an omen for the tragedies to come.

PART II

MODERN TIMES

5

SEVERED SYMBIOSIS AND NEW SAVIOURS: COLONIALISM AND NEW ALLIANCES IN THE LONG NINETEENTH CENTURY, 1789–1914

Radical changes in France impacted Jewish–Muslim relations. In 1789, French revolutionaries abolished the monarchy and executed the king, disestablished the Church, nationalised its revenue and property, and closed churches and monasteries. They established a dechristianised Republic based on the principle of the equality of all citizens no matter their religion. They emancipated the Jews. The French established a system of rule based on the will of the people and freedom of speech. They unleashed nationalism and made devotion to the fatherland a guiding principle. They abolished the slave trade. How could anyone accept servile status after this?

The French took these ideas abroad, launching their colonial empire in the Middle East and North Africa, gaining local allies for their endeavour. On 1 July 1798 the French Army of the Orient, under the command of General Napoleon Bonaparte, landed near Alexandria, in Ottoman Egypt, as the French aimed to cut off the British passage to India and disrupt the commerce upon which their empire depended.[1] The French entered Cairo on 25 July, hoping to benefit from the trade and agriculture of the country by bringing Enlightenment. But the French controlled only from Alexandria to Cairo. A month later a British fleet commanded by Lord Nelson destroyed the French navy at anchor northeast of Alexandria, isolating Bonaparte's army.[2] Bonaparte, to reinforce the capital, ordered the destruction of the gates separating residential quarters and demolished the homes near the citadel, and imposed heavy taxes on Egyptians, leading to resistance. In August 1799 he realised the French situation had deteriorated, and left control in the hands of Jean-Baptiste Kléber, who was assassinated in June 1800.[3] His successor, a French convert to Islam, General Abdallah Jacques Menou, faced an Ottoman–British march on Cairo in spring 1801, and the French occupation was over that autumn. When Napoleon invaded and occupied Egypt, he placed a local Christian in charge of finance and taxation, and presented himself as Christians' protector, allowing them to bear arms, ride horses, wear turbans, and dress as they pleased.[4] A Christian headed a military battalion, and another became a magistrate.[5]

Egypt had become a sphere of interest for the great powers, as had the rest of the Ottoman Arab provinces. Napoleon's conquest and occupation of Egypt and the subsequent rise to power of Governor Muhammad Ali of Kavala and his dynasty, and then the British, opened the country to European influence. By that point there were approximately 5,000 rabbinic Jews and 1,000 Karaite Jews in Cairo.[6] The prosperity which European occupation introduced caused Arab and Sephardic Jews to migrate to Egypt from around the Mediterranean basin, and Ashkenazim from Eastern Europe. It is in this period we witness the rise of influential Jewish families, most of whom had origins outside of Egypt, such as the Suarès, Cattaoui, Mosseri and Menasce.

Muhammad Ali was one of the commanders of the Ottoman army charged in 1803 with restoring and consolidating Ottoman rule after the defeat of the French two years earlier.[7] Promoted to viceroy in 1805, he established his own independent power, eliminated his rivals, and created a formidable military, helping the Ottomans put down the Greek rebellion in 1820, until the Battle of Navarino in 1827 where Europeans destroyed his navy.[8] Yet in 1831 he conquered Ottoman territory as far as Adana. During the second war against the Ottomans from 1838 to 1841 Muhammad Ali's defeat of Ottoman troops and the desertion of the Ottoman fleet to his benefit provoked a new European intervention to keep the Ottoman dynasty in power. In 1840 the UK, France, Russia, Prussia, and Austria aligned to end Muhammad Ali's rule over Syria. In 1841 he and his family obtained the hereditary right to rule Egypt under the sultan.

Muhammad Ali introduced reforms modernising the land.[9] He improved the system of agricultural irrigation, introduced new crops such as cotton, reorganised government administration to ensure control of the economy, promoted industry to transform raw materials, created a fleet and an army made up of peasant conscripts, established medical and engineering schools, and sent Egyptians on educational missions to Europe to learn modern techniques.[10] His reforms set Egypt on a modern, independent path that especially benefited Jewry. Muhammad Ali also ordered the magistrate of Jerusalem to allow the Ashkenazim to return and to be given back their properties that had been distributed among the leading Muslim Husseini and Nashashibi families over a century earlier.[11] In 1836 the Ashkenazim restored the Hurva synagogue in the Jewish quarter of the Old City.[12] The jizya was abolished in 1855 and Christians enrolled in the military.

In Algeria, the French intervened on behalf of the Jews following a famine in 1805. Two Livornese (Italian) Jews, Bacri and Busnach, who were appointed the financial advisors of the Dey of Algiers in 1792, had become wealthy by selling wheat. Rioters blamed the famine on them. Busnach was shot dead. Jews took refuge with the French consul, synagogues were burned down, homes were pillaged, and women were raped. Three hundred Jewish families fled Algiers. Following this the dhimma laws were strictly applied. It was this situation that the French observed, compelling local Europeanised Jews and French Jews to seek to help them.[13]

Before the French conquest, Jews in Algeria, numbering 25,000, were little different from Muslims, although they were subject to the laws of the dhimmi, including not being allowed to go out at night in Algiers.[14] In each city they lived in a special quarter, the *hara*. They occupied certain professions: in Algiers, living in Bat Azzoun, El Biar, Bouzaréah, and Bab el Oued, they worked as tailors, coral jewellers, goldsmiths, and minters. At Constantine, host of the most important Jewish community, they lived in Bab el Djabia and then at Souk el Asser and El Kantara.[15] Like the Jews in Morocco, Jews in Algeria were Amazigh-, Arabic- or Spanish-speaking.

The Sephardic Jews and Livornese, the elite of Jewish society, living in Algiers and Oran, engaged in international trade and diplomacy; their clientele were local rulers, diplomats, and consuls.[16] Influenced by European culture and connected to the latest political trends in Europe, fluent in multiple languages (French, Spanish, English, Italian, Hebrew, Arabic, Turkish), families such as the Douran, Bacri, Busnach, and Stora called upon their European allies to improve the lot of their co-religionists in Algeria. But the mass of Jews in Algeria were native, religious, and poor. They owned small clothing, hosiery, or haberdashery stores, or were shoemakers, hawkers, and goldsmiths. Unlike in Morocco or Tunisia, Algerian Jews were spread across the land.[17] There were some nomadic Jews in Mzab who shared customs and culture with Berber Muslims.

Severed Symbiosis and New Saviours

France conquered Algeria, which was an autonomous part of the Ottoman Empire, in 1830 and made it a department, a part of France even before some areas which are today in France (such as Nice). Despite their anti-Jewish sentiment, the French military officers who invaded Algiers considered Jews as valuable potential allies, due to their dhimmi status.[18] The General Count de Bourmont, commander of the French expedition, put Jews and Muslims on an equal footing. Jacob Bacri, leader of the Jewish community in Algiers, became one of the general's most trusted advisors. Livornese Jews played the same role in the camp of the elite Muslims. The French expeditionary force recognised the existence of the 'Hebrew Nation' and considered Bacri as its representative. Already the next year the colonial administration restructured the 'Hebrew Council', beginning the secularisation of Algerian Jewry.[19] In 1839 the French government created a commission to reform Jewish worship and education, the last vestiges of Jewish autonomy. In 1841 and 1842 the rabbinic courts were abolished, and jurisdiction over Jews was transferred to French courts.[20]

Aware of the changes occurring in the United States and France following their revolutions, Ottoman reform decrees issued in 1839 and 1856 made all subjects equal under the law, regardless of religion, ending the dhimmi status of Jews (and Christians). Sultan Abdülmecid I (r. 1839–61) and his reformist grand vizier, Mustafa Reşid Pasha, intended to sweep away the nearly six-century-old social order.[21] The sultan introduced new state schools, open to all, irrespective of religion. Prior to this, each religious community was responsible for educating its own children in its own religion and language. Law was also secularised. Whereas formerly Islamic law courts were supreme, secular courts were introduced, and as their jurists grew in prominence, Islamic jurists began to lose their power.

In 1839, Sultan Abdülmecid I promulgated the Noble Decree of the Rose Garden. The decree guaranteed 'security of life, honour, and property' to all subjects, and a 'regular system of assessing taxes'. The decree also called for an 'equally regular system for the conscription of troops', which was meant to be universal conscription, what it refers to as 'the inescapable duty of all the people to provide soldiers for the defence of the fatherland'.[22] What was most radical about the decree was its affirmation that 'the Muslim and non-Muslim subjects of our lofty Sultanate shall, without exception, enjoy our imperial concessions'.

The Period of Reforms (*Tanzimat*) began to replace the religious hierarchy by equality between different religious groups. The decree aimed to sap the strength of ethnic nationalism by increasing the patriotism of the empire's subjects.[23] The sultan desired to create an Ottoman nation. Ottoman nationalism was a new ideology that advocated the loyalty of all subject peoples to his person and to the empire. The sultan wanted to be able to distinguish the religious differences of his subjects only when they entered their houses of prayer, as in France, where all citizens were equal, and Jews were referred to as 'French of Mosaic persuasion'.[24] Whereas the path to integration as an Ottoman had been conversion to Islam, this new ideology was based on loyalty alone.[25]

The decree of 1839 was promulgated as the Ottomans faced a rising tide of nationalism that began to break the bonds between the sultan and his subjects and caused the loss of territory in Southeastern Europe and the Middle East.[26] It failed. The reforms exacerbated diverse nationalist movements and did not increase Ottoman patriotism. Less than two decades later a new decree was promulgated.

The Imperial Reform Edict of 18 February 1856 came at the

end of the Crimean War (1853–6).[27] Although the Ottomans were on the victorious side against Russia, the sultan's allies Britain and France insisted that he ensure the full legal rights of Christian (and Jewish) Ottoman subjects. The 1856 edict – issued by Abdülmecid I one week prior to the beginning of the peace talks at Paris – made that which was implied by his 1839 decree explicit: complete religious freedom, no forced conversion, and genuine equality.[28] The decree relinquished, in theory, the predominant role of Muslims. Not all the Muslim ruling elite were happy about this. According to the intellectual and government minister Ahmed Cevdet Pasha, 'Many Muslims began to grumble: "Today we lost our sacred national rights which our ancestors gained with their blood. The Muslim community used to be the ruling community, but it has been deprived of this sacred right. This is a day of tears and mourning"' for Muslims.[29] As an expression of such sentiment, in 1859 there was a coup attempt in Istanbul by a group of officers and Sufis, but it was suppressed.

One year after the 1856 Ottoman edict, on 9 September 1857, Sidi Mohammed Bey, the ruler of Tunisia, nominally part of the Ottoman Empire yet in fact independent, issued the Pact of Security in front of a French admiral, European consuls, and Tunisian dignitaries. He promised 'complete security' to all his subjects and to all inhabitants of his land 'without distinction of religion, nationality, and race', equality in taxation, and equality before the law, which abrogated the dhimma pact. However, the same pact issued by Sidi Mohammed Bey permitted Jewish magistrates a seat on the criminal tribunal to decide cases involving Jews.[30]

The Pact of Security was understood to abolish the dhimma pact in Tunisia. It came six months after a major international scandal involving a Jewish man, Batto Sfez, who was accused of blasphemy and executed.[31] Pressure from foreign consuls and reformist Tunisian ministers and intellectuals helped bring about the Pact of Security in its wake. Ahmed Ben Diaf, chief secretary to the bey, and author of the Pact of Security, defended the abolition of discriminatory measures against Jews to reluctant members of the ulema, reminding them that sartorial rules were not imposed by Muhammad at Medina. He railed against 'the ignorant people of the capital, who considered that this measure heralded the end of the world, not realising that the decline of the country can be explained, to a large extent, by the oppression of our dhimmis and the abandonment of the recommendation of our Prophet (in their favour)' and called Jews 'our brothers in the homeland'.[32] These reforms were instituted in the constitution promulgated four years later by the next bey of Tunis, Sadok Bey.

In Egypt, Muhammad Ali's son Isma'il, fourth viceroy since Muhammad Ali's death in 1849, ruled from 1863 to 1879, and was granted the title khedive (viceroy) by the Ottomans, as were all successors descended from him.[33] Isma'il launched further reforms: modernising customs and the postal system, creating a sugar industry, building a new European-style quarter of Cairo. He spent greatly on education, created specialist and professional schools, sent more students to Europe, and constructed the Suez Canal, completed in 1869.

Khedive Isma'il's banker was Joseph Cattoui Pasha. It was in his villa boasting a rose marble staircase that France's Emperor Napoleon III (r. 1852–70) and Empress Eugenie celebrated a ball inaugurating the canal – the same canal the nationalisation of whose company less than a hundred years later would lead to a war which would spell the end of the Egyptian Jewish community.[34]

To pay for his projects, Khedive Isma'il took out loans from European powers.[35] They profited by obtaining concessions.

Severed Symbiosis and New Saviours

Unable to repay his debts, Isma'il found Egyptian finances controlled by Britain and France. Colonel Ahmad Urabi led a revolt. Britain and France installed Isma'il's elder son Tawfiq Pasha in his place. Urabi's revolt was crushed in 1882 as the British bombarded Alexandria and then occupied Egypt. Britain established a protectorate in 1914, ending symbolic Ottoman rule, which had positive implications for foreigners and Jews.

More important, Muhammad Ali's successors abrogated the dhimma laws. Economic growth led to the immigration of Arab Jews from North Africa and Yemen, Ashkenazim from Poland, Romania, and Russia, and Sephardim from the Ottoman Empire, Greece, Southeastern Europe, and Italy.

The Damascus Affair of 1840 gave British and French Jewry their first opportunity to intervene on behalf of Eastern Jewry, as part of a new Jewish internationalism, saving Jews themselves, or compelling their imperial governments to do so.[36] In that year, Jews were accused by Franciscan monks of the blood libel, supported by the French consul in Damascus. A dozen Jews were tortured to confess to the murder of a Catholic and his Muslim servant boy. Some died in prison. Syria at the time was under the control of Muhammad Ali. A Jewish delegation first travelled to him, who ordered the remaining imprisoned Jews released, and then to Sultan Abdülmecid I in Istanbul, who issued a decree declaring that Jews, in fact, do not murder Christian boys to drain their blood for use in baking matzah. A decree issued by Sultan Abdülmecid in 1840 condemned the blood libel: 'For the love we bear to our subjects, we cannot permit the Jews, whose innocence of the crime alleged against them is evident, to be worried and tormented as a consequence of accusations which have not the least foundation in truth.'[37] The sultan remained their saviour for the time being.

A blood libel occurred weeks later on the island of Rhodes. The deputy magistrate and Muslim religious scholars decided that 'in the absence of any grounds for suspicion, it could not be proven that the case merited further investigation; they also concluded that the Jews deserved to be freed and their persecution halted immediately'.[38] The chief rabbi, Haim Moses Fresco, informed Grand Vizier Reşid Pasha of the episode; who decreed that all the Jews should be released because 'the allegations were declared to be falsehoods and libel'.[39]

Another decree issued in 1866 by Sultan Abdülaziz ordered his grand vizier and Shaykh al-Islam and head of police to 'take all the necessary measures for preventing the Jewish people from being harassed by other religious groups and prejudiced people who pretend that Jews add human blood to matzot'. The sultan confirmed that in Judaism:

> not only blood is forbidden, but also that all kinds of meat has (*sic*) to be purified of all traces of blood in accordance to dietary laws before being consumed. This accusation therefore has no foundation and is a purely subversive invention. We forbid those evil persons from troubling our Jewish people whose innocence is obvious ... All accusations and attacks must cease and be severely punished. Orders are to be issued by the religious authorities to stop this scandalous behaviour ... No one has the right to trouble them, they are under my decree's protection.[40]

One important British Jew to intervene on Eastern Jewry's behalf was Moses Haim Montefiore, an illustrious member of the Bevis Marks synagogue in London. Montefiore was born into a Livornese Sephardi family, established in London in the 1740s, which became rich from the England–Italy trade.

Severed Symbiosis and New Saviours

Moses Haim made his fortune on the London Stock Exchange, enhanced by marrying into the English branch of the Ashkenazi Rothschild family. He became a director of the Bank of England in 1824 and used his enormous wealth to benefit poor and persecuted Jews around the globe. Still today Bevis Marks supports Jewish study in the four holy cities of Jerusalem, Tiberias, Safed, and Hebron, thanks to Montefiore's bequest. He was knighted by Queen Victoria, who took holidays in an adjacent home to his in Ramsgate, where he designed his own synagogue. In 1831 he became only the second Jew to serve as sheriff of the City of London. He was knighted in 1837 and in 1846 was made a baronet. In 1840 he was sent by the British government to intervene on behalf of the Jews accused of ritual murder in Damascus. Two decades later he established Mishkenot Sha'ananim (Peaceful Habitation), the first modern Jewish settlement outside the walls of the Old City of Jerusalem. He led the Board of Deputies of British Jews, founded in London in 1859, for four decades.[41]

Another Jew to intervene on behalf of Middle Eastern Jews and side with Muslim powers reflecting the old Jewish–Muslim alliance was the Conservative politician and prime minister of the United Kingdom Benjamin Disraeli, first Earl of Beaconsfield. He promoted the glory of Spanish Jewry and was a descendant of such a family. His father was Isaac d'Israeli, whose Italian Sephardic father migrated to London in 1748 and became one of the founders of the London Stock Exchange. Isaac was a member of Bevis Marks synagogue. His son Benjamin was baptised instead of celebrating a bar mitzvah there at thirteen.

Disraeli was fascinated by the East, and keen to promote a patronising, imperialist dominion over it. At the same time, like other Jews, he felt a romantic kinship for Muslim-ruled lands, and he and others considered him to be a proud Oriental.[42] On his voyage to the Middle East in 1830 and 1831, this man with olive skin, dark eyes, and curly black locks boasted of being 'quite a Turk' who 'wears a turban, smokes a pipe six-feet long, and squats on a Divan'.[43] Yet he also believed in the superiority of Judaism and of the Jewish race.[44]

Disraeli supported the Ottoman Empire against Russia. His enemies labelled his policies 'Jewish policies', as they understood why his sentiments compelled him to side with the tolerant Ottomans rather than the Russians, who persecuted Jews.[45] Jews were allies of Muslims, not Christians, even when someone such as Disraeli professed Christianity. He was even an apologist for, or denier of, Ottoman atrocities against Christians. His political opponent William Gladstone condemned Ottoman massacres of Bulgarian Christians.[46] It was England under Gladstone which occupied Egypt, not Disraeli. Nevertheless, Disraeli was an imperialist, yet one who 'felt a romantic kinship for the Empire's distant subjects', for he was 'in his eyes and those of many others, himself an Oriental'.[47] He proudly dressed as a Muslim to visit the Haram al-Sharif in Jerusalem. Disraeli believed in the British imperial project, which allowed him to rise to the top despite his Eastern origins.[48] He aimed to unite East and West under British rule cemented by the 'Semitic' Oriental spirit, which he represented.

Algerian Jews played an important diplomatic role as intermediaries in the first decade of French rule, helping to sign treaties with Emir Abd el-Kader,[49] leader of the resistance to the French occupiers, who employed Jews as his interpreters as well: Juda ben Duran and Salomon Zermati, immortalised in a portrait by Salomon Assus.[50] Zermati was part of the emir's delegation to France in 1839.

Jews in Algiers welcomed the French as liberators. Jewish merchants became the exclusive agents of the French army.

But on the other hand, Jews in the east in Constantine and in the south in Laghouat allegedly fiercely opposed the French alongside the Muslims. There is a myth about the capture of Constantine in 1837, according to which the Jews fought alongside the Muslims, participating in the defence of the city, and fired on the French. Evidence points in the opposite direction, that Jews aided the French.[51]

From the French occupation of Algiers in July 1830, the French deployed Jews as military interpreters for the army because they spoke the local Arabic dialect.[52] In that campaign Nathan Mouthy, an Algerian Jew, and Abi Tebal (Abitbol), a Moroccan Jew from Gibraltar, who served Napoleon Bonaparte on the Egyptian campaign of 1798–1801, appeared again.[53] The French introduced a change: these Jewish men became soldiers of the French army to fight against Muslims. A Jewish observer in 1865 noted that 'almost all the expeditionary forces had Jews as interpreters, sometimes children aged 12 to 15, who, in a short time, had learned French, and made themselves extremely useful'.[54] These men were attached to the Interpreter Corps, or the Arab Bureau. Amram Darmon, born in Oran to the well-known Darmon and Bacri families, offered his services to the French military at age eighteen, and served as an interpreter for thirty-three years. He took part in many diplomatic negotiations as well as several battles, such as against Emir Abd el-Kader in 1836 during the Tlemcen expedition.[55] Having also served at the taking of Laghouat in 1852, he was the first Jewish interpreter to receive the Legion of Honour.[56]

French and Muslims opposed these Jewish interpreters being honoured. Muslims did not accept receiving orders from Jews. In 1832, a defeated shaykh, Ali ben Baza, declared, 'We are offended by the power that you grant to a few Jews in your government, because if we consent to be governed by you, we do not want the Jews to serve as intermediaries for us in any circumstances.'[57] A small number of these interpreters became French citizens. In becoming military interpreters, these Algerian Jews chose their camp: France. They wanted to integrate into the colonial society that was being established, and citizenship was the symbol of this.[58] From the 1840s French, French Jewish, and Algerian Jewish voices called for citizenship to be granted to Algerian Jews.[59]

In 1832, the French delegation to Morocco needed a spokesperson, as Sultan Abd al-Rahman (r. 1822–59) could not be addressed directly by a foreigner. He appointed the Jew Abraham Benchimol of Tangier to fill that role, the subject of a painting by Delacroix now in the Museum of Fine Arts, Dijon. The sketches made prior to the painting placed Benchimol at the centre of the scene, in front of the sultan, but he disappeared from the final 1876 version of the painting, although his role was indispensable.[60]

That some Jews rallied to the French led to violent retaliation against Jews in the interior, who fled that region for the coastal cities which housed French garrisons. French colonisation fractured intercommunity relations.[61]

Jews in France recognised that their social rise followed their political and legal liberation in the French Revolution. The French occupation of Algeria gave them an opportunity to serve as intermediaries between France and Algerian Jews.[62] Motivated by fraternity with the Jews and French patriotism, they aimed to relieve their co-religionists of their poverty and ignorance as they had been by subscribing to the values of the French Revolution. They aimed to moralise, regenerate, Frenchify, and assimilate what they saw as their unfortunate co-religionists through their own Jewish colonialism, a civilising mission of their own, tied up within the French civilising mission. According to the Algerian rabbi Itzhak Zerbib, chief rabbi of Constantine in 1959, who migrated to Israel in 1962, where he became chief Sephardic rabbi in 1986, the French ameliorated the condition of Algerian Jewry, but denied its religiosity by secularising it according to the French model, replacing Jewish law regarding private matters such as marriage with French civil law.[63] After 1845 the French Jewish press and metropolitan rabbis began to report on Algerian Jewry. While accentuating their attachment to France, they attacked Algerian Jews' apparent preference for studying Judaism rather than French, not letting girls and women become French, their superstition, and their alleged backwardness that made them fanatical and fundamentally different to Europeans.[64] French Jews aimed to liberate Algerian Jews from the control of their rabbis, whom they judged fanatical, and illiterate because they wrote in Arabic and Hebrew. The Central Consistory of the Jews of France, the representative body of French Jews established by Napoleon I in 1808, asked the government to allow it to organise Algerian Judaism. It succeeded: 'France colonised Algeria, French Judaism "colonised" Algerian Judaism.'[65]

The French statesman who led the effort was Adolphe Crémieux, born Isaac Moïse Crémieux. He was a lawyer, politician, longtime president of the Central Consistory (from 1843), and a Mason who rose to be president of the Supreme Masonic Council of France.[66] French, Jewish, and Mason, he was a universalist and anti-communitarian, a rationalist and a fervent supporter of the Republic. Crémieux fought his entire life for the oppressed: he defended Jews accused of ritual murder at Damascus in 1840, engaged in the battle for the abolition of slavery, signed the decree of abolition in 1848, mobilised against forced Jewish conversion in Italy in 1858, and created the Alliance Israélite Universelle in 1860 and became its president in

1864, with the objective of diffusing French republican culture and values among those he saw as the most miserable Jews in the world.[67] He was appointed minister of justice during the Revolution of 1848 in the provisional government which declared the Second Republic.[68] That year witnessed the abolition of the last discriminatory laws against Jews in France. In 1870 Crémieux again became minister of justice.

On 24 October 1870, Crémieux submitted decrees, which the government ratified, the most important naturalising all Algerian Jews in the northern departments of Algeria, but not those in the Mzab oases, the military-ruled southern territories, whose Jews were classified as indigenous and treated like Muslims. Those in areas annexed by France after 1870 were also not included.[69] The naturalisation of the Jews of Algeria is remembered as the Crémieux Decree: 'The indigenous Jews of the Departments of Algeria are declared French citizens; consequently, their real status and their personal status are from the promulgation of this decree governed by French law, all rights acquired to date remaining inviolable. Any legislative provision, any *senatus-consulte*, decree, regulation or order to the contrary are abolished.' It went into effect in 1871. Crémieux served as deputy of Algeria from 1872 to 1875, then as a senator until his death. The decree, which turned the world upside down, was criticised by the army chiefs, some Europeans, especially the settlers (the *pieds noirs*), and Muslims.

Christians, like a bad parent choosing between two siblings, supported and allied with Jews. The collective naturalisation of the Jews of Algeria ruptured the symbiosis with the Muslim population. Most Jews changed sides and showed solidarity with the invader.[70] The Jew was no longer ally of the Muslim. Registered in the civil registry, they learned to read and write in French, and abandoned traditional trades to embrace new professions. The granting of French citizenship signifies the true end of dhimmi status under which they had lived for centuries.

The religious leaders were hesitant, as they understood how with the arrival of the French in Algeria, there was such great messianic hope, which was the consequence of obtaining French nationality, that people believed that the Messiah had come.[71] But it was not the long-awaited Messiah of Judaism. It was the secular French messianic vision. It was only in the cities of the interior, such as Constantine, that they could maintain the Jewish–Muslim symbiosis. Those who still lived in contact with believing Muslims maintained their own traditions.

In 1870, 35,000 Algerian Jews became citizens, 'united in a community of destiny' with the French.[72] This put them at odds with French racists and eventually most of the Muslims of the country, subjecting them to hostility. The Jews of Algeria proclaimed their patriotism, but in the organisation of their family life, in their religious practices, in their social networks, in their daily life, they preserved traditions of the past. They engaged in selective acculturation, gradually abandoning the old Jewish neighbourhoods, traditional dress, and the Judeo-Arab language, and chose French names for children, yet they retained the old Jewish or Judeo-Arabic family names.[73]

The granting of citizenship to Jews in Algeria was opposed by the far right.[74] There were pogroms in Tlemcen and Mostaganem.[75] Twenty years after the decree was established, Algeria witnessed a wave of unprecedented anti-Semitism culminating in riots in Oran. The rioters demanded the revocation of the Crémieux Decree. In 1898, the anti-Semite Édouard Drumont was elected representative of Algiers. Max Régis, leader of the Anti-Jewish League of Algiers, was elected mayor.[76] Behind the anti-Semitism lay fear of the Arab peril. Behind it all was denunciation of the native.

In Morocco, the Spanish minister at Tangier, threatening a new military intervention, demanded the public execution of four young Jews at Safi accused of having poisoned a Spanish customs agent in July 1863.[77] Based on the torture-induced confession of a fourteen-year-old, three other Jews, two Moroccan subjects, and one Ottoman, were also arrested and caned, and confessed to murdering the Spaniard, and nearly a dozen other Jews, including two women, were also arrested and whipped. But the Muslim magistrate of Safi declared the confession obtained under duress void. Under threat, the sultan relented to the Spanish demand to immediately execute the two Moroccan Jews. A Franciscan priest offered them life in prison rather than death if they converted. The Ottoman Jew was executed in Tangier. The two Moroccan Jews were sent there as well, causing Moroccan Jews to seek foreign intervention.[78]

Moses Parienté, wealthy trader, president of the Jewish community of Tangier, and dragoman and consul general of the United States, through a compatriot at Gibraltar, Judah Serfaty, asked the directors of the Board of Deputies of British Jews to solicit the intervention of the British and French governments. The *Jewish Chronicle* (established in 1841), the voice of the Board of Deputies, denounced the Spanish.[79] Its president, Sir Moses Montefiore, journeyed to Madrid, where he gained the pardon of the two Moroccan Jews condemned in Algiers by the Spanish minister. He continued to Tangier on board a ship put at his disposal by the French government.[80] He took part in the inauguration of a new synagogue, never mind the dhimmi pact. He presented a letter from the Spanish government to the Spanish consul at Algiers, who immediately released the two men and agreed to inform the Moroccan government to release those imprisoned in Safi.[81] The minister posed as the protector of Moroccan Jews, writing a missive to this effect for publication in the *Jewish Chronicle*. The Jews detained in Safi were also freed. The Moroccan consul at Gibraltar was a Jewish convert to Islam, Said Guessous.[82]

Montefiore demanded that Sultan Sidi Mohammed (r. 1859–73) abolish the dhimma pact.[83] His wish was partially fulfilled. Jews were promised justice and an end to corporal punishment, but not granted equality, nor the ending of the jizya. The only way to escape the dhimma pact was to become a protégé of a foreign power.[84] On 5 February 1864, Sultan Sidi Mohamed declared that 'all men are, in our eyes, equal in justice', delivering the decree to the English consul. Muslims and governing officials expressed opposition to the change forbidding public caning of Jews (but not of Muslims).[85] The Montefiore visit 'was a symbolic turning point for the Jewish communities', which from then on 'sought the intervention of foreign governments in disputes with the Muslim authorities, increasing tensions between Muslims and Jews'. The dhimmi system remained intact, but Jews' status began to change, because of consular protection and European Jewish organisations' actions.[86] Jewish leaders appealed directly to foreign consular courts to ensure extraterritorial rights but could also still appeal to Muslim authorities as the sultan's protégés, depending on who they thought would rule in their interest.[87]

One of the European Jewish organisations that played an important role was created by French Jews led by Crémieux, who, in 1860, established a network of schools for boys and girls, the Alliance Israélite Universelle (AIU). The first AIU school opened in Tétouan in 1862.[88] The three-fold aim of the AIU was 'to work throughout the world for the emancipation and the moral progress of the Jews; to help effectively all those who suffer because they are Jews; and to encourage all publications designed to achieve these results'. The goal was to emancipate and promote the moral progress of local Jews, male and female, by combating their poverty, and assumed ignorance through acculturating them in French secular education. Such an education in 'equality, fraternity, and liberty', along with the AIU's diplomatic efforts to stand up for persecuted Jews by appealing to foreign governments to intervene on their behalf, changed the self-perception of these Francophone Jews.[89] The effect was as profound for boys as for girls, as the teachers combined pedagogy with promoting social change. They battled against polygamy and arranged marriage, and promoted family planning. Female AIU teachers and directors were the first Jewish professional women in the Middle East.[90]

As French education swept across the Jewish communities of the Maghreb and Middle East, it gave Jews a new mindset, not just literacy, a new language, and other skills; it connected them intellectually and politically to a reformed, modern Judaism, as well as to the idea that they could be equal citizens.

Modern education was one of the key factors driving Jew and Muslim apart from Morocco to Iran. Modern French education turned them culturally towards France. It allowed them to consider their social and legal place in their homeland and reject it, or demand improvement. The first wave of education reform came in the Maghreb in the form of the adoption of the secular French model of organisation of Jewish communities, the consistory, which already in 1845 was adopted in Algiers, Oran, and Constantine, placed under the tutelage of the Central Consistory in Paris, which aimed to make the community Francophone and reform the traditional schools.[91] Unlike Muslims, most Jews became literate and Francophone, and entered the professional class as civil servants, physicians, and lawyers. At the beginning of the twentieth century, only 9 per cent of the Algerian Jewish army recruits could not read or write, while four decades later, on the eve of the Second World War, 75 per cent of the Algerian Muslim conscripts were still illiterate.[92] The Jews of Morocco, Tunisia, and Egypt joined those of Algeria in being the most educated and Francophone communities in their homelands.[93]

The AIU 'did not only educate, it induced a new self-image and created new expectations', giving Jews a new attitude demanding equality rather than any longer accepting dhimmi status.[94] The French overturned relations by making the Jews equal to Muslims – and in Algeria, superior to Muslims rather than inferior.

In 1910, Yomtov Sémach, sent by the AIU to Yemen, claimed that Jews there 'lack self-confidence and under Arab oppression they crawl, prostrate, through the dust. They are despised and are indeed despicable.'[95] For this reason the AIU, as enunciated by the director of the school at Amara, Iraq in 1909, was on a mission to 'raise the prestige of the Jews amongst the general population and raising the Jews' human dignity in their own eyes'.[96] Those who read the reports of Europeans and European Jews about Middle Eastern Jews absorbed their view and repeated their tropes: 'All lives were fragile, but none were as precarious' as those of Jews, attacked by fanatic barbarians.[97]

AIU reports describe the extreme poverty and destitution and deplorable sanitary conditions of Middle Eastern and North African Jews, while teachers described their students as filthy and hungry. The AIU's Casablanca director in 1904 described the Jewish quarter as 'provoking disgust and deep pity', where 'families are crammed into hovels', 'at doorways, the piles of bodily waste emit asphyxiating odours' from 'latrines that are but open holes in the middle of some street, or at any possible or imaginable place; and practically no water'.[98]

The perceived misery of Eastern Jewry compelled Western Jewry to act on their behalf. They believed they could civilise the

Jews by making them French and rescue them from their abasement and humiliation. What drove the AIU was the French Revolution, which emancipated the Jews, giving them the idea to bring liberty to the world, as French Jews believed their enlightened position allowed them to act on behalf of world Jewry and to regenerate communities outside Europe while also working for the expansion of the French Empire. In 1866 the AIU's secretary general declared that 'the destiny of the [French] Jews is to open up the Orient to Western civilisation' and that the Jewish elites of the Muslim-majority region supported the endeavour, seeing themselves as the agents of Western civilisation, which was incompatible with their status.[99]

From 1862 when the first AIU school was established at Tétouan for boys, and three years later, at Tangier for girls,[100] a modern education in French gave Moroccan Jews a new mentality, new ambitions, and new behaviour.[101] The local rabbis and merchants were opposed because it threatened the traditional order and social hierarchies, not least by educating girls, who had previously not been allowed in schools and were generally illiterate. The revolutionary act of learning to read and write prepared them for professions including that of teacher.[102] Regenerating the Jews would prepare them for all the transformations wrought by European penetration in the kingdom, unlike the Muslims.

The AIU alliance with European colonisers exacerbated the split with Muslims. By teaching hygiene and literacy, French language, literature, and culture, the ideas of the Enlightenment, a Judaism shorn of superstition, Jewish history, and Hebrew, and thus eroding tradition, the AIU aimed to make modern Jewish subjects in charge of their destiny.

The educated elites called for French citizenship to be extended to Moroccan and Tunisian Jews, but their voices were not heeded. Regardless, the establishment of the French protectorate in Morocco in 1912 exacerbated the increasing division between Muslims and Jews in the country. Moroccan and Tunisian institutions such as the Moroccan sultanate remained intact, while true power rested in the hands of the French resident general. Two systems of administration now ruled over Jewish–Muslim relations, depending on whether individuals were granted French nationality or remained subjects of the Muslim ruler. Regardless, the Jewish community as a whole and especially the rabbinical courts lost much of the power they once had. While the AIU and its schools were not officially part and parcel of colonialism, the primacy given to Francophone language and values meant that Jews became allies of French colonial interests. Louis-Hubert-Gonzalve Lyautey, army general and colonial administrator, who established the French protectorate over Morocco, serving as resident general until 1925, told the AIU Marrakesh school director in 1913 that 'your interests are the same as ours'.[103] They became 'the Jews of Empire'.[104]

In the Maghreb this divide-and-rule strategy deepened societal divisions, created new hierarchies, and alienated the two communities, which had had favourable relations. The lack of a Christian minority in North Africa caused the French to turn towards the Jews for their divide-and-rule strategy, despite their widespread anti-Jewish sentiment. The French attempted to cultivate relations with Jews to create commercial connections, as they dominated lucrative trades, such as that in ostrich feathers.[105]

As Britain was the major colonial and imperial power in the Persian Gulf, the elite Jewish merchants of Baghdad and Basra connected themselves to it.[106] From the eighteenth century,

Arab Jews established themselves in India. In 1830 several dozen settled in Bombay (today Mumbai), where they constituted the core of the Baghdadi community. The most eminent family was the Sassoons, who acted like medieval traders, keeping their business records in Judeo-Arabic and relying on credit, which is based on the trust and reputation of their multireligious business partners, along with their family, which in turn relied on far-flung networks of information gathering, a world captured in the scraps that make up the Cairo geniza. What was new was how the Sassoons were a family concern that hitched its coat-tails to a global empire in a rapidly globalising economy. Their global firm rose with the British Empire's expansion in the East and its promotion of free trade by force.

The family's progenitor, Shaykh Sassoon ben Saleh Sassoon, was chief money changer of Davud Pasha, governor of Baghdad, while also serving as the *nasi*, lay leader of the Jewish community.[107] With the fall of the Baghdadi Jew Ezekiel Gabbay in 1826, when the Ottoman dynasty annihilated the elite Janissary corps and murdered their wealthy Jewish quartermasters, Shaykh Sassoon was jailed.[108] A bribe released him.[109] Sassoon and his son David fled Baghdad with their family and settled in the British port of Bombay, which King Charles II had received from the Portuguese a century and a half earlier, and which he leased to the East India Company, who made it the greatest centre of trade on the west coast of India. In 1833 the Company's last monopolies were ended, opening the way for independent merchants allied with British officials to become wealthy.[110] David Sassoon was one of them.

David became head of 'an Arab Jewish family who settled in India, traded in China and aspired to be British'.[111] He began exporting textiles to the Ottoman Empire, in the mid-1840s partnering with an Aleppine Jewish family, the Altaras, who settled in Marseille.¹¹² Father of fourteen children through two marriages, David trained his eldest sons, Abdallah and Elias, to run the family business, by sending them to work in the bazaar in Baghdad, and hiring English tutors to educate them in Bombay. He sent his younger sons to China and England, and every land in between.¹¹³ Elias ran the business in Shanghai, Abdallah (his Muslim name was Anglicised to Albert) worked in Bombay alongside their father, and the third son, David, was the first to reside in London and adopt Western dress.¹¹⁴ His younger sons displayed the Jewish–Muslim symbiosis as well as the family's global reach, for they were named Reuben, Abraham Shalom (Anglicised to Arthur), and Suleiman.¹¹⁵ As in the days of the Cairo geniza, their primary business agent in Bushehr, Iran, was a Muslim, Haj Ali Akbar.¹¹⁶ At the same time, members of the family did not work on Shabbat. All Sassoons learned how to slaughter chickens so they could eat kosher while travelling.¹¹⁷

After Suleiman's death, his wife, Farha Gabbay (Anglicised as Flora), was named a full partner and was operational head of the family's global business in Asia based in Bombay, a modern Doña Gracia Nasi (Mendes).¹¹⁸ This senõra was senior partner. Along with the textiles that were the calling card of her wealthy woman merchant predecessor, Farha's portfolio included opium, real estate, cotton and cotton mills, and import and export to Europe, the Persian Gulf, and China.¹¹⁹ Her great-grandson, Siegfried, was the famous gay, anti-war poet of the First World War, whose brother died fighting the Ottomans at Gallipoli for the British.¹²⁰

The Opium War of 1839–42 was the opportunity the Sassoons needed. China attempted to stem the flow of the dangerous narcotic into the country from British India. Britain waged war to force China to continue the lucrative trade. After being defeated, China ceded Hong Kong to Britain, and opened

Shanghai, Canton, and other cities to foreign trade, granting Britain favoured nation status, and its traders extraterritoriality. Soon after the war David sent his son Elias to register as an agent in China, and to set up branches of the family business in the treaty ports, Shanghai becoming the second hub of the family business after Bombay.[121] Following the Second Opium War in 1858 and the beginning of direct British rule of India, no restrictions remained for the expansion of the opium trade.

The celebration of the transfer of power from the East India Company to the Crown was held at David Sassoon's Bombay mansion, 'Sans Souci', whose 'tinkling fountains blended with the chatter of green parrots in the banyan trees'. Today it is the Masina Hospital, although the family coat of arms inscribed in Hebrew and Latin is still visible on the main staircase.[122] The family had close ties to the empire, offering ships for the use of the British invasion of Abyssinia in 1867, and erected a statue in Bombay to commemorate the Prince of Wales's visit a little over a decade later.[123] The Prince of Wales's first visit to a synagogue was to Abraham Shalom/Arthur's wedding in London in 1873, where Prince Albert signed the couple's *ketubah* (wedding contract) and toasted the happy couple along with Prime Minister Disraeli at the wedding reception.[124] Abdallah/Albert, made a baronet by Queen Victoria in 1890, entertained King Edward VII (r. 1901–10), with whom he had been close friends, at his mansion in Scotland.[125]

The close relationship between Albert and his brother Reuben with the king drew allegations of the Sassoons' 'judaising' of the English aristocracy.[126] Like an Andalusi courtier, Albert mediated between Britain and Iran, where the family had long traded opium and where the shah granted him membership of the Order of the Lion and the Sun.[127] The Middle Eastern nature of the family was not forgotten: the decor of

Severed Symbiosis and New Saviours

Ashley Park, the family mansion in Surrey, is described as having 'a decided dash of Oriental taste' as portraits of family members 'in their Oriental habiliments form a quaint contrast with the Renascence' character of the home.[128] Albert's son Sir Edward, president of Bevis Marks synagogue, inherited his baronetcy and served as an MP.[129] Another member of the family, Sassoon Jacob David, served as sheriff of Bombay and was knighted by the Prince of Wales (later George V), receiving a baronetcy in 1915.[130] Sassoon family wealth grew in turn; the opium trade was a mainstay in their profits from their dominance of the trade by the 1870s to the First World War.[131]

The Sassoons and other Baghdadi Jewish families in British Bombay 'grew prosperous by aligning themselves and their businesses with the British Empire and its interests'.[132] This was like the situation in French Algeria. In both British India and French North Africa, the coloniser aligned itself with Jews.

As his interests were tied to British imperialism and colonialism, in 1853 David Sassoon, referred to as a 'Jew merchant', was granted British citizenship.[133] He signed his oath of allegiance in Hebrew but continued to speak Arabic. A photograph of him shows him dressed as a Baghdadi Jewish merchant, with turban and kaftan, two decades after leaving his native land. Jews described him as they had described the Babylonian exilarch: 'The whole [Jewish] community has a single Prince' who 'is the aristocrat, the most upright among men, both wealthy and righteous' and 'generous and philanthropic', whose 'robes are long and wide, and he has a great turban on his head, exactly as he dressed in the city of Baghdad, and purity and glory hover over him'.[134]

Like his Middle Eastern and Andalusi predecessors, he endowed schools and synagogues. The 1861 sky-blue Magen David synagogue is used by Mumbai Jews today and the grounds of the red-brick Ohel David synagogue in Pune completed in 1867 contain his mausoleum.[135] A statue of an 'Oriental'-looking, robed, turbaned, bearded David Sassoon was displayed first at what is today the Victoria and Albert Museum. The flower-garlanded figure, who looks like a holy man, is now at the David Sassoon Library in Mumbai, established by Abdallah, knighted as Sir Albert, the first Jew to receive the freedom of the City of London for his public service and philanthropy, in 1870.[136]

We see a similar story in Egypt. For Goitein, who first conceptualised the Judeo-Islamic symbiosis, medieval Jews were a Mediterranean society because they were 'representative of their class in the Mediterranean world in general and its Arabic section in particular'.[137] Composed of native Jews and immigrants from the Levant, in the modern period they maintained their international connections, as well as their languages, adapting the lingua franca of the region, French, yet they never assimilated into French culture as did the Jews of Algeria. The Sephardic elements and their family business ties connected them to the port cities around the Mediterranean; they were 'resourceful; mobile; enterprising; and highly pragmatic', the Mediterranean society par excellence.[138] In the modern period, Egyptian Jews – Arab, Karaite, Sephardi, Ashkenazi – were 'overwhelmingly urban, multilingual, middle-class merchants and professionals', but the majority had no Egyptian citizenship.[139]

The period of the khedives and kings, from 1860 to 1950, was a prosperous one for Jews in Egypt.[140] It was a period of economic expansion. Jews had been moneychangers, moneylenders, pawnbrokers, traders, craftsmen, and artisans such as tailors and silk weavers.[141] Karaites continued in these fields to the mid-twentieth century. In the first phase, to 1880, moneychanging and moneylending transformed into banking and credit, in which rabbinic Jews played a major part. From the

In the seventh century, the first Believers prayed toward Jerusalem like the Jews. The Masjid al-Qiblatayn, mosque of the two directions of prayer, one facing Jerusalem and one facing Mecca, Medina, Saudi Arabia.

Twelfth or thirteenth-century Judeo-Arabic text from the geniza collection in Cairo. It is the first and second sura of the Qur'an, the Fatiha, written in Hebrew letters.

Édouard Moyse, 'École juive à Miliana, Algérie', 1861.

Théodore Chassereriau, 'Intérieur d'école arabe à Constantine', 1846.

Ninth-century Moses coin from the Turkish Jewish Khazar kingdom. Rather than declaring, 'There is no God save God and Muhammad is the Messenger of God', the coin states, 'There is no God save God and Moses is the Messenger of God'.

Statue of the greatest medieval Jewish intellectual, Musa ibn Maimun, known as Maimonides or Rambam, Córdoba, Spain.

Alhambra's fourteenth-century Palace of the Lions, Granada, Spain. The lions represent the twelve tribes of Israel and were made by a Jewish artist for the Ibn Naghrelas' Red Palace (al-Hamra') in the eleventh century, over whose ruins the Alhambra was built.

Miniature of a Jewish lady from Enderunlu Fazıl's Zenan-name (Book of Women), 1793.

'Man in Oriental Costume', Rembrandt van Rijn, 1635. The man is Samuel Pallache of Fez, a Sephardic Moroccan Jew entrusted by a Muslim Moroccan sultan to serve as mediator with Christian European powers.

Salomon Assus, 'Portrait de Salomon Zermati', 1876. Algerian Jews played an important diplomatic role as intermediaries in the first decade of French colonial rule in the nineteenth century.

Portrait of David Sassoon and sons, *c.* 1850. The Sassoons and other Baghdadi Jewish families grew prosperous aligning themselves with the British Empire.

'Adolphe Crémieux', Jean-Jules-Antoine Lecomte du Noüy, 1878. French Jewish lawyer and politician Crémieux, founder of the Alliance Israélite Universelle in 1860, as Justice Minister in 1870 granted citizenship to most Jews, but not the Muslims, of Algeria.

Mufti Al-Hajj Amin al-Husseini meeting with Adolf Hitler in 1941. The Palestinian leader Al-Husseini collaborated with the Nazis against the British and the Jewish community in the British mandate of Palestine.

Portrait of Rector of Paris Mosque Si Kaddour Benghabrit. Benghabrit is credited with saving Jewish lives during the Nazi occupation of Paris.

David Ben Gurion declaring the establishment of the State of Israel, 14 May 1948.

Tents at Pardes Hanna, an Iraqi Jewish transit camp in Israel in the 1950s.

André Azoulay paying homage to Moroccan King Hassan II.

1880s to the 1920s the sector developed, and Sephardi families in Cairo (Suarès, Cattaoui), and Alexandria (Aghion, Rolo, Mosseri, Menasce), whose members were already presidents or members of lay councils, evolved from being moneychangers and pawnbrokers to bankers and creditors, as major investors in real estate, construction, and industry, land development, and cotton and sugarcane cultivation. At the beginning of the twentieth century, they entered large enterprises such as transport, infrastructure, and the sugar industry, whereas families of immigrants entered the import–export trade, formed commercial societies, transport agencies, invested in infrastructure, and ran the most lucrative stores.

The Sephardi Menasce family of Palestine and Morocco was descended from Ya'qub Menasce, who began as a moneychanger in the Jewish quarter of Cairo and rose to be private banker of Khedive Isma'il , but later moved to Alexandria, where he built a synagogue, cemetery, school foundation, and hospital. He was 'rich, cosmopolitan, and European-educated, linked by marriage to the best Jewish families', and his heirs 'gave the Alexandria community three presidents, who together held office for thirty-four years' between the 1870s and the 1930s.[142]

The Cattaouis (Qattawi), who emphasised their close links with the Muslim elite, were also Sephardic, and may have been in Egypt since the Fatimid era. Their name may derive from the village of Qatta (present-day Zamalek). The first historical figure is Ya'qub Menasce Qattawi, who was chief moneychanger and director of the mint under Khedive Abbas I and a customs farmer. Khedive Isma'il made him head of the moneychangers and founded banking and trading firms. He served as lifelong head of the Cairo community, was one of the first to move out of the hara (Jewish quarter) to a suburb, the first Egyptian Jew to be made a bey (lord), and an Austro-Hungarian baron as well.[143] His eldest son, Aslan Bey, helped create the sugar industry together with the Suarès family. His son Moise de Cattaoui Pasha was a banker who served as president of the Cairo community for forty years, and with the Menasces, Suarèses, and Rolos, he was involved in the railways, waterworks, and Cairo's public transport. Communal leadership passed to his nephews Yousef (Joseph) Aslan de Cattaoui Pasha and then to his son René, the fifth member of the family in a row to hold that position.[144]

Capital accumulated in finance and credit, and connections to European bankers and industrialists, many of whom were also Jewish, facilitated the rise of such families in Egyptian society. Most department stores, including Cicurel, Chemla, Cohenca, Gattegno, Adès, Lévi-Benzion, Orosdi-Back, and Stein, were Jewish owned, and most stockbrokers were Jewish by the 1930s. The Jewish role in the economy 'was not only highly significant, it was also highly visible'.[145] Nevertheless, as elsewhere in North Africa and the Middle East, most Jews were impoverished. By the late 1940s, 10 per cent of Jews were well to do; 15–20 per cent were middle class; and 70–75 per cent were poor.[146]

At issue was nationality. Egyptian Jews had been Ottoman subjects until 1914, when Egypt became a British protectorate. The constitution of 1923 gave equal citizenship to all, regardless of religion.[147] At the end of the 1930s and beginning of the 1940s only 25–30 per cent of Jews were Egyptian citizens. A quarter were foreign citizens or protected persons, and 45–50 per cent were stateless.[148] As many as 70 per cent of the estimated 60,000 Jews were French- or Italian-speaking Sephardim, including the wealthiest, most powerful families, living in the new suburbs of Isma'iliya, Heliopolis, Giza, Zamalek, Abbasiya, and Garden City, and most of them were stateless or foreign citizens.[149] About 15 per cent were poor, Judeo-Arabic-speaking Arab Jews who resided in the hara, which was 'neither a ghetto nor a mellah', although it had four iron and wood gates.¹⁵⁰ Half that number were Yiddish-speaking Ashkenazim, also largely poor, who worked as cigarette rollers, artisans (tailors, shoemakers, opticians, gold- and silversmiths), clerks, or salespeople, or kept bars and brothels.¹⁵¹ The same number were Egyptian-Arabic-speaking Karaites, established in the city since the ninth century, integrated into Egyptian society, residing in their own hara, which bordered the Jewish neighbourhood. Most were poor craftsmen working with gold, silver, precious stones, and perfume, although some Karaites entered the middle class and there were several wealthy families.¹⁵²

The wealthy and community leaders promoted Egyptian patriotism and emphasised their loyalty to king and country despite their international ties and foreign citizenship. Their attempts to promote the adoption of Arabic and Egyptian citizenship by Jews were not successful.¹⁵³

An astonishing funeral took place in British Shanghai in the summer of 1931, attended by 5,000 mourners. One hundred Taoist monks and priests officiated, as Chinese orchestras performed funeral music. Three thousand mourning gifts were exchanged, and paper figures were burnt in celebration of the spirit of the deceased. Mourners kowtowed before pictures of the family of the deceased. The funeral garden was draped in white silk. At its centre was a wax effigy of the deceased, Silas Aaron Hardoon, chopsticks in hand.

Hardoon was the richest foreigner in Shanghai, with an estate estimated at $150 million. This Baghdadi Jewish man went to China by way of India in the late nineteenth century. In Calcutta he worked for the mercantile firm of David Sassoon. This resident of Shanghai, Ottoman subject, British Protected Person, and Baghdadi Jew born to a father naturalised in India lived sixty years in Shanghai, amassing a real estate empire, formed close ties with Chinese politicians, merchants, and the educational elite, served as life president of Shanghai's Beth-Aaron Synagogue, and sat on the councils of the Shanghai Municipality, French Concession, and International Settlement.[154]

Most of the Sassoon employees in the first decades were Iraqi émigrés from small communities of Baghdadis.[155] Alongside the Sassoons in India were other Baghdadi families, such as the Kedouries (whose Baghdad-born scion, Elie, was a professor at the London School of Economics and Political Science from 1953 to 1990), and others, who established important enterprises in India, China, Burma, and Singapore (the latter had been a British colony since 1824). Towards the end of the nineteenth century, members of these families began to settle in England, where they integrated into British life. Despite their diaspora, they maintained their ties to the natal land and continued to make their mark on Baghdad, especially by establishing schools, synagogues, and yeshivot, and hiring the city's educated sons, as they continued to take spouses from their mother city and to speak the Baghdadi dialect of Judeo-Arabic.[156]

The Hardoon family became rich in China thanks to British colonialism. The story of the Hardoon, Kedourie, and Sassoon families is emblematic of the radical changes that occurred in the nineteenth century across the Middle East.

While allowing for differences in regions and social class, in North Africa, modernisation and French colonialism rendered continued Jewish–Muslim intimacy a dead end. Where for a millennium Jews had been subjected to Muslim power in a binary relationship, the arrival of the French colonial empire – occupying Egypt; ruling Algeria directly and Morocco and Tunisia indirectly – meant Muslims lost political control. Jews and Muslims were henceforth entangled in a triangular relationship with France where the French held power, and the will to share it with Jews or Muslims.[157] They were 'together, but different' in colonial society. And as in earlier historical eras, such as in Al-Andalus, when Christians formed the third point of the triangle, relations between the other two points, Jews and Muslims, worsened.

With the rise of Western European colonialism and empire in the eighteenth and nineteenth centuries, and the concomitant invention of race, modern science, and nationalism, we witness the birth of anti-Semitism. Anti-Semitism has been seen as 'an exclusively Christian phenomenon'. According to some commentators, the history and culture of Muslims offers nothing 'even remotely approaching the anti-Jewish venom or actions' of the Christian West.[158] 'Arab anti-Semitism' is considered an impossibility, a projection of Jews of their own history in Christian lands.[159]

If one is to argue that anti-Semitism is not found among Muslims, one cannot make the claim that there was no anti-Jewish sentiment in Muslim-majority lands, as Ottoman Muslim views of Jews demonstrate. The anti-Judaism of Christians in the Ottoman Empire is well documented.

The turning point in modern Ottoman Muslim accounts of Jews occurred in 1888 when the political journalist Ebüzziya Tevfik published the first Turkish-language history of the Jews, *Millet-i Isra'iliye* (*The Jewish Nation*). Its author retained neither the prototypes nor the stock characters from the past 400 years of Muslim cautionary tales about Jews.[160] He introduced new concepts and terminology derived from French anti-Semites. Like other Ottoman Muslim and Jewish intellectuals, Tevfik was immersed in European, especially French, language and literature, which included the anti-Semitic promotion of the idea of inferior Semitic and superior Aryan (Indo-European) races.[161] Unlike any other Ottomans, Tevfik's study was 'coloured by anti-Semitism'.[162] He is labelled 'the earliest anti-Semitic writer in Turkey'.[163]

What distinguishes modern anti-Semitism from older forms of religious-based anti-Judaism is its insistence on allegedly biological Jewish character traits. Anti-Semitism is an ideology that came into being in the nineteenth century. It is not pre-modern anti-Judaism in Christian-ruled lands, which was based on theology – the idea that Jews, if they convert to Christianity, can rid themselves of all the negative aspects of Judaism and Jewishness that Christians disdain. Modern anti-Semitism is based instead on the idea that Jews are a racial group, and a Jew cannot escape his or her origins, can never leave Jewish characteristics behind, even if they convert to Christianity.[164] Tevfik argued that 'conversion may gild one's morals, but it does not change one's nationality', inasmuch as 'religion and nation are one'.[165] To him, Jews were a separate, rootless people, with an unchanging nature marked by obstinacy, conceit, and the drive to earn money.[166]

The term anti-Semitism is based on the false idea that there is a Semitic race. Race is a modern concept developed in the eighteenth century. The claim of the existence of Aryan and Semitic races first derived from Orientalist philologists who divided languages into these categories. Linguists imbued with the concept of race sorted languages into the Aryan and Semitic categories: Sanskrit, Latin, Old Slavic, and Gothic in the former group, and Hebrew, Aramaic, and Arabic in the latter category. Once they divided languages, they divided people. The European Christian scholars distinguishing the peoples of the world in this fashion placed themselves in the Aryan category and Jews and Arabs (Muslims) as Semitic. The leading French Orientalist

Severed Symbiosis and New Saviours

Ernst Renan attacked Muslims and Jews. Renan claimed that 'Semitic' Oriental minds were inferior to Indo-European 'Aryan' ones, as they lacked creativity and were dogmatic, closed to knowledge and reason, and uninterested in philosophy and science. The Hungarian Jewish scholar Ignaz Goldziher, who taught at Al-Azhar university in Cairo and felt comfortable praying to the one God in a mosque in Damascus, promoted the Jewish–Muslim symbiosis, defending Jews and Muslims together in response.[167] Despite such efforts, linguistic divisions were converted into alleged racial differences between peoples. Empires and nation states used these ideas to justify colonialism and genocide.

Only Jews were politically targeted in Europe when anti-Semitic political parties emerged. Across Europe, in France, Austria-Hungary, and Germany, political organisations were founded in the 1880s which called themselves anti-Semitic. This includes Édouard Drumont's Anti-Semitic League of France. Anti-Semites were Jew-haters. Although the term is based on pseudo-science, the phenomenon is real. As nationalism emerged, anti-Semitism arose: the belief that Jews are inferior to the majority and cannot belong to the national culture. The aim was to exclude Jews from politics and culture, to protect the imagined purity of the ethno-national nation state. For despite being inferior, and a numerical minority, Jews, according to the conspiracy theory of anti-Semites, supposedly wield secret power to control the world.

The anti-Semitic idea that there is an eternal Jewish type, as expressed by Tevfik in Ottoman, and communicated in their own language by Christian and Muslim Arabs, became a prevailing trope in the twentieth century, as did applying the Jewish or crypto-Jewish label to one's enemies. These anti-Semitic beliefs played a role in the rupture in Jewish–Muslim relations. Those relations were put to the test in the maelstrom of the First and Second World Wars, the expanded European colonisation of Muslim-majority lands, and the rise of nationalism.

6

ENEMIES AND ALLIES, PERSECUTORS AND PROTECTORS: JEWS, MUSLIMS, AND NAZISM IN EUROPE AND THE MIDDLE EAST, 1933–45

How did individual Muslims, or groups of Muslims, and Muslim-majority nation states respond to fascism, Nazism, and the persecution of Jews from 1933 to 1939, and the Holocaust during the Second World War? Despite the variety of responses to the horrors of that era, commentators do not shy away from making generalisations about Muslims, Arabs, and Palestinians to support myth and counter-myth about Jewish–Muslim relations. Israeli Prime Minister Benjamin Netanyahu claimed falsely that the grand mufti of Jerusalem, Al-Hajj Amin al-Husseini, gave Hitler the idea to annihilate the Jews rather than allow them to emigrate to Palestine.[1] What is the true story?

Largely because of the partisan politics of history and memory produced by the Israeli–Palestinian conflict, we do not yet have an answer to the question of how Muslims responded to the Nazis and the Holocaust.[2] The story told about Muslims in Nazi Germany is focused on Arabs, and for that matter on a single Palestinian, Al-Husseini, who was the guest of Hitler in Berlin and whose notoriety for working closely with the Nazi regime overshadows the activities of all other Muslims in

Germany, and indeed elsewhere as well.³ The British appointed this former Jerusalem AIU student who fought as an officer in the Ottoman army in the First World War as Palestinian mufti in 1921.⁴ He was the leader of the Palestinian national movement in the 1920s and 1930s, and fled to Iraq in 1939, taking part in the 1941 anti-British uprising.

An anti-Zionist nationalist, from at least as early as 1941 when he took refuge in Berlin and met with Hitler, Al-Husseini sided with the Nazis against the British and the Jewish community (Yishuv) in the British Mandate of Palestine. He became a notorious anti-Semite and collaborator with the Nazis who broadcast pro-Nazi propaganda from Berlin warning about an alleged Judeo-Bolshevik and Judeo-British conspiracy to the Arabic-speaking world. He was on close terms with Nazi leaders, including Heinrich Himmler, from whom he learned of the Holocaust as it unfolded. Despite his knowledge, vowing to hinder the creation of a Jewish state, he opposed the emigration of European Jews to Palestine knowing full well what would happen to those who could not escape. At the end of 1942 the Nazis planned to allow the Red Cross to transfer 4,000 Jewish children from Slovakia, Poland, and Hungary to Palestine in exchange for the release of interned German civilians, but the mufti protested in person to Himmler and the idea was dropped.⁵ In 1943 he helped establish a Bosnian Muslim SS division, which also included Catholic Croatians, training the field imams, and was sent on a propaganda tour of the Nazi-occupied Balkans. For his efforts he received an 'Aryanised' villa, offices, including a former Jewish Institute, a salary, staff, and a fleet of cars at his disposal in Berlin.⁶

In his memoirs, Al-Husseini discusses his efforts to hinder the Nazis allowing Jews to emigrate from Europe to Palestine in 1943 and 1944:

Enemies and Allies, Persecutors and Protectors

> We combated this enterprise by writing to Ribbentrop, Himmler, and Hitler, and, thereafter, the governments of Italy, Hungary, Rumania, Bulgaria, Turkey, and other countries. We succeeded in foiling this initiative, a circumstance that led the Jews to make terrible accusations against me, in which they held me accountable for the liquidation of four hundred thousand Jews who were unable to emigrate to Palestine in this period. They added that I should be tried as a war criminal in Nuremberg.[7]

Statements like this, from someone who knew what the Nazis were doing, constitute a powerful argument against Holocaust deniers. Al-Husseini reported that Reichsführer-SS Heinrich Himmler, for whom he felt admiration and affection, told him in summer 1943 that the Germans had 'already exterminated more than three million' Jews. Himmler 'asked me on this occasion, "How do you plan to resolve the Jewish question in your country?" I answered: "All we want is to see them go back to the countries they came from." He responded: "We will never let them return to Germany."'[8] Moving in the highest circles of the Third Reich, Al-Husseini knew about the genocide.[9] Rather than allow the Nazis to send the Jews to Palestine, he suggested they go to Poland instead, where he knew they would be gassed.[10]

After the Second World War, as Al-Husseini claimed leadership of the Palestinian movement, supporters of the establishment of a Jewish state presented him as their arch-enemy. They began campaigning to delegitimise the competing Palestinian national movement by claiming that Al-Husseini's anti-Semitic views and collaboration with the Nazis represented the view of all Palestinians, and of all Arabs.[11] The entry for the mufti in the *Encyclopaedia of the Holocaust* published by Yad Vashem, the Israeli Holocaust Memorial and Museum in

Jerusalem, is more than twice as long as those for Joseph Goebbels and Hermann Goering, longer than the entries for Heinrich Himmler and Reinhard Heydrich combined, and longer than the one for Adolf Eichmann. It is exceeded in length, slightly, by the entry for Adolf Hitler.[12]

Such preconceptions about Arabs and Muslims prevail even today. Others reject such a one-sided depiction, finding that Arab intellectual elites – Christian, Jewish, and Muslim – overwhelmingly rejected fascism and Nazism as ideology and practice and condemned the persecution of European Jewry, and that Al-Husseini's views were peripheral in Palestine, Syria, the Maghreb, and Egypt.[13] The Egyptian nationalist and intellectual Taha Hussein wrote in 1940 how he opposed Nazi barbarism and hated Hitler, and declared, 'It is therefore a duty more than a right for anyone who believes in spiritual, moral, and religious values, and in liberty, to stand up as the adversary of that man and that regime.'[14] The liberal press including *Al-Ahram* (*The Pyramids*) in Cairo denounced Nazism for being imperialistic, totalitarian, and racist.[15]

Fascist Arab movements that boasted paramilitaries, such as Young Egypt, Al-Futuwwa in Iraq, and the Lebanese Kataeb (Phalange), the latter made up of Christians, were marginal in the Arabic-speaking world. Where Arab Muslims wished for the victory of the Nazis, it was most often not out of ideological conviction, but out of a hope that a German victory would end British or French colonial rule.[16] That is what the Nazis promised them, despite Hitler referring to Arabs as racially inferior in *Mein Kampf*.[17] Because the category 'Semite' includes Arabs as well as Jews, the Nazis ceased using it, referring to their policies as anti-Judaism or anti-Jewish instead of anti-Semitic.[18] The Nazi regime promoted itself as friend of Muslims and defender of Islam, propping up Islamic institutions and religious authorities in offering alliances with Muslims against their alleged common enemies, the colonial British, the atheist Soviets, and the Jews. The Nazis aimed to politicise Islam for their side and to gain Muslim support.[19] They promoted their propaganda on radio, and in pamphlets such as *Islam and Judaism*, distributed by the tens of thousands in the Balkans in 1943, which proclaims that since the time of the Prophet, Jews and Muslims have been enemies.[20] Some Muslims joined. The First Eastern Muslim SS Regiment (made up of Soviet Muslims) was sent to Poland to suppress the Warsaw Uprising in the summer of 1944 along with a regiment of the Azerbaijani Legion of the Wehrmacht. There was also an Eastern Turkic SS Corps headed by a German convert to Islam.[21]

Most Muslims did not take the bait. In most cases, 'fascination with fascist ideas' and politics 'did not stretch to include racism and anti-Semitism'.[22] Arabs – especially Jewish Arabs – were also victims of the Nazis.[23] Enough ink has been spilled about Al-Husseini. Instead of the mufti, it is time we consider the Ahmadiyya mosque community of Berlin, and Dr Mohammed Helmy, and the Jews they saved, Hugo Marcus and Anna Boros.

Berlin's first and only mosque established by Muslims was built and, from 1923 to 1939, controlled by the South Asian Ahmadiyya, and German converts. From its establishment, the Ahmadiyya mission in Berlin attracted German avant-garde intellectuals, preaching interreligious tolerance, practising inclusion of gays, and speaking out against racism, nationalism, and war. When German society was Nazified, the Ahmadiyya, like the other Muslims in Berlin, found themselves needing to make accommodationist overtures to the regime. Yet in helping the gay Jewish convert to Islam and community leader Hugo Marcus to escape from Germany, they managed to thwart this instance of the Nazi reign of violence. Their actions in saving the life of their formerly Jewish co-religionist call into question the claim that contemporary Muslims shared the Nazis' deep-rooted anti-Semitism.

From 1923 to 1935, Hugo Marcus was among the leading German Muslims in Berlin. The gay son of a Jewish industrialist, he studied at the Friedrich Wilhelm University in Berlin in the first decade of the twentieth century. To support his family after financial reverses caused by the First World War, he tutored foreign Muslim doctoral students in German. This led to his conversion to Islam, and for a dozen years, under the adopted name Hamid, he was the most important German in Berlin's mosque community. Nevertheless, he did not terminate his membership in the Jewish community, nor his ties to friends in the world's leading gay rights movement. One of Marcus's brothers, harassed by Nazis, committed suicide, and the other died at the Theresienstadt concentration camp. The Nazis incarcerated Marcus in the Sachsenhausen concentration camp as a Jew in 1938, and he claimed to have remained there until a delegation led by his imam, Dr Shaykh Muhammad Abdullah, gained his release. Abdullah obtained a visa for Marcus to travel to British India, where a sinecure at a Muslim organisation awaited him. Just before the outbreak of the Second World War, using travel documents secured by the imam, Marcus escaped to Switzerland instead, where he intended to establish an Islamic cultural centre. However, after using his gay and Muslim ties to spirit his elderly mother out of Berlin and to safety in Zurich, he devoted the rest of his life to publishing fiction and non-fiction in the world's leading gay magazine, *Der Kreis* (*The Circle*). He lived to the age of eighty-six, financially supported by the Ahmadiyya into the mid-1950s, and succeeded in getting reparations from Germany for having been persecuted as a Jew.[24]

Enemies and Allies, Persecutors and Protectors

Anna Boros, a Hungarian Jewish teenager in Nazi Berlin, also survived the Holocaust thanks to Muslims. In her case it was the Egyptian Muslim Mohammed Helmy. Helmy came to Berlin from Egypt to study medicine in 1922. In 1933 he was promoted to senior doctor at the Robert Koch Hospital in the Moabit neighbourhood in the place of a Jewish man who was forced out after being made by Nazis to crawl on all fours, bark like a dog, and shout 'Heil Hitler', then put against a wall as they fired a pistol around his silhouette like a knife thrower at a fair.[25] Nazi racial laws only targeted Jews, not Muslims.[26] Yet in 1937 the Nazis expelled Dr Helmy from his post. He set up a private practice in his home in Moabit, where he lived in an apartment building surrounded by Jewish-owned businesses and neighbours.[27]

In autumn 1943 when the Gestapo raided the practice, which had moved to Charlottenburg, they found a pretty young Muslim woman with dimples wearing a headscarf sitting at the reception desk, sorting blood and urine samples.[28] The Gestapo men commented that she 'radiated energy and good health'. Helmy introduced his assistant as Nadja, his Egyptian niece.[29] It was Anna, a Jewish teenager. The disguise worked. The Nazis had been deporting Berlin Jews to their deaths for two years by this point and had recently come after Anna. But this Jewish woman survived the war thanks to Dr Helmy hiding her in plain sight at a time when transports of Berlin Jews were sent from Moabit's train station to Riga, where they were shot, and later to Auschwitz, where they were gassed.[30]

It was a precarious existence for Anna, as she could be recognised on the street by other Jews. Her disguise was bold, but foolish; she spoke no Arabic. They explained that she had grown up in Dresden and not learned Arabic.[31] There was a close call in 1943. Dr Helmy was called to the former Prinz-Albrecht-Palais on Wilhelmstrasse, converted into the headquarters of the

Gestapo and SS, from which the SS chief Heinrich Himmler planned the annihilation of Europe's Jews. He was asked to bring his assistant, 'Nadja', to SS Headquarters in Berlin.[32] Worse, they were to treat an honoured Arab guest of the SS for the past two years, Mufti Al-Hajj Amin al-Husseini.

Anna survived the war and migrated to the United States. Dr Helmy married his German fiancée, returned to his medical practice, and spent the rest of his life in Berlin. Anna's daughter Carla later gave the journalist Ronen Steinke a letter to deliver to Dr Helmy's relatives in Cairo, stating, 'I just want you to know that there is a family on the other side of the world that has gratitude and love for Dr Helmy. We continue to marvel at his actions, and we hope his heroism will inspire others.'[33]

From 1963 to 2024 Yad Vashem recognised nearly 30,000 people who risked their lives to save Jews during the Nazi period. Among them are dozens of Muslims, almost all of whom are from Albania, and one from Turkey. In 2013 Dr Helmy became the only Arab recognised as a 'Righteous Among the Nations'.[34] At first, Dr Helmy's relatives refused to accept an honour given by the Jewish state of Israel.[35] Finally, in 2017, Dr Nasser Kotby, a great-nephew of Dr Helmy, accepted the recognition on his behalf.[36] He spoke of how all Egyptians should be proud of the medieval Jewish scholar Maimonides, who wrote in Arabic, after whom a synagogue in Cairo is named, and whom Kotby called by his Arabic name, Ibn Maimun. Kotby mentioned that one of Dr Helmy's cousins married a Jewish woman in Cairo, and spoke nostalgically about how 'Jews were almost always persecuted in Europe. In the Middle East, under a Muslim majority, they lived in peace.'[37]

Following France's fall to Nazi Germany in 1940, as Germany occupied northern France and Paris, the Vichy regime was established as a Nazi ally in southern France and the French North African colonies. Vichy abrogated the Crémieux Decree granting French citizenship to Algerian Jews and implemented anti-Jewish laws in the colony in 1940.[38] It incarcerated thousands in labour and concentration camps. Tunisian Jews were subject to racist laws from 1940 to 1943, and Germany occupied the country for six months in 1942 and 1943. Local Jews were barred from school and work. Five thousand Tunisian Jews were deported by the Germans to a labour camp in the desert, where some were shot on the spot, while others died in camps in Europe.[39] Despite these policies, Tunisian leaders hindered Muslims from being provoked into launching pogroms against Jews, and individuals such as the wealthy landowner and government minister Khaled Abdelwahab, although not recognised as a Righteous Among the Nations by Yad Vashem, was commended for acting admirably towards the two dozen Jews of the Boukris and Ouzzan families who sought his help.[40] Prime Minister Mohammed Chenik sheltered Jews, or publicly supported them.[41] The local Tunisian rulers during the Vichy period, Ahmed Pasha Bey and his successor, Moncef Bey, who took power in June 1942, are remembered as being sympathetic to their Jewish subjects, their dhimmi. Infuriating Vichy, Moncef Bey awarded twenty Tunisian Jews the highest Tunisian state honour.[42]

The loss of legal status and persecution during the Second World War caused Algerian Jews to question being French. Vichy anti-Semitism was traumatic, because it made Jews realise that they had been deceived. The Republic did not treat them as equals: it was not their saviour, but their oppressor. Expelled from French schools, they were traumatised to imagine their figurative return to being dhimmi, not citizens or protected persons.[43] They were astonished that they could be denied after displaying their patriotism, as during the First World War, around 14,000 Algerian Jews (20 per cent of a population of 70,000) were mobilised to fight for France along with 173,000 Muslims (32.5 per cent of a population of around 563,800) and close to 92,000 French and naturalised French (12.5 per cent of the 752,000 Europeans in Algeria). Of the 12,000 Algerian French citizens (Christians or Jews) who died during the war, 1,700 were Jews (14 per cent).[44]

Vichy opened dozens of camps to house 150,000 Spanish Republicans, members of the International Brigades, opponents of the Vichy regime, communists, labour unionists, and Jews; the latter comprised 10 per cent of the camp population.[45] The 'completely pointless tasks they were assigned most often consisted of chores intended to occupy, test, humiliate, destroy their self-esteem, push the internees to revolt the better to break them'. The cruel and sadistic guards imposed on them difficult exercises, and chose, 'in the event of incapacity or refusal to obey, to apply graduated sanctions, brutality, abuse, cruel punishments: exhausting chores, deprivation of water, food, solitary confinement with dry bread and salt water, caning, beatings ... The height of refinement was the "tomb", a hole dug by the inmate who was condemned to spend 2, 4, or 8 days there, in the sun, sometimes without eating.'[46] In such poor conditions they succumbed to epidemics such as typhoid, dysentery, and malaria. As inmates were considered subhuman by their guards, wounds were not attended to, and they rarely had access to doctors or medicine.[47]

The Anglo-American troop landing on the coast between Casablanca and Algiers on 8 November 1942 upset Nazi plans for mass deportations. At Algiers young resistance fighters organised as commandos facilitated the Allied occupation, and two-thirds of the organisers and dozens of the fighters were

Jews.[48] But only on 1 September 1943 was the Crémieux Decree reinstated. Most prisoners were released from the camps, but not the Jews. The first Jewish prisoners were released in January 1944. It was not until the end of the war in May 1945 that all camps were liberated and all measures against Jews rescinded.[49]

In France, Algerian Jews were victims of the Holocaust. On the eve of the Second World War, there were 10,000 Jews in Marseille out of a population of 1.5 million.[50] A quarter of these Jews were born in Algeria.[51] Before the Nazi occupation in November 1942, Marseille had an equal number of Jews, and Muslims.[52] During the round-up in the centre of Marseille from 22 to 29 January 1943, of the 1,642 people sent to the camp of Compiègne, there were at least 782 Jews; 254 of them were French Jews born in North Africa, of whom 225 were born in Algeria.[53] They were deported on 23 and 25 March to Sobibor, where only five of 1,000 people of all nationalities survived.

As Jews fought for their lives during the Nazi occupation of France, some Arabic-speaking Jews passed themselves off as Muslims, others were saved by Muslims, such as the rector of the Paris Mosque, Si Kaddour Benghabrit, and yet others were turned over to the Gestapo by them. Some Muslims joined the Resistance, saving Jews, and many more battled to liberate France at the end of the war, sometimes alongside Jews.[54]

The Grand Mosque of Paris, with its prayer room modelled on a mosque in Fez and minaret inspired by one in Tunisia, was inaugurated by France in 1926 in part to honour the Muslims who fought for the Republic during the First World War, and includes gardens, a tearoom, restaurant, shops, and a hammam. In the mosque today, colonial France is never far away. There are memorial bilingual marble plaques in French and Arabic devoted to the Muslim Algerian, Moroccan, Tunisian, and other African soldiers who gave their lives for France in the First and

Second World Wars. In the historical exhibition on display at the mosque, we learn that 500,000 African soldiers, a majority of them Muslim, served France; and that in 1914, 172,000 Algerians, 80,000 Tunisians, and more than 40,000 Moroccans were sent to the front. Of the 300,000 Muslims who fought for France, 100,000 died, including 70,000 at Verdun.

On the other hand, Algerian Jews who served in the military displayed their patriotism as French citizens. Moroccan and Tunisian Jews volunteered, hoping to be granted French citizenship. Nearly 40,000 French and North African Jews fought for France.[55] Jews were present in almost all the North African Muslim units; more than 10 per cent of Jewish soldiers in Algeria served in the same units as Muslims, while a far higher percentage of Muslims served in regiments that had Jews.[56] The war service of North African Jews accelerated their integration into France, thanks to their level of education and mastery of French, which was far greater than that of Muslims. The mobilisation of Jews 'validated their adherence to France' whilst for Muslims, conscription 'reinforced the stigma of subjection and exploitation by leading to progressive radicalisation in emerging nationalisms'.[57]

Jews and Muslims were far from equal, even within the same unit. Because of their mastery of French and Arabic, and the fact they were considered loyal, Algerian Jews made up a large contingent of the military interpreters in Muslim-majority units.[58] Many Jewish medics serving in the same regiments received honours for aiding their Muslim comrades under enemy fire.[59] French generals, awarding Jews medals for bravery, praised their patriotism and acts of self-sacrifice, and told Muslim soldiers to be brave like the Jews and imitate them.

A gate of the Paris Mosque is named for Si Kaddour Benghabrit. It stands between the memorials to the deceased Muslim soldiers. Benghabrit of Tlemcen, Algeria, was appointed by the French government as the first rector of the Muslim Institute of the Grand Mosque of Paris. The panel devoted to him in the mosque mentions that he was interpreter for the French legation to Tangier and worked closely with colonial officials. There are many photos on display of him with Marshal Lyautey, resident general of the Moroccan Protectorate, and the laying of the first stone of the mosque in Paris in 1922. The panel mentions that Benghabrit was named the mosque's first head in 1926, then skips to his death almost thirty years later. No mention is made of the claims that he had good relations with Jews before the war and saved Jews during the Nazi occupation of Paris. He made the mosque into a space for Jewish–Muslim dialogue between the wars, even commemorating Maimonides in 1935 with a speech celebrating the 'golden age' of Jewish–Muslim symbiosis.[60] Benghabrit is credited with sheltering Jews in the mosque during the war, issuing false papers disguising their Jewish identity, and arranging for their passage to a safe country. He is depicted as a hero in films and children's books.[61]

Michel Tardieu relates how his Moroccan Jewish mother Oro Boganim of Essaouira was saved by Benghabrit: 'My mother told me on several occasions that Si Kaddour Benghabrit visited her at the Franco-Muslim hospital in Bobigny where she worked as a nurse [because she spoke Arabic], and told her: "The Germans are looking at the files of the hospital staff, they will realise that you are Jewish. Run away now!"' She fled to unoccupied southern France and then to Casablanca, where Michel was born in 1944. In Morocco, Benghabrit introduced Boganim to the royal family and its entourage, whom she served as nurse, including the sultan (later King Mohammed V), who bestowed upon her the title of Knight of the Order of Ouissam Alaouite, the Moroccan equivalent of the Legion of Honour.[62] An archival document written by the Vichy administration to the director of the Franco-Muslim hospital on 21 July 1941 bears witness to the fact that in June 1941 Si Kaddour Benghabrit requested that she be allowed to return to her job, but the administration explained that because she was Jewish, it could not comply with his request due to Vichy laws. He likely prepared false certificates for her so that she could return to work.[63]

Benghabrit was only human. He was no angel. One word, or a signature from him, would have saved a woman who, like numerous others, would be saved if someone could attest they did not have Jewish ancestors. On 17 June 1944, Benghabrit was asked whether Germaine Roland née Marzouk of Tunisia was of Jewish or Muslim origin. She claimed that her grandparents were not Jewish but Muslim, and that her father was Muslim.[64] By 12 July it was determined she was of Jewish origin.[65] She was interned at Drancy on 5 August 1944 and subsequently murdered. Benghabrit had confirmed that she was Jewish.[66]

According to a former rector of the mosque, Dalil Boubakeur, it was probably the imam Mohammed Benzouaou who gave false papers to people to attest they were Muslim, not Benghabrit.[67] Albert Assouline narrates how 'the first imam Si Mohamed Benzouaou took considerable risks to camouflage Jews by providing them with certificates attesting that they were Muslims'. But he also relates other stories, which are not true, such as that the mosque sheltered a young girl by the name of Simone Jacob.[68] She is known today as Simone Veil – French politician, women's rights activist, and a former president of the European Parliament. However, according to her, it was a beautiful legend, but it was not true. She had never set foot in the mosque.[69]

The fact that Jewish North Africans and Muslim North Africans are so similar allowed some Jews to pass as Muslims and saved their lives during the war. Their closeness exposed the absurdity of Vichy and Nazi racial policies. Maghrebi Jews and Muslims were nearly indistinguishable because of their shared religious and secular Judeo-Muslim culture. False Nazi race science could not tell them apart.[70]

What mattered was the view of Benghabrit. He and other Muslims in the mosque were repeatedly called upon by Mohammed el-Maadi, who during the war worked for the General Commission on Jewish Questions, to determine whether a person was Jewish or Muslim. Benghabrit's identification of Algerians living in the Marais in Paris and other North Africans as Jews according to their surname in 1943 and 1944 was a death sentence for them and made his legacy more ambiguous than is usually remembered.[71] In Paris immediately after the war, he gave an iftar feast in honour of a guest who, like him, was appointed to his post by colonial authorities. That man was the mufti Al-Husseini.[72]

In 1930 Algerian Jews commemorated the centenary of the French conquest, offering a vision of their history as a model of emancipation, progress, and patriotism, a story of ever-advancing civilisation and attachment to France.[73] The future French chief rabbi Zadoc Kahn called the occasion 'the anniversary of our deliverance, the anniversary of our social emancipation, it is our Exodus from Egypt, it is our modern Passover!'[74]

However, the municipal campaign in Constantine in summer 1934 displayed the anti-Semitism of political life. The Europeans discouraged Jews from voting, and desired to take the mayoralty and to banish Jews from office. On Friday, 3 August, a Jewish soldier in the French army, named Elie Khalifa, exchanged insults with several Muslim men at the mosque next to his home, leading to Muslim and Jewish crowds fighting in the streets with guns, clubs, stones, bricks and knives.⁷⁵ On 5 August, Jews shot three Muslims, including a twelve-year-old boy, and Muslims attacked, looted and set fire to Jewish homes and businesses. They slit the throat, shot, or fractured the skull of twenty-five Jews, including a three-year-old girl.⁷⁶ The historian Benjamin Stora's mother Marthe was an eyewitness: 'They slit their throats. They broke the windows. It was awful. I was fourteen, I was there. I have photos of the destroyed stores ... They killed a lot of Jews that day.'⁷⁷ The police and military did not intervene.

It was not ancient Muslim anti-Jewish antagonism that caused the murderous riots in Constantine, but French anti-Semitism set within the context of the battle between fascism and communism in Europe and North Africa. The agitators were directed by the MP and mayor, Émile Morinaud, who despite being anti-Semitic relied on Jewish voters, who formed a quarter of the electorate, although only 12 per cent of the population, as Muslims, who formed half of the population, were denied citizenship.⁷⁸ But as anti-Semitism rose in the 1930s, Morinaud found the Jewish voting bloc and municipal councillors less useful. The murders during the riots appear to have been premeditated and organised by a Muslim soldier, who served in the same French army unit as Elie Khalifa, whose actions had triggered the violence, named Mohammed el-Maadi. El-Maadi had connections with the far right and with allies of Morinaud. El-Maadi sought to use the violence to discredit the moderate Muslim political elite, including the reformist politician Mohamed Salah Bendjelloul, and to incite more Muslim attacks on Jews.⁷⁹ He joined a far-right terrorist organisation that committed assassinations and bomb attacks in France. During the war he rallied to the Vichy cause, worked briefly in the General Commission for Jewish Questions, the main means of anti-Jewish repression, assisted the Gestapo in Paris, formed a North African Muslim brigade that committed war crimes and ended the war as a captain in the SS in the circle of Hajj Amin Al-Husseini in Berlin before fleeing to Cairo.[80]

Jews believed anti-Semitism among the Muslims was as new as it was superficial, and that the unfortunate condition of the Muslims was not caused by the Crémieux Decree, which granted Algerian Jews French citizenship, but by its being limited to Jews alone. If they wanted to win over most of the population, to end the violence and pacify the country, what could be better than making them French?[81]

Kaddour Makaci, head of the elected Muslim officials' association, held a conference in May 1939 on anti-Semitism and Islam at which he condemned anti-Semitism, racism, and fascism, and recounted historical examples of Islam's tolerance, mentioning good relations between Jews and Muslims in Al-Andalus, and condemning the anti-Semitism of Europeans in Algeria. He expressed pleasure that Jews spoke against the racist regime which subjugated the Muslims of Algeria. He ended his speech proclaiming his faith in human brotherhood.[82] His counterpart was Élie Gozlan of Constantine, a Jew who believed in the fusion of Algerian Judaism and the French Republic and battled for the integration of Algerian Muslims.[83]

When the Second World War broke out, the Jews of Algeria supported France.[84] But what they faced in Algeria was an anti-Semitism more widespread than that in France.[85] The swastika was displayed freely among Europeans, on the front pages of newspapers, as jewellery, on neckties, on cigarette brands, and painted on cars. The far right increased its calls for the abrogation of the Crémieux Decree.[86] They argued that it turned Muslims against France. But the Muslim elite did not fall for it.

When France fell to Nazi Germany the Europeans in Algeria

were relieved that the colonial empire was maintained, and most rallied to Marshal Pétain's Vichy regime. Anti-Semitic violence followed. On 11 and 12 September Algiers witnessed a mini night of broken glass. Beginning in July 1940 and lasting until the Allied landing in November 1942, Pétain promoted a 'National Revolution' to create a 'new man' and to battle against the 'Anti-France' incarnated in the figure of the Jew.[87] A series of laws were passed restricting Jewish rights, barring them from certain professions and holding public office, and on 7 October 1940 the minister of the interior, Marcel Peyrouton, abolished the Crémieux Decree, claiming falsely that it was the anti-Semitism of the Muslims that propelled him to repair an injustice.

The measures destroyed the Jewish middle class and hit an overwhelmingly poor population hard, driving all towards misery.[88] The 'Aryanisation' by means of forced seizure of Jewish property based on a pretext of Jewish wealth is proven false by actual records showing how little Jews owned, a situation worsened by the professional restrictions.[89] Thankfully, the Muslim elite did not acquire Jewish property, except in agreement with other Jewish families.[90] The Europeans, by contrast, had no scruples about acquiring property seized from Jews, and did not return it after Vichy fell.

Ahmed Boumendjel, solicitor of the Algerian independence leader Messali Hadj, sent a letter to the Algerian Jewish leaders in November 1942, expressing his empathy, as both Muslims and Jews were victims of anti-Semitism, declaring:

> The Muslims have understood that it would be inappropriate for them to rejoice in the special measures of which the Jews of Algeria are the victims. They cannot reasonably get behind those who are attempting to practise a racial policy

when they themselves are struck down on a daily basis in the name of racism. Our adversaries did not expect that in making the Jews inferior, they could only bring them closer to the Muslims.[91]

The landing of the Anglo-American troops saved Algerian Jews from a tragic fate. They would have been sent to Auschwitz, claims Chief Rabbi Avraham Hazan. 'It was truly a miracle ... we would have been shipped as all the others, as those of Salonica, of which 85 per cent never returned.'[92] Seven forced labour camps were established in Algeria, incarcerating 2,000 men including Algerian Jewish soldiers. Harsh treatment led to Algerian Jews supporting the Free French and General de Gaulle.[93] Jews welcomed the American troops when they landed.

It took close to a year after the arrival of the Anglo-Americans to re-establish the Crémieux Decree. General Giraud, civil and military leader, was driven by anti-Semitism and displeasure with Jewish support for the Anglo-Americans. He appointed as new governor of Algeria Peyrouton, the former Vichy minister who had abrogated the Crémieux Decree.[94] He announced the abrogation of all Vichy legislation in Algeria and re-abrogated the Crémieux Decree.[95] His excuse was that the decree displeased the Muslims. The Algerian leader Ferhat Abbas declared in April 1943, 'We do not oppose the actions of the Jews to recover their rights as French citizens.'[96] The new government did not want to have trouble with the Muslims, nor to offend the Pétainist European majority. Having accepted the practice of religion in the private sphere, universalism and the rights of man, and the promise of citizenship of the Republic, Jews could not conceive of a return to the past. They were supported by those on the left, who called for equal rights for all.[97]

On 22 October 1943 the decree was re-established, and

Algerian Jews became French again.⁹⁸ The wound remained. They would never forget it. Taking the side of the Algerian Muslims, they preferred Abbas, a reformist who linked Algeria to France, to Messali Hadj, leader of the Étoile nord-africaine (the North African Star), and founder in 1937 of the Parti du peuple algérien (Algerian People's Party), a radical separatist. Only the far-left minority sympathised with the independence seekers.⁹⁹

Vichy's efforts to pit Muslims against Jews had failed. If the Algerian independence war had broken out at the end of the Vichy era, it would have attracted the sympathy of many Jews, because Muslim Algerians did not act in a hostile manner towards them and very few Muslims purchase 'Aryanised' Jewish property.¹⁰⁰

Their relations were tested by the massacres at Sétif and Guelma in the Constantine region in 1945.¹⁰¹ At Sétif 4,000 Jews lived together with 7,000 Muslims and 10,000 Europeans.¹⁰² The town is known for its famous son, Abbas, who would become president of the provisional government from 1958 to 1961. The seeker of independence Messali Hadj was deported on 23 April 1945, and on 8 May 1945, armistice day, Algerian Muslims protested against fascism and colonialism.¹⁰³ At Sétif, police fired on the demonstrators, who turned on the police and Europeans, killing hundreds. General Duval launched a war of reprisal in response, slaughtering 15,000–20,000 Algerians according to the French, and 45,000 according to Algerians, in Sétif and Guelma. The French utilised torture, summary executions, and aerial bombardment.¹⁰⁴

Jews did not take part in the attacks on Muslims. Jewish leaders intervened on behalf of the Muslim victims of the repression; Gozlan and a Muslim counterpart raised funds for their care.¹⁰⁵ In July 1945, the Jewish deputy José Aboulker in the provisional legislative assembly at Algiers blamed the police for firing first and defended the Muslims, saying it was not an instance of religious fanaticism, for Islam did not promote murder and attacks, and resisted all European provocations.[106]

The insecurity caused some young Algerian Jews to emigrate to Palestine.[107] But while Jerusalem was a place in their religious imagination, Algerian Jews were not drawn to political Zionism, because their lodestar was France. Their French patriotism hindered a sense of Jewish nationalism. Their Jewishness was intellectual and spiritual, religious not political. The situation changed somewhat with Vichy, but Zionism did not begin to attract Algerian Jews until after the war and the knowledge of the death camps.[108] Very few joined the Zionist movement.[109]

Disappointment with the motherland caused other young Jews to leave their traditional world behind to join the Algerian Communist Party in unprecedented numbers. Together with like-minded Muslims, they sought to create a secular, democratic society, governed by reason, where everyone was equal, pursuing social justice, imbued with the philosophy of the Enlightenment.[110]

Algerian Jews wanted to identify with the nation – but which one? The metropole, France, which most had never seen, and which revoked their citizenship during the war? French Algeria, where European anti-Semitism reigned? Or the new Algeria – but would they be considered native by Muslims?[111]

As in Algeria, Moroccan Jews and Muslims declared loyalty to France with the outbreak of war in 1939, and hundreds of thousands served on the side of France, as in the First World War.[112] Singers put their voices to the service of promoting the cause of the democratic powers, including M.I. Knafo, son of the chief rabbi of Essaouira, who produced a series of satires and pamphlets in Judeo-Arabic and French ridiculing Hitler, Goering, and Goebbels called *Les Hitlériques*. Matiah Simhun composed a *Qasida di Hitler*, published by the Moroccan government. Moroccan Zionists played a pre-eminent role in mobilising Jews to oppose the 'new Pharaoh' and support the British in the war. Jewish traders were encouraged to end contracts with Germany and Jews were encouraged to boycott German products.

While much of the French army in Morocco was Muslim, at the outbreak of the war large numbers of Jews volunteered to join.[113] But the French in Morocco were reluctant to send Moroccan Jewish troops to war under the French flag, due to both worry about Muslim responses and French anti-Semitism. Only a few dozen naturalised Moroccan Jews were enrolled in the army.[114] Members of the richest Jewish families sought to emigrate.

Nazi agents and supporters of Vichy tried to stir up animosity between Muslims and Jews, by encouraging boycotts of Jews, posting anti-Semitic signs on storefronts, and agitating against allowing European Jewish refugees in Morocco.[115] Due to fascist pressure, 7,700 refugees, mostly Jews, were sent to a dozen detention and labour camps. The French Moroccan resident, General Noguès, was worried the Jewish background of his wife would be revealed.

The French Residence was obligated by Vichy to issue a decree, based on the Jewish Law of 3 June 1941 in France, with the seal of Sultan Sidi Mohammed ben Youssef (the future King Mohammed V), who had no choice but to rubber stamp it, instituting racial discrimination by imposing a *numerus clausus* in the liberal professions (2 per cent of doctors and lawyers) and education (10 per cent at secondary level), the 'Aryanisation' by expropriation of Jewish wealth, and the expulsion of those Jews who had moved into European quarters after 1 September

1939.[116] The Jews protested to the sultan, arguing that the decree violated the spirit and the letter of the dhimma pact. The nationalists also opposed the classification according to race, as they had since the 1930s.[117]

Facing these dangers, Jews turned to the sultan to thwart the implementation of these decrees, but also pleaded with the Residence, reiterating their loyalty and attachment to France. The presidents of the Jewish communities of Casablanca, Rabat, Salé, and Meknes addressed a letter to the sultan on 23 June 1941 invoking the dhimma pact, expressing how 'Muslim tradition has always prided itself on protecting the Jews'. When they presented their grievances at the palace, the Jews were accompanied by Muslim notables and members of the government, asking for protection, while offering animal sacrifices.[118] The sacrifices conferred symbolic significance, reminding the authorities of Islamic obligations, which included the free exercise of religion and the protection of people and property.[119]

From the summer of 1941 through to the first six months of 1942, the sultan publicly expressed 'his attachment to the traditions that his ancestors were almost all keen to respect, and his own desire to protect his subject Jews'. Sidi Mohammed's invitation of Jewish notables to the official ceremonies of presentation of vows, at religious festivals, or the Feast of the Throne, was the symbolic prelude to this process. A telegram from the French Information Agency entitled 'Dissidence', written to discredit the sultan,[120] alleged on 24 May 1941 that when the French expressed their astonishment at the presence of Jews at the banquet, where they were given seats of honour, next to the Vichy officials, the sultan remarked: 'I in no way approve of the new anti-Semitic laws ... I wish to inform you that, as in the past, the Jews remain under my protection, and I refuse to allow any distinction to be made among my subjects.'[121]

Jewish notables were again received in the palace in May, June, and August 1942, when the sultan reaffirmed their right to his protection. A delegation of Jews consisting of notables and rabbis from Fez was officially invited to a grand reception given in Rabat in July 1942 by the pasha of the city. His majesty declared to them, 'My palace is open to you ... Come and find me, if necessary,' and his steward served them tea and cake. In August 1942, a Jewish delegation was presented to the sultan by the pasha of Casablanca. One of the rabbis said a benediction in Hebrew, which was translated into Arabic for the sultan, who declared, 'Be like your ancestors ... I consider you equal to other Moroccans, without any distinction.'[122]

The Vichy measures were adopted, but mitigated because Noguès chose not to apply them rigorously. Both he and the sultan saw the implementation of Vichy laws as destabilising society and undermining their authority, which in the case of the sultan was merely symbolic. The sultan's actions allow Moroccans to remember him as protector of his loyal and grateful Jewish subjects.[123] The AIU schools continued to function. Jewish students attended French lycées. The only Jews expelled from European quarters were those who had moved in after 1 September 1939. The order to declare wealth was only for values above 5,000 dirhams and excluded furniture and jewellery. Muslims gave assistance to Jews seeking to protect themselves against the sequestration. Jews sometimes made fictitious transfers of real estate to Muslim friends, reviving the tradition that previously allowed the former to evade the payment of taxes, and the latter to conceal property which they feared would be ransacked in times of unrest, by giving their word.[124] Relations built on trust remained.

The sultan supposedly refused to make the Jews of Morocco wear the yellow Star of David, although Morocco was a protectorate of Vichy France and subject to its anti-Semitic laws. Noguès prepared 200,000 yellow stars for all the Jews of Morocco to wear, but the sultan apparently told him he needed to prepare fifty more for him and the members of his family. Noguès abandoned the idea.[125]

The Anglo-American landing in 1942 was celebrated as a deliverance from certain death by more than 50,000 Jews in Casablanca, who instituted a special Purim.[126] But the Americans were cautious to intervene in favour of the Jews, for fear of German propaganda among Muslims.[127] The United States' Jewish secretary of the treasury Henry Morgenthau intervened on behalf of his co-religionists, and to push for the normalisation of their situation he travelled to Algiers.[128] The sultan wished to ascertain the American attitude towards Moroccan Jews and their demands. The Americans would not intervene in the affairs of the protectorate, he was told, due to the risk of alienating Muslims, and because they were confident that the sultan, as he had for centuries, would take care of his protégés.[129]

At the Feast of the Throne on 18 November 1944 the sultan repeated his calls for Jews to remain and not migrate to the nascent Jewish state in the British Mandate of Palestine:

> Just like Muslims, you are my subjects, and as such, I protect and love you ... Muslims are and always have been your brothers and your friends ... My illustrious ancestor, Moulay Hassan, was a true friend of the Jews and he repeatedly showed clear concern for them ... I can assure you that, for my part, I intend to maintain the same consideration towards you and your co-religionists and to make you benefit from the same concern.[130]

*

Twenty thousand Bosnian Muslims joined a special Nazi SS division named *Handžar*, an Ottoman word meaning dagger, to fight on behalf of Germany in Serbia and Croatia, committing war crimes and crimes against humanity.[131] Other Bosnian Muslims saved Jews.

Sarajevo is nicknamed the 'Jerusalem of the Balkans'. In the Old Town, established by the Ottomans in 1461, mosque, Greek Orthodox Church, and Sephardic synagogue are steps away from each other. Bosnians today pride themselves on their tolerant past. In 1581, half a century after Gazi Husrev Bey built the city's main mosque at the heart of the city, Sephardic Jews, who settled in the city by 1550, were granted permission by the Imperial Council in Istanbul to build their synagogue near the mosque. The Grand Synagogue rose after the governor-general of Ottoman Europe, Siyavush Pasha, built them an inn in which to reside.

Jews thrived in Ottoman Sarajevo and were granted equal rights when the dhimma pact was abolished in 1856. A generation after Sarajevo became part of Austria-Hungary in 1878, Ashkenazi Jews built a splendid synagogue in Moorish style on the other side of the Miljacka river in 1902. Today the synagogue, unlike other Jewish houses of worship in Europe, has no visible security guards, gates, or cameras, and its Menorah stands proudly outside the building.

Before the Second World War, Jews made up 15–20 per cent of Sarajevo's population, with 12,500 community members. After the Axis powers invaded, occupied, and divided Yugoslavia in spring 1941, Bosnia and Herzegovina came under the control of the Nazi puppet state of Croatia, headed by the fascist Ustaše. Although they were controlled by the Nazis, the Ustaše murdered 350,000 Serbs, 30,000 Roma, and 30,000 Jews under their own initiative from 1941 to 1945, establishing their own concentration camps. The Jews who survived did so by joining the communist partisans or fleeing to partisan-controlled territory. The Ustaše and Nazis murdered 12,000 of Sarajevo's Jews and looted and demolished the Sephardic synagogue (along with that in the Old Town of Mostar, of which but a Star of David on a fence post remains), but spared the Ashkenazi synagogue, which was Oriental in style.

As the Nazis rounded up Jews to send them to their deaths, many Muslims in the city risked their lives to save their Jewish friends and neighbours. Zeyneba and Mustafa Hardaga were an observant Muslim couple on whose land the Sephardic Jew Joseph Kabilio built a factory. The Hardaga and Kabilio families were close. When Sarajevo was bombed, the Kabilio home was destroyed. Without hesitation, Zeyneba invited the Kabilios, Joseph, Tova, and their daughter Rivka, to move in with them. The Hardagas helped the Kabilios flee to the Italian-occupied zone, saving their lives. Forty years later, during the war in Bosnia, when Muslims were subject to genocide, the Kabilios welcomed the Hardagas to their home in Israel, returning the favour of decades earlier. The Hardagas were the first Muslims honoured by Yad Vashem.[132]

Sarajevan Muslims also rescued Sephardic cultural and religious heritage. A beautiful, illuminated haggadah, the prayer book used during the Jewish ritual meal (Seder) commemorating the Exodus and liberation of Jews from slavery in Egypt during Pesach (Passover), composed in around 1350 in Barcelona, arrived in Sarajevo along with the expelled Sephardim by way of Italy and Dubrovnik.[133] As soon as the Nazis occupied Sarajevo in 1941, they demanded that Jozo Petrović, the director of the National Museum, give them the haggadah. Petrović, aided by the Muslim curator and scholar Derviš Korkut – who a year later hid a young Jewish partisan fighter, Donkica Papo, in his home for several months disguised as a Muslim servant, until she could be spirited to safety outside the city to rejoin the partisans – instead secreted the haggadah in a mosque in one of the Muslim villages on Mount Bjelašnica until the end of the Second World War. During the war in the 1990s it was kept safe in the vault of the National Bank. Korkut and his wife Servet's daughter, Lamija Jaha, fleeing the war in Kosovo in 1999, were welcomed in Israel by Papo's son, Davor.[134]

Occupied by Italy from 1939 and Nazi Germany from 1943, Albania saw first-hand incitement to persecute Jews. According to the Bektashi Sufi leader Haxhi Dede Reshat Bardhi, during the German occupation of his nation, the Albanian prime minister, Mehdi Frasheri, who was a Bektashi Sufi, refused to register the Jews in the country, as the Nazis demanded, organising instead a network of Sufis to shelter Jews. He allegedly gave a secret order to Muslims: 'All Jewish children will sleep with your children, all will eat the same food, all will live as one family.' Albanian Muslims, many of whom were Sufis like him, 'who see God everywhere, in everyone', 'in every pore and in every cell, therefore all are God's children', collectively saved the lives of thousands of foreign Jews, especially Sephardim from Yugoslavia, but also Ashkenazim taking refuge in their land, which had very few of its own Jews.[135]

They were motivated by the cultural concept of *besa* ('to keep the promise'), which included protecting dhimmi. 'Our parents were devout Muslims and believed, as we do, that every knock on the door is a blessing from God. We never took any money from our Jewish guests. All persons are from God,' explained brothers Hamid and Xhemal Veseli, who along with their brother Refik sheltered two Jewish families for nine months during the war.[136] They added:

> With the coming of the German occupation in 1943 both Jewish families [Joseph and Mandil] were moved to our family home in Krujë. Xhemal walked the parents night and day for 36 hours to our family home. We dressed them as villagers. Two days later we transported the children to Krujë. During the day we hid the adults in a cave in the mountains near our village. The children played with other children in the village. The entire neighbourhood knew we were sheltering Jews. There were other Jewish families that were being sheltered.[137]

Albania, one of only three European nations – alongside Bosnia and Herzegovina and Kosovo – with a Muslim majority, is the only country whose Jewish population increased during the Second World War. Seventy-five Albanian Muslims, including Hamid, Xhemal, and Refik, were recognised as Righteous Among the Nations by Yad Vashem.

Meanwhile, Egyptian Jews, despite their statelessness or foreign citizenship, had integrated into and played a leading role in modern Egyptian society. Jews were comfortable. According to an observer from the Jewish community in Palestine, 'the Jews enjoy equality'.[138] 'There was no Jewish question in Egypt in the interwar period.'[139] In the late 1930s, however, relations between Jews and Muslims in Egypt began to deteriorate because of the rise of nationalism, anti-colonialism, and political Islam, the influence of fascist propaganda on nationalist youth, and the impact of the worsening conflict over Palestine.[140] The most influential Egyptian Jew, Joseph Aslan Cattaoui, member of the Senate, and president of the Jewish community of Cairo, like the other leaders of the community, did not support the Zionists. Nevertheless, in 1936 the Muslim Brotherhood called for a boycott of Egyptian Jews, who were seen as a fifth column of

Zionism.[141] The Young Egypt movement and its paramilitary Green Shirts, founded in 1933, modelled on Italian and German fascism, encouraged Muslims to expel Jews from their lands. From spring 1938 Young Egypt led anti-Jewish and anti-Zionist demonstrations in Cairo and Alexandria, shouting 'Down with the Jews' and 'Throw the Jews out of Egypt and Palestine'. Students at Al-Azhar University declared a hunger strike protesting against Zionism, attempted to enter the Jewish quarter, and called for a boycott of Egyptian Jews for 'supporting Zionists'. Forty members of the government, led by the education minister, called on Egyptian Jews to repudiate Zionism.[142]

Jews held mass meetings to protest the Nazi rise to power and to counter Nazi propaganda. They organised boycotts of German goods, businesses, and films. Sephardic Jews including Léon Castro established the Egyptian League against German Anti-Semitism (LICA) as a branch of the worldwide movement.[143] Young Jews in Alexandria assaulted the German consul.[144] Yet the leaders of the community, including Haim Nahum – who had fled the new Turkish Republic for Egypt, where he was appointed chief rabbi, was granted Egyptian nationality in 1929, and appointed by the king to the Senate in 1931 – and Joseph Aslan Cattaoui condemned the boycott efforts and the LICA, preferring to not engage in public demonstrations, which they worried would worsen relations between Jews and Muslims.[145]

Rather than German anti-Semitism, or local fascist youth, it was the Palestine conflict that jeopardised Jews in Egypt.[146] Cattaoui, president of the Cairo community, sent a telegram in 1938 to the Zionist leader Chaim Weizmann: 'As Egyptians we urgently appeal to you to recommend moderation all around and a spirit of conciliation; with firm determination we realise that loyal union alone is capable of assuring a durable future peace and concord among populations made to understand each other and already united in a common origin and by long-standing fraternal feelings.'[147]

The government opposed anti-Semitism. In April 1938 the liberal and nationalist Wafd (The Delegation) party newspaper, *Al-Balagh* (*The Report*), editorialised: 'May our Jewish compatriots be reassured. Egypt's sympathy for Palestine contains no offence and no desire to hurt them. They, too, are children of Egypt. As such, they carry the same rights and the same obligations. Their conduct in Egypt has always been excellent. Egyptians feel for them nothing but affection and loyalty.'[148] In spring 1939, the government banned the Nazi news service and proscribed anti-Semitism in general, seized offensive publications, offered Jews police protection, and condemned violence.

Jewish anxiety was acute at Alexandria as Nazi Field Marshal Erwin Rommel's forces advanced across North Africa in the summer of 1940 and in 1942. The city was bombed, as was the Jewish hospital. Most Egyptians opposed the British army stationed in Egypt.[149] King Farouk, nationalist youth, and the junior officer corps were sympathetic to the Nazis. When Rommel advanced toward Libya in 1941–2, King Farouk sent a telegram to Hitler declaring that 90 per cent of Egyptians supported the Nazis, and that 'he was filled with highest respect for the Führer and the German people, whose victory over England he was fervently wishing for', seeing the Nazis 'as liberators from unbearable, brutal English yoke'.[150] But the British army in Egypt controlled who were the nation's political and military leaders. In early 1942, as Rommel continued towards the Egyptian border, the British compelled the king to install a Wafdist cabinet. Accusations were levelled against the Jews for profiteering by hoarding essential commodities as the British placed them in charge of the distribution of food and materials.¹⁵¹ Hundreds of thousands of Alexandrians, including Jews, fled to Cairo.

In July 1942, when Alexandrians heard the cannons of Rommel, opposition to the British increased.¹⁵² As British government officials prepared to evacuate Cairo, more Jews left for Upper Egypt, and most Jews feared for their lives if political conditions worsened.¹⁵³ While Zionist emissaries from Palestine were prepared to ask the British to evacuate Zionists and anti-Nazi activists, Chief Rabbi Nahum told them that the prime minister, Nahhas Pasha, assured him that if the Nazis occupied the country, Jews who had arrived before 1933 would be safe.¹⁵⁴

After the defeat of Rommel at El Alamein, from November 1942 the situation appeared favourable. The Allies landed in Morocco and Algeria, liberating them from Vichy, and in 1943 conquered Libya and liberated Tunisia. The Jews of Egypt rejoiced, for Allied victories assured their safety from the Nazi threat. However, there were ominous signs in Egypt, especially rhetoric from the Muslim Brotherhood, which included anti-Semitic tropes.¹⁵⁵ Its leader Hasan al-Banna promoted the reimposition of the dhimma laws.¹⁵⁶

Jewish leaders were not worried. In November 1944, when the World Jewish Congress met for an emergency session in Atlantic City, New Jersey, René Cattaoui and Edwin Goar sent a memorandum on behalf of Egyptian Jewry. Mentioning the suffering of Central and East European Jewry, they emphasised that the Jews of Egypt benefited from a favourable status: while Jews were massacred in Europe, the country set a precedent in positive human relations. In comparison with Syria and French North Africa under Vichy, 'the Jews of Egypt were relatively protected' by the government and the British, even if in November 1945 there were anti-British, anti-Zionist riots and looting that targeted Jews.¹⁵⁷

The rioters looted Jewish-owned department stores near

Al-Azhar University and on Imad al-Din Street, and attacked, pillaged, and burned the synagogue on Al-Amir Faruq Street. The Ashkenazi synagogue was burned down.[158] Jews pointed the finger at Young Egypt and the Muslim Brotherhood. Afterwards the government posted guards at the entrance to the Jewish quarter and promised to indemnify the victims. Nahum had an audience with the king. Two days later he presented a letter to the prime minister protesting the profanation of the Ashkenazi synagogue.[159] The letter underlined how much the Jews had always contributed to the intellectual and economic prosperity of the country, recalling that the authorities had granted them the same rights as the Muslim population. According to its authors, who compared the troublemakers to the Nazis, such brutal threats had never been made against Jews in Egypt since the country was ruled by Muslims. They reaffirmed Jews' loyalty to their country, where they faced no danger.[160] Nahum, pressed to denounce Zionism, declared that Egyptian Jews were loyal citizens who demanded that the Allies 'find the homeless Jews a refuge other than narrow Palestine', as there was no other solution 'but close cooperation between Arabs [Muslims] and Jews, in an atmosphere of complete agreement, imbued with confidence and mutual understanding' – the first public repudiation of Zionism by an Egyptian Jewish representative.[161]

Seven thousand Jewish men and women from Palestine serving in the British army were stationed in Egypt. They propagated Zionism, trying to convince the youth to emigrate to Palestine, but they had no influence on the elite. Emissaries sent from Palestine were more successful in recruiting some youth to migrate between 1942 and 1948.[162] From 1945 to 1947 Zionist emissaries offered weapons training to young men in Cairo and sent dozens to Palestine for further paramilitary and martial arts training so they could defend their communities.[163] Yet the elite regarded the Zionist colonisation in Palestine as 'historical errors that would haunt the Jewish people'.[164]

President of the Cairo community René Cattaoui upbraided local Zionist leader Léon Castro in 1944 for compromising relations with the government. He tried to mediate between Zionists and Palestinian Muslims.[165] Cattaoui and his father, Joseph, and Chief Rabbi Nahum emphasised the racial affinity of Arabs and Jews as Semitic 'cousins'.[166] Their efforts to Arabise and Egyptianise the community failed, notwithstanding the role some Jews played in patriotic politics, particularly joining the Wafd party.[167]

Authorities viewed Zionism, leading to the exodus of Egypt's Jews, as less dangerous than communism, which would overthrow the state. Jews, especially migrants from Russia, had played a leading role in socialism and communism in Egypt from the 1890s. The Russian Jewish jeweller Joseph Rosenthal, born in Beirut in 1867, active in the trade union movement in Alexandria in the 1890s, formed the first socialist organisation in Egypt in 1920 and then the Egyptian Socialist Party in 1921, which became communist as it joined the Third Comintern in 1922–3.[168] Because of numerous arrests the party ceased to function by the late 1920s. In the 1920s and 1930s the government tried to stop the immigration of Russian Jews from Palestine because they viewed them as communists. During the same period Jews also supported anti-fascist groups, and the pacifist movement.[169] Jewish businessmen played a prominent role in the local Italian anti-fascist groups.

The fortunes and activities of communists, such as Jews Henri and Raoul Curiel, rose in the 1930s with the growth of anti-fascism in the country, and Jews remained in prominent positions in the most influential communist groups of the 1940s, until mass arrests in 1948.[170]

Enemies and Allies, Persecutors and Protectors

The presence of so many Jews, stateless or foreign nationals, in these movements, and their promotion of interreligious coupling, compromised them in the eyes of the majority and the government. Perhaps in response, Ezra Harari, member of the central committee of the Spark, an Egyptian communist organisation established by an Ashkenazi Jew, and others formed the League against Zionism – Egypt in 1945, with branches in Cairo and Alexandria, declaring Zionism to be a tool of British imperialism and calling for one secular Palestine for Jews and Muslims. They aimed to make Egyptians aware that not all Jews were Zionists.[171]

When Britain united the three Ottoman provinces of Mesopotamia – Mosul, Baghdad, and Basra – to form the Mandate of Iraq granted by the League of Nations in 1920, which by agreement lasted until 1932, a new economic and political golden age began for Iraqi Jewry. The Jewish community grew from 87,000 in 1919 to 118,000 in 1949. In fact, the number was greater, as Israel records 135,000 Iraqi immigrants in the early 1950s. Most Jews left the countryside and Kurdistan for Baghdad and Basra, where they spread beyond their traditional Jewish quarters.[172] The Jewish population of Baghdad, where Jews settled in the new city, expanded from 50,000 in 1919 to 77,000 in 1947, or even as much as 90,000. The 1920s witnessed the birth of a large middle class working in public administration and the growing wealth of the upper class. Jews were represented in the two assemblies. One of twenty representatives in the Senate was Jewish, as were four deputies in Parliament, rising to six in 1946. It seemed all the dreams of Iraqi Jewry promised with the abolition of the dhimma pact in Ottoman times had been realised. Secularisation and modernisation lowered barriers to Jewish progress, as did the adoption of Iraqi culture. Jewish intellectuals and the middle class integrated in the economic, social, and political life of the country, as well as its literature and art.

Britain had established Iraq as a constitutional monarchy, creating the Hashemite dynasty and enthroning its first king, Faysal, son of Hussein, the sharif of Mecca, in 1921, but when he died in 1933, the position of Jews became more difficult. In 1937 a military putsch deposed the government. It was led by Colonel Salah al-Din al-Sabbagh, who dominated until 1941. Increasing conflict between Jews and Muslims in Palestine between 1936 to 1939 influenced their nationalism and desire to expel the British. This period also witnessed the rise of the fascist youth paramilitaries Al-Futuwwa and Kataeb al-Shabab.[173] The arrival of Syrian and Palestinian dissidents, including the Palestinian Mufti Al-Hajj Amin al-Husseini in 1939, demonstrated the predominance of the Arab Muslim nationalist view in the 1940s, which excluded Christians and Jews, the latter seen increasingly as a fifth column identified with the British colonisers. Although Jews made up only 3 per cent of the Iraqi population, their concentration in Baghdad, where they were more than 30 per cent of the population, and their predominance in the country's economic life gave them an economic and social weight beyond their demographic presence.[174] But it could not hinder what happened in 1941.

Iraq witnessed a notorious pogrom, the Farhud (looting, robbing), in Basra in May 1941 and in Baghdad in the first two days of June, carried out by police, soldiers, and members of youth organisations on the first day and the urban poor on the second. In spring 1941, it appeared that the Allies were about to lose the war, and the Middle East would fall to the Axis. Syria and North Africa were ruled by Vichy France. On 2 April the pro-Nazi former Prime Minister Rashid Ali al-Kaylani took power in a coup. His government lasted only two months, but it was a terrifying time for Iraqi Jews, who were overwhelmingly pro-British.

The Farhud occurred within the context of anti-Zionism, where Iraqi Muslims equated Iraqi Jews with Zionists; animosity towards Jews stirred up by the presence of Palestinian nationalist exiles including Al-Husseini in 1939; and the spread of Nazi propaganda. All these views, however, were opposed in public, on the radio, and in the press, by Iraqi Muslims and Jews. It was Kaylani's coup that turned the tide in favour of the Nazis and against the British and the group most seen as their allies, the Jews. The British soon reoccupied Iraq, forcing Kaylani to flee at the end of May. It was in this power vacuum that the pogrom occurred.

On 1 June 1941 Jews celebrated both Shavuot – by dressing in white and making pilgrimage to the tombs of prophets – and the victory of the British over the pro-Nazi insurgents.[175] A mob led by Al-Futuwwa and Kataeb al-Shabab militant youth attacked the Jews of Baghdad, killing, wounding, and looting Jewish homes and businesses in the old Jewish quarter as police refused to fire on the rioters and instead joined them.

Jews blamed the British for abandoning them, despite their loyalty, for not intervening to stop the riots, as they let public anger against the British be taken out on the Jews as scapegoat. Elie Kedourie, who was born in Baghdad and was a child during the riots, stressed that it was a British policy of minimal intervention in internal affairs provided that imperial interests were guaranteed. In Iraq this meant the military bases outside Baghdad and Basra, transport routes to India, and oil. The British saw no reason to occupy areas non-essential to the security of their soldiers.[176] In Basra the troops were quartered in the Al-Ashshar neighbourhood, without occupying the other quarters, allowing the looting of the commercial quarter and the violence, despite pleading by the notables, merchants, and middle class for them to intervene. The same policy was applied in Baghdad.[177]

In the afternoon of 2 June, the Iraqi army fired on the rioters and put an end to the rioting. Between 139 and 180 Jews were killed, mostly from the Jewish neighbourhood of Abu Siffin. Hundreds of rioters were killed by the army on the second day of the unrest. Seven hundred to one thousand Jews were wounded. There were at least ten rapes. Around 550 stores and 900 apartments were looted.[178] The Jews of Iraq had never experienced such violence directed at them. It was the first pogrom against Jews in a modern Arab state (there was a pogrom against Jews in Turkey in 1934). Jews had been discriminated against but had been protégés of Islamic rulers who defended them from attacks. Nevertheless, Muslim neighbours, acquaintances, and notables intervened to save Jews.

The lives of Jews in Basra were spared thanks to the actions of local notables, of whom the most eminent was Shaykh Ahmad Bash-A'yan, the ex-mayor. The shaykh gathered his former bodyguards into a militia, and they put an end to the pillage and defended the Jews until soldiers could arrive.[179] Shi'i Muslims, including shaykhs, hajjis, imams, and muftis were motivated by Islam to protect the dhimmi, their Jewish brothers and sisters.[180] More important were personal relations. Most of the killing took place in neighbourhoods that were majority Jewish while in mixed neighbourhoods almost no Jews were killed, because shared intimacy compelled Muslim neighbours, friends, and business partners to protect them.[181] The dhimma pact, no longer valid in a secular state, whose constitution granted all citizens equality, compelled Muslims to stand up to modern nationalist violence.[182]

Like the revocation of the Crémieux Decree in wartime

Algeria, the Farhud shook Iraqi Jews' sense of security and stability and harmed their sense of belonging. They were betrayed by their colonial ally, the British, who had not wanted to risk their soldiers to save their lives. Jews felt betrayed by the nationalists, whom they considered partners in the building of an Iraqi nation state, as some had joined their organisations. Yet few turned to Zionism at the time.[183] The chief rabbi and Jewish intellectuals expressed solidarity with their 'Arab brethren', the Muslims of Palestine.[184]

While some youth migrated illegally to the British Mandate of Palestine, the majority of Iraqi Jews remained and integrated, and the economic and political situation improved. The British took control of the country, established the pro-British Nuri Said in power, punished the coup leaders, and restored stability. A new pro-British journal, *Sawt al-Haqq* (*The Voice of Truth*), condemned Kaylani, Nazism, and fascism, and promoted Islam as a Semitic religion, meaning that Muslims, as Semites, were naturally anti-Nazi.[185] Iraqi officials told Jews of their sense of shame that some had acted contrary to Islam, and they had not protected the Jews. A shaykh spoke on the radio about respecting one's neighbours and protecting dhimmi. Religious authorities issued fatwas urging Muslims not to fight for the Nazis. The new Iraqi regime donated money to the Jewish community and expelled Kaylani supporters and Palestinians.[186]

Rabbi Sasson Kedourie, Jewish members of the Senate and Parliament, the wealthy, the elite, and all those believing in Iraqi nationalism considered themselves to belong to Iraq, identified with the state and society, and desired to remain.[187] They had cordial relations with the political and social elite and the monarchy, kept a low profile, and worked behind the scenes to express their concerns rather than provoke the militants by public confrontations. Others migrated. Some armed themselves and created self-defence organisations. Despite the violence and the betrayal, 'most Jews continued to believe Iraq was their homeland' and sought political solutions within its borders.[188] Jewish youth, however, turned against the conservative politics of their elders in favour of two radical solutions: Zionism, aided by the arrival of secret emissaries in 1942, and communism.[189]

The Ottoman Empire, defeated in the First World War, fell in 1922 as Sultan Mehmed VI was sent away on a British naval vessel. The empire was replaced in Anatolia by the secular, nationalist Turkish Republic in 1923, which abolished the caliphate in 1924. Chief Rabbi Haim Nahum had been part of Ottoman diplomatic delegations from 1918 to 1922, and in 1923 he served as advisor to the Turkish delegation at the Lausanne Peace Conference. Yet he did not see a future for Jews in his homeland and fled to Egypt. Nevertheless, the Jews retained a chief rabbi and the dhimmi attitude towards the secular government, repeating the myth of interfaith utopia and gratefulness to the Turks for having welcomed them after they were expelled from Iberia in the fifteenth century, although Jews have lived in what is today Turkey since ancient times.

The changes accompanying the transformation from empire to nation state adversely affected the Turkish Jewish community, especially government-encouraged Turkification. Jews, like other citizens in the new Republic, were granted equal rights and the freedoms of belief and religion as individuals, as Jews as a community were hindered from organising and possessing autonomous institutions. The Republic aimed to create equal Turkish-speaking, Turkish citizens. But discrimination against Jews in practice did not allow them to become full citizens. Jews were not made candidates for political office, nor could they serve in municipalities or state economic institutions. They were not allowed to be policemen, judges, prosecutors, diplomats, government ministers, or bureaucrats. Jews were not allowed into the military academies to become officers.

Jews in the Turkish Republic, echoing their Ottoman and Mediterranean ancestors, emphasised the positive aspects of their relations with Turkish Muslims. Jewish Member of Parliament and Professor Avram Galanti (Galanté) penned dozens of works, including *Türkler ve Yahudiler* (*Turks and Jews*, 1928). It was published in the wake of the murder of a young Sephardi woman, Elza Niyego, by a Muslim man whose advances she spurned, which sparked unprecedented demonstrations by Jews; after the alleged sending of a telegram by Sephardic Turkish Jews to Spain pledging loyalty to their former homeland; and during a violent campaign to force Jews, who preferred French and Ladino, to speak Turkish. Galanti pleaded that despite what the Muslim public might think, Jews were loyal to the Republic. He wished to prove that the history that Ottomans and Turks shared with Sephardic Jews had always been a peaceful and mutually beneficial symbiosis. Considering the context in which the Turkish patriot was writing, it is understandable why he promoted this thesis.

From 1923 to 1927, the Turkish press attacked Jews for economic exploitation, alleged disloyalty to the Republic, and inability to speak Turkish. Anti-Semitic depictions of Jews were prevalent in Turkish daily newspapers and humour magazines.[190] The government stripped Jewish schools of their independence and outlawed Jewish institutions. Muslims in the cities of Thrace boycotted Jewish merchants. Some demonstrated to have Jews expelled. Those Jews who did not emigrate in response decided to defend the name of their community and ensure its survival. Journalist David Fresco responded to attacks with a spirited defence of Jews. Chief Rabbi Haim Becerano, a former AIU teacher, did his best to keep alive a community suffering financial ruin and legal constraints on its institutions.[191] Galanti and the super-patriot Tekin Alp, born Moiz Kohen, who despite his efforts would end his days penniless and broken in France, acted to influence Turkish leaders and opinion-makers, as well as Jews. While Galanti served on delegations sent by Jews to the government to express their concerns, both men also tried to make Jews into Turks.

Galanti published the pamphlet, *Vatandaş! Türkçe Konuş!* (*Citizen, Speak Turkish!*) for the majority of Turkish Jews who continued to speak French and Ladino. Tekin Alp also wrote to convince Jews of the importance of Turkification. He depicted himself as a modern-day Moses, publishing a new Ten Commandments for Jews to follow:

1. Turkify your names.
2. Speak Turkish.
3. Pray at least partly in Turkish at the synagogue.
4. Turkify your schools.
5. Send your children to state schools.
6. Become involved in public affairs.
7. Maintain close relations with Turks [Muslims].
8. Uproot the spirit of the religious community [give up the dhimmi mentality].
9. Perform your specific task in the domain of the national economy.
10. Know your rights.[192]

Despite such efforts, throughout 1933 measures promoting the speaking of Turkish in public led to Muslims assaulting Jews, and efforts to Turkify Jewish schools prompted the growth of underground Jewish schools and police raids on synagogues and confiscation of Hebrew-language books.

Despite the claim that Turks rescued many Jews during the Nazi period as part of a continuous Turkish Muslim role as saviour of Jews, Turkey did not give permission to German Jews to immigrate in 1933 when approached. The only Jews allowed were those who could fill positions at Istanbul University. A total of fifty-eight academics were accepted.

In 1934, events took a sharp turn for the worse for Jews living in Thrace. At the beginning of July, the homes and stores of Jews in Kırklareli were destroyed, their goods were looted, and men were beaten as no help came from police. Golden crowns were ripped from Jews' mouths and rabbis' beards were cut, as they were forced to watch their wives being stripped and attacked.[193] Along with such violence, other haunting vignettes include families sitting on the bare floor in the ruins of their homes on the morning after, silently making Turkish coffee over a coal brazier. Many Jews of Kırklareli fled to Edirne, which caused many Edirne Jews in turn to seek safety in Istanbul. Fearing for their lives, all the Jews of the town of Uzunköprü, near Edirne, also fled to Istanbul. On the same night, Jews were attacked in Silivri, Babaeski, Lüleburgaz, Çorlu, and Lapseki. According to official government reports, the following day thousands of Thracian Jews fled to Istanbul. At the rail stations they had to run the gauntlet of large, jeering crowds of Muslim Turks.

The 1934 pogrom was part of a government plan to discourage Jews, viewed as a potential fifth column, from living in the sensitive border region. According to the Statute of Relocation, passed in Parliament two weeks before the pogrom, the government planned to deport Jews from Thrace and replace them with Muslims.[194]

The anti-Semitic inspector general of Thrace, Ibrahim Tali, initiated the expulsion of the Thracian Jews, whom he labelled 'parasites who suck Turks' blood'. To Tali, Jews were gold-worshipping, greedy, disloyal agents of foreign powers who controlled the economy and intended to establish communism. He aimed to solve this 'Jewish problem', as he called it, as quickly as possible by putting all economic resources into Muslim hands.[195] After the pogrom, Recep Peker, general secretary of CHP (Cumhuriyet Halk Partisi, the Republican People's Party), and prime minister in 1946 and 1947, wrote that the decision to transport the Jews of Thrace out of the region had got out of hand.

The pogrom occurred in the context of the adoption of Nazi ideology by Turks such as the fascist agitator Cevat Rifat Atılhan. His writings appeared in newspapers, along with a series of anti-Semitic books printed in serial form, arguing that Jewish spies caused the Ottomans to lose the First World War. In 1934, Atılhan spent several months in Munich as the guest of the Nazis. He returned to Turkey after training in Nazi propaganda techniques and published a newspaper that printed anti-Semitic material in translation. He also published articles by Turkish writers such as the self-declared racist Nihal Atsız, who argued that 'just as we never expected [Jews] to be Turkified, nor do we want it. For just as no matter how long you bake mud, it will never turn into iron, so a Jew can never become a Turk, no matter how much he struggles.'[196]

In 1938, Turkey prohibited foreigners from entering Turkey for purposes of transit if they did not possess visas to their destinations. A law the same year disallowed people who were not 'members of the Turkish race' from receiving residence permits.[197] Jews were not considered to belong to the 'Turkish race'. Officials made it clear in 1938 and 1939 that they would not accept Jewish refugees: Turkish consulates received an order not to give visas to Jews with German, Hungarian, Italian, or Romanian passports unless they could help Turkey. Some Turkish consular officials managed to save Jews. But many more Jews in German-occupied France who had their citizenship cancelled or whose passports were not renewed by the Turkish government were sent to Nazi death camps.

The position of Jews worsened between 1941 and 1943, after Turkey signed a Friendship Pact with Germany. Parliament approved a wealth tax on 11 November 1942. The government presented it to seize revenues held by profiteers. Those who could not pay the exorbitant tax were sent to concentration camps. In practice, the tax was directed against Jews (and Christians).[198] Of the first eighteen people arrested in January 1943, twelve were Jews and the rest Armenians and Greeks.[199] Of the 1,500 people sent to break stones at the camp at remote Aşkale in eastern Turkey, over half (800) were Jews. Some died in the camps, and others never overcame the humiliation they endured.[200]

Many Muslims claimed it was a 'blood tax' since Jews (and Christians) had allegedly not spilled blood for the nation in the past, but become wealthy at Muslims' expense.[201] To prevent this situation, the government had to put an end to Jews' profiteering and hoarding.[202] Prime Minister Şükrü Saraçoğlu stated that the tax would be implemented 'with all due severity' on those who 'benefited from the hospitality of this nation and became rich', yet avoided fulfilling their duty during the war years.[203] Many Jews at the time believed that the second half of the Ladino proverb *Ni mujer de la Romanya, ni mülk en la Turkiya* ('Neither take a Romanian bride, nor own possessions in Turkey') was verified.[204] Saraçoğlu argued that the wealth tax was 'an opportunity to win our economic independence. Removing the foreigners [including Christians and Jews] who control our market, we will turn the Turkish market over to

Turks [Muslims].'[205] A CHP official declared that the tax would force Jewish (and Christian) merchants to leave.[206]

Nearly 800 passengers on board the Romanian Jewish refugee ship *Struma* wished to disembark in Istanbul and travel overland to Palestine in 1941, but they were refused haven. Vehbi Koç, one of the two wealthiest men in Turkey, intervened to save Standard Oil's Jewish Romania director and his family, who were on board. Koç was on the blacklist in England for trading with Nazi Germany. But thanks to this intervention to save the director, Koç was removed from the list. A tugboat towed the ship back out to sea in February 1942, where it was hit by a torpedo and sank. There was only one survivor.

The Twentieth Reserve Corps was established the same year. Christian and Jewish men were sent to camps to break rocks and build roads while their Muslim officers told them they would never see their families or Istanbul again and that the ditches they dug would be their graves. Many perished in the harsh conditions.[207]

Turkey was neutral until the end of the war, adhering to its Friendship and Non-Aggression Pact with Nazi Germany and its Treaty of Mutual Assistance with Britain.[208] Some Turkish newspapers in Istanbul, such as the liberal *Vatan* (*Fatherland*), whose editor was the Dönme Ahmet Emin Yalman, and the leftist *Tan* (*Dawn*), whose writers included the Dönme Sabiha Sertel, voiced opposition to fascism and Nazism.

Close relations were established between the Nazi foreign ministry, the Nazi Party, and scholars in Germany and Turks advocating for the unity of all Turkic peoples in Eurasia, who included the main decision-makers in Turkish foreign policy. This included the Turkish general staff, which distributed copies of an anti-Jewish novel written by Turkey's leading anti-Semite to Turkish officers.[209] The Turkish ambassador to Germany,

Enemies and Allies, Persecutors and Protectors

Hüsrev Gerede, the foreign minister and then prime minister Saraçoğlu, and the foreign minister Numan Menemencioğlu supported the Nazis. Beginning in 1941 they promoted the effort to recruit Turkic Soviet POWs to fight for the Nazis. Two hundred thousand served on the Nazi side, helping to suppress the Warsaw Uprising in 1944, and as late as May 1945, Turkic Waffen-SS units defended Berlin.[210]

Gerede saw the German invasion of the USSR as a 'joyful opportunity to assist his Turkic blood brothers in Russia to be freed from Soviet despotism'.[211] But he bemoaned the behaviour of the SS, which disregarded the fact that the Turkic peoples saw the Nazis as their saviours from the Soviet 'dictatorship', as the Nazis murdered Turks, mistaking them for Jews.[212] During the Barbarossa campaign against the Soviet Union in 1941, SS squads executed Muslim POWs 'on the assumption that the fact that they were circumcised proved that they were Jews'. This caused Reich Security Main Office head Reinhard Heydrich (assassinated in 1942) to order the SS to be aware that the circumcision and 'Jewish appearance' of Turkic Muslims did not mean they were Jews. The two groups were not to be confused. Muslims were not to be persecuted.[213]

Throughout the end of the war, approximately 400 Turkish students pursued advanced degrees in the Third Reich, many becoming 'supporters of Hitler', expressing 'open admiration for the Nazi regime' when they returned to Turkey in 1945 to establish departments in the Turkish Republic's two universities.[214] This was despite the fact that they were eyewitnesses to the humiliation and physical assaults on German Jews, including the pogrom of 9–10 November 1938, where they saw synagogues burned and Jews beaten to death. When they learned that their 'dark-skinned' female landlords, or women who wished to date and then marry them, were Jewish, they expressed disgust, and moved out of their rented accommodation, or left their companions to their fate. They did not want to continue the centuries-old tradition of the Jew as ally of the Muslim and Muslim as saviour of the Jews. They became targets of violence, as they were mistaken for Jews on account of what they reported as their own dark skin and large noses.[215] Being mistaken for Jews did not lead to solidarity with Jews, however, but distancing and disdain.

When, shortly after Hitler became Chancellor, the Turkish cultural attaché Cevat Bey was severely maltreated 'because he had dark skin and an aquiline nose', it was the last straw for the Turkish ambassador, Kemaleddin Sami Pasha. He donned his military dress uniform and First World War medals, including the highest German honours, and met with the authorities. Sami Pasha was 'the only ambassador admitted to Hitler at any time without an appointment', because 'Hitler had great respect for such war heroes'. Their ambassador demanded 'that dark-skinned Turks be left alone' and that 'SA men, before they bludgeoned a Jew, first examine [his] identification to make sure that they were not mistakenly laying their hands on a Turkish student'.[216] Far from insisting that Turkish Jews not be harmed, the ambassador (and the students) assumed that Turk equated with Muslim, and expressed no opposition to the persecution of Jews.

In 1933, Jews constituted 45 per cent of the 1,673 Turkish citizens in Germany.[217] More than half of the Turks in Berlin were Judeo-Spanish-speaking Jews. The fate of Turkish Jews in Nazi Germany is best illustrated by the life of a single person. Isaak Behar, a Turkish Jew in Nazi Berlin, was stripped of his citizenship by his own government. Turkish consular officials refused to repatriate him to Turkey as Germany requested, although they were aware of the deadly consequences awaiting him and thousands of Turkish Jews in the same circumstance in Nazi-occupied Europe. Like the others, Behar was condemned to Auschwitz. When the Gestapo came to his home to arrest him at the end of 1942, Turkish officials did nothing to save him. At the same time, though, the Turkish government allowed select German Jews temporary refuge in Turkey.[218]

In 1937, the Behar family still had not faced anti-Semitic persecution in Berlin. As Behar relates in his autobiography, 'our Turkish citizenship still protected us'.[219] The family witnessed the burning of the Moorish Fasanenstrasse synagogue during the pogrom of 9 November 1938, from the window of their third-floor home.[220] Behar's family's Oriental carpet business on the first floor was not attacked by the mob. Behar wondered whether this 'was because we were considered Turks first and not primarily Jews'.[221] But that November night was a bad omen for the family. A cousin was arrested and sent to Buchenwald concentration camp.[222] His father had to surrender his business to a non-Jew.[223]

The next year, of Jews residing in Germany who were Turks, only one-third (263) were recognised as Turkish citizens. Of the Turkish Jews in Berlin, only one-fifth (101) were considered Turkish nationals.[224] The decline in the number of Turkish Jews was because Turkey stripped most Turkish Jews living in Europe of their Turkish nationality. In this way, over 90 per cent of the 20,000–30,000 Turkish Jews in Nazi-occupied Europe became stateless.[225] As Behar recounts, in April 1939, the Turkish government 'ordered us to have our Turkish citizenship verified. It was immediately clear to all of us that this was fatal, for it meant our passports would be cancelled during this "verification". Other Turkish Jews had already explained to us that they had never seen their passports again.' Indeed, 'We received German alien passports in their place, with the notation "Citizenship:

Turkey". Soon after, this was changed to "Citizenship: Undeclared". Finally, it was replaced by "Stateless". We had lost our final protection.'[226]

The Gestapo was immediately notified of those who lost Turkey's protection. Stateless Turkish Jews of Berlin were among the first to be deported to the Nazi death camps. The second transport from Berlin, on 24 October 1941, carried more than a dozen Turkish Jewish women and children to their deaths in Łódź or the nearby death camp of Chelmno.[227]

Less than two months later, on 3 December 1941, Turkish Ambassador Gerede informed his superiors in the foreign ministry in Ankara of the mass murder of Jews in Poland and the Ukraine: 'Nearly one million Jewish men have recently been killed in Lemberg (Lviv) and Kyiv. Twenty to thirty thousand people are made to congregate in a field, which is encircled by gunmen who annihilate them with machine-gun fire. The SS is responsible for the process of annihilation, and according to the eyewitness, these deadly operations will continue.'[228]

In December, Nissim, Lea, Alegrina, and Jeanne Behar were arrested at their home, deported to Auschwitz, and murdered.

In 1943, 'as part of the solution of the Jewish question in Europe', neutral states, including Turkey, were given an ultimatum: repatriate their Jewish citizens found in Nazi territory by the end of July because 'all foreign Jews found in the German area of control after that time would be subject to the general measures taken against Jews'.[229] By that point, most Turkish Jews had either already been deported or were subject to deportation. In September 1943, the Turkish embassy in Berlin informed the German foreign ministry that it had been instructed by Ankara to prevent a mass return migration of Turkish Jews.[230] Despite this, Turkey was given another month to repatriate its citizens, but it did not act on behalf of the Jews waiting to be deported.[231]

Enemies and Allies, Persecutors and Protectors

At the end of October, the Nazis informed the Turkish authorities that they would deport the remaining Turkish Jews from Berlin to concentration camps: women and children to Ravensbrück, men to Buchenwald, and the elderly to Theresienstadt. The Turkish authorities once again did nothing to stop them, despite being able to repatriate them to Turkey. After their deportation, Turkish authorities were granted an additional month to demand their release, but they did not act on this opportunity to save Turkish Jews, either.

Turkish officials imagined other ways to solve the 'Jewish problem' in Turkey. Istanbul's chief of police, Nihat Halûk Pepeyi, and the chief of the police division concerned with foreigners and minorities, Salahattin Korkud, travelled to Berlin at the beginning of 1943 to meet with their Gestapo counterparts.[232] As guests of the Gestapo and SS, they travelled from Nazi-occupied Holland and France in the west to Poland and Crimea in the east. They visited the Krupp and IG Farben factories, run on slave labour. In Berlin, they stayed at the SS guesthouse in Wannsee, where only one year before their visit high-ranking representatives of the SS and Nazi Party, including Adolf Eichmann and Heydrich, met to coordinate the ongoing genocide of European Jewry. On 1 February 1943, 'due to their special request', the two Turkish police officials visited the Sachsenhausen concentration camp outside Berlin, where 200,000 people were held in barbarous conditions, and 30,000 were gassed, hanged, shot, and tortured to death.[233]

Sachsenhausen was set up by Heinrich Himmler as a model for other camps, and was used by the SS to train and prepare people such as Rudolf Höss, the camp commandant of Sachsenhausen and then Auschwitz, who had first shed blood for the Ottomans during the First World War. It was the centre of operations for all concentration camps in Nazi-occupied Europe.[234]

At the SS club at Sachsenhausen, adjacent to 'the screaming, the stench, the cramped conditions, and the violence', the Turkish police dined on a six-course lunch, including goose liver, and drank wine with SS officers.[235] They were given a VIP tour of the camp, which would serve as a model for what they planned to construct in Turkey. When they returned, large buildings were erected in the main Jewish neighbourhoods of Balat and Sütlüce in Istanbul and Bahri Baba in Izmir. The rumour spread among Turkish Jews that they were enormous crematoria that would be used to incinerate them if Germany, which already occupied Greece and Bulgaria, took over Turkey.[236] Although the rumour proved to be false, the fact that many Jews believed it illustrates their fear and distrust of Turkish authorities.

The top Turkish army generals travelled to Europe that summer, meeting with Hitler in Berlin and touring the Western and Eastern Fronts.[237] As Nazi troops occupied Poland, Russia, and Crimea, the SS and Gestapo sought guidance on whether to persecute the roughly 10,000 'non-Jewish people of Jewish belief' that had come under their control. Officials at the Reich Office of Genealogy of the interior ministry, responsible for determining the 'racial identity' of peoples, sought scholarly opinion on the 'racial origin' of the Karaites, Mountain Jews of the Caucasus, and Krimchak Jews of Crimea, a Turkish-speaking people that had become Jewish. Their opinions could be the difference between life and death, since Jews considered Turkic in origin, and not Semitic, and who had not intermarried with Jews, could be spared from the Holocaust. The Karaites were generally considered to share only their religion in common with Jews, and were not murdered by the SS in Crimea, whereas the Krimchaks were annihilated. The Semiticists Dr Holz and Dr Kuhn discussed the origin of the Karaites in the summer of 1942. Dr Kuhn argued that it was most likely that the Karaites were people of Turko-Tatar descent who were converted by Jewish missionaries, did not intermarry with Jews, and therefore had very little 'Jewish blood' and were not Jews. He pointed to the similarity of the Mountain Jews of the Caucasus, a Caucasian people that had converted to Judaism, and the Krimchaks. None of the three, Karaite, Mountain Jews, nor Krimchaks, he argued, were 'Jewish by race'.

He claimed that Eastern European Jews falsely presented themselves as non-Jewish, reasoning that they were descendants of the Khazars who converted to Judaism in the ninth century. According to Dr Kuhn, however, the Khazars themselves so intermarried with Jews, and had such a high proportion of 'Jewish blood', that one could not distinguish between the descendants of the Khazars and the Eastern European Jews.[238]

Turkish Jews such as the Behar family were targeted for persecution and murder with the collaboration of Turkish consular officials, who systematically stripped them of their citizenship, rendering them stateless and defenceless before Nazi genocidal policies. The Behars lived near Erich Auerbach, whose son Clemens was born the same year as Isaak. Auerbach was a member of a small group of eminent German Jewish intellectuals allowed conditional refuge in Turkey: the Behars, who had tried to find a better life in Germany, became the victims of the Nazis. The Auerbachs were allowed to leave Germany, finding refuge in the Behars' home city.[239]

Turkey's actions regarding German Jewish academics were motivated by state interest in improving its educational system rather than humanitarianism, or an intention to help Jews.[240] Officials did not see Turkish Jews as either Europeans useful for Turkey, or Turks worth saving. Ankara told its diplomats in Europe 'not to send trains full of Jews to Turkey', 'particularly of those Jews who had correct Turkish papers but have not had any contact with Turkey for decades'.²⁴¹ The consular officials acted accordingly. This fact should finally invalidate the claim that Turkey's policy was to save Jews during the Shoah, that it 'struggled and fought to protect Turkish Jews from racist attacks', and that when Jews lost their Turkish citizenship, there was nothing Turkey could do to save them.²⁴²

Of Turkish Jews in France, eighty were saved by Turkish diplomats, 500 were repatriated to Turkey, and 2,000 were sent to Auschwitz.²⁴³ Most Turkish Jews of France who survived the Holocaust did so with the help of the Turkish authorities. This demonstrates that they could have saved them when it was desired in Turkey. But most of the time they did not act, and the Jews, whether of Turkish or French citizenship or stateless, were deported, never to return. There is no evidence for the supposed heroic action of the 'Turkish Schindler' of Marseille.²⁴⁴ No Jewish eyewitnesses or Turkish documents corroborate Necdet Kent's account of his saving trainloads of Jews. The consul on Rhodes, Selahattin Ülkümen, saved forty-two Jews, but 1,820 were sent from there to Auschwitz.²⁴⁵ In contrast, an Iranian diplomat in Paris, Abdol Hossein Sardari, saved hundreds of Iranian Jews in France.²⁴⁶

The Sephardic Turkish community of Berlin was completely destroyed by the Holocaust. More than 100 of its members were deported to concentration camps, and most of them were murdered.²⁴⁷ The last leader of the community – Davisco Asriël, who wore a Turkish flag pin on his lapel, and had been a member of the Turkish Chamber of Commerce, in whose minutes one finds the signature of this Jew next to that of the Turkish consul – pleaded with the embassy in Berlin to reinstate his Turkish citizenship, revoked in 1940, and to repatriate him to Turkey, but was refused. He was arrested and deported to his death in Riga in January 1942.²⁴⁸ The Sephardic synagogue built in 1911 did not survive the war.

Enemies and Allies, Persecutors and Protectors

Thanks to the assistance of non-Jews, and several strokes of good luck, Isaak Behar escaped death, including from a transport from Berlin to Auschwitz, and survived.[249] Behar's opinion of Turkey was pessimistic. As he related in his memoir, in the mid-1950s:

> Obtaining a Turkish passport appeared to be an absolutely simple process. But with complete bitterness I thought back about how Turkey had withdrawn our citizenship when we needed it the most. How easy it would have been at that time, with a Turkish passport, for me and my family to have been delivered to safety. And how easy was it for me [after the war], to get my Turkish passport back! Shortly afterward, I decided, however, to relinquish my Turkish citizenship ... I decided to become German.[250]

Because the government promoted Turkish racial superiority and distinguished citizens by religion and many believed that the term Turk denoted a Muslim, efforts at making Jews into Turkish citizens failed. The aim of winning a 'second War of Independence' by 'liberating' the economy from Jews (and Christians) and creating a Muslim Turkish bourgeoisie also hindered the full realisation of the project to create equal citizens.

Anti-Semitic public opinion, incited by newspapers such as the government-mouthpiece *Cumhuriyet* (*Republic*) and humour magazines that depicted Jews with grotesque anti-Semitic stereotypes, along with humiliation of Jews in public and print for speaking heavily accented Turkish, hindered their efforts and discouraged them. Another stumbling block was that the leaders of Turkish Jewry emphasised that the Ottomans had welcomed their ancestors in 1492, so Jews owed Ottomans and Turks an everlasting debt of gratitude. Emphasising their being foreign and having guest status encouraged the public to view Jews as non-Turks and to consider them ungrateful for not speaking Turkish.

To prove their loyalty, Jews raised funds for public institutions, but they were accused in the press of making these donations for their own financial gain, not because of loyalty to the nation. Jews were considered incapable of true patriotic feeling and accused of celebrating national holidays only because they were opportunities to make money, for example by selling Turkish flags. The CHP's view of Jews (and Christians) hindered their ability to be considered full members of society. A 1944 CHP report claimed that Jews did not integrate, spoke their own languages, played no role in the foundation of the Republic, served the interests of foreign powers, and never demonstrated loyalty to Turkey.[251]

The report also proposed that Turkey should not permit the Jewish population to grow, and should instead ease restrictions on Jews' emigration, decrease their population, and remove them from important spheres of the Turkish economy. After Israel's establishment in 1948, most Turkish Jews, except the upper class, fled to the Jewish state. The categories Turk and Jew were sundered prior to 1948 and the establishment of Israel, however.

To this day in Turkey, Jews are marked as foreigners by the 'non-Turkish' names, often Spanish, they bear and are not regarded as Turks.[252] Although being considered a stranger may no longer have the grave consequences that it did for Turkish Jews in the Second World War, this shows how the process of exclusion, distinguishing Turk from Jew, and determining who belongs to the nation, was completed before Israel was established, and is still operative.

7

TRANSFORMING JEWISH–MUSLIM RELATIONS: JEWISH NATIONALISM AND THE ESTABLISHMENT OF ISRAEL

Prior to 1920, in Jaffa, Jerusalem, and Hebron, Jews and Muslims lived together in the same buildings or courtyards in the same neighbourhoods, spoke Arabic (while Muslims learned a few Hebrew blessings and joined the Jewish parties on Purim), sang the same songs at weddings, visited the same tombs of holy men, went to school together (Muslims at the AIU school, Jews at modern madrasas), befriended each other, and socialised together in the same coffee shops. Jewish musicians played Andalusi music at the weddings of Muslim families nostalgic for al-Andalus 'whose culture was preserved by the descendants of the Spanish expulsion'.[1] The founders of the Red Crescent included the Muslim Khalidi and Husseini families along with the Jewish Antébi, Mani, and Elyashar families.[2] The Nashashibi and Husseini families purchased villas on the outskirts of Jerusalem where they threw parties at which wine was drunk and hashish was smoked as Jews and Muslims found lovers from members of the opposite religion. Jerusalem's Muslim mayor, Raghib Nashashibi, known for having a Jewish lover, later had a Jewish wife named Palomba Marudes. The conviviality made it seem as if it was Al-Andalus reborn.

Jews and Muslims respected each other's religious obligations. Arab Jews recall how the Muslim pilgrimage to the alleged tomb of Moses (Jews do not accept that Moses entered the promised land) 'induced in us a feeling of bonhomie and joy. We knew that they were honouring the memory of a prophet, a man of God, who is accepted by us.'[3] An Arab Jew remembers how prior to 1920, 'when young and old alike took up position already in the morning next to the gate of the wall to welcome the [Muslim] Nebi Musa celebrants with fanfare, as their flag-bedecked processions passed along the lanes of the Jews to the sound of drums and cymbals, the Jews of Jerusalem and Hebron cheered them and sprinkled rosewater on them'.[4] When the Muslim pilgrims returned to Hebron, the descendants of Muhammad greeted them with all other residents of the city. The descendants raised the banners of Abraham, Isaac, and Jacob, which are kept in the Cave of Machpelah. Another Arab Jew recalls how, 'For the [banner] all the residents turned out onto the streets of the city, both Arabs [Muslims] and Jews. The procession enters the Cave of Machpelah, where a special prayer is conducted and the celebrants then disperse ... Upon the pilgrims' return home a festive mood spreads throughout the city, in the Jewish compound and beyond.'[5]

Muslims 'invited their Jewish neighbours to their festivities and in summer also got together with them in their vineyards, took meals together, drank and slept. And vice versa. There was not a joyous occasion in a Jewish home without the presence of [an] honoured Arab [Muslim] guest' in Hebron. 'Jewish peddlers would find accommodation in village mosques, just like Arabs [Muslims], or in the home of the *mukhtar* [village leader]. And when the villagers descended to the town on Fridays to pray at the Cave of Machpelah they found accommodation in Jewish homes.'[6] In great contrast to this level of trust and intimacy,

Jews avoided the Church of the Holy Sepulchre in Jerusalem at Easter, fearing attack. From the late nineteenth century to the 1920s, some Arab Jews like Muslims were considered Palestinian patriots and *abna al-balad* – that is, natives.[7] Arab Jew and Muslim lived side by side in mixed neighbourhoods, interacting daily at the market, the cinema, the brothel, at restaurants and playgrounds.[8] Yet many of these Arab Jews were killed in the riots of 1929 when Muslims slaughtered 133 and wounded several hundred more in Hebron and Safed. What caused this sudden turn to violence?

When the Romans destroyed the Second Temple in 70 CE, leaving only the Temple Mount and Western Wall still standing, and crushed the final Jewish rebellion three years later, they ended Jewish sovereignty in Israel. From the seventh century until modern times a succession of Muslim dynasties controlled Palestine, except for periods of European Christian Crusader control. From 1099 to 1187, when Saladin reconquered Jerusalem, to 1291 when the last holdout knights at Acre were expelled, Crusaders prohibited Jews and Muslims from residing in their holy cities, including Jerusalem. Muslims, by contrast, allowed Jews to live amongst them according to the dhimma pact. Relations between Jews and Muslims in Palestine did not begin with European Zionist settlements at the end of the nineteenth century.

From birth to death, Jews, wherever they find themselves in the world, are attuned to the land of Israel. Religious holidays and festivals are based on the agricultural seasons in ancient Israel. Every year at Passover, Jews conclude the ritual dinner, the Seder, with the wish 'next year in Jerusalem' – may the Messiah come and transport us to the Holy Land. At every Jewish marriage ceremony, the groom breaks a glass to commemorate the destruction of the Second Temple in Jerusalem. Jews in the diaspora have a handful of earth from Israel thrown over their body when they are buried. To focus only on the last century, to not discuss the centrality of Israel in Judaism, to dismiss the spiritual focus of Jews to the land, is misleading.

My own great-great-grandfather Israel Isaac migrated from the Russian Empire to Ottoman Palestine towards the end of his life to be buried in Jerusalem on the Mount of Olives in 1898.[9] He had a wish to be as near kingdom come when it comes. To dismiss his desire, to dismiss the long history of Arab Jews and Sephardic Jews who flourished under Muslim rule, to pretend that Jewish focus on Israel began with the birth of political Zionism at the first Zionist congress in Basel in 1897, or to begin the story with the occupation of the British army in 1917 is to misrepresent a significant element in the history of Jewish–Muslim relations. What is different is that people like my great-great-grandfather or the tens of thousands of Yemeni Jews who migrated there before the First World War had no political aim. My forefather wanted to be buried in Israel so he would be resurrected on the Day of Judgement. The idea of *politically* resurrecting Jews was the aim of Zionism.

In pre-modern times, Jews living in Muslim-ruled Palestine practised Judaism in the context of the legal discrimination of the dhimma pact, as those promoting an antagonistic view enumerate.[10] They were at times compelled not to wear ostentatious jewellery, not to visit the public baths at the same time as Muslims, or to wear distinguishing markers if bathing together with Muslims. From the ninth century they were at times required to wear a yellow badge on their clothing to mark them as distinct. The latter practice was adapted by Christians at the Fourth Lateran Council held by Pope Innocent III in 1215 for use in Christendom.[11] Christians also made

Muslims wear the badge, as they perceived the Jew as the ally of the Muslim.

Jews participated in the economic life of the society and practised their religion with a minimum of restrictions, appealing to the local magistrate or imperial authorities when they needed assistance or when they were wronged. As in other pre-modern Muslim societies, they were allowed 'to live in relative calm and to develop as they wished within Arab Muslim society and under Ottoman authority'. One finds that 'numerous historical testimonies ... testify that, during the 400 years of the Ottoman Empire, the Jews lived happily alongside the Arabs [Muslims]'.[12]

When the Ottomans defeated the Mamluks in 1516 and 1517 they incorporated Palestine into their empire, which had a positive reputation for the dynasty's relations with Jews. Ottoman sultans and sultanas launched economic development projects in Jerusalem, restoring old markets and constructing new ones.[13] A flourishing and growing community of Jews participated in the economic life of the city from the beginning of the empire's rule. By the end of the sixteenth century, most of the merchants in the new spice market were Jews. Jews engaged in the olive trade in the countryside and the soap trade with Egypt and played a significant role in the new jewellers' market as well.[14] Jews were appointed by the local magistrate as head of the jewellers' guild, 'the most important profession of Jerusalem'. One also found Jewish butchers, millers, bakers, blacksmiths, coachmen, vintners, cheesemakers, moneychangers, and financial managers for Muslim endowments, as well as wealthy doctors and surgeons who were on a par with their Muslim colleagues and named as chief physicians of the city, working in the main hospital. Sephardic weavers established a textile industry in northern Palestine in Safed, as Jewish fabric merchants sold their and others' wares in Jerusalem. In the nineteenth century were added the professions of banker, lawyer, and watchmaker. Yet the Jews' financial situation was lamentable, as witnessed by the sending of emissaries abroad to collect funds.[15]

During the Ottoman period, Jews and Muslims 'shared an inextricable common history'.[16] Yet over the centuries, Jews in Palestine were sometimes accused by Christians or Muslims of conducting ritual murder, of abducting Christian or Muslim boys, of murdering them, and using their blood to bake matzot (unleavened bread) during Passover. In 1544, following such an accusation by a Muslim, Sultan Suleiman I sent a decree to the magistrate of Jerusalem and all Arabic-speaking regions of his empire declaring that Jews were protected people and any attempt to harm them, under any pretext whatsoever, would be considered contrary to Islamic law and secular Ottoman law. Such accusations were rejected by Ottoman authorities, who served as saviour of the Jews from calumny and persecution.[17]

In 1586 a complex of four adjoining Sephardic synagogues was established in Jerusalem. The innermost is named the 'Estambouli' after its Istanbulite founders. They were built in the heart of the Jewish quarters to the west of the Temple Mount where all Jews lived. Despite being referred to as Jewish quarters, the neighbourhoods had Muslim majorities, so they were Jewish sections of Muslim neighbourhoods, although Muslim homes backed onto Jewish houses, and often there was no separation between them.[18]

In the seventeenth century Ottoman authorities recognised a Sephardic Jewish majority and an Ashkenazi ('German') Jewish minority with its own synagogue, liturgical music, and style of dress.[19] The Ashkenazi community fell into debt to Muslim creditors, leading to bankruptcy. Its synagogue and homes were sacked by a mob in 1720, causing the Ashkenazi Jews to flee

Jerusalem and leave all their wealth behind to their creditors.[20] The Ashkenazim were forbidden from residing in Jerusalem.

When the Ottomans engaged in reforms from 1789 to the First World War, including abolishing the dhimma pact, relations changed. The French Revolution, emancipation of the Jews, and French and British occupation of Algeria and Egypt led to the first stirrings of Arab nationalism. A Sephardic Jew of Italian background, Yaqub Sanu, was the most outspoken Jew in the Arab world. He allegedly converted to Islam and under the name Shaykh James Sanua Abou Naddara he was active as a journalist, politician, and a prolific playwright.[21] But his theatre was closed by Khedive Isma'il in 1872, and he was expelled to France in 1878 following two attempted assassinations after his criticism of the ruler.[22]

Sanu's publications were the first to promote a new idea, an inclusive Arab nationalism. His slogan was 'Egypt for the Egyptians' as he promoted the French republican spirit among the Egyptians and sought to compel the peasants to rise against their overlords. He called on Egyptian officers to rebel and backed the 1882 Urabi revolt against the British.[23] His slogan became the rallying cry for all nationalists in the region, who substituted the name of their own land and its people for 'Egypt'. In his writing he never revealed his Jewish origins. Unlike his contemporary Arab Christian nationalists, he could not encourage his co-religionists to join the cause, as did Greek Orthodox, Maronites, and Copts.[24] He was buried in the Jewish section of Montparnasse cemetery in Paris in 1912, without a Hebrew inscription or mention of religion.[25]

Jewish nationalism, Zionism, also emerged at the end of the nineteenth century. Jews were pushed out of Russia and Poland by a wave of persecution in the late nineteenth and early twentieth century, and were drawn to Palestine by the revolutionary ideology of Zionism.[26] The proto-Zionist movement of the Lovers of Zion (Hovevei Zion) called for the rejection of *Galut* (exile from the Land of Israel) by a national Jewish renaissance and the rebirth of the Hebrew language in Palestine. The manifesto of the Bilu group of Ukrainian and Russian Jews who migrated and established their own settlement in 1882, referencing Judah Halevi, called to Jews: 'Hopeless is your state in the West; the star of your future is gleaming in the East.' What they demanded was 'a home in our country [Ottoman Palestine]. It was given to us by the mercy of God, it is ours as registered in the archives of history.' To obtain it, they asked the sultan that Jews 'may be allowed to possess it as a state within a larger state; the internal administration to be ours, to have our civil and political rights, and to act with the Turkish [Ottoman] Empire only in foreign affairs, so as to help our brother Ishmael [the Muslim] in his time and need'.[27]

Writing in the London *Jewish Chronicle* in 1896, summarising some of the main arguments of his book *Der Judenstaat* (*The Jews' State*), published the same year, the Viennese journalist Theodor Herzl promoted a 'national movement' which would lead to the 'restoration of the Jewish state', where 'we shall live at last, as free men, on our own soil, and die peacefully in our own home'.[28]

In 1897, fifteen years after the beginning of the first migration (*aliya*, 'going up') to Palestine, these new ideological movements and popular associations popping up across Europe merged in the Zionist movement. Its first congress in Basel, led by Herzl, declared that 'the aim of Zionism is to create for the Jewish people a home in Palestine'. It was to be attained by 'the colonisation of Palestine by Jewish agricultural and industrial workers', the uniting of world Jewry in this purpose, 'the strengthening and fostering of Jewish national sentiment and consciousness', and taking steps to obtain '[Ottoman] government consent' for the project.[29] From the beginning the movement needed the aid and support of the Ottomans. Herzl tried in vain to gain support for the project from Sultan Abdülhamid II. He believed that 'supposing His Majesty the Sultan were to give us Palestine, we could in return pledge ourselves to regulate the whole finances of Turkey [the Ottoman Empire]'. Perceiving the Zionist project as a European one, whose 'continued existence' would be guaranteed by Europe, he argued that in Palestine the Jewish nation 'should also form a portion of the rampart of Europe against Asia, an outpost of civilisation as opposed to barbarism'.[30] The fact that the land of origin of the most immigrants was the traditional enemy, Russia, along with reticence to increase the number of European subjects, who would have extraterritorial status, not to mention the fact that Jerusalem is the third holiest Muslim city, meant the appeal fell on deaf ears.

The previous year, in 1896, an agent of the sultan had suggested to Herzl that he marshal 'Jewish power' on the Ottoman Empire's behalf, to temper international outrage regarding the massacres of Armenians. Herzl gave a one-word response: 'Excellent!'[31] As European sympathy for the Armenians was at its greatest and pressure on the Ottoman sultan was most intense, Herzl used all his contacts, as Zionist leader and as journalist, to turn the tide. In a journal entry from June 1896, Herzl wrote that 'this is the service he demands of me: that I prevail upon the newspapers of Europe (in London, Paris, Berlin and Vienna), to present the Armenian question in a fashion friendly to Turkey [the Ottoman Empire], and that I convince the Armenian leaders themselves to surrender to him, whereupon he will be willing to meet all sorts of their demands'.[32] When interviewed in the English press that July, and asked whether he had gained the sultan's support for his programme at the cost of Jewish support against the Armenians, he rejected this claim, but added that 'people in England have not been entirely fair towards the Sultan. He personally abhors brutality, and he honestly yearns to live in peace with all his subjects.'[33] In August 1896, as Armenians were massacred in Istanbul, Herzl feared this would lead to the deposition of Abdülhamid II, which would mean the end of the Zionist dream to settle Jews in Palestine. Herzl continued to rouse public opinion to support the sultan despite the worsening atrocities.

Herzl and the sultan imagined Jews could silence negative opinion about the Ottomans and hinder Christian rebellion. Both Herzl and the sultan were using each other to fulfil their own aims. Both lived in a world of fantasy. In Herzl's view, 'the Sultan gives us the piece of land, and for that we will put everything in order for him, regulate his finances, and determine public opinion of the entire world in his favour.'[34] Abdülhamid II turned to the historical trope and real fact of the Jews as allies of the Muslims to oppose the common Christian enemy. At the same time, he invoked an anti-Semitic conspiracy theory, imagining a Europe controlled by Jews.

For their part, the Zionists continued to praise Sultan Abdülhamid II. Only a few months after the latest massacres of Armenians in 1901, the Fifth Zionist Congress held in Basel expressed gratitude for Ottoman tolerance of Jews. This was how Ottoman Jews publicly viewed the sultan. That year Sultan Abdülhamid II and Herzl met for the first time; they met twice in 1902.[35]

With the freeing of the press after the 1908 revolution – when the Committee of Union and Progress (CUP) forced the sultan to reinstate the 1876 constitution and recall Parliament, which had been opened in 1877 but suspended the following year – the public debate over Zionism among Jews and in the empire accelerated. The Ottoman Chief Rabbi Haim Nahum felt Zionists to be a threat, as support for Jewish nationalism in the empire was increasing, and opponents of the CUP debated Zionism in Parliament.[36] Nahum was concerned that Zionism would turn authorities against the Jews, a community which 'had hitherto been considered loyal to the central power and enjoyed relative tranquillity, for which it paid by remaining silent'.[37]

Nahum ensured that a French-language anti-Zionist pamphlet written by the Ottoman Jewish journalist David Fresco, editor of the popular Istanbul Judeo-Spanish newspaper *El Tiempo*, was distributed 'to all the ministers, senators, deputies, and newspaper editors' confirming Ottoman Jewry's rejection of Zionism, as was publicly voiced by the communities of Salonica and Izmir.[38] In a series of articles in *El Tiempo* entitled 'Is Zionism Compatible with Ottomanism?', Fresco denied that Jews are a nation, claiming they are only members of a religion, and blamed Zionists for inciting Ottoman Jews against their empire: 'I think the central leadership of Zionism is committing a huge crime in its desire to drag the Ottoman Jews after their crazy movement.' He argued that Zionist leaders 'should think a little about the existence of half a million Jews who live quiet and peaceful lives without any pressures, faithful to their homeland'.[39] Three of four Jewish deputies in the Ottoman Parliament declared that they were against the Zionist movement, as they were Ottomans first and Jews second.[40]

To fight 'the rising tide of Zionism' Nahum came up with a plan in autumn 1909: a declaration in the Ottoman Parliament by a friend of the Jews who would ask in part, 'Does the government not think that this movement is of a nature to damage the unity of the Ottoman homeland?'[41] Nahum envisaged the minister of the interior rising to 'speak of the loyalty of the Ottoman Jews … of the patriotism with which they welcomed the military law that now makes them the equals of their co-citizens ... He would denounce the creation of a separatist nationalist movement as a very grave danger to the Jews, which could alienate the sympathies of their co-citizens.'

Nahum was also assisted in his efforts by the passionate Ottoman patriot Moiz Kohen/ Munis Tekinalp. Speaking at the Ninth World Zionist Congress in Hamburg in 1909, Tekinalp contrasted an antagonistic vision of life for Jews in Christian lands with an interfaith utopian account of Muslim rule. He declared: 'Turkey [the Ottoman Empire] is the only land that has been spared from the plague of anti-Semitism, appearing to us as a modern Canaan, the promised land for today's Jews, who flee from the modern Egypts, the lands of slavery and grief [Romania and Russia].'[42] Tekinalp mentioned how 'the legendary tolerance of the Turks' was so well known it had become a truism.[43] Arguing against Zionism, he supported Jewish immigration into the empire on the condition that the Jewish immigrants became Ottoman patriots and were not concentrated in Palestine alone. He contended that loyal Jews would serve to offset disloyal Christian groups because 'the respective interests of the Jews' and the empire coincided.[44] He ended his speech quoting Bayezid II inviting Iberian Jews to his land and Itzhak Tzarfati declaring, 'Here every man may dwell at peace under his own vine and fig tree.'[45] In a later article he claimed that Tzarfati referred to the empire as an 'earthly paradise for the world's persecuted Jews.'[46]

The Ottoman Jewish journalist Fresco warned against the danger of Zionism, proclaiming in 1910 his loyalty to the homeland in contrast to the Zionist who would

> be seen as a rebel against the state and traitor to his partner brothers he will cause shame and dishonour and provoke

an awful hatred against the Jewish people in the empire. All the Ottoman Jews and Arabs are related to each other so it is incumbent upon us to prevent this rebellion, to ban this disgrace, and to take refuge from the catastrophe that can fall on our heads.[47]

Fresco's counterpart in Palestine was Albert Antébi, Damascus-born and Paris-educated director of an AIU school in Jerusalem, who was an outspoken anti-Zionist and proponent of unity with Muslims and Christians, yet director of the Jewish Colonisation Association promoting Jewish immigration.[48] The Ottoman Muslim press also began to distinguish between Ashkenazi immigrants, who caused problems, and local Ottoman Jews, who were seen as loyal and patriotic.

The ally of the Jews, the Ottoman government, also tried to stamp out the fire of Zionism. It first limited, then banned the immigration of Jews to Palestine, although small numbers of religious pilgrims were permitted to visit for a well-defined period. These measures were not effective. Jewish immigrants, bearing foreign passports, continued to arrive and settle in Jerusalem and in the north of Palestine and to benefit from the protection of European powers, which hindered their expulsion.[49]

Jews also aimed to buy land in Palestine for their settlement, which was sometimes forbidden. To avoid such restrictions, they purchased land in the name of Ottoman Jews of Palestine. The most important support in land purchases came from European Jewry, such as the Baron de Rothschild of Paris, who offered financial backing to immigrants from 1882, and in 1891 Baron Maurice de Hirsch established the Jewish Colonisation Association in London, which purchased land in northern Palestine from Muslim families in the name of Ottoman Jews to create agricultural settlements for Russian Jewish immigrants. Of

Palestine's total area of 27 million dunams, Jews owned 22,000 dunams in 1882, whereas by 1900 they owned 200,000 dunams, and by 1914, 400,000 dunams.[50] The aim was to transform Jews from their contemporary mode of existence into a new society of productive, self-sufficient agriculturalists. From the late 1870s they established cooperative settlements of individual farms (moshavot). After 1909, Marxist and socialist ideas were propagated in the new socialist agricultural collectives (kibbutzim), along with gender equality and self-defence. Although the kibbutzniks made up only 15 per cent of the Jewish population, they stood in stark contrast to the urban Jews from the Arab and Sephardic community.[51]

Muslim opposition to the newcomers was fed by the inability of the Ottomans to limit Jewish immigration, which was especially noticeable in urban areas, the establishment of kibbutzim in the countryside, and Jews purchasing land from absentee landowners and then expelling Muslim peasants.[52] In 1891 several Muslim and Christian notables from Jerusalem sent a telegram to the Ottoman grand vizier demanding that he end Jewish immigration to Palestine and block Jews' purchase of land.[53] Others followed suit.

The dethronement of Sultan Abdülhamid II in 1909 led to more democracy and representative government. In the new Parliament sixty of 288 deputies were from Arabic-speaking regions, including two from Jerusalem, one from Jaffa, and two representing northern Palestine.[54] Nationalist separatism was seen as a threat to the integrity of the empire, and the Zionists were seen in the same light as other nationalist movements. Beginning with the parliamentary session of 1909, the Arab deputies of Palestine depicted the Zionists as a threat to the new regime and to the Arab presence in Palestine through land purchases and Jewish settlements. Some Jewish farmers were assassinated in the Tiberias area.⁵⁵ The removal of censorship led to the flourishing of journalists who targeted the Zionists.

Najib Nassar, founder and editor-in-chief of *Al-Karmil* in Haifa, who was previously employed by Jews to purchase land in Tiberias, became the most vehement anti-Zionist journalist prior to the First World War. The journal *Filastin* in Jaffa played a similar role, gaining the attention of the press in Damascus and leading to the sale of some land being blocked. Already in 1914 the paper's Greek Orthodox editor Isa al-Isa wrote an editorial worried about 'a nation threatened with disappearance by the Zionist tide in this Palestinian land'.⁵⁶ After the First World War, when Palestinian nationalism developed in full force, Muslims and Christians held congresses opposing the British and Zionists from 1919 to 1928, after which al-Isa called his people 'strangers in our own land'.⁵⁷

In 1934, Jacques Bigart, secretary general of the AIU, asked, 'After having struggled for so many years for emancipation, can we now support a movement which undermines the achievements of all our efforts? The process of emancipation, in my view, involves the complete adaptation of the Jews to their new homelands. Zionism, with its dishonest approach, condemns this adaptation.'⁵⁸ AIU leaders were anti-Zionist up to 1939, warning that Zionism was a false solution 'which can lead all of Judaism into danger'.⁵⁹ Already in 1904 the AIU's president, Narcisse Leven, had warned that Zionism would establish 'a Jewish nationalism which would be more fanatical than the others, since history ... shows us that the first use which peoples newly liberated from their yokes make of their freedom is to persecute the foreign elements existing amongst them'. The aim of the AIU was to promote progress and civilisation, which would allow Jews to live with non-Jewish people. Jewish elites feared the Zionists would question their integration into society.

In the second half of the nineteenth century and early twentieth century, as the Jewish population of Jerusalem grew – by 1910 it was the second largest Ottoman city with a Jewish majority, after Salonica – so did the urban communities of Jaffa, Safed, Tiberias, Haifa, and Hebron, at the same time as more than 10,000 Jews settled in the countryside.[60] The Jewish population shifted from a Sephardic majority to an Ashkenazi majority, building new neighbourhoods outside the walls of the Old City of Jerusalem. Baghdadi Jews established a small colony in Ottoman Jerusalem and in Hebron and contributed to the welfare and religious life of Jews of the land, such as the Baghdadi-born Calcutta donor Yossef Abraham Shalom, who inaugurated the Sephardic yeshiva Porat Yossef overlooking the Western Wall in the Old City of Jerusalem. Its foundation stone was laid in 1914, and it was inaugurated in 1923.

Palestine witnessed the arrival of Jews who had never lived with Muslims, and had never experienced the Jewish–Muslim symbiosis because they were from Russia, where they had antagonistic relations with Christians, or from Germany. They arrived in a land where there were Arab Jews. They were all Palestinian, but the Arab and Sephardic Jews were soon outnumbered by these new arriving nationalist Jews, who were there to create an exclusive Jewish state, and looked down upon the local Jews and their good relations with Muslims.

A representative nineteenth-century Arab Jewish family was the Chelouches, whose patriarch Avraham migrated from Oran in Algeria to Jaffa in 1840. Avraham's son, Aharon, who wore a *jalabiya* and *tarboush*, expanded the port city, established relations with the Ottoman governor, with whom he smoked a nargila and drank Turkish coffee, founded industrial enterprises, and took part in government infrastructure projects.[61] At the end of the Ottoman period Aharon developed a new residential quarter for the expanding Jewish middle class in Neve Tzedek outside Jaffa's ancient city walls in 1887, which led in 1909 to the founding of the first Jewish city, Tel Aviv.[62] The Chelouches were apolitical. In his memoir, Aharon's son, Yosef Eliahu, contrasts the bloody conflicts at the end of the 1920s and the long peaceful coexistence of Jews and Muslims before the British arrived, and he violently criticises the Zionist movement for the deterioration of intercommunal relations.[63] 'Many of those who came from abroad ... did not understand the importance of good neighbourly relations.'[64]

What was happening was the growth of a new Jewish society in Palestine from 1882 to 1917, distinct from the ancient one. Between 1881 and 1904, in the first immigration wave, 25,000 Jews arrived; from 1905 to 1914 around 30,000 immigrated. By 1914 there were around 100,000 Jews in Palestine, about 15 per cent of the population.[65] By 1917 half of the Jews in Palestine were new immigrants, a third of them living in around thirty rural settlements, self-sustaining farming communities, and the rest joining Jews in urban areas including Jerusalem, Jaffa, Ramle, Hebron, Gaza, Haifa, Acre, Safed, and Tiberias.[66] The Jewish population growth occurred despite Ottoman policy from 1880 to 1908 not to allow Jews to immigrate to Palestine. By 1901 they were allowed three-month visas, but none, apparently, were expelled before the First World War.[67]

If only between 1908 and 1913, Muslims, Christians, and Jews sought a common future in a reformed empire. Members of the urban intellectual class saw each other as Ottoman brothers.[68] In the wake of the 1908 revolution, which reinstated the constitution and Parliament, Muslim, Christian, and Jewish men gathered in public squares throughout the empire to proclaim, 'Long live the homeland! Liberty, equality, brotherhood!' Men of different religions publicly embraced each other, proclaiming that all were united as brothers of the Ottoman family. In 1912, one of the two main Armenian political organisations promoted the shared interest of all Ottoman citizens. In 1912, the Ottoman governor of Jerusalem, Mehdi Bey, visited the decades-old Jewish Zionist colony of Rishon LeZion along with the Muslim mayor of Jerusalem, Hussein al-Husayni, the chief rabbi of Jaffa, the Arab Jew Albert Antébi, from the AIU, and other Jewish colonists, including the Zionist representative Arthur Ruppin. They were met with an orchestra playing the Ottoman anthem.[69] The governor applauded them for bringing economic progress to Palestine, and visited a Jewish farming school, a synagogue, and Tel Aviv. In 1913, an Arab congress upheld the integrity of the empire. On the eve of the First World War, most Ottoman Jews viewed the Zionist programme to create a Jewish state in Palestine with indifference or hostility.

Yet by 1914, few of these men promoted a reinvigorated empire, Ottoman patriotism, or interconfessional imperial union. The majority supported ethnonationalist claims. During the First World War the rulers of the empire abandoned interconfessional solidarity in favour of religious and racial unity. One result was that in 1915 the Armenians were deported to their deaths. The Greek Orthodox were expelled from Anatolia. Arabs and Turks, once vital partners in the imperial project, viewed each other as oppressor or traitor. And in Palestine, Christians and Muslims united against Zionists, who began establishing a Jewish national home that would segregate native Jews from their neighbours and their empire. Ottomanism failed to keep the empire and its citizens together.

Ottomanism was not mere propaganda, an official imperial project that had no impact on its citizens, or political opportunism by Muslim Turkish rulers driven by reason of state, or even the origin of Turkish nationalism. The newly emergent Muslim,

Christian, and Jewish urban middle and upper classes – lawyers, doctors, businessmen, journalists, schoolteachers, government clerks – engaged in the task of strengthening and solidifying imperial citizenship. They were members of the same branches of the revolutionary Committee of Union and Progress (CUP) and Masonic lodges, launched boycotts of the Ottoman enemy Austria-Hungary, engaged in parliamentary elections and politics, served in the provincial councils and local chambers of commerce, engaged in economic and commercial partnerships to build public works, expressed their views in a newly free press, and extolled the necessity of universal conscription. Jewish lawyer Shlomo Yellin, known also as Suleiman Effendi, son of an Arab Jewish mother and Ashkenazi father, member of the Beirut branch of the CUP, declared to a gathering of like-minded men in 1909 that 'in the Ottoman Empire the different peoples are equal to one another and it is not lawful to divide according to race; the Turkish, Arab, Armenian, and Jewish elements have mixed one with the other, and all of them are connected together, moulded into one shape for the holy *vatan* [fatherland]'.[70] Yet the irreconcilable differences between individual and ethno-religious interests and gap between the promises and shortcomings of Ottomanism led to conflict.

Despite sincere intentions to save the homeland by linking its citizens together regardless of religion, ethnicity, or mother tongue, structural constraints ensured that the project failed. The Ottoman Empire remained a Muslim-ruled state that was wary of enfranchising and arming Christians, and promoted Muslim and ethnic Turks above all others. Vocal Muslims declared that equality between Muslims, Christians, and Jews contravened Islamic law. Christian and Jewish religious leaders abhorred giving up their power and privilege and demanded proportional representation of their communities in Parliament. Christian and Jewish youth avoided conscription. The Jewish–Muslim alliance provoked a split between society's constituent elements.

The Ottoman MP Riza Tevfik supported the mass movement of Jews to the empire, to bring prosperity and serve as an ally and counterweight to the allegedly disloyal Greeks:

> The Jew in Turkey [Ottoman Empire] is no stranger, and we have need of him. I say this, not merely as a Philo-Jew, but from my conviction as a Turkish [Ottoman] patriot. We need [the Jew] as a powerful counterweight to another alien element. This is the Greek against whom we can only hold our own ... Only the Jew can hold his own with the Greeks, because the Jew is much more capable, industrious and reliable.[71]

The changed demographic realities ensuing from the Balkan Wars of 1912–13 – the removal of Muslims from Southeastern Europe and the expulsion of Christians from western Anatolia, all while the Zionist movement proclaimed support for the Ottomans – and the Armenian Genocide of 1915 and the massacres of Assyrians in 1916 – made a union of Christians and Muslims a dead letter. Islamic propaganda including the call to jihad, or holy war, was used openly in politics thereafter, as the empire was reconceived as a union of Muslim peoples. Arabs complained that they were treated as colonised peoples, not on an equal footing with their Turkish masters. An increasing number of Ottoman Jews sided with the Zionists. Palestinian Muslim peasants and Christian and Muslim nationalists united to protest against the sale of land for the purpose of settling Jewish immigrants. The Balfour Declaration of 1917 guaranteed that Britain, which began its internationally sanctioned occupation of Palestine after the First World War, supported the

Zionist effort to establish a state for the Jewish minority and not a shared homeland for all its citizens.

Whilst the First World War raged, on 2 November 1917 the British foreign secretary and former Conservative prime minister Sir Arthur James Balfour wrote a letter to Lionel Walter Rothschild, 2nd Baron Rothschild, a leader of Anglo-Jewry:

> I have much pleasure in conveying to you, on behalf of His Majesty's Government, the following declaration of sympathy with Jewish Zionist aspirations which has been submitted to, and approved, by the Cabinet:
> 'His Majesty's government view with favour the establishment in Palestine of a national home for the Jewish people, and will use their best endeavours to facilitate the achievement of this object, it being clearly understood that nothing shall be done which may prejudice the civil and religious rights of existing non-Jewish communities in Palestine, or the rights and political status enjoyed by Jews in any other country.'
> I should be grateful if you would bring this declaration to the knowledge of the Zionist Federation.[72]

It was thanks to the efforts of the Manchester-based Zionist leader and future president of Israel Chaim Weizmann that the Balfour Declaration referred to the 90 per cent of the population that was Muslim and Christian as 'non-Jewish' and not deserving of political or national rights.

Prime Minister David Lloyd George supported Zionism and believed it was a just cause. He was motivated as much by Christian biblical sentiment to resurrect the Jewish nation of ancient Israel as by the anti-Semitic belief that Jews are disproportionately influential, so much so that Jews in the neutral US and Russia would rally their government to support the Allies in the ongoing war effort. Lloyd George also wanted to limit Jewish immigration to Britain, as did Balfour, whose government in 1905 authored the Aliens Act for that purpose.[73] Despite this fact, Lloyd George's Parliamentary Private Secretary was Philip Gustave Sassoon, of the Baghdad Jewish merchant family, whose home was noted for its 'Moorish courtyard'.[74] Sassoon was castigated by Chaim Weizmann for being 'the only man to ignore the whole business' of the Palestine Mandate, despite being 'the only Jewish member of the British delegation'.[75] Lloyd George also aimed for the British Empire to control Palestine as a bridge between its colonies in Egypt and India.[76]

The Ottoman alliance with Germany during the war meant they had chosen the losing side, with catastrophic consequences for Jewish–Muslim relations. After defeating the Ottomans, the commander-in-chief of the British forces in Palestine, Field Marshal Edmund Allenby, entered Jerusalem on 11 December 1917. He was a man whose daily habit was to read the Bible and *The Historical Geography of the Holy Land*, whose frontispiece was a map entitled 'The Semitic World'.[77] Its author, George Adam Smith, noted that 'Israel belonged to "the Semitic race"', for whom the 'Arabian peninsula and the deserts obtruding from it upon Syria have been from time immemorial their breeding ground and proper home'.[78] Referring to the dhimma pact, abrogated more than half a century earlier, Allenby declared to Jerusalemites:

> Since your city is regarded with affection by three of the great religions of mankind, and its soil has been consecrated by the prayers and pilgrimages of multitudes of

devout people of these three religions for many centuries, therefore do I make it known to you that every sacred building, monument, holy spot, shrine, traditional site, endowment, pious bequest, or customary place of prayer will be maintained and protected according to the existing customs and beliefs of those to whose faith they are sacred ... in remembrance of the magnanimous act of the Caliph Omar.[79]

Never mind such declared magnanimity, the World Zionist Organisation understood what this meant:

The Declaration of His Majesty's Government [the Balfour Declaration] coincides with the triumphant march of the British Army in Palestine ... It is at such a moment, while the army of Great Britain is taking possession of Palestine, that Mr Balfour assures us that Great Britain will help us in the establishment of a National Home in Palestine. This is the beginning of the fulfilment.[80]

For those promoting an antagonistic view of Jewish–Muslim relations, it is not that the conflict over Palestine brought about 'a situation overwrought with violence'. It *revealed* it. Palestine only darkened an already sombre picture. And what darkened it was not Palestine per se: what 'the Arab world refused to accept' was rather 'the Jews' emancipation'.[81] Once subjugated and humiliated, the Jews were always to be subjugated and humiliated. It was the overturning of the master/servant relationship and the restoring of the Jews' humanity that so riled the Muslims.

Their differences led to a mutual clash of misunderstanding, as well as stubborn competition for the same land. Local observers saw the writing on the wall. According to the Lebanese

Maronite intellectual Najib Azoury, author of *The Awakening of the Arab Nation in Turkish Asia* (1906):

> Two important phenomena, of the same nature but opposed, which have not yet attracted anyone's attention, are emerging at this moment in Asiatic Turkey. They are the awakening of the Arab nation and the latent effort of the Jews to reconstitute on a very large scale the ancient kingdom of Israel. These two movements are destined to confront each other continuously, until one prevails over the other. The outcome of this struggle, between two peoples that represent two contradictory principles, may shape the destiny of the whole world.[82]

The correctness of his premonition was verified at the end of the First World War with the Balfour Declaration promising a national home for the Jewish people in the British Mandate of Palestine. The troubles that this decision generated in Palestine stirred up tension between Jews and Muslims in all the lands around the Mediterranean. Against a backdrop of cultural and political alienation aggravated by the consequences of European colonisation and the appearance of anti-Jewish myths belonging to Christian anti-Semitic heritage, relations between Jews and Muslims had never been as bad since the intrusion of Europe in North Africa and the Middle East. For Palestinian Muslims the Balfour Declaration in 1917 and thirty years later the establishment of the Jewish state led to a view that Israel is the 'bitter fruit of the collusion between European imperialism and Jewish Zionism'.[83] Anti-Semitism peddled by Europeans and local Christians found favour in this environment.

Throughout history, when there is a triangular relationship among Jews, Muslims, and Christians, and Christians are on

Transforming Jewish–Muslim Relations

top, relations between Jews and Muslims worsen. This was the case in Palestine beginning in 1917, which has been called 'the first declaration of war on Palestine'.[84] European colonialism was one of the factors in the modern world that transformed relations between Jews and Muslims. In the case of Palestine, it was British colonialism that had the most profound effect, for the British ensured the creation of a Jewish state in Palestine. In the words of Lord Balfour, Zionism 'is rooted in age-long traditions, in present needs, in future hopes, of far profounder import than the desires and prejudices of the 700,000 Arabs who now inhabit that ancient land'.[85]

What critics of Israel see is a process whereby Jews escaped their Orientalisation by the West, identified with European colonialism, and colonised and Orientalised Muslims, the Palestinians. This simplistic view is countered by the argument that Zionism itself gave political independence to a persecuted minority (which in turn persecutes a people which became a minority in the land they took over). In so doing, the state of Israel missed a chance to resurrect the historical bond of Jew as ally of the Muslim united in a Jewish–Muslim symbiosis.

After conquering the land in 1917, on 25 April 1920 Britain was granted a mandate over Palestine at the San Remo Conference, just as France received the mandate over Syria. According to article 22 of its covenant, the League of Nations created mandates so that 'civilised' and 'advanced nations' could see to the 'well-being and development' of 'people not yet able to stand by themselves'.

In the immediate post-conquest period, the British and French aimed to bring together the 'Semites', Arab and Jew – the 'racial thread[s] that bound the post-Ottoman tapestry'.[86] In 1917 the Zionist executive member Nahum Sokolov confirmed:

Our membership of the Semitic race, our title to a place in the civilisation of the world and to influence the world and take our share in the development of civilisation, have always been emphasised. If racial kinship really counts, if great associations exist which must serve as a foundation for the future, these associations exist between us and the Arabs.[87]

In 1918 Chaim Weizmann met with the nationalist Arab leader Prince Faysal in Jordan, both wearing the keffiyeh, publicly proclaiming Arab–Jewish amity.[88] In 1919 the two signed an agreement to implement the Balfour Declaration while Zionists assisted the economic development of the proposed independent Arab kingdom of the Hijaz, 'mindful of the racial kinship and ancient bonds existing between the Arabs and the Jewish people'.[89] The alliance was short-lived.

On 24 July 1922 the League of Nations ratified the British Mandate of Palestine. The British were the 'advanced nation' that would develop Palestine until its Jewish inhabitants were prepared to govern themselves. Recognising 'the historical connection of the Jewish people with Palestine and to the grounds for reconstituting their national home in that country', the preamble of the British Mandate stated the responsibility of Britain (the Mandatory) to establish a Jewish state in Palestine, incorporating the Balfour Declaration. Article 2 states:

> The Mandatory shall be responsible for placing the country under such political, administrative and economic conditions as will secure the establishment of a Jewish national home, as laid down in the preamble, and the development of self-governing institutions, and also for safeguarding the civil and religious rights of all the inhabitants of Palestine, irrespective of race and religion.[90]

The Zionist executive of Palestine became the Jewish Agency, officially recognised by the British to represent all Jews in the Mandate, a de facto Jewish proto-government.[91] Neither the word 'Arab' nor 'Palestinian' appeared in the articles of the Mandate, nor were Muslims or Christians given political rights or similar self-governing representatives and institutions as the Jews, who made up only a small minority of the population.[92] Hebrew was made an official language of the country along with Arabic, and the Mandatory was enjoined to facilitate Jewish purchase of land in fertile and strategic areas, ease Jewish immigration, and allow the new arrivals to acquire citizenship.

Like the French in Algeria, the British divided and ruled native Jews and Muslims, promoting the former over the latter, worsening relations between the two. Unlike the French, however, Britain was not interested in making Jews into British citizens, but in preparing them for their own sovereign state. While preparing Jews for statehood, Britain only allowed for a religious leader and religious council to represent Muslims.

The British continued late Ottoman transformations in the status of Jews, making them equals. Muslims could not understand why they were playing such a pre-eminent role in the eyes of the new rulers. There were anti-Jewish riots in the Jewish quarter of Jerusalem in April 1920 and in Jaffa in May 1921.[93] Late in 1920 a national Palestinian congress was held in Haifa which aimed to create an autonomous Palestine under British rule and created an executive committee to serve as an intermediary between the Muslim population and the British, mirroring the Jewish Agency. The British recognised it in 1929, although it had little influence. It ceased to exist in 1935.[94]

In 1922 the British government created the Supreme Muslim Council, headed by the young mufti of Jerusalem, Hajj Amin al-Husseini (see Chapter 6).[95] In 1923 the Nashashibi family founded the Palestinian Arab National Party. Awni Abd al-Hadi established the Independence Party in 1932, but he was discredited for selling land to Jews.[96] A Liberal Party also existed briefly, as did other anti-Zionist parties in the 1930s. Muslim Palestinians had many political venues to influence the British and to organise against the Jewish Agency.

Opposition to the Zionist project turned violent in August 1929, fomented by the mufti, on the pretext that Jews intended to seize the prayer area in front of the Western Wall, and the entire Dome of the Rock.[97] Muslims attacked Jews in the Jewish quarter of Jerusalem and massacred hundreds of Jews in Hebron and Safed.[98] It was this turn to violence that caused many Arab Jews in Palestine to turn to the Zionists, whose military leaders found them useful in security and intelligence operations because they spoke the local Arabic dialect.[99] Al-Husseini became the uncontested leader of the Palestinians in the 1930s as Palestinian Muslim nationalism rose to the fore in place of old Muslim–Christian associations of notables.

By 1936, because of the rise of Hitler, hundreds of thousands of Jewish refugees had fled Europe and settled in the Mandate; Jews formed one-third of the population of Palestine.[100] By that point the British dropped the category of the 'Semite' altogether. A royal commission sent by the British cabinet declared in 1937 that Jews and Muslims are of different races, the former European, the latter Oriental, and only territorial partition and racial separation would lead to peace. The Jewish national home is Western, the Palestinians are Asians, and one could not expect them to coexist, for they 'shared no common ground'.[101]

Muslims organised boycotts and general strikes to protest British policy. This turned to open revolt between 1936 and 1939. The mufti secretly supported Izz al-Din al-Qassam's clandestine military, which began attacking Jewish villages in the

Galilee.[102] He was killed by the British in 1935, and his funeral in Haifa demonstrated how all Muslim political parties viewed him as a hero.[103] Muslims realised their political efforts to stop Jewish immigration were futile, especially as the rise of the Nazis increased the number of Jews seeking refuge in Palestine. They turned to a general strike demanding an end to Jewish immigration, the prohibition of land sales to Jews, and establishment of a national government responsible to a representative council.[104] The general strike shut down the railways and the ports of Jaffa and Haifa for six months, but harmed the Muslim labour force while helping Jewish workers and the Jewish economy by boosting a new Jewish port at Tel Aviv.[105]

Muslims attacked government buildings and the British military. The British suppressed the revolt violently in such towns as Nablus and Jaffa.[106] Attacks in urban areas were joined by attacks in the countryside as militants arrived from Iraq, Syria, and Jordan directed by a former Iraqi officer, Fawzi al-Qa'uqji, who set up his base in the north, serving as commander-in-chief of the revolt.

The British established a royal commission to investigate the roots of the troubles. The high commissioner accepted Muslims' (and Arab Christians') demand to stop Jewish immigration during the work of the commission, which was accepted by the British cabinet.[107] To re-establish public order the British decided to send another military division to Palestine. The Muslims responded by calling off the general strike and military actions. Despite earlier agreement, the Peel Commission, named for its head, Lord Robert Peel, began its work in Palestine without the British ending Jewish immigration, so the general strike resumed. The Peel Commission published its conclusions in July 1937. The main recommendation, adopted officially by the British government, was the end of the British Mandate in

Palestine and its replacement by a land divided into a homogeneous Jewish state and a homogeneous Arab (Muslim) state, which would be accompanied by an exchange of populations, and a neutral territory that contained areas important to Christians including Nazareth and Jerusalem, and a corridor to the port of Jaffa. The Arab state would comprise 85 per cent of Palestine, made up of the West Bank and the Negev desert, and would be reunited with Transjordan to form an independent state.[108] The Jewish state would possess the coastal plain from Haifa to Tel Aviv, and the northern Galilee. Muslims rejected the report. Jewish leaders were divided. While the Twentieth Zionist Congress rejected it, David Ben Gurion, president of the executive committee of the Jewish Agency, accepted it. Some months after proposing it, the British government rejected its own report as unrealisable. But the idea of partition was established.

The second stage of the revolt broke out with the assassination of the British commissioner of the Galilee. The British responded by announcing a warrant for the arrest of the mufti, outlawing the Arab High Committee, and arresting or deporting most nationalist leaders. The mufti escaped to Lebanon, from where he directed the revolt, attacking the British and Jews alike.[109] The reprisals against Muslim civilians by the Irgun, a Jewish paramilitary organisation that split from the main clandestine Jewish defence organisation, the Haganah, founded in the 1920s, incited more Muslim attacks on Jews, which reached their apogee in summer 1938. By the end of 1939 the British had violently retaken control of Jerusalem, Acre, and Jaffa and ended the revolt at the cost of many Palestinians killed, wounded, imprisoned, or exiled.[110]

The British realised that without taking into consideration the views of the Muslims they would not be able to resolve tensions. In February 1939 the Conference of St James in London invited Jewish and Muslim delegations from Palestine as well as Arab states including Egypt.[111] The Muslim delegations refused to meet directly and officially with the Jewish delegation, as they did not recognise the Jewish Agency.[112] As the two sides had opposite views on the question of Jewish immigration, agreement was impossible, and the conference ended without any progress towards compromise or agreement.

The White Paper published in May 1939 by Neville Chamberlain's government presented a new British approach which managed to alienate both Jews and Muslims. It foresaw the creation of a Jewish home within an independent Palestinian state in ten years, but limited the immigration of Jews to 75,000 people over the next five years, after which it would be dependent on the consent of the Muslims, and forbade the Jewish purchase of land in most of the country.[113] The government's aim was not 'that Palestine should be converted into a Jewish State against the will of the Arab [Muslim and Christian] population of the country'.[114] These planks were incompatible with the Balfour Declaration, which was incorporated into the Mandate. Facing an impending world war, where Muslims in India and the Middle East would be crucial to the British war effort, the UK government turned away from the pro-Zionist policy it had promoted since 1917. The Jewish Agency rejected the White Paper and organised clandestine immigration, to which Britain responded by blockading Palestine, leading to the death or arrest and imprisonment of Jewish refugees from Nazi Europe. David Ben Gurion declared, 'We will fight in the war against Hitler as if there was no White Paper, and we will fight against the White Paper as if there were no war.'[115]

The Arab High Committee also rejected the White Paper. The mufti fled to Iraq and then to Nazi Germany, where he was the honoured guest of Hitler, and from where he notoriously promoted Muslim support of the Nazis and the genocide of the Jews (see Chapter 6). At the same time, many Jews served in the British army, leading to the creation of the Jewish Brigade in September 1944, which saw combat in Italy in 1945. The Jewish Agency vociferously supported Britain.

The Holocaust changed the way Western Jews viewed Arab Jewry. With most of the Ashkenazi population annihilated, they looked towards the Islamic world to recruit Jews to boost the population of the Jewish community in Palestine. From 1943 the Jewish Agency considered 'the entire Zionist project now at risk of coming to naught for lack of a living nation in search of a state'.[116] In 1944, when his dream of welcoming two million Jews to Palestine had been destroyed in the gas chambers, Ben Gurion asked, 'Where are we going to find Jews in order to populate Palestine?'[117] In June 1945 the Jewish Agency asked the British High Commission to issue visas to Jews in Muslim-majority lands.

Yet the Agency still had a pejorative view of Arab Jews. They arranged two types of housing for immigrants: camps on the coastal plain set up for a maximum three-month stay for European Jews, and transit camps in the desert set up for a one- to two-year stay for the Arab Jews. After 1948 the Arab world's Jewish communities were viewed as a 'demographic reservoir', a guarantee of the continuity of the Jewish people.[118] After the war not only French Zionists but also the AIU changed their view. Genocide and French anti-Semitism during the war caused the AIU to support more Hebrew instruction and contacts with the Jewish Agency.[119] According to a French Jewish intellectual, 'the mellah of the Maghreb constitutes the last biological reserve in the world of the Diaspora', and its people were necessary for Israel.[120] Yet Zionism was not strong even after the war in these countries. Few desired to leave their homeland.

After the war, the Jewish Agency continued its efforts to purchase land and to bring in survivors of the Holocaust who could not immigrate to Palestine. Those who attempted to run the British maritime blockade were interned in camps on Cyprus. The Jewish Agency did its best to smuggle them illegally to Palestine, as its official position was no longer to seek a Jewish state under British rule, but an independent Jewish state.[121] As neither the US nor UK would accept them, the American President Harry Truman asked the UK to allow 100,000 Jewish concentration camp survivors living in displaced persons camps in Europe to immigrate to Palestine, but the British refused.[122] In 1946 Truman repeated his support for a Jewish state, but the British foreign secretary, Ernest Bevin, was opposed.

The Palestinian nationalist movement was characterised by disunity and infighting. It was little supported by the surrounding newly independent Arab states such as Transjordan, whose King Abdullah (assassinated by a Palestinian in Jerusalem in 1951) secretly met with Zionist leaders to plan the division of the territory.[123] The Palestinians were not helped by the fact that the mufti returned from a defeated Nazi Germany and was considered the leader of the Palestinian movement from 1946.[124]

In contrast, the Zionist movement in Palestine was well organised, well financed, diplomatically astute, internationally supported, especially by the new global powers the US and Soviet Union, and well armed. In 1946 Zionists blew up British military headquarters in the King David Hotel in Jerusalem at a cost of ninety-one lives. They were confident and not afraid of the coloniser.

On 14 February 1947 the British prime minister, Clement Attlee, announced his decision to hand Palestine to the United Nations. In April 1947 the United Nations formed a committee made up of eleven members, two Muslim (from India and Iran), two from the Soviet bloc (Yugoslavia and Czechoslovakia), and seven from neutral nations to find a solution to the question of Palestine.[125] The Arab High Committee refused to cooperate, precluding any Palestinian Muslim voice from being heard, but the Jewish Agency met with the committee. The commission recommended ending the Mandate as soon as possible but concluded that 'the development of a solution fully acceptable to both Jews and Arabs seems totally impossible'.[126] The majority of the commission (seven of the eleven members) presented a plan for the partition of Palestine divided into a Jewish and an Arab (Muslim) state linked in an economic union and a special international status for Jerusalem. The two sides had irreconcilable demands, and partition could only partially fulfil the national aspirations of each.[127] The Iranian, Indian, and Yugoslav members of the committee proposed instead a federal solution 'that unites Arabs and Jews as loyal and patriotic citizens of an independent Palestine'. Muslims rejected the plan. Jews accepted it, as it was the first time international blessing was given to their state. The Soviet Union supported partition, despite the anti-Zionist activity of communist Jews in Arab countries.

In the second major turning point since the Balfour Declaration, on 29 November 1947 the UN General Assembly adopted Resolution 181, with thirty-three states in favour, including the US and the Soviet Union, thirteen against, and ten abstaining, including the UK.[128] Palestine was divided between a Jewish community and an Arab Muslim and Christian community that was twice its size. The Arab state comprised 42 per cent of the Mandate and included the West Bank, Gaza, a strip of the Negev bordering Gaza, and half the Galilee including Nazareth. The Jewish state consisted of 56 per cent of the Mandate and was made up of the Negev desert, the coastal plain from Haifa to Jaffa, and half the Galilee including Safed and Tiberias. The remaining territory, including Jerusalem and Bethlehem, was to be governed by an international regime. A new phase in Jewish–Muslim relations began.

From the time of Muhammad in seventh-century Medina, to 1947, Jews had almost always lived under Muslim (or Christian) rule in the Middle East and Europe. From 1948, Jews ruled over Muslims (and Christians). At the same time, Ashkenazi Jews, who had never ruled over anyone, were superior to Sephardi and Arab Jews in the Jewish state. For the first time in history since the Khazar kingdom 900 years earlier, Jews ruled over Muslims in a Jewish state. For the first time the state had a Jewish majority and was ruled according to Jewish law.

On 14 May 1948 the last British High Commissioner of Palestine steamed away from the port of Haifa on HMS *Euryalus*. On the same day the head of the Jewish Agency, Ben Gurion, stood beneath a portrait of Theodor Herzl at the Tel Aviv Museum, and proclaimed the establishment of the Jewish state of Israel as a philharmonic orchestra played the national anthem ('Hatikvah', 'The Hope').[129] The following day Egyptian planes bombed Tel Aviv and five Arab armies attacked: the Lebanese and Syrians from the north, the Jordanians, whose Transjordanian Arab Legion was trained and commanded by the British, and Iraqis from the east, and the Egyptians from the south. The Soviet Union gave full backing to Israel, supplying it with weapons, fighter jets, military equipment, and military training, while the US began to promote the creation of a single state under UN tutelage.[130] Nevertheless, the US, followed by the Soviet Union, Eastern bloc, and Latin American states, recognised the new state of Israel.[131] Arab nationalist Fawzi al-Qa'uqji formed an army in Syria financed by the Arab League, founded in Cairo in 1945, to attack Israel.[132]

During the six months between the partition resolution in

November 1947 and Israel's declaration of independence in May 1948 the main protagonists were the 600,000 Jewish Palestinians and the 1.2 million Muslim (and a minority of Christian) Palestinians.[133] In the 1880s, when political Zionism and Arab nationalism first emerged, there were 25,000 indigenous Jews of Palestine. According to Ottoman sources, there were approximately 600,000 inhabitants in 1914. When Britain conducted its first census after the Palestine Mandate was established in 1922, they counted 750,000 inhabitants, of whom 589,000 were Muslims, 84,000 were Jews, and 71,500 were Christians.[134] Over the course of the British Mandate, from 1922 to 1947, as Palestine's population rose from 650,000 to 1.7 million, the proportion of Muslims decreased from 76 to 59 per cent as the Jewish population rose from 13 to 32 per cent.[135]

Attacks on a Jewish bus in Lydda and on the Jewish commercial heart of Jerusalem immediately followed the resolution. The Jews of Haifa were also targeted. Jews engaged in reprisals, conducted by the Haganah, as the Etzel and Lehi paramilitaries attacked Muslim civilians and British soldiers.[136] In the north, Qa'uqji's forces attacked kibbutzim, causing Haganah reprisals on Muslim villages.[137] Each side attacked each other's means of transport, blocking routes and laying mines.[138]

The Jewish side knew the withdrawal of the British in May would lead to invasion by the surrounding Arab states. The Haganah accordingly adopted a new strategy, becoming a regular army known as the Zahal (Israel Defense Forces, IDF). Their plan in March 1948 was to capture key positions and strategic areas to give them military advantage, such as occupying Arab villages north and south of Jerusalem to lift a siege of the Jewish half of the city.[139] One of these villages, Deir Yassin, occupying a strategic hilltop location 5 kilometres from Jerusalem, was occupied by Etzel and Lehi. The Jewish irregulars carried out a massacre of around 100 civilians on 9 April.[140] A reprisal by Muslim forces a few days later killed eighty Jews in a convoy to the Hadassah hospital in Jerusalem.

In mid-May, the Israeli army occupied other mixed cities including Haifa, Safed, and Tiberias, most of the Galilee, Acre, Jaffa, and West Jerusalem, expelling more than 100,000 Muslim and Christian inhabitants. The Jewish army won this pre-war war, controlling an almost uninterrupted chain of territories peopled by Jews and the major urban centres peopled and then de-peopled of Muslims and Christians. Prior to the declaration of independence, the army met its goals. It was the result neither of divine intervention, nor of collusion with the British, but of its own strategy.[141] Unlike the divided Muslim population, the Jews spent the thirty years of the Mandate preparing for the eventuality of national autonomy, establishing political and military institutions and state structures and governmental organs throughout the country.[142] Good political organisation allowed the Jewish community to concentrate its activities on the precise objectives of its well-planned projects despite its numerical inferiority.[143]

When the armies of the surrounding nations attacked, they failed to save the Muslims and destroy Israel. The IDF stopped their assault on the Jewish urban centres of Tel Aviv, Jerusalem, and Haifa with small arms, as well as on most of the kibbutzim.[144] After a month of fighting, a one-month ceasefire was agreed, after which fighting resumed.[145] Israel repelled the Syrian army and defeated Qa'uqji's forces in the north, and expelled the Arab Legion from Lydda and Ramle, 20 kilometres east of Tel Aviv. Its soldiers massacred hundreds of civilians in Lydda and expelled the 50,000 Muslims of the two towns and occupied other Muslim villages to relieve the siege of Jerusalem.[146] The Druze of the Galilee and Christians and Muslims of Nazareth surrendered to the Jewish forces.¹⁴⁷ Most of the Muslims of the north, fearing reprisals for having supported Qa'uqji or the Syrian or Lebanese armies, fled to Lebanon. The conquest of Muslim villages and mixed cities situated within the future state of Israel led to the expulsion or flight of hundreds of thousands of Muslim and Christian inhabitants to Gaza, the West Bank, and Lebanon in May and June.

The UN imposed a three-month ceasefire from July through to October.¹⁴⁸ Jordan, boasting the most formidable Muslim army, made a secret agreement with Israel to end hostilities.¹⁴⁹ In October the Israelis expelled Egypt from much of the south but not from Gaza, where 200,000 Muslim refugees arrived, and took over most of the Galilee. At the end of November Israel and Jordan signed a ceasefire, allowing Israel to keep West Jerusalem and the Hebrew University's campus on Mount Scopus, while Jordan controlled East Jerusalem including the Old City.¹⁵⁰ In December the Israelis pushed Egyptian troops back into the Sinai, causing Britain to give an ultimatum to Israel to stop its advance and withdraw, and causing Egypt to sign a ceasefire in January 1949.¹⁵¹ Syria withdrew its troops and signed an armistice in summer 1949. Iraq never signed one but evacuated its forces as well.

Between 100,000 and 150,000 Muslims fled at that time, and a further 10,000–20,000 were expelled by Israel in 1949–50, after the war. Israel viewed Muslims in sensitive border areas as a potential fifth column and aimed to decrease the Muslim population and increase the Jewish population of the state.¹⁵² Majority-Muslim Palestine became majority-Jewish Israel. For Jews, recognition by the UN of Israel as a member state in 1949 was the attainment of a dream. As Ben Gurion declared, establishing the nation, 'the State of Israel will be open to the immigration of Jews from all countries of their dispersion' yet will also 'promote the development of the country for the benefit of all its inhabitants', as Muslim (and Christian) citizens in Israel would have 'full and equal citizenship'.[153] For Palestinian Muslims and Christians, it was a nightmare. In the term coined by Constantine Zureiq, professor of history at the American University of Beirut, the loss of Palestine was a *nakba*, a catastrophe.[154] Today it is commemorated annually by Palestinians as the dispossession of their land and the displacement and ethnic cleansing of a people.[155] Most Muslims became refugees, although those in Israel became Israeli citizens and those in Jordan became Jordanian citizens. Between 600,000 and 750,000 ended up in Gaza, ruled by Egypt; the West Bank and East Jerusalem, annexed by Jordan; Syria; or Lebanon. Between 150,000 and 160,000 remained in Israel as a minority among three-quarters of a million Jews in 1948.

Six hundred thousand Jews arrived from Muslim-majority countries by 1951. It was a de facto population exchange, or ethnic cleansing, as most of the Muslims of Palestine/Israel became refugees, and the Jews of the Muslim-majority states mainly went to Israel. Israel's Law of Return (1950) declared that 'every Jew has the right to immigrate to the country' and become a citizen.[156] No such right exists for the Muslims (and Christians) and their descendants who were expelled from or left Israel since 1948.

Israel remained in a state of war with all of its Muslim-majority neighbours and refused to allow the return of Muslim refugees without a peace agreement.[157] Until 1966 Muslim citizens were ruled according to martial law, a system inherited from the British.[158] Seen as potential enemies, Muslims were treated as second-class citizens and every aspect of their lives was controlled. They were discriminated against, viewed as hostile by the government, and given fewer public services and financial resources. Their land and homes were confiscated and given to Jews. The centuries-old relationship was reversed: Muslims became the dhimmi tolerated by Jews, although Israel does not permit interfaith marriage. Yet it is dhimmitude with a twist: legally citizens, but exempt from conscription, small numbers of Muslims (as well as Druze and Christians) have been elected to Parliament since the first sitting in 1949. They have represented parties across the political spectrum, including left- and right-wing Zionist parties, as well as the communists, whose leadership is mainly Jewish but rank and file largely Muslim.[159]

The establishment of Israel inaugurated the fourth time in history when Jews have been more powerful than the Muslims with whom they live. This transformation in Jewish–Muslim relations has led to one of the worst periods, characterised by a great rupture, ongoing antagonism, strife, and some of the worst violence in the history of their relations on the largest scale.

On 5 June 1967, responding to Egypt moving troops into the Sinai peninsula, the Israeli air force launched simultaneous attacks destroying most of the fighter jets and radar systems of Egypt, Jordan, and Syria. Having taken control of the air, the Israeli army launched its ground forces into Gaza, Sinai, East Jerusalem, including the Old City, the West Bank, and the Golan Heights. On 8 June at the Western Wall of the Temple, Rabbi Shlomo Goren, Israeli army chaplain, blew the *shofar*, the ram's horn blown on the Jewish High Holy Days, and declared, 'This is the first time since the destruction of the Second Temple that all the Land of Israel is in our hands.'[160] Israel tripled in size. On 29 June Israel annexed East Jerusalem and proclaimed the city, divided into an Israeli West and Jordanian East since 1948, the reunified, eternal capital of the state of Israel.[161] Israel began to control the Jewish holy city of Hebron, site of the graves of the common prophetic ancestors of Jews and Muslims. Israel began to rule over 1.2 million Palestinians in the conquered territories.[162]

Of all the Arab–Israeli wars, the 1967 war had the greatest significance for Jews and Muslims alike. For religious Jews the capture of the holiest city in Judaism, the ancient Jewish capital and cult centre at the Temple Mount, was a miracle, an omen for the arrival of the Messiah, accompanied as it was by the re-establishment of ancient Israel from the Sinai Desert to the Sea of Galilee, from the Jordan Valley to the Mediterranean Sea. Jews rebuilt the Hurva synagogue and the Sephardic yeshiva Porat Yossef, established by Baghdadi Jews, both of which were destroyed by Jordan when it occupied East Jerusalem between 1948 and 1967. Among the yeshiva's notable alumni are Sephardi chief rabbis of Israel and several South American countries, leaders of Sephardi communities abroad, and leaders of the Israeli Sephardic religious movement and political party Shas (*Shomrei Sepharad*, the Guardians of the Sephardim). Shas was founded in 1984 by the purple-turbaned, golden-brocaded black gown-wearing, Baghdad-born Sephardi Chief Rabbi Ovadia Yosef. Shas, predominantly made up of Moroccans, plays a major role in Israeli politics, being the third largest party in the country, and coalition partner in governments of the left and right.

As a result of the war of 1967 hundreds of thousands of Muslims came under Israeli military rule, as Israeli military rule on its own Muslim citizens ended. The reunification of the territory of Palestine under one authority abolished frontiers for Israeli Muslims but opened new vistas for Muslims newly under Israeli rule. A resurgence of Palestinian identity and resistance to Israeli rule increased in the 1960s especially among educated, leftist, middle-class youth. They were angry at traditional leaders such as the mufti of Jerusalem and the other notables from Ottoman times who still shaped politics, and at the leaders of neighbouring countries who were more concerned about their own stability, such as Jordan and Saudi Arabia, or revolutionary changes, such as Egypt, than about the Palestinians, to whose cause they merely paid lip service.

In 1964 the Arab League in Cairo established the Palestine Liberation Organisation (PLO) headed by Yasser Arafat. Arafat – along with other Palestinian engineers, teachers, and professionals – had established Fatah in Kuwait five years earlier; its leaders called for 'direct and immediate action by Palestinians'.[163] By this they meant guerrilla attacks launched from Egyptian-occupied Gaza into Israel, which was a contributing factor to the 1967 war. The original PLO charter declared that only Jews living in Palestine before 1917 would be recognised as citizens. It argued that because Jews do not form a nation, they do not have the right to a state. Only the liberation of all Palestine will suffice, which includes the expulsion of Jews who are descended from people who arrived after the Balfour Declaration.[164] The PLO charter as amended in 1968 declared that all Palestinians residing in Palestine before 1947 and their descendants would be citizens of the future Palestinian state. Jews could also reside there, but the internationally recognised state of Israel and the ideology upon which it is based, Zionism, would be disestablished and replaced by a democratic Palestine where Jews, Muslims, and Christians would have equal rights.[165]

Arafat was invited to address the United Nations General Assembly in 1974, two years after Fatah took Israeli athletes hostage and murdered eleven of them during the summer Olympics in Munich.[166] Arafat ended his UN speech by declaring, 'Today I have come bearing an olive branch and a freedom-fighter's gun. Do not let the olive branch fall from my hand. Do not let the olive branch fall from my hand. Do not let the olive branch fall from my hand.'[167]

Denying the existence of the Israeli people and nation, repeatedly promoting the myth of interfaith harmony, Arafat distinguished between Zionists and Jews. Arafat criticised Zionism for the 'severing of Jews from their various homelands and subsequently their estrangement from their nations' without mentioning which nations or the existence of Arab Jews.[168] He claimed that when Zionist settlement of Palestine began in 1881, there were 10,000 Jews in Palestine, who 'enjoyed the religious tolerance characteristic of our civilisation'.[169] He waxed romantic about how the Palestinian Arabs set an example 'in the practice of religious tolerance and freedom of worship, acting as faithful guardians of the holy places of all religions', treasuring 'beautiful memories and vivid images of the religious brotherhood that was the hallmark of our Holy City' before the establishment of Israel.[170] He argued that 50,000 European Jews had settled in Palestine between 1882 and 1917, ignoring the wave of Yemeni and other Arab Jewish migrants. He mourned the fact that thirty years later the Zionists had succeeded in securing a state and settling more European Jews on the land, to the detriment of Muslims and Christians.

No mention was made of the more than half a million Arab Jews who arrived between 1948 and 1968. He contrasted the 600,000 Jews residing in the land in 1947 with 1.25 million Arabs. Arafat could not conceive of Jews being Arabs, although he condemned Israel's 'racial discrimination against Oriental Jews'.[171] He argued that 'Israeli law treats [Palestinians in Israel] as second-class citizens – even as third-class citizens since Oriental Jews are second-class citizens'.[172] He asserted that the causes of the clash 'do not stem from any conflict between two religions or two nationalisms', denying Jews the right to form their own nation, imagining them as dhimmi.[173] He claimed that the Palestinian movement 'has not been motivated by racial or religious factors. Its target has never been the Jew, as a person,' but the Zionist movement. Arafat insisted that Palestinians 'distinguish between Judaism and Zionism', maintaining opposition to the latter, but 'we respect the Jewish faith'.

In his 1974 speech, Arafat condemned Israel for committing 'acts of barbarism and terrorism' against Palestinians and calling the PLO terrorists, and not revolutionaries who had no other choice but to engage in justified armed struggle.[174] One could ask whether this justified the PLO and Palestinian Front for the Liberation of Palestine (PFLP) and offshoots going on a murderous rampage in Europe, hijacking civilian airliners, killing Jews at a Parisian synagogue (1980), Antwerp's Spanish and Portuguese synagogue (1981), a Viennese synagogue (1981), a Jewish restaurant in Paris (1982), and Rome's grand synagogue (1982), assaulting a cruise liner and throwing a wheelchair-bound American man overboard (1985), and attacking Istanbul's Neve Shalom synagogue (1986) as well. None of these were Israelis or had anything to do with Israel's oppression of Palestinians. Did their murders promote the Palestinian cause? Were they killed in the name of 'progress, justice, democracy and peace'?[175] Did it show that the Palestinians were 'neither vindictive nor vengeful' and 'have not lost the true method by which friend and foe are distinguished'? Were these, too, not 'crimes committed against the Jews' which Arafat ostensibly deplored? Declaring in 1974 that 'we do not wish one drop of either Jewish or Arab blood to be shed; neither do we delight in the continuation of killings for a single moment, once a just peace, based on our people's rights, hopes, and aspirations has been finally established', he implied the bloodshed would go on, including the slaughter of innocents, until Palestinian independence was achieved.[176] According to a leading Palestinian intellectual, the PLO's terrorist attacks 'did little to advance the Palestinian national cause, if indeed they did not harm it'.[177]

In 1975 the UN General Assembly passed a resolution declaring Zionism 'a form of racism and racial discrimination'.[178] Semite had been split from Semite; Jews and Muslims were no longer considered siblings.

In Israel, the announcement of the appropriation of 20,000 dunams of land in the Galilee in March 1976 led to the first mass protests by Israeli Muslims, when half a dozen young people were killed. This became the annual Land Day commemoration.[179]

Expanding settlements, continued discrimination, and politicisation by the PLO and other Palestinian groups contributed to the outbreak of the Palestinian uprising (intifada) in the Jabaliya refugee camp in Gaza in December 1987. It was triggered when an Israeli lorry struck two vans carrying Palestinian workers, killing four of them, which was perceived by Palestinians as a deliberate act of revenge for the murder of an Israeli in Gaza days earlier. The uprising spread to the West Bank and Jerusalem and was organised by a secret, grassroots leadership, outside the control of the PLO based in Tunis. It lasted six years, during which Israeli forces killed 1,000 Palestinians and Palestinians murdered 100 Israelis. It convinced Jordan to renounce all claims to the West Bank in 1988. Daily televised images of Israeli soldiers firing rubber bullets at rock-throwing Palestinian youths or beating them, like the pictures of civilians killed by the IDF in Lebanon in 1982, led to a decrease in the support of Israel by Jewish Americans, the largest and most influential Jewish community in the world, and increased support for the peace movement in Israel.

UN Resolution 247, passed nearly six months after the war of 1967, called for Israeli withdrawal from the territories it occupied as a result of that war in exchange for peace with the surrounding nation states, never once mentioning Palestinians:

(i) Withdrawal of Israel armed forces from territories

occupied in the recent conflict; (ii) Termination of all claims or states of belligerency and respect for and acknowledgement of the sovereignty, territorial integrity and political independence of every State in the area and their right to live in peace within secure and recognized boundaries free from threats or acts.[180]

It did not call for the creation of a Palestinian state.

Over two decades later, in 1988, Arafat and the PLO accepted UN Resolution 242 recognising the sovereignty of Israel, renounced terrorism, and declared the PLO charter claiming the entirety of Palestine to be obsolete, accepting a two-state solution.[181] Israel refused to negotiate with the PLO, or to accept the possibility of the creation of a Palestinian state, but agreed to talks with Jordan which included Palestinians at the Madrid Peace Conference in 1991, preceded by the UN revoking the resolution condemning Zionism as racism. The talks were limited to exploring Palestinian autonomy, and did not cover the most important topics, including sovereignty, refugee return, or the status of Jerusalem.[182]

Secret negotiations in Oslo between Israel and the PLO led to the Declaration of Principles of 1993 signed by Israeli Prime Minister Yitzhak Rabin and Arafat at the White House. Although Israel recognised the PLO as the representative of the Palestinians, and the PLO recognised the state of Israel, after a generation fighting against it, Palestinian grievances were not resolved and their hopes and dreams were not realised, as Israel did not recognise the need to create a Palestinian state alongside Israel.

New forms of Palestinian opposition to Israel emerged, spearheaded by the Islamist groups Hamas (Islamic Resistance Movement) and Islamic Jihad. Although the Palestinian

Authority was given control over education, health, taxation, and police, the questions of refugees, settlements, and the status of Jerusalem were not debated.[183] Jewish settlements expanded. Nothing was accomplished when Prime Minister Ehud Barak and Arafat met at Camp David in 2000. When Arafat passed away four years later, his supporters, reflecting an anti-Semitic canard, claimed Israel had poisoned the seventy-five-year-old.

The emergence of Islamist rather than secular guerrilla and political organisations, the assassination of Rabin by a far-right Israeli in 1995, and the outbreak in 2000 of the second intifada, in which Palestinians engaged in suicide bombings, led to further radicalisation of Israel's Muslim minority.[184] The second intifada was triggered by the actions of Likud Party leader Ariel Sharon, former minister of defence, culpable for the massacre of 1,300 Palestinians in the Sabra and Shatila refugee camps by Christian militias during the Israeli occupation of West Beirut in 1982. Accompanied by fellow right-wing politicians and hundreds of riot police, he spent forty-five minutes atop the Haram al-Sharif/Temple Mount and was met by rioting youths, whose violence quickly spread to the rest of Jerusalem and Ramallah.[185] According to Sharon, who would be elected prime minister a few months later, 'The Temple Mount is in our hands and will remain in our hands. It is the holiest site in Judaism, and it is the right of every Jew to visit the Temple Mount.'[186] The following day, 20,000 Muslims gathered on the Haram al-Sharif and rained stones down on riot police and Jews praying in the plaza of the Western Wall below. They were met by deadly force and the intifada by Israeli citizens and Palestinians in the territories began.[187] It lasted five years and was much more violent than the first intifada: more than 1,000 Israelis were killed, mostly civilians murdered at cafes, on buses, and in shopping malls by Palestinian suicide bombers, members of Islamist Hamas and

Islamic Jihad, or secularist Fatah. Nearly 5,000 Palestinians died, most killed by Israeli security forces but some by other Palestinians.[188]

Israel unilaterally decided to evacuate its military and civilians from Gaza in 2005, where the following year Hamas won the vote. Hamas has not held another poll, just as the secular Palestinian Authority headed by Fatah has ruled in part of the West Bank and not held an election since 2005. The Hamas military wing was named the Al-Qassam Brigades after Izz al-Din al-Qassam. Almost continually since 2009 the right-wing Benjamin Netanyahu has been Israeli prime minister. With Hamas representing the Palestinians, and Netanyahu the Israelis, Israel and Hamas went to war in 2012, 2014, and from 7 October 2023. In the war begun in 2023, Israelis and Palestinians alike have suffered the highest civilian and combatant death tolls and greatest civilian displacements since the 1948 war.[189]

Following the 1967 war a messianic dimension was added to the nationalist ideology of the Israeli–Palestinian conflict. For Arabs and Muslims, the traumatic defeat in 1967 of secular, revolutionary, anti-colonial regimes such as Egypt and Syria and colonialist-installed regimes such as Jordan contributed to the rise in popularity of religious extremists from Sayyid Qutb (executed by Egypt in 1966), who promoted war against 'crusaders and Zionists', to Iran's Islamist revolutionary leader Ayatollah Ruhollah Khomeini, Al-Qaeda leader Osama bin Laden (assassinated by the US in 2011), and Hamas. For Israelis, victory in the same war led to religious messianism becoming mainstream, as evidenced by the rise of Menachem Begin and Likud to power in 1977, followed by Ariel Sharon and Benjamin Netanyahu.[190]

After the 1967 war, at the instigation of a group of nationalist religious students, the first Jewish settlement was established in the West Bank, the first time since the creation of the state that religious Jews had become involved in questions of national security.[191] Strongly tinted by messianism, they were disciples of Rabbi Zvi Yehuda Kook's yeshiva in Jerusalem. Kook viewed the miraculous victory in the war and the Jewish conquest of the holy places in Jerusalem in Hebron and the biblical lands as a precursor of the arrival of the Messiah.[192] His disciples and their ideological descendants Gush Emunim (Bloc of the Faithful, founded in 1974) became the fiercest advocates of the creation of Jewish settlements in the occupied territories of Gaza, the West Bank, Jerusalem, and the Golan.[193] A right-wing religious and political movement, it was established to pressure the government to allow new Jewish settlements in the West Bank and Gaza. Its motto is 'The Land of Israel, for the people of Israel, according to the Torah of Israel'. It was favoured by Israel's first right-wing government, that of Menachem Begin which was voted into power in 1977, promoting an Israel 'from the river to the sea'.[194] Whereas in 1977 only 5,000 Jews lived in the West Bank, their number quintupled by 1983 and reached 160,000 by 2000, passing 250,000 in 2008 and 400,000 in 2012.[195] In 2025 there were an estimated 200,000 Israeli citizens living in East Jerusalem and more than 500,000 in the West Bank.

These religious zealots were countered by Shalom Achshav (Peace Now).[196] Founded in 1978, Peace Now grew in influence, holding mass protests against the crimes committed by Israel's Christian allies against Palestinians following the invasion of Lebanon to dislodge the PLO in 1982, at a time when media reports of IDF killings of civilians drew condemnation from American and Israeli Jews as never before.[197]

Bloc of the Faithful and Peace Now represent the two poles of Israeli society, conservative religious right and secular liberal left. The right-wing religious nationalists have proven dangerous to Palestinians – such as Baruch Goldstein's murder of thirty Muslims at prayer at the Cave of the Patriarchs in Hebron in 1994 – and to Israelis, notably when the Yemeni Jew Yigal Amir, who believed he was acting on God's orders, assassinated Rabin in 1995 for signing the Oslo Accords with the PLO. That event recalled how the Egyptian leader Anwar Sadat was assassinated by an Islamic fundamentalist in 1981 for signing peace accords with Israel in 1979, despite having surprised Israel in 1973 with Operation Badr, taking back the Sinai peninsula.

Unlike the religious nationalists, the secular leftist and member of Peace Now Amos Oz did not feel ecstatic in 1967. He remembers how he felt as a soldier patrolling the streets of the Old City of Jerusalem, city of his birth, in combat gear, several days after its capture:

> I perceived hostility and opposition, sycophancy, amazement and fear, humiliations and pitfalls. I wandered East Jerusalem like a man breaking into a forbidden place. It was painful. My hometown. The city of my dreams, the city invoked in nostalgia by my ancestors and by my people. And I am condemned to walking through its streets with a machine gun, as if I were one of those characters who haunted the nightmares of my childhood. To be a stranger in such a strange city.[198]

The 1967 war was a turning point.[199] It made Israel and Palestine the centre of preoccupation for world Jewry and world Muslims. In the Middle East it led to a decline in secular socialism in Israel and the loss of power of the Mapai (Labour) party, which had been in office from 1948 to 1977, with the concomitant rise in religious nationalism and messianism and Herut/Likud (Conservatives). Among Palestinians it led to an increase in religious fundamentalism, which contributed to the rise of religious nationalist movements (Hamas, Islamic Jihad) at the expense of secular ones (PLO, PFLP), a process seen across Muslim-majority societies.

Thirteen centuries after the Believers' exodus from Mecca to Medina, and the establishment of the first Muslim polity at the expense of local Jews, fate turned in the Jews' favour: the wars of 1948, 1956, and 1967 were 'theologically inconceivable and psychologically unbearable defeats for Muslims: the despicable dhimmi of the past became the arrogant victor of the present'.[200]

A book by the Egyptian fundamentalist thinker and Muslim Brotherhood leader Sayyid Qutb, *Our Struggle with the Jews*, published in the early 1950s and reprinted by the Saudi Arabian Government Press in 1970 displayed this new thinking about Jews, connecting 'European anti-Semitic ideas with Muslim sacred texts',[201] which would later be expressed by Islamist figures ranging from the Shi'i Ayatollah Ruholla Khomeini, who established the Islamic Republic of Iran, to the terrorist leader Osama bin Laden and Turkey's President Receb Tayyib Erdoğan (in power since 2003).[202] In his influential contemporary Islamic doctrine, Qutb linked past to present in a history marked by the Jews' war on Muslims. He blamed Jews for leading Muslims astray from Islam, for having deceived them and plotted against them in a conspiracy that lasted from the first Muslim community to his own day, when they imposed leaders and regimes to rule over Muslims. He argued that political leaders and Muslim religious authorities were 'manufactured by Zionism'.[203] Whether actual Muslims or crypto-Jews, Conversos, the 'agents of Zionism' were secretly plotting to destroy Islam, he claimed.[204] Whether it was the Jews at Medina siding with the hypocrites, or Jews in his day imposing secular leaders in Muslim-majority countries, the aim was the same: for Jews to annihilate Muslims.

Guided by the Qur'an, which 'elucidated their evil psychology', he argued there was no other group in human history with the Jews' degree of 'mercilessness, moral shirking and ungratefulness' to God. They were a people who 'killed, butchered, and expelled many of their prophets', he alleged, invoking the Christ-killer calumny. The Jews are evil, and not even human, for their 'black fury', 'narrow selfishness', and 'fanaticism' did not 'allow them to feel the larger human connection which binds humanity together'.[205]

Qutb invoked the classic anti-Semitic tropes of Jews being behind both capitalism and Marxism, and fomenting wars for their own profit. At the dawn of Islam they sided with Muhammad's polytheist enemies, the hypocrites, while in modern times they established communism to destroy Islam. Marxism is a branch of world Zionism. Qutb cited the Qur'an (5:82) – 'You will surely find the worst enemies of the Muslim to be the Jews and the polytheists' – as confirmation.[206]

Agreeing with Jews who promoted an antagonistic view, Qutb argued that the war that Jews supposedly have launched against Muslims from the time of Muhammad 'has not been extinguished, even for one moment, for close on fourteen centuries, and ... continues until this moment'. Citing the myth of tolerance, he claimed that even though Muslims treat Jews better than any other people, the Jews offer treachery in return. Worse, they lead an anti-Islamic, 'Crusader-Zionist war' that is behind the abolishment of dhimmi status for Jews through the replacement of Shariah with a constitution during the reign of Abdülhamid II, and behind secular Turkey's ending of the caliphate in 1924. In Qutb's view, the struggle against the Jews had become 'more deeply entrenched, more intense and more explicit' since the establishment of Israel. The Jews had been expelled from the Holy Land, and they had been expelled from

Arabia, but returned. Promoting genocide, he argued that 'Allah brought Hitler to rule over them' as revenge. Despite everything, the Jews live and they have 'returned to evil-doing, in the form of Israel'.[207] He wished for God to 'bring down upon the Jews people who will mete out to them the worst kind of punishment, as a confirmation of His promise, "If you return, then We return"' (Qur'an 17:8). Because God had twice punished Jews in the Holy Land, by destroying the First and Second Temples, after their alleged evildoing, God would again do so for what they had done to the Palestinians.

To the initial turn-of-the-twentieth-century cultural misunderstanding between Russian and Eastern European secular socialist Zionists and Palestinian Arab nationalists was added the mid-twentieth-century exodus of Jews from Arab lands to the fledgling Jewish state, where they had no influence over the political or cultural order and its lack of connection to Arabs, Muslims, and the Middle East. Few remained in the wider region to serve as a bridge between Israelis and others, if that was even any longer possible, when considering such views as that expressed by Qutb. The era of the Arab Jew was over.

8

THE ARAB JEW IN THE MIDDLE EAST AND EUROPE AFTER 1948

How do you pack 2,000 years of Jewish history and culture, existence even, into the few suitcases permitted per family?[1] Albert Memmi stated it bluntly: 'They allow them to leave, on condition that they do so entirely naked.'[2]

Arab Jewish identity, which was marked by a hyphen (Arab-Jew), had now to be separated by a comma (Arab, Jew).[3] After the establishment of the Jewish state of Israel in 1948, Arab and Jew became separated 'as enemy identities'. In a historic shift, Arab Jews 'suddenly became simply "Jews" or Israelis'. One could not be an Arab and a Jew in most Muslim-majority countries, because they ceased to distinguish between Israelis and local Jews and discriminated against or persecuted the latter. At the same time, Israel, dominated by Ashkenazi Jews, discriminated against Arab Jews, and made that identity no longer a possibility there either.

Israel rejected an Arab and Muslim context for Jewish history, just as Arab countries erased a millennium of Jewish existence from their national stories.[4] For Algeria, colonialism led to the impossibility of perceiving of a local Jewish presence. For Egypt and Iraq, anti-Zionism led to the impossibility of perceiving Jews as loyal citizens. The distinction between Jews and Israelis dissolved. Because these nation states were at war

The Arab Jew in the Middle East and Europe after 1948

with Israel, Jews were perceived as traitors. Jews were deemed Western, and Arabs Eastern, which for Israel was seen as positive, but for the Arab states, a problem. As a result, there are fewer Jews in all the Arab countries today than lived in Arabia at the time of the Prophet Muhammad.[5] After 1948 the Jewish presence was no longer desired in most of the Arab world, just as one can argue a Muslim (and Christian) presence was not desired in Israel.[6]

Jewish population by country in 2021[7]

	1948	1966	1969	1972	2000	2021
Morocco (90% to Israel, 5% to France, 5% to Canada)	250,000	70,000	50,000	35,000	3,000	2,100
Algeria (90% to France, 10% to Israel)	130,000	3,500	1,500	500	0	0
Iraq (90% to Israel, 10% to the UK)	130,000	3,000	2,000	500	0	0
Tunisia (50% to Israel, 50% to France)	90,000	23,000	10,000	7,000	2,500	1,000
Egypt (40% to Israel, 40% to France, 20% to UK/USA)	65,000	8,500	400	300	100	100
Yemen (95% to Israel)	54,000	2,500	500	300	300	6
Libya (90% to Israel, 10% to Italy)	35,000	6,000	100	0	0	0
Syria/Lebanon (80% to Israel, 20% to Europe/USA)	30,000	10,000	2,000	1,000	100	100

Jews in non-Arab Muslim-majority lands tend to fare better, except for Afghanistan

	1948	1966	1969	2000	2021
Iran (70% to Israel, 30% to USA)	90,000	65,000	60,000	25,000	9,400
Turkey (70% to Israel, 30% to Europe)	80,000	40,000	39,000	20,000	14,500
Afghanistan (100% to Israel)	5,000	800	600	0	0
Azerbaijan	?	?	41,300	10,000	7,000

In July 1830 Algerian Jews made their first contacts with the French army in Algiers. In July 1960 more than 90 per cent of Algerian Jews left Algeria for France. Between these two dates, the Jews of Algeria repressed their Berber–Arab identity, the identity of a dhimmi, to adopt the French identity, for them the symbol of a liberated person, until departing for France with their religious identity confined to the private sphere.[8]

According to an Algerian Jewish French historian, Algerian Jews experienced three major ruptures, or exiles.[9] The first was a separation, the Crémieux Decree of 1870, which sent them into an internal exile in their home country. The second rupture was an external exile, as they were stripped of their French citizenship seventy years later in 1940 by the fascist Vichy regime. The third exile was an external one, and it came less than two decades later in 1962, as they left newly independent Algeria, never to return. When the Front de Libération Nationale (FLN) launched its war of independence in 1954, for most Jews, assimilation into a secular French identity accomplished its goal, and the idea of living again under Muslim rule was inconceivable. These three ruptures or exiles help explain why most Algerian Jews chose to settle in France rather than Israel.

The prime minister of France when the FLN began its

anti-colonial war was the socialist Parisian and former undersecretary of state for economic affairs in the socialist Jew Léon Blum's Popular Front government (1936–7), Pierre Mendès-France. Arrested by Vichy during the Second World War, he had escaped, fought for the Resistance, then took refuge in Britain, where he flew bomber missions with the Free French.[10] He was scion of a Sephardic Jewish family, married to an Egyptian Jewish woman, the niece of Salvator Cicurel, the last leader of the Sephardi community of Cairo.[11]

In October 1956 the FLN addressed the Jewish community in a letter to the chief rabbi of Algiers asking them to express their belonging to the Algerian nation, 'which would eradicate the seeds of hatred maintained by French colonialism'. The FLN reminded Jews of the anti-Semitism of the Europeans in Algeria and the crimes of Vichy to pull them away from either being neutral or choosing French citizenship. They appealed to the myth of interfaith utopia regarding Jewish–Muslim relations to get them to side with the FLN. They considered Jewish Algerians as sons of the fatherland, and they hoped the leaders of the Jewish community would have the wisdom to contribute to creating a free and brotherly Algeria and to condemn French colonialism and proclaim their choice of Algerian nationality.

The religious authorities declared that since all Algerian Jewish institutions were cultural and religious, and not political, none could speak in the name of all Jews.[12] They reiterated their attachment to France and to an Algeria where all would live together in peace. They praised Muslim behaviour towards Jews during Vichy. They hoped that France would raise the status of the Muslims. They promoted a just solution that would assure the liberty and equality of all.[13] Despite their apparent apolitical position, they called for the equality of citizens in the same republic: the French Republic.[14]

The response did not vary to the end of the conflict. And neither would violence against Jews, or attempts by the FLN to get the Jews to commit to their struggle. Following numerous deadly FLN attacks on Jews at the end of the 1950s, the emergence of far-right terrorists in 1960, and the return to power of de Gaulle, perceived as the saviour of the Jews, Jews opted to openly side with France.[15]

Violence worsened: on 12 December 1960 Muslim rioters sacked the Great Synagogue of Algiers, desecrating the Torah scrolls, looting the furniture, and tearing the gates off the building. 'Death to the Jews' and swastikas were graffitied on the walls. The rioters planted the Algerian independence flag on the ruins of the synagogue.[16] In Oran rioters pillaged the Jewish cemetery. These acts pushed Jews to openly declare fealty to French Algeria and to oppose Algerian nationalism.[17]

Algerian Jews narrate how the moment of choice arrived when a Muslim assassinated oudist and singer Raymond Raoul Leyris, known as Shaykh Raymond to his legions of Jewish and Muslim fans, one of the greatest masters of Arabo-Andalusian music, in the heart of the Jewish quarter of Constantine on 22 June 1961. Raymond was a Jew with a French name who sang in Arabic.[18] He was the son of a Jewish father who died in the First World War, and a French mother who abandoned him. An orphan raised by a poor Jewish family, he studied Andalusi music with leading Constantine musicians. Starting his professional career in the 1930s, playing for Muslim and Jewish weddings, and then concert halls, by the 1950s he had recorded hundreds of records, and appeared on the radio and television with his mixed Muslim and Jewish orchestra. He would not be honoured in his own country until fifty years after the assassination.[19]

The FLN's assassination of this beloved musician, bombings of synagogues, and attacks on Jewish cafes at the end of

1961 caused panic. Scorched-earth policies of the far-right paramilitary terrorists of the Organisation armée secrète (Secret Army Organisation, OAS) from January to June 1962 accentuated the despair and flight. It was established in 1961 to keep Algeria French, and made up of former soldiers, former Resistance members, former Gaullists, and anti-Semites. Jews were at equal distance to both extremes. Yet they did not want again to figuratively become dhimmi.

Friend of the Jews Ferhat Abbas returned to Algeria in 1962 after six years' absence (the provisional government was in Tunisia). Élie Stora, deputy mayor of Khenchela, home of the kahina (see Chapter 1), said to him, 'Now, Ferhat, you are going to build us our beautiful Algeria.'[20] But he was thrown out of his post leading the provisional Algerian government. Attacks on Jews multiplied.

The new leaders, Ahmed Boumendjel and Mohamed Benyahia, conceived of there being no place for anything that was not Muslim, Arab, or Islamic in the future Algeria.[21] Words matter. At Oran on Rosh Hashana 1961 a Jewish man was murdered by a Muslim on his way to the synagogue. Jews attacked the suspects, killing two Muslims. It was the first case of intercommunal violence in Oran since the start of the war.[22] The Jewish community was also attacked by the OAS. On 20 November 1961 William Lévy, secretary general of the Socialist Federation of Algeria (SFIO), whose son was assassinated by a FLN militant in 1956, was killed. Adolphe Lévy, president of former prisoners of the Second World War at Algiers, was assassinated, as well as David Zermati, president of the Jewish community of Sétif. The assassination of Zermati, symbol of understanding and friendship between Jews and Muslims, caused most Jews to flee Sétif.[23]

By the end of the war young Jews swelled the ranks of the OAS, just as at the beginning of the war other Jews joined the

FLN.[24] As a former Jewish OAS fighter declared twenty years after the end of the war, Jews were caught between the rock and hard place of the Franco-Arab and Franco-French war, and war against the Jews in each camp. Some Jews, such as Lucien Hanoun, member of the Algerian Communist Party, remained loyal to the FLN to the end.[25] Élie Gozlan, who had spent decades working to bring Muslims and Jews together, was forced to leave his country and settled in France, where he passed away 'disconsolate for the heartbreaks of the land that he had defended with so much passion and determination'.[26]

Algerian Jews were each allowed two suitcases. They wore as many clothes as they could, despite the heat of summer. They left as if they were going on vacation, but they knew they would not go back. Unlike Tunisian and Moroccan Jews who held on to their Jewish identity, Algerian Jews were less inclined to claim a religious identity: 'They are *French*, and *French despite everything*.' Their attachment to France and French culture meant Zionism in Algeria was a marginal movement. Even the few who migrated to Israel after living in France described themselves as having a triple identity that was always French: French from Algeria, French from France, French outside France.[27]

In the weeks prior to independence on 2 July 1962 there was a sudden exodus of Algerian Jews who chose France, not Israel. Jerusalem was their celestial city, not their real one. Some young people became Zionist, but they were marginal. It was only after the 1967 war that secular Algerian Jews chose Israel, joining their more traditional co-religionists from such cities as Constantine who had migrated to the Jewish state since 1948.[28] In October 1962 no more than 25,000 Jews remained in Algeria. In 1971 there were no more than 1,000. In 1982 there were no more than 200. By the 1990s there were practically no more Jews in the country.[29]

What awaited these North African Jews in France? Algerian Jews, who were French citizens, arrived in a territory which was their homeland (they were French), but not their country.[30]

Moroccan Jews had a different experience from Algerian Jews despite the common denominator of French colonialism. After the creation of Israel, and especially following Moroccan independence in 1956, almost the entire population of 250,000 migrated to the Jewish state. Today one in every seven Israelis is of Moroccan background. As in Turkey, Muslims and Jews in Morocco today market the Jewish heritage and alleged pre-Zionist tolerance to an international audience made up partly of nostalgic Israelis and North Americans (Montreal has one of the largest Moroccan Jewish populations in the world). According to this myth, Moroccans are good Muslims who get along with their Jews, and maintaining sites of Jewish pilgrimage, especially cemeteries and the tombs of saints, is key to producing this image. The current king of Morocco has a Jewish man, André Azoulay, as senior advisor, a symbol of this historical relationship. Whereas from 1948 to 1960 AIU schools across the Middle East closed, in Tunisia and Morocco they remained open. In Morocco they were nationalised and renamed Ittihad-Maroc (Alliance-Morocco). Arabic language classes became part of the curriculum, yet the main language of instruction remained French, and modern Hebrew and Judaism were still taught.[31] Such practices raise the question of how to practise tolerance when hardly any Jews are left, and as anti-Zionism and anti-Semitism rise among newer generations who have never known Jews personally, unlike their grandparents.

After the Second World War, as the independence movement accelerated, and France dug in its heels, the Zionist movement made strong inroads among Moroccan Jewry, as the country suffered drought and famine.[32] When the sultan returned to

Tangier, he was alarmed and called representatives of the Jewish community to the palace to encourage them to remind their co-religionists that they were Moroccans.[33] He gained legitimacy in part by being the protector of the Jews.

Jews who were members or sympathisers of the Moroccan Communist Party took part in the independence struggle. The MCP was close to the UGSM, the General Association of Confederated Trade Unions of Morocco, a number of whose officers were Jews.[34] The context was formed by the massacre of civilians in Casablanca on the eve of the sultan's return to Tangier, the deterioration of relations with the resident general, the call by the nationalists for co-sovereignty with the French, the presentation of the Moroccan case at the UN, the UN vote for the partition of Palestine, and the unleashing of passions after the creation of Israel.[35] Such a climate produced panic and precipitated the exodus of Jews as incidents with Muslims increased.

As a climate of fear was created in Morocco, the sultan tried to re-establish calm after rumours spread about Jews poisoning the wells; he issued a communiqué on 23 May 1948 calling on the population to preserve the traditional links of symbiosis and not to be drawn into the conflict which had broken out in Palestine. Muslims were pressed to 'not molest Moroccan Jews even if Zionists attack their brother Arabs in Palestine'. He directed his speech to the Jews, saying that they 'had lived in the country for centuries, were placed under its protection' and were 'different from those wandering Jews who came from various countries, converged on Palestine, and sought to unjustly take possession of it'.[36] They needed 'not to forget ... that they are Moroccan, are entitled to his benevolence and have found in him the best defender of their rights'. They must, he insisted, abstain from 'any action aimed at helping the Zionist aggressors', under penalty of 'calling into question their status and their Moroccan nationality'.

Yet intercommunal violence in June 1948 in Oujda, site of clandestine emigration to Algeria and then to Israel since 1947, exacerbated the flight of Moroccan Jewry. Marcel Amsellem, born in Oujda in 1942, recalled how Jews and Muslims had harmonious, neighbourly relations. Friendships were 'frequent and warm'. His father, Rabbi Salomon, was regularly invited to speak at the madrasa, with whose students he memorised Qur'anic suras. Marcel remembers how it was difficult to even distinguish Jew from Muslim because both wore *djellabah* and *tarboush*. These good relations seemed to evaporate in 1948 in the pogrom of 7 June, after the state of Israel had declared itself.

Mobs attacked the Jewish quarter of Oujda armed with knives, axes, and clubs. Marcel and his father were spared when Muslim shop owners recognised his father and told the rioters to leave 'Taleb (seeker of knowledge) Shlomo' and his boy alone. After that, life returned to normal. Muslim scholars were again welcomed into the Amsellem home for discussions over sweet mint tea with his father. He remembers Muslims and Jews exchanging well wishes on Ramadan or Passover. But the rising tide of nationalism swept Morocco, and Oujda faced another pogrom in 1953, the masses associating the Jews with the French, whose army crushed the rioters. Amsellem claims that at independence three years later all the Jews of Oujda left, including the Amsellems, not for France, because they were not its citizens, but for Israel.[37]

Sultan Sidi Mohammed ben Youssef was deposed and exiled on 20 August 1953, leading to an armed fight for independence, backed by Egypt.[38] The government in Paris brought the sultan back to the throne as the king. The Jewish masses in the mellahs were pushed to emigrate by the Jewish Agency, when Israel realised it needed manpower and developed a plan to settle them on the nation's insecure borders. Ninety thousand Jews emigrated between 1948 and 1956, principally to Israel, prior to Moroccan independence.[39]

Sidi Mohammed ben Youssef returned to Rabat on 16 November 1955, after he was visited in Paris by Moroccan delegations, including those of Jews. Independence was announced by France on 2 March 1956. That Jews were given posts in the first government and in various ministries was recognition of Jews as equal citizens. When the king returned, two million people filled the streets to greet him in Rabat, and Jews shared in the joy, despite doubts about their future.[40] Pleased, the king declared to them that 'Moroccan Jews are full citizens like their Muslim compatriots' who 'will live in the most absolute equality and freedom'.[41]

Notwithstanding mass emigration, and the 1956 British, French, and Israeli attack on Suez, Jews were hopeful about the establishment of an independent, democratic, prosperous Morocco with equal rights for all, where all individuals were assured of their freedoms, as the king declared.[42] At their congress after the king's return, the Istiqlal (Independence) Party confirmed that Jews were equal under the law and had the right to maintain their religion and culture, and that Morocco would be governed without distinction of class or religion.[43] A Jew was nominated as a government minister, just as in neighbouring independent Tunisia André Baruch and André Bessis became government ministers.[44] Morocco's actions integrating Jews, nominating Jews to high posts in government, and making being Jewish not incompatible with being considered a member of the nation were in stark contrast to what prevailed in most other Arab Muslim countries (other than Lebanon), where laws denaturalised Jews who were citizens, sequestered their wealth and property, prosecuted individuals for Zionist conspiracies, and issued them with distinctive identity cards.[45] By contrast, in 1955 and 1956 the Moroccan ministerial cabinet boasted Jewish solicitors, engineers, and others, as did the embassies of the kingdom in Europe and America, and many other central or regional posts.[46]

For the first two years after independence in 1956, Jews played a significant role in the king's government and modernisation policies. The wealthy businessman Jo (Joseph) Ohana of Meknes was head of the nationalist Mouvement national marocain. Dr Léon Benzaken of Casablanca was named minister of the post and telegraph in the first and second governments of the new constitutional monarchy. As he was an apolitical physician, his appointment ruffled no feathers and demonstrated the king's support of Jewish citizens.[47] The king named him president of the Jewish community, reflecting the many Moroccan and other Arab Jews who had served in this capacity over the preceding centuries. It was considered a golden age for Jews.[48] It would be more accurate to call it a short-lived honeymoon.

Jews were appointed to important leadership positions in the national economy and in finance, such as Raphael Toledano as secretary of the National Commission of Investments, or Paul Ohana, director of a new refinery at Mohammedia. Influential members of Istiqlal, members of both the Jewish and Muslim elite, established the association Al-Wifaq (Entente) at the beginning of 1956, promoting Muslim and Jewish Moroccans building a new nation state, unified in heart and spirit, for the good of their country.[49] Crown Prince Moulay Hassan was honorary president. His aim was to show how Morocco was an exception, a model of intercommunal concord and stability in an Arab environment marked by the passions unleashed by the Israeli–Palestinian conflict. The government took concrete measures, playing Jewish music, sacred and profane, on national radio. The singers Samy El Maghribi, Salim Halali, and

Zohra Fassiya were as popular among Jews as among Muslims. The ministry of education allowed Hebrew to be taught in the Arabic Department at the University of Rabat.

Jews were wary of the writing on the wall, however, such as the king's support for the FLN. In 1958 Morocco joined the Arab League, which was at war with Israel. The new government formed in 1958 did not have any Jewish ministers and cut off postal connections with Israel.[50]

The massive clandestine exodus continued, so that only 160,000 Jews remained in the country in 1960.[51] Hoping to stem the tide of emigration, through which more than a thousand Jews left per month, the government mobilised Jews to intervene. Community leaders were asked to tell Israel and international Jewish organisations to stop facilitating the secret emigration.[52] As Morocco drew closer to Egypt and the other nationalist Arab countries opposed to Israel, the Israeli intelligence agency, Mossad, took over the emigration through Gibraltar, which had a significant Moroccan Jewish population, and whose British governor, Joshua Hassan, was a Jew.[53]

On 10 January 1961 the boat *Pisces* sank off the Moroccan coast, with around forty Jewish migrants on board.[54] It marked a turning point in the history of emigration of Moroccan Jews to Israel and occurred near the time of the death of King Mohammed V (26 February 1961). Jews deplored 'the disappearance of the one who had protected them against the exceptional laws of the Vichy government, and had made them citizens, recognising them at the time of independence with rights equal to those of Muslims'.[55]

Mohammed V was replaced by his son, Hassan II (r. 1961–99). Hassan II attended Yom Kippur services in Casablanca every year, while he was a prince, to receive a blessing from the chief rabbi for him and his dynasty. When Rabbi Shalom

Messas departed Morocco for Israel in 1978, he was escorted to the airport by the king, who asked for his blessing one last time.[56]

The 1960s were punctuated by revolts, uprisings, and the earthquake at Agadir which caused the emigration of the Jewish survivors.[57] In July 1961 Moroccan and Israeli representatives met secretly in Paris, agreeing to the emigration of 50,000 Moroccan Jews to Western Europe, Canada, and the US.[58] By the beginning of 1964, fewer than 90,000 Jews remained.[59] The war of 1967 marked a third historic peak in emigration of some 65,000 Jews who still lived in Morocco. The Arab loss in 1967 radicalised politics. One new movement was Ila al Amam (Forward), which included Marxist-Leninist Jewish members such as the Casablancan anti-Zionist Maoist engineer Abraham Serfaty, who published *Souffles* (1967–73), promoting cultural and political revolution, supported by students, leading to many arrests of militant leftists.[60]

As calls were made to boycott Jewish businesses, a new wave of mass departures resulted. From July to October 1967, nearly 7,000 Jews, wealthy and educated professionals, left for Canada, France, and Spain. Within a few years, fewer than 40,000 Jews remained. Like previous waves, the choice to leave was theirs, unlike in other Arab countries, such as Egypt, Iraq or Libya, which expelled their Jews, accusing them of collaborating with the Zionist enemy.

A similar story played out in Lebanon. The Lebanese community was decimated in the wake of the 1967 war, with half of the 6,000 remaining leaving for France in that year alone. The influx of Palestinian refugees and guerrilla fighters instigated more sectarianism and polarisation in the country. Jews realised that their traditional protectors, Maronite Christian politicians and militias, were losing power to Muslims. Many more Jews left in the early 1970s. The breakdown of the Lebanese political system which balanced Christian and Muslim interests led to civil war breaking out in 1975. By 1978, as leading Jews were assassinated in the civil war, 500 were left. The Jews of Lebanon suffered especially due to the 1982 Israeli invasion, and public Jewish life in Lebanon became untenable following the Israeli withdrawal from Beirut in 1984 and the south of the country in 1985 when the leading Jews were abducted and murdered. By 2000, sixty were left.[61] Although the main synagogue in Beirut has been restored, the remaining Jews are reportedly too afraid to pray in it.

In Egypt, until the late 1930s political Zionism was supported by the Ashkenazi and Arab Jewish lower classes, not the prosperous Sephardi and Arab Jewish upper classes. It gained favour among middle-class youth after the Second World War. Despite all the Zionist emissaries' educational efforts to recruit Egyptian Jewish youth for migration to Israel and a Hebrew-speaking socialist agricultural life on a kibbutz, only 1,500 Egyptian Jews were members of Zionist organisations in 1947.[62] From 1945 to 1947 several hundred Egyptian Jews, including a young Zionist elite, played a key role in recruiting Jewish migrants from Egypt and North Africa in the following years.[63]

A communist appeal distributed in May 1947 in Arabic and French declared, 'Down with Zionism! Long live the brotherhood of Jews and Arabs! Long live the Egyptian people!'[64] The Soviet Union's support of the UN partition of Palestine in 1947 marked a change in position, favouring the creation of a Jewish state, which in turn triggered Muslim communists to attack Jewish leaders, accusing them of being Zionists.[65]

In 1947 the government census recorded 65,639 Jews, a likely undercount by 10,000 or 15,000. Most of them lived in Cairo and Alexandria. Statelessness was prominent among former Ottoman subjects. In 1947, the stateless were declared foreigners.[66] After 1948 Jews were no longer granted Egyptian nationality. The 1956 law fixed 1900 as the date for having established nationality. It prohibited granting nationality to 'Zionists', which was used for any Jews, and included provisions for withdrawing nationality from 'Zionists'. When Jews left the country, they had to surrender their Egyptian nationality, if they had it. Knowing that stateless Jews could only migrate to Israel, Egyptian officials were declaring that Jews have a state, and that state was not Egypt.[67]

The establishment of Israel and war with the Arab states affected the Jews of Egypt. The Muslim Brotherhood recruited volunteers to fight in Palestine. Muhammad Hussein Haykal, head of Egypt's UN delegation, declared a year earlier, 'The lives of Jews in Arab countries will be jeopardised by this partition … If Arab blood is shed in Palestine, Jewish blood will necessarily be shed elsewhere in the world despite all the sincere efforts of the governments concerned to prevent such reprisals.'[68] The Egyptian press began to question the loyalty of the nation's Jews. At the beginning of May 1948 King Farouk declared most of the Jews of the country were loyal to Egypt and that no measures were contemplated against them, only against Zionists. On 16 May 1948, *Al-Ahram* published a letter from René and Aslan Cattaoui declaring that 'their religion was Judaism, their homeland Egypt, and their nationality Egyptian'.[69]

The Egyptian prime minister, Fahmi al-Nuqrashi, conflated Zionism and communism and ordered mass arrests when Egypt went to war with Israel in May 1948. The communist groups were disbanded and their members arrested. Hundreds of Zionists and communists, mainly Jews, were interned in camps along with members of the Muslim Brotherhood. The Jewish internees, who included non-Zionists and non-communists as well, numbered in the thousands and included women. The internees were freed in the second half of 1949 on condition they leave the country.[70]

From May 1948 to early 1949 sixty Jewish private, commercial, and communal assets and enterprises, including those belonging to Zionist or communist activists, such as Henri Curiel, were sequestered by the government. Some were returned a year later.[71] From May 1948 Jewish gatherings were forbidden, and Jewish organisations had to provide the government with the names and addresses of their members. Zionist organisations were outlawed. Jews who were foreign citizens were expelled. To limit migration to Israel, no Jews were allowed to leave the country in summer 1948.[72] These measures were accompanied by violence. On 20 June 1948 ten homes in the Karaite quarter were destroyed by a bomb which killed twenty-two Arabic-speaking Jews and wounded forty-one.[73]

On 15 July an Israeli plane bombed one of the poor quarters of Cairo, after which rioters stormed the Jewish quarter, which was protected by young Jews trained in self-defence by Zionist emissaries, but the police arrested them, and the rioters trashed homes and stores.[74] Four days later a bomb damaged the Italian-Sephardic-owned Grands Magasins Cicurel et Oreco department stores. Five hundred other stores were damaged and several people were killed and wounded, including Salvator Bey Cicurel, the head of the family firm, a highly influential businessman and leader of the Cairo Jewish community from 1946.[75] In September several buildings were bombed in the Jewish quarter, killing nineteen Jews and wounding sixty-two.[76] The government blamed the Jews, Israel, and then the Muslim Brotherhood for this terrorism. In December 1948, after the organisation was banned, a member of the Muslim Brotherhood assassinated Prime Minister Al-Nuqrashi. In February

1949 the Brotherhood's leader Hasan al-Banna was murdered by the secret police.

From summer 1948 to summer 1952, large-scale emigration was organised by Zionist emissaries, and a quarter of the community, mainly the lower classes, migrated to Israel via Marseille or Genoa with little government interference.[77] Twenty thousand Jews, at least a quarter of the population, left Egypt, 14,000 of them for Israel.[78] The establishment of Israel was one of the elements undermining Jewish–Muslim coexistence in Egypt and contributing to the end of Jewish life in the country. But even if in the 1940s all Jews had become Egyptian patriots, learned Arabic, and applied for Egyptian nationality, 'it would still not have changed the basic fact that they overwhelmingly are not of Egyptian origin, not "real Egyptians", not Egyptian citizens, and not Muslim', which mattered more than ever before.[79] In 1950 Henri Curiel was expelled as a dangerous foreigner, despite being a citizen, and Marcel Israel, Hillel Schwartz, and other prominent Jewish communists were arrested and deported.[80]

In 1951 and 1952 Egypt's political situation turned to chaos as political parties opposed both the king and the British, nullifying treaties with the UK, and British troops stationed in the country were attacked, turning into open battle in Isma'iliya. A mass protest against Britain on 26 January 1952 evolved into anti-British and anti-foreigner riots targeting Greek-, Armenian-, and Jewish- but also Muslim-owned stores, cinemas, hotels, and offices.[81] On 23 July a coup installed revolutionary military officers whose Revolutionary Command Council was headed by Colonel Gamal Abdel Nasser. King Farouk was deposed in 1952. The monarchy was abolished in 1953, ending the dynasty established by Muhammad Ali, and Egypt became a republic with a new constitution. As a secular republic, Egypt abolished the religious courts, including the Jewish one, in 1955.[82]

What worsened life for Jews in Egypt was Operation Susannah in 1954. In 1951 Israel sent intelligence agents to Egypt to establish contacts with Egyptian Jews and to train them in clandestine operations and sabotage techniques, including improvising explosives. The agents established cells in Alexandria and Cairo, some of whose members received further training in Israel.[83]

Between 1952 and 1954 an Israeli military intelligence officer formerly in charge of clandestine operations in Iraq, Meir (Max) Binnet, and Austrian-born Israeli intelligence officer Avraham Seidenberg arrived in Cairo.[84] Their aim was to sabotage American and British bases in Egypt to convince those nations, involved in negotiations to evacuate their military forces, that Egypt was unstable and they should not withdraw. Israel feared Britain handing over its bases and military hardware to its biggest enemy.

Operation Susannah was launched in July 1954. After bombing the American libraries connected to American embassies and consulates in Cairo and Alexandria, the underground planned to bomb two cinemas showing Western films in the two cities on 23 July, the national holiday celebrating the 1952 revolution, so that blame would be placed on the Muslim Brotherhood.[85] One cell of militants was charged with placing explosives inside the toilet tanks at the Métro and Rio cinemas in Alexandria. But in the lobby of the Rio cinema the explosives hidden in the trouser pocket of one of the militants ignited and flames shot out, and he was arrested.[86] All of the other militants were arrested, including Max Binnet. Seidenberg was a double agent who had alerted authorities to the plot.[87]

Rather than admit to the existence of the spy ring established by Israel, and its crimes, Israel and its allies in Europe and North America used the trials of the accused to blame Egypt for Nazi-style anti-Semitism, fitting in with the myth of an antagonistic view of Jewish–Muslim relations.[88] The Egyptian government's *Story of Zionist Espionage in Egypt*, published to explain the trials to an international audience, in arguing that Zionism and communism share 'one political objective: world domination', reinforced the view of Israel and its supporters that the Egyptian government was motivated by anti-Semitism.[89]

The Egyptian Jewish members of the underground were put on trial at the beginning of 1955 for espionage and sabotage. Binnet admitted his role in Iraq and Iran and then committed suicide in his cell.[90] Two other Israeli handlers were tried in absentia. The Egyptian government was careful to distinguish between the spies accused of treasonous criminal activity, and Egyptian Jewry.[91] Two of the accused, Shmuel Azar and the Karaite Moshe Marzuq, were sentenced to death and executed.[92] Six were sentenced to prison terms from seven years to life, including a woman, Marcelle Ninio, and two were acquitted.[93] Israel launched a retaliatory raid in Gaza in 1955, and Egyptian and Israeli counterstrikes contributed to the outbreak of war in 1956, after which Egypt pressured Egyptian Jewry to leave and expelled foreign Jews.

In 1955 President Nasser, who occupied Gaza, sent his forces to infiltrate Israel, engaging in acts of sabotage and killing civilians.[94] Israel launched bloody reprisals. In 1956 Egypt blockaded the Gulf of Aqaba. Israel continued its reprisals. That same year the US refused to finance the construction of the Aswan dam, and Egypt responded by nationalising the Suez Canal Company on 26 July. France and Britain, which had financial interests in the canal, planned a military attack together with Israel.

France was angered by Nasser's support for the FLN in Algeria. Israel attacked on 29 October and by 2 November it had advanced on the canal. By 5 November Israel had occupied the southernmost point of Sinai and ended the Egyptian blockade, and its forces took Gaza City, along with thousands of Egyptian prisoners.[95] The Anglo-French air campaign began on 1 November.[96] By 6 November the British and French took Ismaʻiliya. Due to pressure from the US, the Soviet Union, and the UN, the French and British removed their forces by the end of the year, whereas Israel stayed in occupation until spring 1957. But the attacks did not lead to Nasser's downfall. Instead, he turned his military defeat into political victory.

The war pushed the Egyptian government to declare a state of emergency, leading to mass arrests and denaturalisation of entire groups.[97] Jews were subject to police detention, sequestration of their companies and wealth, expulsion, and a new law which deprived Jews of their citizenship. Nearly a thousand Jews of Cairo were arrested. The assets of several hundred Jewish-owned firms were sequestered and those of 800 others were frozen.[98] The people and enterprises affected by this measure were the economic foundation of the community and its institutions. It intensified the pressure on Jews to leave the country. The government also engaged in expulsions and encouraged emigration. From November 1956 several hundred Jewish heads of households, whether they held Egyptian, British, or French citizenship, or were stateless, were told to leave the country in two to seven days.

After the 1956 war, 13,000–14,000 Jews, or 35 per cent of the remaining population, left Egypt for Israel.[99] By 1958, it is estimated that half of the Jews had left.[100] The situation was chaotic from November 1956 with thousands of Jews flocking to the offices of the rabbinate, consulates, and embassies seeking assistance and means of escape. The port of Alexandria and Cairo's airport were overflowing with those trying to leave for Europe to transit to Israel or to gain asylum there. In the confusion many could depart with only the clothes on their backs, while government officials arbitrarily confiscated valuable items.[101]

A new nationality law promulgated by Nasser in November 1956 affected Jews, because 'only those resident in Egypt before 1 January 1900 and who maintained their residence in Egypt until the present decree and are not under the jurisdiction of a foreign state are Egyptians'.[102] Article 1 of the law declared that Zionists and traitors could not be citizens, giving the government another means of stripping Jews of citizenship.[103] Jewish life became nearly impossible in a state where in 1958 the leader promoted the notorious anti-Semitic forgery, *The Protocols of the Elders of Zion*, as a way to understand Jewish aims.[104]

In the 1950s Jewish writer Jacqueline Kahanoff's parents in Cairo rented spare rooms to Tunisian and Algerian independence fighters. When one of the guests was arrested by the French, they learned his identity: he was Ahmed Ben Bella, Marxist revolutionary, leader of the FLN, and future prime minister and president of independent Algeria. Kahanoff wrote about this encounter in *Rebel, My Brother* (in Hebrew, 1959).[105]

Ben Bella lived in their home off and on from 1954 to 1956 after fleeing prison in his home country. Habib Bourguiba, leader of the Tunisian independence struggle in 1952–6 and first president of independent Tunisia, stayed in Kahanoff's 'Tunisian, Levantine, and Jewish' cousin Julian's home in Cairo. At that time the Tunisian embassy in Cairo issued Tunisian passports to Egyptian Jews with North African connections, allowing them to stay in the country when Egypt wished to expel them. The Egyptian press accused the Tunisian embassy of serving as a Jewish consulate, but the Tunisians 'went on helping Jews as much as they could'. Reflecting their age-old symbiosis, these nationalists chose to live with Jews in Egypt with whom they could converse and who supported them.[106]

Her parents told her that Ben Bella owned right-wing Israeli politician Menachem Begin's book *The Revolt*, which tells the story of militant Jewish resistance to British colonial rule in Palestine, and felt that Begin was his model in politics; he admired Israel, supported the Jews' right to have their own state, and declared that when Algeria became independent it would follow Israel's example to solve its social and economic problems. He told them that as he had the key to their home, 'whatever might happen and whatever he might do he knew there was always a place he could return to', and when he left 'there were tears in his eyes, real tears. Terrorist, yes,' his mother concluded, 'maybe, but the sweetest and most sensitive young man in the world', a Muslim revolutionary whom this Jewish woman loved like her own son.[107]

After the Sinai campaign, when her parents told the Tunisians of their plans to leave, the Tunisians claimed the Kahanoffs had nothing to fear because they were under their protection; besides, Nasser knew who the Kahanoffs were and how loyal they had been to the cause of independence and how happy Ben Bella was with them. They could even be granted Tunisian passports if needed.[108] They did not. They left for Israel in 1958.

Before the Suez crisis, Egyptian authorities, the press and the radio distinguished between Jews on the one hand, and Israelis and Zionists on the other. Beginning in 1958 when Egypt and Syria formed the United Arab Republic and promoted pan-Arabism, these differences disappeared. They spoke of 'international Jewry' and its plots against Egypt.[109] These ideological changes appeared together with socialist nationalisation measures from 1961, which hit Jews hard, as they were concentrated in the industries most affected: banking, insurance, and the import trade.

From 1950 Jews were banned from leading Egyptian

communist parties, although Jews remained rank-and-file members, just as the exiles in France continued their communist activities on behalf of Egypt until after the Suez war in 1956 when their émigré organisation was expelled from the Egyptian communist movement and they were excluded from membership in the party.[110] One issue was that that the Jewish communists in France promoted a resolution of the Arab–Israeli conflict. Another was the fact that Jews were no longer considered Arabs in Egypt, and could not be accepted as sincere Egyptian nationalists.[111] Curiel and other Jewish Egyptian communists in France reoriented themselves to support Algerian independence and the FLN instead. Curiel was imprisoned from 1960 to 1962. He donated his family mansion in Zamalek, Cairo to the newly independent Algerian state for use as its embassy, a function it still serves today.[112] Thereafter, funded by the Algerian government, Curiel established Solidarité to support anti-colonialist communist revolutionaries around the world, including the African National Congress in South Africa.[113] Throughout the 1960s and 1970s, along with the Arabic-speaking journalist Eric Rouleau, a Cairo-born Jew and communist, Curiel helped facilitate contacts between the Egyptian government and Egyptian leftists such as 'Adil Rif'at, a Marxist convert to Islam who was the communist activist Hillel Schwartz's nephew, and Israelis interested in peace; in the 1970s it was the PLO and leftist Israelis and French communists, including Rif'at's half-brother, the Maoist Benny Lévy.[114] In 1968 Curiel was assassinated by unknown assailants.[115]

In 1960 Haim Nahum, more a mediator for Jews with Egyptian and foreign authorities than a spiritual guide for them, passed away aged eighty-eight.[116] He was the first and last chief rabbi of Egypt. His replacement, Haim Dwek, did not inherit all his powers.[117] Jews faced a crisis of religious leadership, and were vulnerable to the caprices of the regime and its police measures. Further nationalisation measures in 1961 and 1962 affected the remaining community, which was ended almost without a trace remaining of 2,000 years of history following the 1967 war.

Two or three days after the outbreak of that war, the police rounded up most of the Jewish men of Cairo and Alexandria, rumoured to include the chief rabbi and other notables. At least 425 were arrested and imprisoned. Seventy-five holding foreign citizenship were expelled from the country. Most of the remaining 350 citizens and stateless Jews were transferred to other prisons, and foreign governments and international Jewish organisations managed to get 112 released before the end of the year. They were expelled.[118] The rest were incarcerated for up to three years. Four still imprisoned spies were freed in 1968 in exchange for Egyptian prisoners of war captured in June 1967.[119] The last were released and expelled from Egypt in 1970 along with their families. Those who were not imprisoned but were citizens were required to renounce their citizenship and promise never to return, and were expelled, leaving all their assets behind.[120] By the end of 1968 or beginning of 1969, only a thousand Jews remained in Egypt.[121] By the mid-1970s there were only around 200 rabbinic Jews and 100 Karaites in Cairo and a similar number in Alexandria, many of whom were elderly, disabled, or poor.[122] Alexandria's last chief rabbi had long since migrated to Buenos Aires.

A similar fate befell Iraqi Jews despite their eagerness to integrate into Iraqi society and be a part of the Iraqi nation, reminiscent of how French or German Jews assimilated. They were active in centrist and leftist political parties, particularly the Communist Party, and present in all the ranks of the administration and economy and in the army. No less impressive was their participation in the birth of modern Iraqi literature. Novelists, poets, playwrights, translators: a third of the novels published in Iraq at the end of the 1920s were by Jews. Most Jews were against Zionism. In 1922 the Jewish Iraqi politician Menahem Daniel claimed Zionism endangered Jews in his country, because it 'undermines good Jewish–Muslim relations' as it aimed to transform local Jews into 'a completely foreign element'. Muslims would question all Jews' patriotism and loyalty to the country. It would denationalise them, he warned.[123] Most Iraqi Jews had no intention of uprooting themselves.

Iraqi Jews were associated with Zionists and accused of being traitors, nevertheless. They were compelled to publicly distance themselves from Zionism and express their solidarity with Palestinians. The leaders of the community 'repeatedly demonstrated their public support for the Palestinian cause without, however, overcoming the public distrust of Jewish loyalty to the Iraqi state and the Arab nation'.[124]

Iraq did not have a 'Jewish problem'. Its Jews had no need for a refuge.[125] Community leaders believed that Zionism was the problem.[126] In 1935 the few Zionist activists were expelled or migrated to Palestine, and Zionism was not openly propagated in the country thereafter. In August 1938 thirty-three Jewish notables addressed a condemnation of Zionism sent to the Colonial Office in London and the League of Nations.[127] Yet the problem of Palestine affected the Jews of Iraq the most.

Iraqi Jews refused to get drawn into the dispute over Palestine. In 1943 the leaders of the community refused to publicly support Nuri Said's plan of creating a Greater Syria in which the Jews of Palestine would have semi-autonomous status, but no national home. They told him it would have no effect on the Zionists, and that the Jews of Iraq were not interested in international politics or in Palestine.[128] More than once Iraqi Jews were asked to publicly condemn Zionism and pledge their loyalty to Iraq. Nuri Said believed their refusal stemmed from their secret support of Zionism.[129]

Distrust of Jews led to their dismissal from positions in the public and private sector, according to Ibrahim al-Kabir, director of the ministry of finance and one of the leaders of the community.[130] Ezra Daniel argued that the British 'used Iraqi Jews as a pawn in their political games, without considering the consequences for the Jews themselves'.[131]

In 1944 Nuri Said warned that the anger of the masses was likely to turn against local Jews in reaction to events in Palestine. The Iraqi UN delegate Fadhel al-Jamali declared that 'the interests and the well-being of 600,000 Jews in Arab lands' would be affected.[132] The leaders of the Iraqi Jewish community condemned the UN declaration of the partition of Palestine in 1947, reasserting their patriotism and loyalty in a statement circulated in the press and repeated on the radio.

From 1945 to 1948 all Iraqi governments attempted to protect Jews, either out of concern for their safety, or for the reputation of Iraq, or because they feared the anti-Jewish riots could turn against the conservative Sunni regime in the face of Kurdish, Shi'i, and leftist demand for rights. Despite the disquiet, the years 1946 and 1947 were peaceful and the situation for Iraqi Jews remained good. Shalom Darwish, secretary of the community in the 1940s, reported that according to its leaders, 'We have lived in Iraq 2,000 years and we will continue to live there for another 2,000 years, perhaps until the coming of the Messiah, this is why we must coexist in peace with the Iraqi people.'[133]

Thanks to the arrival of Zionist emissaries working clandestinely in 1942, by 1945 there were 500 youth affiliated with Zionism in the country, and their numbers tripled.[134] Rebelling against the conservatism of the community, these idealists believed in a transformation in their social lives, family structure, work, and language, as they prepared to migrate to Palestine and join kibbutzim. These lower- and middle-class young men and women saw a future as liberated Hebrew-speaking, progressive agricultural labourers. Between 1941 and 1948, 3,000 Iraqi Jews immigrated illegally to Palestine.[135] Zionism was not a solution other than for a tiny minority of youth. Emissaries from the Yishuv in Palestine secretly trained and armed several hundred young Jews in Iraqi cities to defend themselves in the case of a repeat of the Farhud. By May 1948 they counted 300 members armed with rifles, machine guns, pistols, and hand grenades.[136]

The war in May 1948 – in which Iraq sent three poorly provisioned brigades to the front against Israel – caused more problems for Iraqi Jews.[137] Soldiers attacked Jews in Fallujah on 28 January 1948. On 15 May, when Israel declared its independence, the streets of Baghdad were filled by masses shouting anti-Zionist and anti-Jewish slogans, calling on their government to crush Israel. Jews who gathered on the sidewalks to watch were stunned, hearing them call for the destruction of the Jews.[138]

Another option taken up by Jewish youth was communism. The communists were anti-monarchy, anti-Nazi, anti-British colonialist, pro-independence. The idea of a separate Jewish nation was antithetical to their secular and egalitarian views, which saw no ethno-religious differences, only those of class. They fought for the interests of peasants and workers in a country that was conservative, divided by ethnicity and religion, and ruled by a coalition of large landowners, capitalists, and the monarchy.[139]

What appealed to Jews was the Soviet Union's victory over fascism in the Second World War, the communist condemnation of anti-Semitism, in the wake of the shock of the Farhud, and the fraternity between peoples of different nations and religions.¹⁴⁰ According to the writer Sami Michael (Salah Mujalid), born to a middle-class Jewish family in Baghdad in 1926, who headed several cells, including those for women and Shi'ites, and was an editor of their secret journals, 'Being a communist does not only mean raising the standard of revolt against the regime, but also raising the standard of revolt against one's father and mother, against one's tradition and superstitions, and fighting against an ancient and mouldy heritage.'¹⁴¹ Thanks to their mastery of English and French, Jews were the main translators of foreign communist material into Arabic and played a large role in publishing communist propaganda. In 1947, the influence of Jews increased, and two among them, Yehuda Sadiq and then Sasson Dallal, became general secretary of the Communist Party.

Michael fled to Iran and then to Israel in 1948, where he became a well-known novelist. In *Storm among the Palms* (1975), *Handful of Fog* (1979), and *Victoria* (1993), the latter translated into Arabic, he described his childhood growing up in the Jewish neighbourhoods of Baghdad. *Equal and More Equal* (1974) and *Tin Shacks and Dreams* (1979) concern life in Israel for Arab Jews in the transit camps. In an interview he argued that

> the entire Zionist story is a myth that has no basis in reality, according to the reality I saw and experienced. The Iraqi Jews were like American Jewry of today, that is, we cared about the well-being of the Jews in Palestine but at the same time we enjoyed the lifestyle of the land in which we were born and had no intention of moving.¹⁴²

The first Iraqi prose literature was written by Jews such as Anwar Shaul and Shalom Darwish, and Jewish poets wrote in Arabic. There was no newspaper editorial staff in Iraq without

The Arab Jew in the Middle East and Europe after 1948

Jews on it. 'Were we not the best Arabic grammarians?' asks Naim Kattan. 'There was neither affectation nor calculation in the love we bore for this language, which we spoke from birth, which was ours just as much as it belonged to the Bedouins of the desert.'[143] He considered himself as a writer first, an Iraqi second, and a Jew third in the 1940s.

It was a period that is erased from history, in both Iraq and Israel, where an antagonistic view of Jewish–Muslim relations is promoted. In 1947 the communists organised mass protests against the anti-Soviet treaty between Britain and Iraq. At their protests, rabbis and shaykhs 'held hands and talked about Jewish-Arab [Muslim] brotherhood … Jews and Arabs fought together against the government and the Jewish community supported it.' There were bloody street battles. The soldiers joined them, and the government fell. The Iraqi Communist Party's head of the central committee was a Jew. 'It was the first case from the time of Muhammad and until today that the head of the opposition in Iraq was a Jew. Several top leaders in the Party were Jews as well, and I personally helped found new cells and organised officers and members of the Shiite community.'[144]

Just as the secretary general of Morocco's Communist Party was a Jew, Léon Réne Sultan of Algeria, so too did Iraqi Jews play an important role in the Iraqi Communist Party (ICP) from 1941 to 1951.[145] As Iraqi patriots who were against imperialism and sectarianism, eight Jewish communists formed the League for Combating Zionism. They opposed Zionism because as self-described Arab Jews they opposed sectarianism, wished Jews to solve their existential problem in the states where they resided, opposed colonialism, and called for a free, democratic Palestine.[146] The League declared Zionism 'a pressing danger for Jewish and Arab masses in their national struggle. Because we are both Jews and Arabs at the same time, we are doubly hostile toward Zionism ... And because the question of Palestine is an issue for the entire Arab world, we place ourselves alongside the Arabs of Palestine.'[147] Under cover of anti-Zionist activity the League propagated communism, which was illegal. It perceived Zionism as a danger to Jews and Muslims alike because it converted Palestine into a base for British imperialism, and hindered national liberation movements in Arab lands elsewhere, and prevented national unity. The League did not conceive of a 'Jewish problem', but held that Jews shared the same problems as others in the Arab lands.

Its leader and the editor of its journal, Yusuf Harun Zilkha, published *Zionism: The Enemy of the Arabs and the Jews* and promoted solving the class struggle as a means of ending racism and anti-Semitism rather than Jewish nationalism, which served British imperial interests. He argued that it was British colonialism that created a Jewish problem in Muslim societies that had not previously existed, dividing Arab (Muslim) from Jew rather than uniting them against outside colonialists.[148] 'As Jews and Arabs at the same time', reads one pamphlet, Arab Jews are 'the enemies of Zionism'.[149] The League received telegrams of support from Arab labour unions from Palestine. When Zilkha was arrested in 1947 (and subsequently expelled from Iraq in 1951), members of the Supreme Arab Committee in Palestine, Syria, and the Arab League sent letters of protest.[150] The League fomented demonstrations in front of the British embassy in Baghdad to support Palestine in 1946. During one a Jewish communist, Sha'ul Tweig, was killed by police in front of the statue of General Maude, symbol of British colonialism in Iraq.[151] The government took away its licence the same year, and arrested its Jewish members, without irony, for being Zionists.

The problem was that the ICP was an illegal organisation. Its leaders, Dallal and Sadiq, were executed not because they were Jews, but because they were communists, which the government perceived as dangerously subversive.[152] The fact that the ICP toed the Party line given by the Soviet Union, which supported the establishment of Israel in 1948, meant that the communists became pro-Israel despite their previous anti-Zionism. At the same time the government persecuted Jews for being Zionists, even if they were communists, and vice versa. For Jews it appeared the only solution was to leave Iraq.

The government started to harass the Jewish community at the same time as Muslims and Jews were fighting over Palestine, according to Sami Michael, 'so this window of time became obscured by the conflict there. So the Iraqi authorities used the Palestine conflict to divert attention' from Iraq's problems, 'and thus attempted to erase this piece of history'.

> The Arabs erased it because the Arab nationalist line after Israel's establishment became that all Zionists and all Jews are monsters and thieves, and that you can't make peace with them. And the Iraqi Communist Party erased this chapter to avoid admitting that Jews and Arabs could cooperate. Israel also has tried its best to abolish this storyline from memory because it does not fit the Zionist narrative in which all the Jews sat on their suitcases and waited for the Zionist redemption. And it did not fit the reality of what was happening in Israel at the time. Few wanted to hear that Jews and Arabs have lived together in peace and harmony and, moreover, were ideologically aligned.[153]

When Michael migrated to Israel, he moved to an Arab neighbourhood in Haifa, and organised Muslims and Jews for the Communist Party, writing for Arabic-language newspapers, and lecturing on communism to Arab Jews in the transit camps, despite being attacked by the left and right. He argued that even the Communist Party was racist against Arab Jews, but then it evolved into an Arab party for Arabs, so the Iraqi Jews were ignored again.[154] The Stalinist anti-Jewish show trials caused him to leave the Party in 1955.[155] Yet he was forever traumatised by the rupture, and his own displacement. He had a recurring nightmare where he was sitting in his favourite Baghdad cafe, but when it was time to pay he reached into his pocket and pulled out Israeli shekels, outing himself as an enemy Zionist. The nostalgic dream became a nightmare.[156]

Many Party members, Jewish and Muslim, fled to Iran, but did not find support, though the regime allowed the Zionists to organise the exodus of Jews from Tehran to Israel, and the communists benefited from this to escape. Ironically, it was the Zionists who got the anti-Zionist Jewish communists out of Iraq, into Iran, and on to Israel, a country whose existence they did not support. In March 1950 Iraq authorised the Jews to depart for Israel. The Communist Party criticised this measure but did not oppose the departure of members of the Party to safety in Israel. The majority of Jewish communists left for Israel. At the end of 1951, after most Iraqi Jews had left the country, practically the only Jews left were the several hundred communist prisoners. When they were freed, they were expelled to Israel, against their will.[157]

The story of the Iraqi Jewish communist militants provides an example of the secular symbiosis between Jew and Muslim. Baghdad in the 1940s was another time and place where Jews were an integral part of the Arab world. Communism was an antithesis to Zionism, the latter being an ideology which refutes and severs the link between Muslim and Jew.[158] As Michael remembers, the 'most amazing thing of all was that it was a sort of Jewish–Shiite–Kurdish coalition against the ruling Sunni minority'. Arrests began in 1943 and continued through 1949, and their newspaper was banned. When Israel was established, 'the Iraqi government was glad to get rid of the Zionists and the Jews in general, and used that event as the pretext for ordering the arrests or executions of Jewish Communists'.[159] Most Jews occupying high positions were arrested and sentenced to prison. Sadiq and Dallal were executed in 1949.

In Israel today, some remember the Iraqi Jewish communists as courageous heroes willing to die for their ideological conviction, fighting against imperialism and nationalism to create a unified nation of Muslim and Jew. Others present them as model secular leftists, contradicting the usual stereotype of Arab Jews as conservative and religious.[160]

On 15 May 1948, as Iraqi troops invaded the new state of Israel, and Iraq closed the oil pipeline to Haifa, Iraq's government declared the imposition of martial law. The military regime lasted a year and a half, to December 1949. It arrested the communists, controlled the press, and repressed the opposition.[161] In mid-July 1948, Zionism, along with communism and anarchism, was declared a crime punishable by seven years' imprisonment or capital punishment. As 'Zionism' was not defined, this opened the path to arbitrary persecution of Jews.[162]

Iraqi Jews played no part in the conflict over Palestine, nor were they responsible for the acts of the Israeli government. While the government protected them from attacks by violent mobs, it subjected them to discrimination and repression. Jews were not allowed to leave the country without paying a large sum and obtaining permission from the ministry of defence. They were forced to make contributions to the Palestinian cause. Jewish banks were closed. Merchants were denied licences. The wealthy were incarcerated and forced to pay heavy fines. Hundreds of Jews were arrested, incarcerated, or fined for relations with Zionists or belonging to Zionist organisations. Higher education institutes stopped accepting Jews.[163]

Ibrahim al-Kabir, who had served the state for three decades, was retired from his post as director general of the ministry of finance. As news of the Arab defeat in Israel arrived in Iraq, the wealthiest Jew in the country, the millionaire Syrian-born Shafiq Ades, who had no links to Zionism or Israel, was arrested in Basra in August. He was accused by a military court of transferring surplus military equipment to Israel. He was convicted of treason in September, sentenced to death, and ordered to pay five million dinars (worth $20 million), then hanged.[164]

At the same time, Nuri Said threatened to expel the Jews of Iraq if Israel did not allow the return of the Palestinian refugees. In July the prime minister proposed an exchange of 100,000 Iraqi Jews who would be transferred to Israel for 100,000 Palestinian refugees who would settle in Iraq. The wealth of the expelled Iraqi Jews would fund the Palestinian resettlement in Iraq in exchange for their wealth left in Israel. The British rejected the idea. In October Said repeated the offer. The Iraqi delegation presented the plan at the UN, but Israel rejected it.[165] They wanted the departure of Iraqi Jews to be free, and for them to be allowed to bring their wealth without Israel giving up the Palestinian wealth it had taken. Moreover, Israel wanted to exchange not Palestinian refugees, but Palestinians who had remained in Israel. The fall of Said's government put an end to this debate.[166]

In October 1949 the head of the community, Rabbi Sasson Kedourie, wrote to the vice-premier that:

> The Jewish community of Iraq, based on its past of 2,400 years of dedication and loyalty to the land of Iraq, was

convinced that the war in the Land of Israel would not influence its existence nor diminish its guaranteed rights and freedoms by law, as long as it obeys the laws of the land and is loyal to the state. However, to our great regret, all our hopes turned out to be in vain. The community suffered because of this war and fell into a hardly enviable situation.[167]

'Despite this, many sensible people continue to have faith and hope that eventually things will return to normal' for the law-abiding, patriotic Jews, loyal to the fatherland and the dynasty ruling it.[168] They appeared to have returned to normal at the end of 1949, as Jews sat at cafes, went to the cinemas, and strolled in large groups on Shabbat, and there were wealthy Jews who still 'live in their beautiful palaces and enjoy the pleasures of life'.[169] The Israeli foreign ministry noted that the situation was not bad, as 'the number of detainees was minor', only hundreds out of a population of 110,000, and that no danger awaited them. The Israelis estimated that so long as the regime held the reins of power, the Jews were safe. They wanted to remain in Iraq.[170]

On 9 March 1950 the new prime minister, Tawfiq al-Suwaidi, announced 'the forfeiture of Iraqi nationality of any Iraqi Jew who would prefer, of his own free will, to leave Iraq definitively, after having signed a special form in front of an official named by the interior minister'.[171] Those who left agreed never to return. The law would be valid until March 1951. This law was not an act of expulsion. The government wanted to get rid of several thousand Zionist or communist youth agitators who would leave via Iran. It knew the majority of Iraqi Jews preferred to remain in Iraq. The government estimated that perhaps 10,000 would leave.[172] It did not envision a mass exodus. Because they were not given passports when they left, Iraqi Jews could only go to Israel. But if Jews considered migration, they only wanted to go to Europe or the USA, not to hazard an uncertain future in Israel, which seemed to offer many fewer opportunities than a secure, stable, prosperous Iraq. Only the poor and the ideological would want to go, not the middle and upper classes who were loyal citizens.[173] The surprise was that within two months 47,000 Jews registered to leave. Within six months their number reached 70,000.[174] Israel was more concerned with Romanian and Polish refugees and delayed the migration of the Iraqis. Tens of thousands registered to leave but could not.[175]

On 14 January 1951 a registration centre in the Masuda Shemtov synagogue was bombed. Four were killed, including a twelve-year-old boy, and twenty wounded. The period to leave was to end three months later. This compelled Israel to act quickly. More than 70,000 Iraqi Jews migrated to Israel, the majority between March 1950 and June 1951, when five bombs exploded. Nineteen thousand middle-class Jews registered after the first bombing.[176]

On 10 March 1951, the day the law of migration ended, the Iraqi Parliament voted to freeze the wealth of Jews who registered to leave the country. Previously, those leaving the country had been able to take their wealth. At that time, 64,000 who had registered were still waiting to migrate to Israel. One of the most comfortable Jewish communities in the Middle East was reduced to poverty.[177] As the former bourgeoisie arrived in Israel, they found themselves impoverished and vulnerable.[178] Permission for each person to leave with fifty dinars was reduced to five dinars.[179]

In mid-May 1951, after the flights to Israel were completed, Iraq arrested two Israeli agents, Mordechai Ben Porat and Yehouda Tadjer. Dozens more were soon detained, including Yossef Batsri, head of an Israeli espionage ring in Iraq, and

Saleh Shalom, responsible for secret arms depots for Jewish self-defence, and were accused of having planted three of the five bombs targeting Jews, not including the one at the synagogue, to sow panic among Jews to incite them to emigrate to Israel.[180] Batsri and Shalom were executed in January 1952. Tadjer was sentenced to life in prison. Ben Porat escaped from jail.[181]

The exodus of Iraqi Jewry remains linked to these attacks. The claim that the exodus 'would not have taken place without Israeli terrorism against Jews thanks to its emissaries, in particular Ben Porat, target of the accusations, was proclaimed by Iraqi authorities, Palestinian spokespersons, even many Iraqi Jews in Israel'.[182] Perhaps these Iraqi allegations cleared it of accusations from the Arab League of having ignored its directives and aiding Israel in increasing its Jewish population. Palestinians have adopted the accusation of Israeli terrorism as counterweight to the Israeli support of the antagonistic account of Jewish–Muslim relations that Jewish existence in Muslim-majority societies became impossible thanks to local anti-Semitism. Left-wing Israelis of Iraqi background blamed Israel and Zionist agents.[183]

Summer 1951 was the end of the Iraqi exodus. Between 1948 and 1951, 130,000 Iraqi Jews arrived in Israel, 105,000 by plane, the totality of Iraqi Jewry, of every social class, ethnicity, and region of origin, urban, rural, rich and poor, including as many as 20,000 Kurdish Jews.[184] Ten thousand Jews who remained in Iraq belonged mainly to the social, cultural, economic, and intellectual elite. Many were owners of land and real estate, bankers and importers, traders, liberal professionals, and public and private office holders, the majority in Baghdad. In 1952 they were allowed passports, and many left Iraq after having succeeded in transferring their wealth outside the country. They lost their nationality when they did not return.

The revolution of 1958 ended the dynasty and ushered in the

four-year reign of Abdel Karim Kassem, the most splendid for Iraqi Jews after the exodus. Their rights were restored, university enrolment was again open, they could travel abroad without losing their citizenship, and they benefited from a prosperous and secure environment. Most Jewish prisoners, including Tadjer, spies, and communists, were freed and expelled to Israel. Numerous Jews became wealthy and bought large homes in the villa quarter in the capital. The wealthy rejoined the social clubs.[185]

In 1963 there was a coup, and the position of the Jews began to deteriorate. New restrictions were imposed, the wealth of Jews travelling abroad was confiscated, and few were allowed to leave the country. They were victims of the nationalisation of businesses, whether they worked in or owned them. The 1967 war worsened the situation for the 3,000 who remained. In July 1968 the Baath Party under Saddam Hussein (president of Iraq, 1979–2003, executed 2006) took power and began a violent campaign of persecution. Hundreds of Jews were arrested and imprisoned. In 1969 dozens were arrested and displayed at a show trial, and forty were executed for allegedly spying for Israel. Seven were tortured to death and nine were executed in prison. Their bodies were publicly displayed in Baghdad (as were two others in Basra) and shown on Iraqi state television. A million Iraqis witnessed the corpses of the nine hanged men, each bearing a placard around the neck stating his name, profession, birthplace, and the word 'Jew'.[186] By 1972 most of the remaining Iraqi Jews had fled to Iran via Kurdistan with the aid of Kurds, the majority travelling to the UK.[187]

From the mid-nineteenth century the centre of Jewish life in Kurdistan was Zakho on the Habur river, where Jews lived in mud-brick homes on an island, the oldest part of the town and its market.¹⁸⁸ Kurds demonstrated the salience of symbiosis as they related the story of the survival of the town to Jewish–Muslim harmony. According to the story, Jews and Muslims lived together in the island town for centuries. Five hundred years ago, a flood wiped out the settlement and all its inhabitants. Nearly a century later, a tribal leader tried to resettle it, 'but every time he built a wall, it collapsed'. He asked a shaman what to do, and the soothsayer told him 'the spirits would not let Zakho rebuild until Jews returned'. The agha brought an Ottoman Jewish timber raftsman family to settle the island. They built walls and houses that stood. Muslims and Jews followed. As the pre-flood balance was restored, the town flourished once again.¹⁸⁹

Relations with their Muslim neighbours were generally good. Jews sought out Muslim wet-nurses, who returned the babies when they were ready for solid food.¹⁹⁰ Muslims shopped at Jewish stores, went to Jewish tailors. They sent the Jews gift baskets of bread, milk, and eggs at the end of Passover. Muslims ate matzah. They sent Jewish neighbours hot tea during Shabbat, when Jews could not light fires. On Shabbat the Muslims in the teahouse even stubbed out their cigarettes in respect as Jews filed past on their way home from the synagogue. Jews gave up smoking cigarettes during Ramadan in solidarity with their Muslim neighbours. The local agha, who employed a Jew as his personal secretary, protected them in exchange for manual labour. 'Neighbouring tribes knew that robbing or murdering a Zakho Jew would invite retributory bloodshed.'¹⁹¹ When a Zionist agent told local Jews that the country was no longer safe for them and that Muslims killed Jews in Baghdad, they responded with disbelief.¹⁹²

When a Palestinian Muslim arrived at the Zakho market in the 1940s to spread word among local Muslims that Jews were killing Muslims in his homeland, a member of the crowd cut the man off, saying, 'We have no problem with our Jews. Why do you come here?' He talked about Jews in Baghdad. Another shopkeeper shouted at him that that was Baghdad.[193] Some in the crowd called him a liar. He told them Jews are the liars, even the ones in Zakho, who may act like friends but will one day rise and slaughter them. Abd al-Karim Agha, the main protector of the Jews, threatened the man and chased him out of town saying, 'Palestine is that way, do you understand me? This is Zakho. If you don't leave now, it won't be our Jews who will kill you. It will be me.'[194] Soon after, the agha confided that in the past a man like that would never dare set foot in Kurdistan, and if he did, Kurds would beat him into silence. But that day, people listened to him. It was a bad omen.[195] The Farhud, the Shafiq Ades hanging, nothing touched Zakho Jews. But the arrest, torture, and imprisonment of fifteen local Jewish loggers in 1948 or 1949 who the Iraqi police thought were Zionist agents because they overheard them singing a Jewish song woke them to the dangers of the era.[196]

In October 1950 seventy Jews left Zakho, the illiterate have-nots – peddlers, porters, beggars, cobblers, and bakers.[197] Later that autumn the middle class left – storekeepers, farmers, butchers, weavers, silversmiths, and schoolteachers – promising never to return.[198] A clerk in the large synagogue drew a black line through their names in the citizenship rolls and entered their names in the list of the denaturalised.[199]

More than half of Zakho's Jews registered to leave, and became stateless, but the buses taking them to Mosul did not arrive. They sold their houses worth 300 dinars for one-tenth that and waited to leave.[200] Of the nearly half-million Jews who migrated to Palestine during the British Mandate, 90 per cent were European. Israel was to be Vienna on the Jordan, not another Zakho on the Habur.²⁰¹ But after the bombing of the Masuda Shemtov synagogue in Baghdad, Ben-Gurion, who had a dim view of Arab Jews, decided to act. Iraqi Jews were flown to Israel in less than a year.²⁰² When the Iraqi Parliament froze all assets and property of denaturalised Jews, the wealthy landowners of Zakho, such as Moshe Gabbay, who had not yet registered to leave, lost almost everything.²⁰³

On 16 April 1951, as the Jews of Zakho crossed the bridge over the Habur to the bus stop, where a fleet of buses waited to take them to Mosul, 'hundreds of Muslims had lined the streets to bid their neighbours farewell'.

> Old women raised cries … ululating as if a loved one had died. A troupe of child musicians played drums and flute. Teenage boys stepped forward to help with suitcases … It was the old grocer, the first one to give him a job, who gave him a box of Turkish delight for the journey. 'Eat them slowly,' he pleaded, 'to remind you of Zakho' and hugged him.²⁰⁴

Trains carried them from Mosul to Baghdad, where at the airport crowds hurled insults: 'die, Jewish dogs', 'rot in Hell', and 'be gone'.²⁰⁵ The irony was that they would not be treated much better in Israel.

From 1948 to 1951, 560,000 of the 688,000 immigrants to Israel were Arab Jews.²⁰⁶ What awaited them? A popular Iraqi immigrant song in Israel in the 1950s was as follows:

> Oh, what did you do, Ben-Gurion?
> You smuggled us all in:
> Because of the past we gave it all

Up and came to Israel!
Oh, if only we'd ridden in on donkeys
and hadn't yet gotten here!
Alas, what a black hour it was –
To hell with the plane that brought us here![207]

Oded Halahmy was born in Baghdad in 1938 and left for Israel in 1951. In his nostalgic memories, 'Everything about Baghdad is beautiful and colourful: the people, food, the city, and its museums and parks, its rivers and landscapes.'[208] His father, a goldsmith, co-owned a coffeehouse with a Muslim partner. In the evenings he took his son there as he sat with Muslim and Jewish friends, drinking tea or coffee, playing backgammon, sharing watermelon seeds and his flask of arak with those seated around him. When Oded was twelve, the family emigrated to Israel. They could not sell their home or business and could take only one suitcase. They were sad to leave their homeland. He remembers that 'the flight was crowded, and we dressed in our most beautiful clothes and the women wore all their jewellery'.

> When we landed at Lod Airport the Israelis sprayed us with DDT out of sheer ignorance, fearing that we'd brought parasites from an Arab land they didn't know anything about. They put us on flat-bed trucks and brought us directly to the transit camp. It was winter. It was raining. We were given two tents, one for the men, one for the women. The bathroom was far away. Harsh winds blew the tents away, and it was very hard work to keep them secured and maintained. The winter was very cold, living in tents with no heat, and we had no running water. We missed our beautiful house in Baghdad [where three generations

lived together in a three-story home with a courtyard] ... Everything was a shock for us because we had grown up being told that Israel was the Garden of Eden. Still today, I feel that the real 'land of milk and honey' was Iraq.²⁰⁹

Another Iraqi immigrant recalls that the transit camp had been a British detention centre beforehand: 'The Israeli security authorities had reinforced the camp's security by doubling the height of barbed wire around it and installing a direct telephone link to the Israeli police.' There were sixty constables and four sergeants 'and an officer to supervise the immigrants, who were housed in tents or tin-roofed barracks ... As I wandered amongst these tents, an elderly Iraqi waylaid me. "I have just one question," he said. "Are we immigrants or prisoners of war?"'²¹⁰

Along with being mistreated, Arab Jews were stripped of their Arab culture. One author relates how after he migrated to Israel from Morocco, when he registered and gave his name as Makhlouf, the school secretary was displeased by its Arabic sound. She shouted at her director to ask what she should write down instead. 'Put down Michael for him,' she said without raising her head from her files. Makhlouf suddenly became Michael.²¹¹ A scion of Spanish Jews, surname Parienté, who arrived in Meknes, Morocco in the fifteenth century, speaking a Judeo-Arabic dialect containing dozens of Castilian words, was stripped of that rich heritage in a single moment.²¹² The irony is that when Arab Jews arrived in Israel, they were cut off from the 'sources of their own culture, not to mention that of the peoples among whom they had lived for thousands of years'. This de-Arabisation meant the loss of Arabic.²¹³ For Abba Eban, South African-born Israeli diplomat and government minister who served in various roles from the creation of the state to the early 1970s:

> The object should be to infuse the Sephardim with an Occidental spirit, rather than allow them to drag us into an unnatural Orientalism ... One of the great apprehensions which afflict us ... is the danger lest the predominance of immigrants of Oriental origin force Israel to equalise its cultural level [i.e. lower it] with that of the neighbouring world.[214]

Israeli Ashkenazim had negative views of these Orientals, the Mizrahim, leading them to discriminate against Moroccans and other Arab Jews. This already began when they boarded ships for Israel, before they even arrived. Once there, the immigrants were sent to transit camps (*ma'barot*) that were temporary but where their stay dragged on, or to slums in Haifa and elsewhere, or to the *moshav* (agricultural collective) in the Negev Desert in place of the comfortable housing, jobs, and well-being that they were promised.[215] Discriminated against and placed at the bottom of the social ladder, only a few degrees above Falashas (Black Ethiopian Jews) and Palestinians, providing cheap labour, and victims of unemployment, they did not benefit from the education offered them by the AIU in Morocco.[216] In Hebrew, migrating to Israel is called ascent (*aliyah*), but for Arab Jews it was a very steep descent (*yerida*) to the margins of Israeli society, for, in the words of one migrant, 'not only did we descend down the social and economic ladder, we also lost our self-confidence, our social status and our proud sense of identity as Iraqi Jews'.[217]

The departure of Jews from Muslim-majority lands meant 'the disappearance of codes of communication, modes of behaviour and thinking which had allowed, in the past, a minimum of understanding between Jews and Muslims, even at the worst moments of their history. Amnesia gave rise, in times of crisis, to the most unbridled fantasies, on one side or the other.'[218] An antagonistic conception of Jewish–Muslim relations took hold in Israel. Israel emphasised persecution in Muslim-majority societies to justify the necessity of a Jewish state as a refuge for the victims of the Nazis in Europe, and for alleged persecution and discrimination in the Middle East since the time of Muhammad.[219] Arab Jews, as represented by the World Organisation of Jews from Arab Countries, make the argument that since Israel absorbed Jewish refugees from Muslim-majority lands, those Arab states have an obligation to absorb an equal number of Palestinian refugees and their descendants, on the model of the population exchanges of Greece and Turkey or India and Pakistan, to solve the Israeli–Palestinian conflict. As Israel had already done its share of the exchange, it was time for the Arab countries to do theirs.[220]

As Ella Shohat argues, Israeli national myth posits a split between Arab and Jew, without accepting a hyphenated Arab Jewish existence: 'The Arabness and the Orientalness of Jews posed a challenge' to Jewish national identity, for 'the cultural affinity that Arab Jews shared with Arab Muslims – in many respects stronger than that which they shared with European Jews – threatened the Zionist conception of a homogeneous nation modelled on the European nationalist definition of the nation-state'. Israel presents itself as Europe *in* the Middle East, but not *of* it. Arab Jews had to choose for the first time between Arabness and Jewishness, as Arabness, Middle Easterners, and Islam are placed on the negative side of the equation, and Jewishness, Europeanness, and Westernness on the positive side.[221] Primitive, backwardness, and pre-modern are attached to the former, and progress and modern to the latter.[222] Cultural dismemberment and rupture was couched as ingathering, a healing and a return, ostensibly tickets to integration. Which would you choose?

When world Jewish life was refocused in the twentieth

century on one nation, to which practically all Asian and African Jews migrated, Arab Jews went through a process of proletarianisation and impoverisation; disconnected, they faced cultural loss. Israel imposed a new culture that is Hebrew-language and Ashkenazi, in the middle of the Middle East, yet cut off from the region and its surrounding Arabic culture.

Arab Jews had closer links to the presumed enemy than to the Ashkenazi Jews with whom they were forced to assimilate. Peace will mean destroying the East/West cultural and linguistic borders between Israel and the rest of the Middle East. As Shohat writes, making Jewishness into a national identity had profound effects on Arab Jews as 'the meaning of the phrase "Arab-Jew" was transformed from being a taken-for-granted marker of religious (Jewish) and cultural (Arab) affiliation into a vexed question mark within competing nationalisms ... The two nationalisms came to view one side of the hyphen suspiciously. In the Arab world "the Jew" became out of bounds, while in the Jewish state "the Arab", hence the "Arab-Jew" or the "Jewish-Arab", came to seem an "impossibility".'[223]

Explaining why he entitled his autobiography *Memoirs of an Arab-Jew*, historian Avi Shlaim declared:

> In Iraq we were Arab Jews, we spoke Arabic at home, our cuisine was Arab cuisine, our culture was Arab culture, my parents' music was a very nice blend of Jewish and Arab music, so I can think of no better way to define myself as a young boy, to define my identity as that of an Arab Jew. I insist that there is such a thing. Zionism tried to erase the notion of an Arab Jew, but I still cling to it.[224]

An antagonistic view of Jewish–Muslim relations was codified recently in Israel, where the myth of the constant persecution of Jews in Muslim-majority countries and their expulsion is promoted, by the passing of a law on 23 June 2014, marking 30 November as the day of commemoration of the hundreds of thousands of Jewish refugees from the Middle East who were forcibly exiled and deported. The thirtieth of November, not coincidentally, is the day when war broke out between Jews and Muslims in Palestine in 1947. All Jews from the Middle East were lumped together, in a new, national narrative that erases the context of decolonisation and makes them all the same victims of persecution by Arabs, like Ashkenazi Jews victimised by Nazis.[225]

9

DUELLING MYTHS, DIVIDED HISTORIES, AND PROMOTING SYMBIOSIS TODAY

Jewish nostalgia for Egypt began in ancient times. In the Torah, after the Exodus, the Israelites wandering in the desert 'wept and said, "If only we had meat to eat! We remember the fish that we used to eat free in Egypt, the cucumbers, the melons, the leeks, the onions, and the garlic. Now our gullets are shrivelled. There is nothing at all! Nothing but this manna to look to!' (Numbers 11:4–6).

Nothing will bring the Jews back, not even the spectacular visit of President Anwar Sadat to Jerusalem in 1977 and his signing of a peace treaty with Israel in 1979, the first normalisation of relations between an Arab Muslim state and the Jewish state. Hundreds of thousands of Israelis, including Egyptian Jews, travelled as tourists or as pilgrims to the only neighbouring country they could visit. For their part, Egyptian Muslims did not reciprocate. Hostility and suspicion of Jews increased, and few made a distinction between Jews and Israelis/Zionists.

The Egyptian Jewish population decreased to eighteen by 2017, mostly elderly women. In June 2020 there were only five Jewish women in Cairo, and a man, who converted to Islam. Another four or five lived in Alexandria. They have not had rabbis for decades. 'This tiny core of elderly people can only remember a prestigious community past, or emblematic figures in what was a cosmopolitan culture.'[1]

For several decades women in Cairo led the community, pushing the government to restore cemeteries and synagogues, resisting foreign Jews' attempts to take the community's assets out of the country, as with the geniza. Until 2004 Esther Weinstein was its head, followed until 2013 by her daughter, Carmen. In 1978 Carmen began efforts to preserve the Bassatine Cemetery, the second oldest Jewish cemetery outside the Mount of Olives. It is more than a thousand years old, built in the ninth century during Sa'adia Gaon's era. After 1967 most of the marble headstones were repurposed for construction and roads were built through it. With the help of international Jewish organisations, it was protected and restored.[2] Carmen's grave was desecrated when she was laid to rest there in 2013.

The next community head, Magda Shehata Haroun, noted that Egyptian Jews are the accidental victims of regional politics as the creation of Israel caused a negative reaction by the Arab states which expelled their Jews or compelled them to emigrate. She intends to remain in Egypt to fulfil her duty to preserve the Jewish heritage of the land.[3] In 2014 her sister, Nadia, who served as deputy community leader, died aged fifty-nine. She was buried under armed police protection in the Bassatine cemetery, which remains a dumping ground for rubbish.[4]

The constitution of 2012 introduced by the Muslim Brotherhood President Mohammed Morsi after the Arab Spring of 2011 endorsed Judaism as a national religion along with Christianity and Islam, guaranteeing Jews the right to practise their religion.[5] After Morsi's overthrow, the secular president of Egypt Abdel Fattah El-Sisi continues the same policy. The ministry of antiquities restores synagogues and cemeteries. Nothing remains of the Jewish quarter at the heart of Cairo, other than a few Stars of David on doors where now Muslims live. This area, which contained more than a dozen synagogues, is today a market for toys and beauty products. Three synagogues remain, one of which is the ancient Ben Ezra synagogue in Fustat, Old Cairo, where the geniza was found. But the other two, despite being in the care of the ministry of antiquities, are in ruins: their walls are collapsing, or they have been eroded by sewage.[6]

The Ashkenazi synagogue, burned in the riots of 1945 and reconstructed in 1950, has not been used for decades. A visitor notes that 'scattered on the floor and full of dust, among various objects, was the candelabra which had once decorated the ceiling. It was difficult to breathe inside the building, which looked more like a storage room than a place of worship.'[7] Eliyahu Ha-Navi synagogue in Alexandria, one of the largest and most beautiful synagogues in the Middle East, was restored in January 2020.

The Jews and much of their cultural patrimony are gone. Egyptian filmmakers have used the figure of the Jew to symbolise cosmopolitanism, Levantism, and a golden age prior to 1952 when nationalism took over. The Jew serves as metaphor for the idealised past characterised by secular, modern, educated, urban, affluent, Westernised elites. In film Jewish women love Muslim men, and friendships are forged no matter the religious differences.

Since the late 1980s, Turkey has embraced the self-image of a righteous Muslim nation that has always been a tolerant host to its Jewish guests, which it uses to foster a sense of moral superiority to Christian Europe. Drawing continuities between the Ottoman Empire and Turkish Republic as saviour of Jews, it has used a propaganda campaign – manifested in model school curricula, academic publications and conferences, university lectures, heritage tourism for Jewish Americans, sponsored trips for journalists and politicians, the establishment of a Jewish Museum in Istanbul, and affiliated travelling exhibits – to promote the message that Turks have always been tolerant of foreign Jews.[8] Turkish film director Burak Cem Arlıel boasted that his film *Türk Pasaportu* (*Turkish Passport*), financed by the Turkish foreign ministry, 'is the only genocide film with a happy ending, because we succeeded in saving these people'.[9] The film narrates how Turkish ambassadors in France saved Jews, assumed to be French citizens, by granting them Turkish citizenship and providing Turkish passports. Since the Jews in the film speak French, the viewer would never imagine that the Jews were Turks.

Repeating stories of European Jews given refuge across the centuries allows Turkey to turn the tables on centuries-old charges of Turkish barbarity, and to silence European criticism of contemporary human rights violations and inherited responsibility for committing genocide. Turkey has no interest in admitting to the discrimination and violence its own population of Jews has been subjected to in the Turkish Republic, or the tragedy of the Turkish Jews left to their fate in Europe during the Shoah by their own government. Such revelations would puncture the myth of tolerance of Jews that Turkey relies on and draw attention to the Turkish (and not foreign) nature of Turkish Jews.

After Israel was established, half of Turkish Jews, mainly the poor, migrated to Israel by 1952. Mob violence in 1955, discrimination, being treated like foreigners, repeated synagogue bombings, assassinations of community leaders, and rampant anti-Semitism – in the press and Parliament and articulated by the president – contributed to the Jewish population dwindling from 80,000 in 1948 to 14,500 today. Declaring the Ottomans and Turks are their saviours, that Turks cannot be anti-Semitic, accusing Christians in the Ottoman Empire and Turkish Republic of treason to boost their own pride in being the ally of the Muslims, repeatedly denying the crimes of the empire and Republic including the Armenian Genocide, no group has been more vocal in promoting the myth of interfaith utopia in the Ottoman Empire and Turkey than the Turkish Jewish community.[10]

Turkish Muslims also play their part in this myth-making. The Turkish government funded the rebuilding of one of the largest synagogues in Europe, the great synagogue in Edirne. At the opening ceremony the deputy prime minister boasted, 'There is no anti-Semitism in Turkey,' a claim belied by the fact that it was the 1934 pogrom in Thrace that caused Jews to flee the city and left the synagogue to fall into ruin.[11] Despite President Erdoğan's claim that 'Turkey has never been anti-Semitic in any time in its history', and his promotion of the Ottoman and Turk as saviour of the Jew, he freely deploys anti-Semitic canards.[12] According to Erdoğan, Jews control world media. He claims the *New York Times* has been campaigning against Turkey's rulers since Sultan Abdülhamid II, and 'now, they are spitting out the same hatred on me ... It is clear who their patrons are. There is Jewish capital behind it, unfortunately.'[13] Erdoğan alleges Jews are so clever at managing money and are such geniuses that Turks should take them as a model, for they 'print money from where they are sitting' and 'still earn dividends from having invented the telephone and the light bulb' (Jews invented neither). He blames unrest in Turkey on either 'the interest rate lobby'[14] or the 'Mastermind' – a codeword for 'the international Jew', who Erdoğan and his followers, echoing both *The Protocols of the Elders of Zion* and Sayyid Qutb, allege 'rules the world, burns, destroys, starves, wages wars, organizes revolutions and coups, and establishes states within states', an evil cabal which has its sights set on annihilating Islam, Muslims, Turkey, and Turks.[15] Believing that the 'Mastermind' has deposed Ottoman and Turkish rulers ever since Abdülhamid II, Erdoğan blamed the 'Mastermind' for ordering the followers of Fethullah Gülen to carry out the unsuccessful coup attempt against his government in 2016.[16] But how could they explain how Gülen – a Turkish-educated, Sunni Muslim religious leader and former ally of Erdoğan who fled Turkey facing indictment for fomenting Islamic revolution prior to the rise of Erdoğan's party, the AKP – could be the cat's paw for a Jewish coup against an Islamist leader? They relied on the oldest conspiracy theory in their book, labelling him a Jew and Dönme, a Converso fulfilling world Jewry's alleged secret agenda.[17]

From 1908 to today, the Dönme character – a secret Jew hiding in the guise of the nation's leader who surreptitiously aims to destroy the Turkish culture, nation, and people on behalf of world Jewry – has been the stock figure in anti-government conspiracy theories promoted by Islamists dispossessed of their authority, extreme rightists, and leftists and secularists divested of their power. Long indoctrinated by official state history's belief that internal Christian enemies allied with foreign Christian powers always seek to destroy Turkey, the secularists are prepared to accept conspiracy theories about local minority puppets of world powers. The Islamists' rise to power with the election of Erdoğan in 2002, and the decline of the secular elite's control of Turkey's wealth, power, and culture, triggered the secularists' acceptance of the idea of a Converso prime minister and president.

Anti-Semitic conspiracy theories gained traction among all elements of Turkish society based on the assumption that only an ethnic Turkish Muslim can have Turkey's interests at heart, while a Jew – here the false convert, the secret Jew Dönme – can only serve foreign interests at odds with those of the Turks.[18] Jews cannot be considered Turks. While the people accused of being Conversos in the Ottoman Empire and Republican Turkey may have changed, the accusation remains the same.[19] It is as if the ghost of Spanish Inquisitional fears of judaisation re-emerged in Turkey and mixed with anti-Semitism.

More recently, President Erdoğan, using the word 'Jew' instead of 'Israeli', called Jews 'murderers, to the point that they kill children who are five or six years old. They are only satisfied by sucking their blood,' an echo of the medieval Christian blood libel. Despite such statements, the leaders of the Turkish Jewish community continue to declare the Turkish leader a friend and ally.[20]

In Morocco, the monarchy and elite, intellectuals interested in tolerance and diversity, some Amazigh activists and those connected to the tourist industry value the presence of Jews. The country promotes the idea of itself as tolerant, the saviour, or protector of Jews. After independence, the positive, protective aspect of the dhimma pact in pre-colonial Morocco – with the role of the sovereign as protector of the Jewish communities – was emphasised in royal discourse and by Jews as an expression of nationalist ideology. Although the legal disabilities of dhimmi status had almost disappeared (Muslim women can still marry only Muslim men) and Jews are Moroccan citizens just like Muslims, Jews are considered subjects and citizens: subjects from the fact of the allegiance connecting the commander of the faithful to the community of Moroccan Muslims, and citizens by virtue of the Moroccan constitution that recognises their rights. The notion of a protected rather than an emancipated Jewish community remains.

Duelling Myths, Divided Histories, and Promoting Symbiosis

The Jews are 'cosmopolitan and local, ambulatory but also rooted in the environment, polyglot yet maintaining the particular linguistic characteristics of the region'.[21] There are elements that recall pre-modern relations. The king employs a Jewish advisor, André Azoulay, 'the most prominent Jew living in the Arab world today'.[22] In 1991 Azoulay was appointed royal councillor to King Hassan II and played a role in PLO–Israel peace talks in Rabat, culminating in the Oslo Accords in 1993. Since 2003, Azoulay has spearheaded the Festival of Atlantic Andalusias in his native Essaouira, where Jews and Muslims sing Andalusi Arabic and Hebrew songs, celebrating Moroccan tolerance and coexistence.[23] One of the expressions of secular Judeo-Muslim culture is music.

From the end of the nineteenth century to the mid-twentieth century, Algerian, Moroccan, and Tunisian Jewish and Muslim musicians rediscovered the Andalusi musical tradition, and took it to the top of the charts performing with mixed orchestras on the radio, in concert halls, and at home, spinning records produced by Jewish-owned companies.[24] Jews 'played an important role in the conservation, promotion, and improvement' of this musical tradition.

In 2020 the king, Azoulay, and Azoulay's daughter, Audrey, former Minister of Culture of France, and current head of UNESCO, inaugurated the Beyt Dakira (House of Memory), a Jewish museum in Essaouira which incorporates a synagogue in the mellah of the same city.[25] The Jews are allowed an autonomous law court employing Jewish judges, all of whom are rabbis, to adjudicate domestic cases – the only one of its kind outside Israel. Muslims take care of abandoned synagogues and cemeteries. Some of these have been vandalised and their tombs broken. The kingdom tries to protect them, and is engaged in a project to restore thousands of cemeteries and shrines. As part of cultural diplomacy, the Andalusi spirit in Morocco is celebrated, and the Jewish heritage of the kingdom is marketed to nostalgic Moroccan Israelis, Europeans, and Canadians, just as youth attack them out of anti-Israeli sentiment. The nostalgia has been especially promoted since the 1991 peace process between Israel and the Arab states and continued after Morocco's signing of the Abraham Accords normalisation agreement in 2020.

In Morocco, Jews no longer have an impact on society and live mainly in Casablanca, where prior to mass migration in 1951 there were 75,000 Jews, one-third of Morocco's total; there are also some in Rabat, Fez, Meknes, Marrakesh, Tangier, and Essaouira, numbering (in 2016) around 4,000 mostly aged people, as the young left from 1948 to 1973.[26] The Jewish dimension of Morocco's heritage has acquired increased visibility in recent years. The multiplication of concrete manifestations of the diversity of the components of the country's identity, culture, and civilisation is one of the main results of the democratic process since Mohammed VI was enthroned in 1999.[27] The official recognition of the Jewish component of this diversity benefits from the presence of a Jewish population in the kingdom, and its involvement in various aspects of the life of the country: the daily functioning of its community institutions, the existence in the national judicial system of a High Rabbinical Tribunal, the attachment to their former homeland of those who left, their status as Moroccans with regard to the Moroccan Code of Nationality, the creation of a museum of Moroccan Judaism, and the Foundation of Judeo-Moroccan Cultural Patrimony (FPCJM). In 2011 the preamble of the new constitution gave credit to the Jewish presence and offered a message of tolerance.[28]

The ministry of education has rehabilitated former AIU schools and added commemorative plaques. Synagogues were restored, such as the seventeenth-century Danan synagogue in Fez, inaugurated in February 1999 by the future king Sidi Mohamed (now Mohammed VI) in the presence of Azoulay. In 2013 another, called Slat al Fassiyine, was restored by the FPCJM and inaugurated with a message sent by the king praising the cultural and spiritual heritage of Moroccan Jews as an example of the diversity, coexistence, and tolerance of the land.[29] It encouraged Muslims to be aware of the importance of the Jewish component of their history and their culture, in a world marked by rejection of differences, as well as by the daily repercussions of the Israeli–Palestinian conflict.[30] Even after terrorist attacks, such as at Casablanca in 2003, Moroccans, Jewish and Muslim, protested, with signs in Arabic and French, 'Jews and Muslims, we are all Moroccans' and 'No to terrorism'.[31] Jewish writer Edmond Amran El Maleh, former head of the Politburo of the illegal Communist Party, became a national icon; Simon Lévy, another former communist activist, and member of parliament, promoted Moroccan Jewish heritage as founder of the Jewish Museum of Casablanca. Both were outspoken patriots and fiercely anti-Zionist.[32]

In a 2015 US news report from Casablanca, which still boasts seventeen synagogues and a Jewish care home for the elderly, along with a Jewish Museum opened in 1997, the reporter takes a viewer into an AIU school. After the Second World War the AIU expanded in Morocco while abandoning most other countries by 1960. In Morocco it still had seventy-seven schools educating 29,000 students in 1960.[33] In 2015 the students, 80 per cent of whom were Muslim, and who were instructed in Arabic, Hebrew, French, and English, are shown preparing matzah for Passover. Director Shimon Cohen, speaking in French, declares that 'In Morocco, historically, Jews and Muslims lived as neighbours in a proximity that was extremely peaceful. They shared not only celebrations, but also traditions, and at the same time, food.' There were terrorist attacks on a Jewish restaurant and community centre in 2003, but Shimon Cohen declares such attacks are out of character for Morocco, as Jews 'benefit from Muslim benevolence towards them ... they are respected, they are protected. They are very close.' All agree intolerance is an aberration.[34]

In Akka, in Saharan Morocco, for young adults who have never met Jews, the notion of indigenous Jews is inconceivable. They tend to see all Jews one-dimensionally as Israeli oppressors of Palestinians, as 'their political and social enemies'. Their grandparents and great-grandparents, however, have fond memories of their interactions with Jews and 'express nostalgic sadness about the absence of Jews'.[35]

At the end of the 1960s, there were 600,000 Jews and 700,000 Muslims in France. Most members of both groups originated in the Maghreb, where they shared a Judeo-Muslim culture.[36] Today France boasts the largest Muslim and Jewish population in Europe, with four to six million Muslims and 500,000–600,000 Jews, at least half of each group made up of immigrants or descendants of those from French Algeria, Morocco, and Tunisia. They live side by side in Paris (in Belleville, Sarcelles, Crétiel, the Marais) and Marseille (in La Rose, Belsunce-Porte d'Aix), where they interact, in cooperation and conflict, not solely motivated by religion, or by what is happening in Israel–Palestine, but with their own history shaped by their dissimilar experience thanks to colonialism.[37]

Jewish and Muslim migrants to France relate to each other as immigrants living in the same neighbourhoods, as customers at the same bars, cafes, cinemas, groceries, and restaurants, speakers of Arabic, employers and employees, victims of racists, religious minorities in a secular state, and citizens.[38] On the rue des Chapeliers in Marseille in the 1950s and 1960s there were thirty-two Muslim-owned businesses including Tunisian restaurants and twenty-seven Jewish ones such as fabric stores. A Muslim woman remembers how 'my mother and all the other women bought cloth at the fabric stores, Arab or not (Jewish or Armenian), but they all spoke Arabic.' According to another resident, 'When there was a party – a baptism ... a circumcision – everyone took advantage, both Jews and Arabs ... When there was an Arab wedding ... everyone went.'[39]

The problem began at arrival. Jews were considered Europeans and Muslims were not. Muslims became 'immigrants of a lower order'.[40] Most Muslims arriving in the 1950s were not educated, while Jews were. Maghrebi Jews experienced rapid social mobility, moving from artisanal, industrial, and commercial employment into salaried positions, the civil service, and the liberal professions, such as law or medicine. Muslims were employed in poorly paid jobs, in building, industrial labour, mines, and cleaning services.[41] Jewish institutions offered a safety net, medical facilities, care for the elderly and children, scholarships, employment, cultural, religious, and education programmes, along with French citizenship, which enabled people to benefit from welfare and access to housing. Young male Muslim migrants lacked financial and social support while facing discrimination.[42]

As citizens, included in the colonial project, Jews were repatriated to France after colonialism, assisted by the ministry of repatriation, which offered them housing and employment. They were welcomed to the metropole, and reinstalled, thanks to state subventions and credit, in nearly the same social and economic ranks they lost. They received compensation for wealth left behind in the Maghreb. By contrast, as immigrants, excluded from the colonial project, Muslims were treated as foreigners in

France, assisted by the ministry of the interior. They were discriminated against, as in the colonies.[43] Jews were met with a 'welcome policy', the latter a 'migration policy', or even a 'labour policy'.[44] Jews were said to return to France, although it was an arrival for them, classified with the other French people, the *pieds noirs*, returning from exile. They claimed a Sephardi identity to distinguish themselves from the Ashkenazim and fellow Arabs.[45] The Maghrebi Muslims were seen as temporary migrants, who, unlike the Jews, could return to their homelands.[46]

In the 1950s and 1960s left-wing Jews and organisations in France supported the Algerian independence struggle and promoted interreligious dialogue, while mainstream Ashkenazi-dominated Jewish institutions promoted an antagonistic view of Muslims as anti-Semites and independence as a threat to Jews.[47]

The idea that Maghrebi Jews are in conflict with Muslims stemmed from French administrators, who imagined the two to be homogenised blocs at odds with each other, which their granting of French citizenship to the former helped solidify.[48] Another source of the idea of eternal conflict came from international Jewish organisations, which sought to help the large number of impoverished Jews. The members of these organisations were motivated by a post-Holocaust, Zionist view that promoted Arab Jews' salvation from dangerous Muslim fanatics in migration to Israel.[49] A final source for this view came from the nationalist movements – the Algerian FLN, Tunisian Neo Destour, and Moroccan Istiqlal – that promoted the integration of local Jews, attracting Jewish supporters, yet considered Jews at least collaborators if not traitors for siding with France, and denigrated Zionism, seeing migration as an act of disloyalty, leading to riots and boycotts against them.[50]

The 1967 Arab–Israeli war did not lead to conflict between Jews and Muslims in France, although tensions rose in Marseille,

Duelling Myths, Divided Histories, and Promoting Symbiosis

which had the third largest Jewish population in Europe (80,000), most of whom were North African, and tens of thousands of Algerian Muslims.[51] The war made Zionism and the Palestinian cause more central concerns for Jewish and Muslim university students.

Disagreements over France's Middle East policy began to effect inter-communal relations as it pitted student activists against each other. Jews depicted Palestinian and Middle Eastern Arabs, even Maghrebi Muslims, as violent and threatening, on par with Nazis. Centuries of symbiosis were forgotten in antagonistic memories of Muslims as persecutors. Nasser was compared with Hitler and the war of 1967 – in the event of an Israeli defeat – was considered a prelude to genocide. It was the 1968 student movement, with its many Jewish leaders, such as Daniel Cohn-Bendit, that brought the Palestinian issue to the centre of Jewish–Muslim relations in the country.[52] Whilst leftists adopting the Palestinian cause as their own led to a further rupture, there were Maoist Jewish militants and Muslim students who saw eye to eye, denouncing racism in France as well.[53] In 1968 the Sephardic former prime minister Mendès-France called for Arab–Israeli peace.[54]

Differences led to riots between Muslims and Jews in Belleville, Paris in June 1968, before religious leaders stepped in to re-establish good relations.[55] Most significant, the two days of rioting in 1968 took place during massive student uprisings and labour strikes, reflecting how high school and university student activists made the Arab–Israeli conflict central to Jewish–Muslim relations.[56]

We see the continuing relevance of secular symbiosis. Trotskyists and Maoists in France, such as the then Algerian Jewish radical Benjamin Stora, or the Egyptian Jewish convert to Islam Adel Rifaat, linked the Palestinian cause to the struggles against capitalism, colonialism, imperialism, and racism, and for the rights of immigrant Muslim workers in France.[57] Far-left activists, North African Muslim students, and Palestinian representatives joined efforts to promote the Palestinian cause. Many of these radicals were Jewish children of Holocaust survivors who saw the Palestinians as the new Jews denied their human rights.[58]

Maoists were the most vociferous supporters of the Palestinians, and Ashkenazi Jews played leading roles in their organisations. The two leaders of the Proletarian Left, banned in 1970, were Alan Geismar, who supported the FLN and compared the French army actions in Algeria to those of the Nazis, and Pierre Victor (aka Benny Lévy, the philosopher and personal secretary of Jean Paul-Sartre and co-founder of the newspaper *Libération*, as well as half-brother of Adel Rifaat, who fled Egypt in 1956). Three of the four most visible student leaders were Daniel Cohn-Bendit, Alain Krivine, and Alain Geismar. Eleven of twelve of the board members of the Revolutionary Communist League, banned in 1973, were Jews, as were most of the Trotskyist Communist Party.[59] They were not the only anti-Zionist Jewish radicals.

Maxime Rodinson, a professor of history and sociology at the École Pratique des Hautes Études, and a Marseille-born Marxist whose communist parents were murdered at Auschwitz, was also a leading critic of Israel.[60] Rabbi Emmanuel Lévyne, whose father was killed in Auschwitz, wrote *Judaism against Zionism*.[61] Journalist Ania Francos, another French Jew whose family was murdered by the Nazis, was close to the PLO and opposed Israel. Trotskyist and Marxist sociologist Catherine Lévy supported the Palestinians, as did Trotskyist Jean-Louis Weissberg, who visited the PFLP in a refugee camp.[62] Geismar and Léo Lévy (Benny's wife) visited the PLO's military wing in

Jordan in 1969. They worked with Muslim students to fuse the Palestinian cause and immigrant workers' rights in the Maoist Comités Palestine in 1970.[63]

The outcome of these radical Jews and Muslims working together, however, was worsened relations between Jews and Muslims in France, as positions on Israel and Palestine hardened among the wider communities, which saw the struggle in ethnic terms. Scuffles broke out on university campuses, and there were fistfights between political sides, but it was not always Jews versus Muslims. Jews clashed amongst themselves.[64] Mainstream Jewish organisations complained that 'anti-Semitism in the guise of anti-Zionism was infecting French campuses and that their *own* co-religionists were helping to *create* tensions'.[65]

By 1969, however, many Jews perceived all Arabs, even the Maghrebis in France, as their opponents. The Palestinian terrorist killing of Israeli athletes at the 1972 Munich Olympics, and more than a dozen attacks against Jewish targets in France, including the main synagogue in Marseille, and Israeli assassinations of Arabs in France, such as the Paris representative of the PLO Mahmoud Hamchari in 1973, worsened Jewish–Muslim relations.[66] The lines conflating Israeli/Zionist/Jew and Muslim/Palestinian/Arab/Maghrebi blurred. In 1976 Mendès-France hosted indirect talks between the PLO and Israelis.[67]

The 1980s witnessed the growth of multiculturalism ushered in by François Mitterrand's Socialist government as well as the rise of Jean-Marie Le Pen's Far-Right Front National. Despite the tensions of the preceding decades, such xenophobia and anti-minority sentiment made Muslims and Jews alike recognise that racism is a common danger to them both. It was countered by the birth of an anti-racist coalition spearheaded by such groups as SOS Racisme (established 1985), which fought against anti-Semitism and Islamophobia. One of its founders was the former Trotskyist Julien Dray, an Algerian Jew from Oran. Its secretary general was Eric Ghébali, president of the Union of French Jewish Students, who promoted Jewish–Muslim reconciliation. It was given media prominence by the support of such distinguished Jewish intellectuals as Bernard-Henri Lévy.[68]

After a series of murders of Muslims and a bombing of a Jewish film festival, Jews and Muslims protested together, crying, 'Arabs in Menton, Jews in Paris, they are killing our friends.'[69] Prominent French Muslim intellectuals such as Tahar Ben Jelloun argued that victims of racism – who include Jews – must unite.[70] These efforts were preceded by such organisations promoting relations between Muslim and Jewish North Africans as Identité et Dialogue, founded in 1976 by André Azoulay.[71]

Jewish–Muslim cooperation collapsed by the end of the decade. Muslims reminded Jews how they had supported the colonialists in Algeria, while Jews wanted Muslims to recognise the attacks on Jews. Muslims wanted their help given to French Jews during the Holocaust recognised.[72] In 1988 Arezki Dahmani founded a new organisation, France Plus, which launched a committee called Shalom-Salem that emphasised common Maghrebi heritage, committed to fighting racism in France, and promoted peace in the Middle East recognising Israel while supporting Palestinian rights.[73] But despite the opportunity for expressing shared concerns for religious tolerance, being anti-racist, and promoting peace, differing responses to the expulsion of headscarf-wearing Muslim girls from a middle school in 1989, one of whom was a Jewish convert, the desecration of a body at the Jewish cemetery at Carpentras in southeastern France in 1990, and the First Gulf War in 1991 brought Jewish–Muslim divergences to the fore.[74] Jews sided with state secularism over the right to wear a headscarf, emphasising Jewish Frenchness

Duelling Myths, Divided Histories, and Promoting Symbiosis

but Muslim foreignness. Anti-Semitism and racism began to be seen as distinct. Taking the side of either Israel or Iraq in the war as well as increased police surveillance of Muslims accused of double loyalty broke apart the anti-racism coalition.[75] Jews and Muslims moved away from republicanism and towards ethno-religious identity politics, making relationships more difficult.[76]

Relations between Muslims and Jews in France worsened. The PFLP bombed the Parisian rue Copernic synagogue in 1980; there was a terror attack on the rue des Rosiers in the heart of the Jewish quarter of Paris in 1982; and Molotov cocktails were launched at a synagogue in Villepinte in the Parisian suburbs in 2000.

The new millennium witnessed the beginning of a two-decade wave of anti-Jewish violence committed by Muslims in France. This includes the 2002 attack on the Lyon synagogue; the 2006 kidnapping, torture, burning, and murder of Ilan Halimi, who had a Moroccan background and whose corpse was found naked on railroad tracks; the 2012 murder of a rabbi and three children aged three, six, and seven at the Ohr Torah Jewish school in Toulouse by an Algerian Muslim; and the kidnapping of a Jewish couple and rape of the woman in Créteil in 2014.[77] In 2015 alone, there were three sad events. Three Jews were stabbed outside a synagogue and another Jewish man was stabbed on the street in Marseille. The office of the satirical weekly *Charlie Hebdo* – which ridicules Muhammad – was attacked by Islamists shouting '*Allahu Akbar*' and that they were avenging the Prophet. They murdered eight writers, many of whom were Jews, and a Muslim policeman and three others. Days later a convert to Islam connected to the *Charlie Hebdo* attackers besieged the kosher supermarket Hyper Cacher in Paris, took hostages, and killed four Jewish customers.[78] In 2017 there was the murder of sixty-five-year-old grandmother Lucie Attal (or Attal-Halimi), whose Muslim neighbour and attacker shouted '*Allahu Akbar*' and crushed her skull with her bedside telephone in her home and threw her corpse off her balcony. She had had good relations with her Muslim neighbours, including a Moroccan man doing work for the Orthodox woman that she could not do on Shabbat. A year later, the same grim fate awaited eighty-five-year-old Mireille Knolle: a Holocaust survivor, stabbed a dozen times and burned. She was also murdered by a Muslim neighbour because she was Jewish.[79] In 2024, 62 per cent of all religious-motivated hate crimes were against Jews although Jews make up only 1 per cent of the population.[80] All led to an increased Islamophobia in society, increasing support for the far right (an Algerian-origin Islamophobic Jew, Éric Zemmour, leads a far-right splinter party), and restrictions on the practice of Islam. The Israeli–Palestinian conflict continued to divide Jews and Muslims, even as French recognition of the horrors of the Holocaust and Algerian War and interfaith dialogue had helped improve relations.[81] And yet, despite it all, daily interactions continue in such places as boulevard de Belleville in Paris, where Tunisian synagogues, kosher cafes and greengrocers stand side by side with Muslim-owned cafes and Algerian restaurants.

Violence in the Middle East hardens views. On Saturday 7 October 2023 Jews were celebrating the holiday of Simchat Torah, which marks the completion of the annual cycle of reading the Torah scroll. It is a joyous synagogue festival, where congregants sing and dance with the ancient scrolls. But on that day, thousands of Hamas and Islamic Jihad militants and Palestinian civilians burst through the border fence separating the Palestinian-administered coastal Gaza Strip and the Jewish state of Israel. Heavily armed, they crossed with motorcycles, pickup trucks, paramotors – and speedboats on the coast – descending on two dozen towns as far as fifteen kilometres inside Israel. These militants also attacked a rave festival. The Hamas guerrillas beat, gang raped, and murdered the people they came across. They killed more than 1,200 Israelis, of whom more than 800 were civilians.[82] The victims included babies, children, women, and the elderly. The militants also assaulted and abducted more than 255 others, taking them as hostages to the Gaza Strip. A year later, while 154 hostages had been returned, 101 were still held, 35 of whom were declared dead. Two years later, the last twenty living hostages were released. The attack confirmed the Islamophobic view of many Israelis and Jews that Muslims are ruthless anti-Semitic murderers.

In response, Israel mobilised several hundred thousand soldiers to launch a military campaign by air, land, and sea. Within a month, relentless Israeli bombing killed an estimated 10,000 Palestinians, perhaps half of whom were children. After two years, at least 67,000 had been killed, an estimated four fifths of whom were civilians, although we do not know how many were Hamas fighters.[83] Israeli forces targeted hospitals, convoys of ambulances, schools, and refugee camps. Israel was accused of committing genocide as it besieged the Gaza Strip, cutting it off from the world, blockading its supply of aid, water, food, fuel, and electricity, silencing its internet and telephone links. Without electricity, desalination and wastewater treatment plants could not run, leading to outbreaks of disease, including polio, and lack of power to hospitals led to further misery and death. Israeli attacks on densely populated urban areas caused most of the civilian population to flee their homes to the southern end of the strip, where they were also targeted in bombings. Israel's response to the Hamas attack confirmed for many Muslims the anti-Semitic view that Jews are bloodthirsty Islamophobic murderers.

Observing this pitiless bloodshed in Israel and Gaza, in which civilians are targeted, and which ostensibly pits Muslims against Jews, many commentators declare that the conflict in Israel and Palestine is a religious struggle. They see it as proof of the myth that Jews and Muslims have always been enemies, that they never have and can never live together.

They quote verses in the Qur'an about Jews such as, 'Wretchedness and baseness were stamped upon them, and they were visited with wrath from God. That was because they disbelieved in God's revelations and slew the prophets wrongfully' (2:61), or 'Indeed, you will surely find that the most vehement of men in enmity to those who believe are the Jews and the polytheists' (5:82), and 'O you who believe! do not take the Jews and the Christians for friends; they are friends of each other; and whoever amongst you takes them for a friend, then surely he is one of them; surely God does not guide the unjust people' (5:51).

Others observe that the founding charter of Hamas, an offshoot of the Palestinian branch of the Egyptian Muslim Brotherhood founded in 1988 by Shaykh Ahmed Yassin (who was assassinated by Israel in 2004), the group that carried out the 7 October terrorist attacks, frames the battle over Palestine as a religious struggle. The group declared it was engaged in a 'battle with the Jews', until Israel is overcome, and God's victory is assured 'on every inch of Palestine'. It cites a *hadith*, a saying attributed to Muhammad: 'The Last Hour would not come until the Muslims fight against the Jews and the Muslims would kill them, and until the Jews would hide themselves behind a stone or a tree and a stone or a tree would say, "Muslim or Servant of Allah there is a Jew behind me; come and kill him."' According to the charter, 'fighting the enemy', the Jew, is obligatory for

Duelling Myths, Divided Histories, and Promoting Symbiosis

every Muslim man and woman everywhere in the world. There is no solution to the Palestinian problem other than Holy War, for the Palestinian cause 'is a religious cause'. Although Hamas's revised 2017 charter 'affirms that its conflict is with the Zionist project not with the Jews because of their religion', the group continues to promote 'armed resistance' to Israel until an Islamic state is established in the entirety of Palestine.[84] In its original charter, Hamas quotes from *The Protocols of the Elders of Zion*, as if it is an actual historical document, proof of a worldwide Jewish conspiracy.[85] Unlike the PLO, the openly anti-Semitic Hamas does not recognise Israel's existence and vows to continue 'armed struggle'. During the first Palestinian uprising (intifada) in 1987, Hamas declared, 'The day of judgment will not come before the extermination of all the Jews.'[86]

Hamas is not alone in making religious statements to justify its actions. Israeli Prime Minister Benjamin Netanyahu referred to the Torah three weeks after the Hamas attack when he declared,

> 'Remember what Amalek did to you' (Deuteronomy 25:17). We remember and we fight. Our brave soldiers who are now in Gaza, around Gaza and in the other sectors throughout the country, join a chain of heroes of Israel that has continued for over 3,000 years, from Joshua, Judah Maccabee and Bar Kochba, and up to the heroes of 1948, the Six Day War, the Yom Kippur War and Israel's other wars. Our heroic soldiers have one supreme goal: to destroy the murderous enemy and ensure our existence in our land. We have always said 'Never again.' 'Never again' is now.[87]

In the Torah, God commands King Saul to kill every person in Amalek (1 Samuel). The prophet Samuel tells King Saul that God says, 'I will punish the Amalekites for what they did to Israel when they waylaid them as they came up from Egypt. Now go, attack the Amalekites and destroy all that belongs to them. Do not spare them. Put to death men and women, children and infants, cattle and sheep, camels and donkeys.' Just as the Amalekites ambushed the Israelites, the prime minister inferred, so, too, did Hamas attack Israelis. The ancient attack led God to tell Moses to wipe out Amalek. Hundreds of years later, King Saul nearly fulfilled the command by killing all Amalekite people, save their king, who kept his people alive by siring a child. Many generations later, one of his descendants, the villain Haman, hatched a plot to kill all the Jews living in exile in Persia, the overcoming of which is told every year in the festival of Purim. Saul's failure to kill every Amalekite posed an existential threat to the Jewish people. Prime Minister Netanyahu vowed he would not make the same mistake facing today's Amalekites, the Palestinians, to prevent Jews falling victim to another Holocaust. And as a result, the Israeli army has waged what has been called a genocidal war, as the ancient Israelites committed genocide against the Amalekites.

Considering the historical religious references made by the main protagonists in the current violence, it seems we are witnessing a Jewish–Muslim struggle, not the battle of two nations over the same land which they both claim. But Benjamin Netanyahu and Hamas's leader Yahya Sinwar (killed by Israel in 2024) do not represent all Jews and Muslims. Jews and Muslims have not always been at each other's throats. Yet if we oppose that view, we do not have to subscribe to the mythical sentiment animating Turkish Jewish historian and Member of Parliament Avram Galanti that 'No Jews in the world have ever been protected as well by their state as has Turkish Jewry. Jews know this and write Jewish history expressing this in golden letters.'[88] We must not have to choose between writing the history of Jewish–Muslim relations in either red (blood) or gold ink. As this book has shown, Jews and Muslims have shared good times and bad, days of onion and days of honey, in the words of a Sephardic and Palestinian proverb.

From 7 October 2023, Israelis and Jewish communities in Europe held candlelight vigils mourning the greatest Jewish loss of life in an attack since the Holocaust. They put up posters of the missing Israeli hostages. From the beginning of Israel's revenge attack on Gaza, mass protests against the immense loss of Palestinian life have been organised in the cities of Europe. Protestors have torn down pictures of the abducted Israelis. They have burned the Israeli flag, which consists of a blue Star of David on a white background, in front of synagogues. They launched arson attacks on other synagogues and assaulted identifiably Jewish people. At the pro-Palestine marches in London, Muslim women held signs declaring 'Keep the World Clean of Jews' with a picture of a stick man throwing a Star of David in a rubbish bin. Other Muslim women at the protests carried photos of paramotors of the type Hamas used to carry out the 7 October attacks.

The outbreak of violence in Israel and the Gaza Strip led to an increase in attacks on Jews and Muslims in the UK. The Community Security Trust (CST) has been reporting anti-Semitic incidents since 1984. It defines anti-Semitism as 'any malicious act aimed at Jewish people, organisations, or property'.[89] The CST's detailed reports of anti-Jewish racism – ranging from damage and desecration of Jewish synagogues, cemeteries, schools, and businesses, to verbal abuse, hate mail and social media, anti-Semitic graffiti, and grievous bodily harm – demonstrate the correlation between the Israeli–Palestinian conflict and attacks on Jews in the UK. The three highest recorded numbers of incidents occurred in 2009, 2014, and 2023–5, all years when Israel and Hamas warred in Gaza.[90]

According to the CST, in the twenty-one days between the Hamas attack on Israel and Friday 27 October, there were at least 805 anti-Semitic incidents across the UK, the highest total ever reported to CST across a twenty-one-day period. In three weeks, CST recorded more anti-Semitic incidents than the 803 reported in the first six months in 2023. This was an increase in anti-Jewish hate acts of 689 per cent compared to the same period the year before. By 7 October 2024, the CST had recorded more than 5,500 anti-Semitic incidents in the UK in the past year, a 204 per cent increase from the year before.

Islamophobia in the UK also spiked in the same period. Between 7 and 19 October, Tell MAMA, funded by the UK government, recorded 291 cases of anti-Muslim hate – a six-fold increase from the same period in 2022. Tell MAMA observed a two-fold increase in London alone. By 7 October 2024, Tell MAMA recorded 4,971 incidents of Islamophobia, the highest total in fourteen years.[91]

In England in 2025, boxes of Passover matzot for sale in several grocery store chains were covered in 'Free Palestine' stickers by activists, as if British Jews are responsible for what happens in Gaza. A British Muslim man drove his car into Jews gathered outside the Heaton Park synagogue in Manchester, England on Yom Kippur, the holiest day of the Jewish calendar, and emerged from the car and knifed a Jewish man to death before police killed him as he tried to enter the barricaded synagogue.[92] Yet at the same time, the leader of the Green Party of England and Wales is a Jew, Zack Polanski, and a deputy leader is a Muslim, Mothin Ali. It is the age-old secular symbiosis, the left-wing anti-Zionist alliance that we have seen in the Middle East and Europe.

Duelling Myths, Divided Histories, and Promoting Symbiosis

On 7 October 2024, UK Chief Rabbi Sir Ephraim Mirvis, Archbishop of Canterbury Justin Welby, and Imam Qari Muhammad Asim, chair of the Mosques and Imams national advisory board, along with other rabbis and imams, issued a letter condemning both 'the brutal Hamas terrorist attacks in Israel' and the 'devastating war in Gaza'. These faith leaders stood 'united in our grief and in our belief that our shared humanity must bring us together ... that we should mourn for all the innocent people who have lost their lives. We must also reject those who seek to divide us. Anti-Jewish hate and anti-Muslim hate have no place in the UK today. We must stand together against prejudice and hatred in all its forms.'[93] At the time of writing, at the end of 2025, it seems there is little space for one who wishes to follow their lead, to mourn the nine-month-old Israeli infant Kfar Bibas and his four-year-old brother Ariel, taken hostage by Hamas and murdered, together with the five-year-old Palestinian girl Hind Rajab, indiscriminately killed by Israeli forces.

CONCLUSION

ABRAHAM'S INHERITANCE: ISHMAEL AND ISAAC, HAGAR AND SARAH TODAY

In her essay 'My Brother Ishmael', written in 1977 in Hebrew when Egyptian President Anwar Sadat visited Jerusalem, the Cairo-born Jewish writer Jacqueline Kahanoff argued against the Islamic and Jewish view that only one son – Ishmael for Muslims, Isaac for Jews – has the right to the Abrahamic inheritance. Jews need to accept Ishmael, representing Muslims, as their brother, just as Muslims need to recognise Isaac, representing Jews, as their brother with equal rights.[1] Kahanoff called on Jew and Muslim to understand that rather than only one son being blessed, there are two rights, and two sons, which deserve equal recognition as the inheritors of Abraham. Arguing against primacy, she was a prophetic voice offering a way for Israelis and Palestinians, Jews and Muslims, sons, daughters, and mothers, to live in peace.[2]

In an earlier essay, Kahanoff imagined that rather than being rivals and victims of patriarchy, Sarah and Hagar's descendants today can 'establish a new covenant for themselves and their children', as Jews and Muslims 'need not be bound forever by the terms set by our ancient myths and holy scriptures'.[3] The solution lies in an Israel which belongs to and is integrated into the

Middle East, part of 'a pluralistic Levant', which, going beyond what she imagines, will hopefully see an independent Palestine alongside Israel.[4]

Today, despite everything, there are Jews and Muslims who insist on having good relations. In France this includes the group Amitié Judéo-Musulmane de France, established nearly two decades ago in Paris, whose goals are to 'develop friendship between Jews and Muslims, fight against anti-Semitism and anti-Muslim racism, say no to all forms of prejudice and discrimination, and promote a peaceful society through better knowledge of others'.[5] They organise lectures, film screenings, visits to a mosque, and Spanish and Portuguese synagogues, iftars, concerts, and vigils for peace. More recently, in July 2024 Nous Réconcilier (Let's Reconcile) was established in France to foster dialogue between Israelis and Palestinians, Jews and Muslims. In 2025 they sponsored a pop-up restaurant in Paris called Sababa (Joy of Living) established by an Algerian-born French–Israeli Jew, Edgar Laloum, and an Algerian-born Palestinian Muslim, Radjaa Aboudagga.[6]

Amid the outpouring of hate, there exist grassroots networks of Muslims and Jews committed to good relations between the approximately 300,000 Jews (over half of whom live in London) and four million Muslims in England and Wales, too. One of them is the Joseph Interfaith Foundation, a joint Jewish–Muslim interfaith charity founded in 2006 which aims to end prejudice, misinformation, and misunderstanding through 'constructive and sustained dialogue, effective discussion and realistic social interaction' between British Muslims and Jews. It provides annual student seminars on university campuses, hosts a recognised national council of imams and rabbis, as well as an academic advisory board, and a national council of Muslim and Jewish physicians. Its executive director is an Iranian British woman, Mehri Niknam, who describes herself as 'an Islamophile Jew'.[7]

Another organisation is Nisa-Nashim, a national Jewish Muslim women's network whose explicit goal is to 'build cohesion and positive change'. Its local branches are co-chaired by a Muslim and a Jewish woman. The group notes that what its members share are 'the challenges of historical immigration, weaknesses in women's empowerment, prejudice from outside, and minority status'. Bridges are built from shared experiences, recognising real differences.[8] The Maimonides Interfaith Foundation, established by an Iranian British Muslim, Professor Sir Nasser David Khalili is another such group. 'Inspired by Moses Maimonides, the great Jewish philosopher who lived and wrote at a time of enlightened religious tolerance', the charity emphasises 'what the Abrahamic faiths share'.

Maimonides is also the inspiration for interfaith efforts in the Middle East. In Abu Dhabi, a synagogue, church, and mosque were built side by side in an interfaith centre called the Abrahamic Family House in 2023. The Moses ben Maimon synagogue has a Torah scroll donated by the Muslim president of the country. The British chief rabbi, Ephraim Mirvis, affixed the *mezuzah* to its door. The synagogue, church, and mosque have the same dimensions, symbolising coexistence and interfaith dialogue. The UAE has been criticised, however, for building the complex merely to improve its image and foster better international commercial and diplomatic relations, especially with Israel. Nevertheless, the fact that the synagogue is named after the great medieval Andalusian and Egyptian Jewish thinker Maimonides bears witness to an important aspect of the history of Jewish–Muslim relations that is as much a part of the past and future as violence and prejudice.[9]

In 2019, as René Trabelsi served as minister of tourism, the first Jewish minister in a Tunisian government since the late 1950s, Tunisia issued a postage stamp with an image of the El Ghriba synagogue, located on the island of Djerba, where half of Tunisia's Jewish population lives, despite a 2002 Al-Qaeda suicide bombing that killed nineteen people.[10] The aim was to promote 'the principles and values of tolerance, openness and dialogue between the religions of Tunisia, throughout the ages and civilisations'. The synagogue was attacked again in 2023 and the annual pilgrimage festival was cancelled.[11] Yet Jews and Muslims who visit proclaim a fervent belief that it is a holy pilgrimage site, built over the tomb of a saintly woman located in the crypt of the synagogue, where women write their prayers on eggs and leave them along with candles so that the saint will make them come true. A fire extinguisher is placed above the burning candles lit by devotees whispering prayers.

Among the whitewashed walls of the homes and mosques on the palm tree-spotted island, not far from the cerulean sea, is the ancient synagogue. The main entrance door to the covered courtyard through which one reaches the sanctuary is a horseshoe arch inscribed with a Star of David at top. Its whitewashed exterior, interspersed with sky-blue window grates, does not ready the visitor for the vibrant decoration of the sanctuary inside. Blue pillars support blue and white banded arches and blue tiles beneath blue, green, and yellow stained glass and ceiling. After removing one's shoes, as Muslims do, the pilgrim enters the sanctuary, whose eastern wall is filled with prayers written on paper and fitted into the cracks of a glass-covered case holding silver amulets, as if this were the Western Wall of the Temple in Jerusalem. Treasures from the Temple destroyed by the Babylonians in 586 BCE were allegedly carried here and buried where the synagogue was built by Israelites arriving on Phoenician boats. As a reminder, the names of the twelve

Israelite tribes are inscribed in gold letters around the sanctuary. Names of Sephardic families, such as the Parienté, are also memorialised on the walls. El Ghriba is a pilgrimage site, where before the recent Israeli–Palestinian war 15,000 Jews, especially Tunisian Jews from France and Israel, celebrated a three-day annual festival.

The synagogue is in the *hara sghira*, the small Jewish neighbourhood on the island. A short distance away is the *hara kbira*, the large Jewish neighbourhood, where thirteen synagogues such as those of Rabbi Pinhas and Sabban hide behind their walls, unbeknownst to tourists, just as the Jewish homes on Raisin Street and Almond Street are not distinguishable from those of Muslims. Arabic- and French-speaking men wearing kippot fry *brik*, a savoury pastry filled with egg and tuna, parsley and harissa, in hot oil at Brik Ishak and Le Roi de Brik, and serve baguettes filled with boiled egg, cucumber, tomato, sardines, and more harissa to hungry boys on their break from nearby yeshivot. In the ancient market at Houmt Souk, a whole row of dozens of jewellers carries surnames like the Portuguese Bitan, along with first names Esther and David, Simon, Daniel, Yonatan, Benjamin, and Ariel. Signs in Hebrew offer welcome to Israeli tourists. Jewish silversmiths serve their veiled and modestly dressed Muslim women customers, buying gold 'at the Jew's', as one elderly woman refers to one shop.

Djerba is one of the only places in the Middle East where Arab Jews, if in much diminished numbers, continue to live as they have for centuries. The pilgrim hostel at El Ghriba, a two-storey, arched caravansary, however, with its blue *hamsa* set into the white entry gate to its courtyard, lies empty and unused, and the jewellers fret about the impact of the current war on their relations with their customers who are their neighbours.

In the middle of June 2024, centenarian Yahya Ben Yossef,

one of six Jews remaining in Yemen, passed away in the village of Madar, north of Sana'a. With no other Jews to be found, dozens of his Muslim neighbours organised the Jewish man's funeral. They wrapped Yahya's body in his black and white prayer shawl and accompanied the deceased to the cemetery.[12] Muslims may have buried one of the last Yemeni Jews in the country, but 'in a moving act of respect', they honoured the man who refused to leave his homeland. Their actions show how the Jewish–Muslim symbiosis lives. According to a Yemeni Jewish Facebook group, 'this powerful moment highlights the power of humanity and compassion that still exists' even at a time when Jews and Muslims are at war.

The recent death of one of the last Jews in Yemen makes us think about what is lost and what can be recreated. Without Jewish–Muslim symbiosis, Jewish thinkers would not have created some of their most enduring works. Without that cooperation, Muslim societies would not have reached their heights. Some biologists argue that 'life did not take over the globe by combat, but by networking. Life forms multiplied and complexified by co-opting others, not just by killing them.' Symbiosis provides benefits to both parties. We can try not to disrupt them, to preserve them, restore them, or create new symbioses in their spirit.[13]

As a scholar writing on Christian–Muslim relations with the intention of promoting 'mutual cooperation' and more 'collaboration' warned, 'there should be no illusions about the extent of the obstacles which militate against the realisation of these hopes', as members of both groups 'see the relationship as being intrinsically and essentially an adversarial one'.[14] As this book has demonstrated, it has not always been so.

The reader has met Muslim warriors who fought for a medieval Turkish Jewish kingdom on the Caspian Sea, rabbis adapting secular Arabic poetry for use in the synagogue, Jewish viziers leading the Muslim sultan's troops in Spain, Jews entrusted by the Moroccan sultan to be his international traders and diplomats, Jewish literary lights and leaders of political parties in modern Egypt and Iraq, like-minded left-wing Jewish and Muslim activists in Europe, and Muslim independence leaders taking refuge in Jewish homes. In Arabic-speaking regions, colonial division, differing modern educations and expectations, Arab and Jewish nationalism, and the creation of Israel and the subsequent separation of Jews and Muslims across the Middle East drove these two peoples apart, and religious nationalism and extremism aggravates their mutual alienation, but it is hoped that knowledge of their long, shared history will allow them to find common purpose once more today, no matter how challenging it is.

Perhaps, rather than a metaphor of brothers, of being children of the same father, another family metaphor is necessary. In the words of the Egyptian-born Jewish novelist André Aciman, 'Alexandria was a city where all the religions and nationalities of the world were represented, and where each religion lived side by side with the others in perfect harmony. Perfect harmony may be an exaggeration, of course, but I mean it no less facetiously than when it is said of married couples living side by side in perfect harmony.'[15] Maybe, instead of being siblings, waiting for the father to restore peace between them, Jews and Muslims can act as adults, whether as a married or divorced couple, and treat each other, if not with love, then with the respect that the other deserves after all those years of togetherness and mutual purpose.

NOTES

Introduction

1. Christians also claim to be the sons of Abraham, but through faith in Jesus. We read in Galatians 3:6 that 'those who have faith are children of Abraham'. According to Galatians 3:29, 'If you belong to Christ, then you are the descendants of Abraham and will receive what God has promised'. They are not 'children born of the same Father and reared in the bosom of Abraham' as are Jews and Muslims, as F.E. Peters claims, but according to Galatians 3:26, 'children of God through faith in Jesus Christ'. F.E. Peters, *The Children of Abraham: Judaism, Christianity, Islam*, new edition (Princeton, NJ: Princeton University Press, 2004), xvii. Judaism and Islam are far more similar than Judaism and Christianity or Christianity and Islam.
2. Brian Catlos, *Kingdoms of Faith: A New History of Islamic Spain* (London: Hurst & Company, 2021), 4.
3. Marc David Baer, *Sultanic Saviors and Tolerant Turks: Writing Ottoman Jewish History, Denying the Armenian Genocide* (Bloomington: Indiana University Press, 2020).
4. Simon Dubnow, *Nationalism and History* (Philadelphia, PA: Jewish Publication Society of America, 1958), 299–300.
5. S.D. Goitein, *Jews and Arabs: Their Contacts through the Ages* (New York: Schocken, 1964), 129–30.
6. Heinrich Heine, quoted in Nissim Rejwan, *Israel's Place in the Middle East: A Pluralist Perspective* (Gainesville: University Press of Florida, 1998), 107.
7. Ammiel Alcalay, *After Jews and Arabs: Remaking Levantine Culture*

(Minneapolis and London: University of Minnesota Press, 1993), 312, note 4.
8   Edward Said, *Orientalism* (New York: Vintage, 1979), 27–8.
9   Ibid., 286.
10 James Renton and Ben Gidley, 'Introduction: The Shared Story of Europe's Ideas of the Muslim and the Jew – A Diachronic Framework', in *Antisemitism and Islamophobia in Europe: A Shared Story?*, ed. James Renton and Ben Gidley (London: Palgrave Macmillan, 2017), 1–6.
11 Ibid., 9.
12 James Renton, 'The End of the Semites', in *Antisemitism and Islamophobia in Europe: A Shared Story?*, ed. Renton and Gidley, 99–100.
13 Mark R. Cohen, 'The Neo-Lachrymose Conception of Jewish-Arab History', *Tikkun* 6, no. 3 (1991), 58.
14 Ibid., 60.
15 Bernard Lewis, *The Jews of Islam* (Princeton, NJ: Princeton University Press, 1984), 3.
16 Ibid., 7.
17 Ibid., 31.
18 Ibid., 46.
19 *Canonici Hebronensis Tractatus de invention sanctorum patriarchum Abraham, Ysaac, et Jacob*, in *The Jews of Arab Lands: A History and Source Book*, ed. Norman A. Stillman (Philadelphia, PA: Jewish Publication Society of America, 1979), 152.
20 Al-Baladhuri, *Futuh al-Buldan*, in *The Jews of Arab Lands: A History and Source Book*, ed. Stillman, 153.
21 *Akhbar Majmu'a*, in *The Jews of Arab Lands: A History and Source Book*, ed. Stillman, 156.
22 Naim Güleryüz, *The History of the Turkish Jews*, condensed from a lecture by the author, revised 2nd ed. (Istanbul: Rekor Ofset, 1992), 5.
23 Fred Astren, 'Re-reading the Arabic Sources: Jewish History and the Muslim Conquests', *Jerusalem Studies in Arabic and Islam* 36 (2009), 83–130.

1. Judeo-Islamic Religious Symbiosis and Pacts of Alliance and Protection, Seventh–Thirteenth centuries

1. Gordon D. Newby, 'The Jews of Arabia at the Birth of Islam', in *A History of Jewish–Muslim Relations: From the Origins to the Present Day*, ed. Abdelwahab Meddeb and Benjamin Stora, trans. Jane Marie Todd and Michael B. Smith (Princeton, NJ: Princeton University Press, 2013), 44.
2. Ibid., 43–4.
3. Ibid., 41.
4. Julie Cohen-Lacassagne, *Berbères juifs: L'émergence du monothéisme en Afrique du Nord* (Paris: La Fabrique, 2020), 131.
5. *The Life of Muhammad: A Translation of Ishaq's Sirat Rasul Allah*, with Introduction and Notes by Alfred Guillaume (Oxford: Oxford University Press, 1955), 104.
6. Fazlur Rahman, Appendix II, 'The People of the Book and Diversity of "Religions"', in Fazlur Rahman, *Major Themes of the Qur'ān* (Chicago: University of Chicago Press, 1980), 163.
7. *The Life of Muhammad: A Translation of Ishaq's Sirat Rasul Allah*, 182, 186.
8. Ibid., 235.
9. Maxime Rodinson, *Muhammad* [1961], trans. Anne Carter (New York: New Press, 2002), 159, 170.
10. *The Life of Muhammad: A Translation of Ishaq's Sirat Rasul Allah*, 240.
11. Rodinson, *Muhammad*, 185.
12. *The Life of Muhammad: A Translation of Ishaq's Sirat Rasul Allah*, 260; Qur'an 3:67.
13. Fred M. Donner, *Muhammad and the Believers: At the Origins of Islam* (Cambridge, MA: Harvard University Press, 2010), 203–4.
14. Ibid., 203.
15. Newby, 'The Jews of Arabia at the Birth of Islam', 48.
16. Steven Wasserstrom, *Between Muslim and Jew: The Problem of Symbiosis under Early Islam* (Princeton, NJ: Princeton University Press, 1995), 19.
17. Rodinson, *Muhammad*, 172.
18. *The Life of Muhammad: A Translation of Ishaq's Sirat Rasul Allah*, 197.
19. Jacob Lassner, *Jews, Christians, and the Abode of Islam: Modern*

Scholarship, Medieval Realities (Chicago: University of Chicago Press, 2012), 162.
20 Rodinson, *Muhammad*, 153.
21 *The Life of Muhammad: A Translation of Ishaq's Sirat Rasul Allah*, 233.
22 Ibid., 231.
23 Ibid., 233.
24 Ibid., 232.
25 Michael Lecker, 'Did Muhammad Conclude Treaties with the Jewish Tribes Nadir, Qurayza, and Qaynuqa?', *Israel Oriental Studies* 17 (1997), 36.
26 Lassner, *Jews, Christians, and the Abode of Islam*, 163.
27 *The Life of Muhammad: A Translation of Ishaq's Sirat Rasul Allah*, 437; Qur'an 59:2.
28 Lassner, *Jews, Christians, and the Abode of Islam*, 167.
29 *The Life of Muhammad: A Translation of Ishaq's Sirat Rasul Allah*, 461–2.
30 Lassner, *Jews, Christians, and the Abode of Islam*, 171.
31 *The Life of Muhammad: A Translation of Ishaq's Sirat Rasul Allah*, 464.
32 Ibid.
33 Rodinson, *Muhammad*, 213.
34 *The Life of Muhammad: A Translation of Ishaq's Sirat Rasul Allah*, 256.
35 Ibid., 511.
36 Ibid., 515.
37 Ibid.
38 Lassner, *Jews, Christians, and the Abode of Islam*, 174.
39 Yosef Yuval Tobi, *Juifs et musulmans au Yémen: De l'avènement de l'Islam à nos jours*, trans. Jean-Luc Allouche (Paris: Tallandier, 2019), 29–31.
40 Ibid., 31.
41 Ibid., 34.
42 Ibid., 36–7.
43 Walter E. Kaegi, *Byzantium and the Early Islamic Conquests* (Cambridge: Cambridge University Press, 1992), 117.
44 Tobi, *Juifs et musulmans au Yémen*, 27.
45 Kaegi, *Byzantium and the Early Islamic Conquests*, 116–17.
46 *Canonici Hebronensis Tractatus de inventione sanctorum patriarchum*

Abraham, Ysaac, et Jacob, in *The Jews of Arab Lands: A History and Source Book*, ed. Stillman, 152.
47 Wasserstrom, *Between Muslim and Jew*, 81.
48 Quoted in ibid., 53.
49 Daniel Schroeter, 'On the Origins and Identity of Indigenous North African Jews', in *North African Mosaic: A Cultural Reappraisal of Ethnic and Religious Minorities*, ed. Nabil Boudraa and Joseph Krause (Newcastle: Cambridge Scholars Publishing, 2007), 164–77.
50 Haim Zafrani, *Two Thousand Years of Jewish Life in Morocco* (Jersey City, NJ: Ktav, 2005), 1, 33.
51 Cohen-Lacassagne, *Berbères juifs*, 71, 83–4.
52 Quoted in Abdelmajid Hannoum, 'The Kahina: Jewish Symbol, Islamic Narrative', in *A History of Jewish–Muslim Relations: From the Origins to the Present Day*, ed. Meddeb and Stora, 995.
53 Zafrani, *Two Thousand Years of Jewish Life in Morocco*, 21.
54 Cohen-Lacassagne, *Berbères juifs*, 93.
55 Ibid., 117–18.
56 Mustapha Saha, *Haïm Zafrani, Penseur de la diversité* (Langres: Hémisphères, 2020), 56. For photos of two of the tombstones, see *L'Arche*, special issue, 'les juifs du maroc', no. 700 (Sept.–Oct. 2023), 17.
57 Saha, *Haïm Zafrani*, 62.
58 Cohen-Lacassagne, *Berbères juifs*, 119.
59 Ibid., 121.
60 Hannoum, 'The Kahina: Jewish Symbol, Islamic Narrative', 996.
61 Ewa Tartakowsky, *Les juifs et le maghreb: Fonctions sociales d'une littérature d'exil* (Tours: Presses universitaires françois-rabelais, 2016), 150.
62 Joëlle Allouche-Benayoun, 'Les juifs d'Algérie. Du *dhimmi* au citoyen français', in *Les Juifs d'Algérie. Une histoire de ruptures*, ed. Joëlle Allouche-Benayoun and Geneviève Dermenjian (Aix-en-Provence: Presses universitaires de Provence, 2015), 27.
63 Hannoum, 'The Kahina: Jewish Symbol, Islamic Narrative', 997.
64 Benjamin Hendrickx, 'Al-Kahina: The Last Ally of the Roman-Byzantines in the Maghreb against the Muslim Arab Conquest?', *Journal of Early Christian History* 3, no. 2 (2013), 47–61.
65 Tartakowsky, *Les juifs et le maghreb*, 152–3.

Notes

66 Quoted in Hannoum, 'The Kahina: Jewish Symbol, Islamic Narrative', 994.
67 Abdelmajid Hannoum, *Colonial Histories, Post-Colonial Memories: The Legend of the Kahina, A North African Heroine* (Westport, CT: Greenwood Publishing, 2001).
68 Joseph Chetrit et Daniel Schroeter, 'Les rapports entre Juifs et Berbères en Afrique du Nord. Aspects historiques et culturels', in *La Méditerranée des Juifs. Exodes et enracinements*, ed. Paul Balta, Caherine Dana, and Régine Dhoquois-Cohen (Paris: L'Harmattan, 2003), 75–87.
69 Cohen-Lacassagne, *Berbères juifs*, 36.
70 Haïm Zafrani, with Paulette Pernet-Galand, *Une version berbère de la Haggadah de Pesah. Texte de Tinrhir du Todrha (Maroc)*, 2 vols (Paris: Éditions Groupe Linguistique d'Études Chamito-Sémitiques, 1970).
71 Zafrani, *Two Thousand Years of Jewish Life in Morocco*, 114.
72 Mohammed Kenbib, *Juifs et musulmans au Maroc, des origines à nos jours* (Paris: Texto, 2023), 16.
73 Al-Turtushi, *Siraj al-Muluk*, 229–30, trans. Bernard Lewis, in *Islam from the Prophet Muhammad to the Capture of Constantinople*, ed. Bernard Lewis, vol. 2, *Religion and Society* (New York: Walker and Company, 1974), 217–19.
74 Abu Yusuf, *Kitab al-Kharaj*, 3rd ed. (Cairo, 1382/1962–3), 140–1.
75 Khaled Abou El Fadl, 'The Place of Tolerance in Islam', in Khaled Abou El Fadl et al., *The Place of Tolerance in Islam*, ed. Joshua Cohen and Ian Lague (Boston: Beacon Press, 2002), 21.
76 Lewis, *The Jews of Islam*, 85.
77 Mark R. Cohen, *Under Crescent and Cross: The Jews in the Middle Ages* (Princeton, NJ: Princeton University Press, 1994), Chapter 2.
78 El Fadl, 'The Place of Tolerance in Islam', 16.
79 Ibid., 100.
80 Ibid., 17–18.
81 Cohen, *Under Crescent and Cross*, Chapter 3.
82 Ibid., Chapter 4.
83 Reuven Firestone, 'Rituals: Similarities, Influences, and Processes of Differentiation', in *A History of Jewish–Muslim Relations*, ed. Meddeb and Stora, 702.
84 Ibid., 703.

85 Goitein, *Jews and Arabs*.
86 Ibid., 130.
87 S.D. Goitein, 'Portrait of a Yemenite Weavers' Village', *Jewish Social Studies* 17, no. 1 (1955), 3–26.
88 'Shelomo Dov Goitein: *In Memoriam*', Institute for Advanced Study, Princeton, NJ, 1985, 23, https://www.ias.edu/sites/default/files/library/Shelomo_Dov_Goitein_1900-1985.pdf; Goitein, 'Portrait of a Yemenite Weavers' Village'.
89 Goitein, *Jews and Arabs*, 10.
90 Wasserstrom, *Between Muslim and Jew*, 11–12, 18.
91 Ibid., 9, 11.
92 Ibid., 223.
93 Ibid., 224.
94 Donner, *Muhammad and the Believers*, 200.
95 Cohen-Lacassagne, *Berbères juifs*, 131–3.
96 'Appendix B: Inscriptions in the Dome of the Rock, Jerusalem', in Donner, *Muhammad and the Believers*, 234.
97 Ibid., 235.
98 Donner, *Muhammad and the Believers*, 202.
99 Michel Cuypers, 'The Jews in the Fifth Sura, *al-Ma'ida*', in *A History of Jewish–Muslim Relations*, ed. Meddeb and Stora, 623–4.
100 Mercedes García-Arenal, 'The Jews of Al-Andalus', in *A History of Jewish–Muslim Relations*, ed. Meddeb and Stora, 126–7.
101 Hava Lazarus-Yafeh, 'Judaism and Islam: Some Aspects of Mutual Cultural Influences', in *Some Religious Aspects of Islam* (Leiden: Brill, 1981), 81–2.
102 Wasserstrom, *Between Muslim and Jew*, 55.
103 Ibid., 56.
104 Ibid., 64–5.
105 Ibid., 124.
106 Ibid., 68.
107 Ibid., 69.
108 Ibid., 84–5.
109 Ibid., 76.
110 Ibid., 82.
111 Sahih Muslim, 4:1525.

Notes

112 Wasserstrom, *Between Muslim and Jew*, 57.
113 Ibid., 94.
114 Ibid., 97.
115 Ibid., 97, 100.
116 Ibid., 101.
117 Ibid., 102–3.
118 Ibid., 182.
119 Ammiel Alcalay, *After Jews and Arabs: Remaking Levantine Culture* (Minneapolis and London: University of Minnesota Press, 1993), 142–3.
120 S.D. Goitein, *A Mediterranean Society: The Jewish Communities of the Arab World as Portrayed in the Documents of the Cairo Geniza*, 5 vols (Berkeley: University of California Press, 1967–83).

2. The Secular Symbiosis and Jews Ruling over Muslims: The Turkish Jewish Khazar Kingdom, Eighth–Tenth Centuries

1 Lazarus-Yafeh, 'Judaism and Islam', 89.
2 Makram Abbès, 'The Andalusian Philosophical Milieu', in *A History of Jewish–Muslim Relations*, ed. Meddeb and Stora, 766.
3 Ibid., 765.
4 Esther Meir-Glitzenstein, *Juifs et musulmans en Irak. Des origines à nos jours*, trans. Jean-Luc Allouche (Paris: Tallandier, 2022), 37.
5 Quoted in Dominique Jarrassé, 'Synagogues in the Islamic World', in *A History of Jewish–Muslim Relations*, ed. Meddeb and Stora, 916.
6 Michel Abitbol and Abdou Filali-Ansary, 'Préface', in Meir-Glitzenstein, *Juifs et musulmans en Irak*, 8.
7 Meir-Glitzenstein, *Juifs et musulmans en Irak*, 41.
8 Wasserstrom, *Between Muslim and Jew*, 19–20.
9 Ibid., 32.
10 Ibid., 125.
11 Meir-Glitzenstein, *Juifs et musulmans en Irak*, 46.
12 Wasserstrom, *Between Muslim and Jew*, 18–19.
13 Ibid., 20–1, 24.
14 Meir-Glitzenstein, *Juifs et musulmans en Irak*, 49.
15 Norman A. Stillman, 'The Judeo-Arabic Heritage', in *Sephardic and Mizrahi Jewry: From the Golden Age of Spain to Modern Times*, ed. Zion Zohar (New York: New York University Press, 2005), 41.

16 Rejwan, *Israel's Place in the Middle East*, 62.
17 Peters, *The Children of Abraham*, 149.
18 Steven Harvey, 'Jewish and Muslim Philosophy: Similarities and Differences', in *A History of Jewish–Muslim Relations*, ed. Meddeb and Stora, 751.
19 Wasserstrom, *Between Muslim and Jew*, 146.
20 Ibid., 147, 207, 212.
21 Ibid., 150, 153.
22 Alcalay, *After Jews and Arabs*, 149.
23 Ibid., 149.
24 Ibid., 160.
25 Michael M. Laskier, *Juifs et Musulmans en Égypte. Des origines à nos jours*, trans. Françoise Bloch (Paris: Tallandier, 2020), 32.
26 Yoram Eder, 'The Karaites and Mu'tazilim', in *A History of Jewish–Muslim Relations*, ed. Meddeb and Stora, 779.
27 Ibid., 782.
28 Jacques Hassoun, 'The Traditional Jewry of the Harā', in *The Jews of Egypt: A Mediterranean Society in Modern Times*, ed. Shimon Shamir (London: Westview Press, 1987), 170.
29 Laskier, *Juifs et Musulmans en Égypte*, 36.
30 Ibid., 38.
31 Ibid., 52–3.
32 Ibid., 58.
33 Ibid., 59.
34 Ibid., 60.
35 Ibid., 62.
36 Ibid., 62–3.
37 Mark R. Cohen and Sasson Somekh, 'In the Court of Ya'kub ibn Killis: A Fragment from the Cairo Genizah', *Jewish Quarterly Review* 80, nos 3–4 (1990), 286, 292, 294.
38 Laskier, *Juifs et Musulmans en Égypte*, 63.
39 Ibid., 65–6.
40 Markus Kohbach, 'Ein Fall von Steinigung wegen Ehebruch in Istanbul im Jahre 1680', *Wiener Zeitschrift für die Kunde des Morgenlandes* 76 (1986), 189.
41 Laskier, *Juifs et Musulmans en Égypte*, 67, 70.

Notes

42 Ibid., 68, 70.
43 Abraham L. Udovitch and Lucette Valensi, *The Last Arab Jews: The Communities of Jerba, Tunisia* (London: Harwood Academic Publishers, 1984), 117.
44 Alcalay, *After Jews and Arabs*, 233.
45 S.D. Goitein, *Letters of Medieval Jewish Traders* (Princeton, NJ: Princeton University Press, 1973), 78.
46 Alcalay, *After Jews and Arabs*, 137.
47 Goitein, *A Mediterranean Society*, vol. 1: Economic Foundations (Berkeley: University of California Press, 1967), 169.
48 Goitein, *Letters of Medieval Jewish Traders*, 6–7.
49 Ibid., 8.
50 Ibid., 308, 310.
51 Ibid., 25, 65–71, 227–9.
52 Ibid., 17.
53 Ibid., 12.
54 Ibid., 14, 181.
55 Ibid., 185–92.
56 Jarrassé, 'Synagogues in the Islamic World', 916.
57 'Panel from a Torah Ark Door', Walters Art Museum, https://art.thewalters.org/object/64.181/#:~:text=This%20rare%20wooden%20panel%20comes,holds%20the%20sacred%20Jewish%20Scripture.
58 Cambridge University Library, T-S (Taylor-Schechter) Ar.51.62. *Bismillaah ar-Rahman ar-Raheem Al hamdu lillaahi rabbil 'alameen Ar-Rahman ar-Raheem Maaliki yaumid Deen Iyyaaka na'abudu wa iyyaaka nasta'een Ihdinas siraatal mustaqeem Siraatal ladheena an 'amta' alaihim Ghairil maghduubi' alaihim waladaaleen.*
59 Cambridge University Library, T-S (Taylor-Schechter) Ar.52.242. The verses included from the Book of Numbers have rebellion as one of the themes (Numbers 14:22–43, 15:19–25, 16:28–34, 20:3–8, 31:54–32:22).
60 *The Spillings Hoard: Gotland's Role in Viking Age World Trade*, ed. Ann-Maria Pettersson (Visby: Gotlands Museum, 2009).
61 Kevin Alan Brook, *The Jews of Khazaria* (Lanham, MD: Rowman & Littlefield, 1999), Chapter 6.
62 Solomon Schechter, 'An Unknown Khazar Document', *Jewish Quarterly Review* 3, no. 2 (1912), 217.

63 Ariel Sabar, *My Father's Paradise: A Son's Search For His Family's Past* (Chapel Hill, NC: Algonquin, 2008), 51.
64 Ibid., 54.
65 Brook, *The Jews of Khazaria*, Chapter 7.
66 Peter B. Golden, 'Khazars', in *Turkish–Jewish Encounters: Studies on Turkish–Jewish Relations through the Ages*, ed. Mehmet Tutuncu (Haarlem: SOTA, 2001), 37.
67 Ibid., 36.
68 Quoted in ibid., 41.
69 'The Book of Ahmad ibn Fadlan', in *Ibn Fadlān and the Land of Darkness: Arab Travellers in the Far North*, trans. and introduction by Paul Lunde and Caroline Stone (New York: Penguin Classics, 2011), 58.
70 Wasserstrom, *Between Muslim and Jew*, 61.
71 Schechter, 'An Unknown Khazar Document', 213.
72 Ibid., 214.
73 Ibid., 215.
74 'Ibn Khurradadhbih on the Routes of the Radhaniya and the Rus c.830', in *Ibn Fadlān and the Land of Darkness*, trans. Lunde and Stone, 111.
75 Ibid., 112.
76 The modern descendant of their Turkic language is Chuvash, spoken in central Russia today.
77 'Ibn Rusta on the Khazars, 903–913', in *Ibn Fadlān and the Land of Darkness*, trans. Lunde and Stone, 116.
78 'The Book of Ahmad ibn Fadlan, 921–922', 55.
79 'Istakhri on the Khazars and Their Neighbours c.951', in *Ibn Fadlān and the Land of Darkness*, trans. Lunde and Stone, 157.
80 'Mas'udi on the Khazars, 943', in *Ibn Fadlān and the Land of Darkness*, trans. Lunde and Stone, 132.
81 'The Book of Ahmad ibn Fadlan, 921–922', 57.
82 Ibid., 58.
83 'Ibn Rusta on the Khazars, 903–913', 117.
84 'Istakhri on the Khazars and Their Neighbours c.951', 155.
85 'The Book of Ahmad ibn Fadlan, 921–922', 58.
86 'Mas'udi on the Khazars, 943', 133.
87 'Istakhri on the Khazars and Their Neighbours c.951', 154.
88 Ibid., 156.

Notes

89 'Mas'udi on the Khazars, 943', 134.
90 'Istakhri on the Khazars and Their Neighbours *c*. 951', 153.
91 Ibid., 154.
92 'The Book of Ahmad ibn Fadlan, 921–922', 45.
93 'Mas'udi on a Viking Raid on the Caspian *c*.913', 145.
94 Cat Jarman, *River Kings: The Vikings from Scandinavia to the Silk Roads* (London: William Collins, 2021), 75, 205–6.
95 Michael Chabon, *Gentlemen of the Road* (New York: Ballantine Books, 2007), 91.
96 'Ibn Hawqal on the Rus Destruction of Itil in 965', in *Ibn Fadlān and the Land of Darkness*, trans. Lunde and Stone, 178.
97 Jarman, *River Kings*, 187, 199.
98 Arthur Koestler, *The Thirteenth Tribe* (New York: Random House, 1976).
99 'Muqaddasi on the Land of the Khazars, 985–990', in *Ibn Fadlān and the Land of Darkness*, trans. Lunde and Stone, 171.
100 Ibid., 172.
101 Doron M. Behar et al., 'No Evidence from Genome-Wide Data of a Khazar Origin for the Ashkenazi Jews', *Human Biology* 85, no. 6 (2013), 860.
102 Ibid., 875.
103 Barry Kogan, 'Judah Halevi', in Seyyed Hossein Nasr and Oliver Leaman, *History of Islamic Philosophy* (London: Routledge, 2001), 718–24.

3. Jewish–Muslim Symbiosis and Alliance: Al-Andalus, Eighth–Seventeenth Centuries

1 Cohen-Lacassagne, *Berbères juifs*, 141–2.
2 Américo Castro, *España en su historia: cristianos, moros, y judíos* (1948); translated and revised as *The Structure of Spanish History* (1954) and revised again as *The Spaniards: An Introduction to Their History* (1971).
3 Vivian Mann, 'Introduction', in *Convivencia: Jews, Muslims, and Christians in Medieval Spain*, ed. Thomas Glick, Vivian Mann et al. (New York: George Braziller in Association with the Jewish Museum, 1992), 2.

4 Mercedes García-Arenal, 'The Jews of Al-Andalus', in *A History of Jewish–Muslim Relations*, ed. Meddeb and Stora, 111.
5 Ibid., 112.
6 Catlos, *Kingdoms of Faith*, 90.
7 García-Arenal, 'The Jews of Al-Andalus', 124.
8 Quoted in Raymond P. Scheindlin, *Wine, Women, and Death: Medieval Hebrew Poems on the Good Life* (Philadelphia, PA: Jewish Publication Society, 1986), 3.
9 Raymond Scheindlin, 'Hasdai ibn Shaprut', in *A History of Jewish–Muslim Relations*, ed. Meddeb and Stora, 134.
10 Catlos, *Kingdoms of Faith*, 151–3.
11 Scheindlin, *Wine, Women, and Death*, 11.
12 Brian Catlos, *Infidel Kings and Unholy Warriors: Faith, Power, and Violence in the Age of Crusade and Jihad* (New York: Farrar, Straus and Giroux, 2014), 35–8, 40–8.
13 Ross Brann, *The Compunctious Poet: Cultural Ambiguity and Hebrew Poetry in Muslim Spain* (Baltimore, MD: Johns Hopkins University Press, 1991), 48.
14 Ibid., 55.
15 Scheindlin, *Wine, Women, and Death*.
16 Quoted in Brann, *The Compunctious Poet*, 41.
17 Ibid., 9.
18 Ibid., 11.
19 Ibid., 21–2.
20 Raymond P. Scheindlin, *The Gazelle: Medieval Hebrew Poems on God, Israel, and the Soul* (Philadelphia, PA: Jewish Publication Society, 1991), 11–12.
21 Saʻid al-Andalusi, *Book of the Categories of Nations*, referring to Abu al-Fadl, quoted in Makram Abbès, 'The Andalusian Philosophical Milieu', in *A History of Jewish–Muslim Relations*, ed. Meddeb and Stora, 765–6.
22 Abbès, 'The Andalusian Philosophical Milieu', 766–7.
23 García-Arenal, 'The Jews of Al-Andalus', 124.
24 Catlos, *Infidel Kings and Unholy Warriors*, 56–7.
25 Quoted in 'Moshe ibn Ezra: The Impossible Task of the Translator', in *A History of Jewish–Muslim Relations*, ed. Meddeb and Stora, 636.

Notes

26 Brann, *The Compunctious Poet*.
27 Quoted in ibid., 87.
28 Alcalay, *After Jews and Arabs*, 173–4.
29 Masha Itzhaki, 'Arabic Ars Poetica in Biblical Hebrew: Hebrew Poetry in Spain', in *A History of Jewish–Muslim Relations*, ed. Meddeb and Stora, 946.
30 Ibid., 949–50.
31 Scheindlin, *The Gazelle*, 18–19.
32 Dwight Reynolds, 'The Music of Al-Andalus: Meeting Place of Three Cultures', in *A History of Jewish–Muslim Relations*, ed. Meddeb and Stora, 973–4.
33 Ibid., 975.
34 Ibid., 976.
35 Scheindlin, *Wine, Women, and Death*, 87, 89. Sometimes the sex was explicit. Moses ibn Ezra's erotic *muwashshah* poem, whose last lines come from a poem written in Arabic by a Muslim, has as the last three stanzas
[Hebrew] Never will I forget the night
We lay together in delight
Upon my bed till morning light.
All night he made love to me,
At his mouth he suckled me.
[Hebrew] Charming even in deceit;
The fruit of his mouth is like candy sweet.
Played me false, that little cheat!
Deceived me, then made fun of me;
I did him no wrong, but he wronged me.
[Arabic] One day when my eyes were filled to the brim
There came to my ears this little hymn,
So I sang my doleful song to him:
'How dear that boy is to me!
Maybe he'll come back to me'.
Quoted in Scheindlin, *Wine, Women, and Death*, 103.
36 Quoted in Scheindlin, *Wine, Women, and Death*, 51.
37 Ibid., 4.
38 Jonathan Ray, 'Beyond Tolerance and Persecution: Reassessing Our

Approach to Medieval "Convivencia"', *Jewish Social Studies*, New Series 11, no. 2 (2005), 1–18.
39 Ross Brann, *Power in the Portrayal: Representations of Jews and Muslims in Eleventh- and Twelfth-Century Islamic Spain* (Princeton, NJ: Princeton University Press, 2002), 1–23.
40 Quoted in Scheindlin, *The Gazelle*, 109.
41 Abraham ibn Daud, *Book of Tradition*, trans. from Hebrew by Gerson D. Cohen, in *Medieval Iberia: Readings from Christian, Muslim, and Jewish Sources*, 2nd ed., ed. Olivia Remie Constable (Philadelphia: University of Pennsylvania Press, 2011), 130.
42 'Abd Allah ibn Buluggin, *Tibyan*, trans. from Arabic by Amin T. Tibi, in *Medieval Iberia: Readings from Christian, Muslim, and Jewish Sources*, 118–19.
43 Ibid., 119.
44 Ibid., 122.
45 Catlos, *Infidel Kings and Unholy Warriors*, 55.
46 Abu Ishaq of Elvira, *Qasida*, trans. from Arabic by Bernard Lewis, in *Medieval Iberia: Readings from Christian, Muslim, and Jewish Sources*, 123.
47 'Abd Allah ibn Buluggin, *Tibyan*, trans. from Arabic by Amin T. Tibi, in *Medieval Iberia: Readings from Christian, Muslim, and Jewish Sources*, 124.
48 Ibid., 125.
49 María Rosa Menocal, *The Ornament of the World: How Muslims, Jews, and Christians Created a Culture of Tolerance in Medieval Spain* (New York: Little, Brown, 2002).
50 Daniel J. Schroeter, *The Sultan's Jew: Morocco and the Sephardi World* (Stanford, CA: Stanford University Press, 2002), 2, 26.
51 Thomas Glick, '"My Master, the Jew": Observations on Interfaith Scholarly Interaction in the Middle Ages', in *Jews, Muslims, and Christians in and around the Crown of Aragon: Essays in Honour of Professor Elena Lourie*, ed. Harvey Hames (Leiden: Brill, 2003), 168.
52 Scheindlin, *The Gazelle*, 37.
53 Brann, *The Compunctious Poet*, 78.
54 Steven Harvey, 'Jewish and Muslim Philosophy: Similarities and

Notes

Differences', in *A History of Jewish–Muslim Relations*, ed. Meddeb and Stora, 742.
55 Menocal, *The Ornament of the World*, 206.
56 Laskier, *Juifs et Musulmans en Égypte*, 45.
57 Saha, *Haïm Zafrani, Penseur de la diversité*, 49.
58 Moses Maimonides, *The Guide of the Perplexed*, trans. and with an Introduction and Notes by Shlomo Pines, 2 vols, new ed. (Chicago: University of Chicago Press, 1974).
59 Goitein, *Jews and Arabs*, 146.
60 Abbès, 'The Andalusian Philosophical Milieu', 772.
61 Maimonides, *The Guide of the Perplexed*, 1:166–231.
62 Abbès, 'The Andalusian Philosophical Milieu', 774.
63 Saha, *Haïm Zafrani, Penseur de la diversité*, 50.
64 Maimonides, 'The Epistle on Martyrdom', in *The Epistles of Maimonides: Crisis and Leadership*, trans. and notes by Abraham Halkin, discussions by David Hartman (Philadelphia, PA: Jewish Publication Society of America, 1985), 30.
65 Ibid., 31.
66 Maimonides, 'The Epistle to Yemen', in *The Epistles of Maimonides*, 102–3.
67 Elisha Russ-Fishbane, 'Respectful Rival: Abraham Maimonides on Islam', in *A History of Jewish–Muslim Relations*, ed. Meddeb and Stora, 857.
68 Scheindlin, *The Gazelle*, 22–3, 142–3.
69 Ibid., 41.
70 Ibid., 42.
71 Ibid., 171, 174.
72 Ibid., 40.
73 Lazarus-Yafeh, 'Judaism and Islam: Some Aspects of Mutual Cultural Influences', in *Some Religious Aspects of Islam* (Leiden: Brill, 1981), 89.
74 Elisha Russ-Fishbane, 'Respectful Rival: Abraham Maimonides on Islam', in *A History of Jewish–Muslim Relations*, ed. Meddeb and Stora, 858.
75 Ibid., 860.
76 Ibid., 861.
77 Rumi, *Masnavi*, Book 4, 406–7, trans. Jenia Jianfar and Abdelwahab

Meddeb, in *A History of Jewish–Muslim Relations*, ed. Meddeb and Stora, 865–8.
78 Diana Lobel, *A Sufi-Jewish Dialogue: Philosophy and Mysticism in Bahya ibn Paquda's* Duties of the Heart (Philadelphia: University of Pennsylvania Press, 2007), 8.
79 Catlos, *Infidel Kings and Unholy Warriors*, 15–16, 58.
80 *Siete partidas*, translated from Castilian by S.P. Scott, in *Medieval Iberia: Readings from Christian, Muslim, and Jewish Sources*, 399–402.
81 Ibid., 399.
82 David Nirenberg, 'What Can Medieval Spain Teach Us about Muslim–Jewish Relations?', *CCAR Journal: A Reform Jewish Quarterly* (spring/summer 2002), 20.
83 Josef W. Meri, 'Introduction', in *The Routledge Handbook of Muslim–Jewish Relations*, ed. Josef Meri (London: Routledge, 2016), 7.
84 David Nirenberg, *Communities of Violence: Persecution of Minorities in the Middle Ages* (Princeton, NJ: Princeton University Press, 1998), 169.
85 Ibid., 174.
86 Ibid., 179.
87 Ibid., 176.
88 Brian Catlos, *The Victors and the Vanquished: Christians and Muslims of Catalonia and Aragon, 1050–1300* (Cambridge: Cambridge University Press, 2004), 147–9.
89 Ibid., 201–2, 205.
90 Ibid., 206–7.
91 Nirenberg, *Communities of Violence*, 180.
92 Catlos, *The Victors and the Vanquished*, 319.
93 Nirenberg, *Communities of Violence*, 181.
94 Catlos, *The Victors and the Vanquished*, 306–7, 311–12.
95 Nirenberg, *Communities of Violence*, 185.
96 Ibid., 186–7.
97 Ibid., 188.
98 Ibid., 189.
99 Nirenberg, 'What Can Medieval Spain Teach Us?', 26.
100 Nirenberg, *Communities of Violence*, 199; Catlos, *The Victors and the Vanquished*, 278, 296.
101 Nirenberg, *Communities of Violence*, 199.

Notes

102 Anonymous, 'Jewish Account of the Expulsion', Italy, 1495, trans. from Hebrew by Jacob R. Marcus, in *Medieval Iberia: Readings from Christian, Muslim, and Jewish Sources*, 516.

103 'Royal Edict of Expulsion' (1502), trans. from Castilian by Dayle Seidenspinner-Nuñez, in *Medieval Iberia: Readings from Christian, Muslim, and Jewish Sources*, 535.

104 Ibid., 535, 537.

105 Ibid., 538–9.

106 Renee Levine Melammed, 'Judeo-Conversas and Moriscas in Sixteenth-Century Spain: A Study of Parallels', *Jewish History* 24, no. 2 (2010), 157.

107 Mary Elizabeth Perry, *The Handless Maiden: Moriscos and the Politics of Religion in Early Modern Spain* (Princeton, NJ: Princeton University Press, 2013), 4.

108 Ibid., 87.

109 Ibid., 157–8.

110 Natalia Muchnik, 'Judeoconversos and Moriscos in the Diaspora', in *The Expulsion of the Moriscos from Spain: A Mediterranean Diaspora*, ed. Mercedes García-Arenal and Gerard Wiegers (Leiden: Brill, 2014), 438.

111 Mercedes García-Arenal, 'The Moriscos in Morocco: From Granadan Emigration to the Hornacheros of Salé', in *The Expulsion of the Moriscos from Spain*, ed. García-Arenal and Wiegers, 286–328.

112 Muchnik, 'Judeoconversos and Moriscos in the Diaspora', 421–2.

113 Nicole Sebag-Sarfaty, 'Notables juifs à la cour des sultans marocains', *L'Arche*, special issue, 'les juifs du maroc', no. 700 (Sept.–Oct. 2023), 35. See also Nicole S. Serfaty, *Les Courtisans juifs des sultans marocains (xiiie-xviiie siècles) – Hommes politiques et hauts dignitaires* (Paris: Bouchène, 1999).

114 Zafrani, *Two Thousand Years of Jewish Life in Morocco*, 6.

115 Kenbib, *Juifs et musulmans au Maroc*, 45.

116 Ibid., 46.

117 Sebag-Sarfaty, 'Notables juifs à la cour des sultans marocains', 35.

118 Mercedes García-Arenal and Gerard Wiegers, *A Man of Three Worlds: Samuel Pallache, a Moroccan Jew in Catholic and Protestant Europe*, trans. Martin Beagles (Baltimore, MD: Johns Hopkins University Press, 2003), 32.

119 Ibid., 40.

120 Ibid., 4.
121 Ibid., 8.
122 Ibid., 18.
123 Ibid., 10.
124 Ibid., 58–60.
125 Ibid., 53–4, 58.
126 Ibid., 55, 71.
127 Ibid., 71.
128 Ibid., 72.
129 Ibid., 99.
130 'Man in Oriental Costume', National Gallery of Art, Washington, DC, https://www.nga.gov/collection/art-object-page.572.html.
131 García-Arenal and Wiegers, *A Man of Three Worlds*, 38.
132 Ibid., 50–1.
133 Allan Harris Cutler and Helen Elmquist Cutler, *The Jew as Ally of the Muslim: Medieval Roots of Antisemitism* (South Bend, IN: University of Notre Dame Press, 1986), 6, 96.
134 Ibid., 93.
135 Maxime Rodinson, *Europe and the Mystique of Islam*, trans. Roger Veinus (Seattle: University of Washington Press, 1987), 11.

4. Muslim Saviours: Jews and Muslims in the Ottoman Empire and Morocco, Fifteenth–Nineteenth Centuries

1 'The Travels of Abu Hamid al-Andalusi al-Gharnati, 1130–1155', in *Ibn Fadlān and the Land of Darkness*, trans. Lunde and Stone, 63.
2 Güleryüz, *The History of the Turkish Jews*, 5.
3 Marc David Baer, *The Ottomans: Khans, Caesars and Caliphs* (London: Basic, 2021), 81, 184, 397.
4 Mark Mazower, *Salonica, City of Ghosts: Christians, Muslims and Jews, 1430–1950* (London: HarperCollins, 2004), 51.
5 Devin E. Naar, 'Fashioning the "Mother of Israel": The Ottoman Jewish Historical Narrative and the Image of Jewish Salonica', *Jewish History* 28, nos 3–4 (2014), 337–72.
6 Translated from Hebrew in Matt Goldish, *Jewish Questions: Responsa on Sephardic Life in the Early Modern Period* (Princeton, NJ: Princeton University Press, 2008), 101.

Notes

7 Cecil Roth, *Doña Gracia of the House of Nasi: A Jewish Renaissance Woman* (Philadelphia, PA: Jewish Publication Society of America, 1948), 116.
8 Ibid., 117.
9 Baer, *The Ottomans*, 159–60, 177.
10 Roth, *Doña Gracia of the House of Nasi*, 180.
11 M. Ertuğrul Düzdağ, *Şeyhülislam Ebussuud Efendi Fetvaları ışığında 16. asır Türk hayatı* (Istanbul, 1972), 94.
12 One can view the painting on the Quincentennial Foundation/500. Yıl Vakfı website, www.sephardichouse.org/Quincentennial-Foundation.html.
13 Esther Benbassa and Aron Rodrigue, *Sephardi Jewry: A History of the Judeo-Spanish Community, 15th to 20th Centuries* (Berkeley: University of California Press, 2000), 192.
14 Marcy Brink-Danan, *Jewish Life in 21st-Century Turkey: The Other Side of Tolerance* (Bloomington: Indiana University Press, 2012), 33.
15 Marc David Baer, *Sultanic Saviors and Tolerant Turks: Writing Ottoman Jewish History, Denying the Armenian Genocide* (Bloomington: Indiana University Press, 2020).
16 'Tolerance and Conversion in the Ottoman Empire: A Conversation with Marc Baer and Ussama Makdisi', *Comparative Studies in Society & History* 51, no. 4 (2009), 930. The statements I cite from this article are my own.
17 Marc David Baer, 'Islamic Conversion Narratives of Women: Social Change and Gendered Religious Hierarchy in Early Modern Ottoman Istanbul', *Gender & History* 16, no. 2 (2004), 425–58.
18 Karen Barkey, *Empire of Difference: The Ottomans in Comparative Perspective* (Cambridge: Cambridge University Press, 2008), 115.
19 Aron Rodrigue, 'Difference and Tolerance in the Ottoman Empire', *Stanford Humanities Review* 5, no. 1 (1995), 81–90.
20 Salo Wittmayer Baron, *A Social and Religious History of the Jews*, 2nd revised ed., 18 vols (New York: Columbia University Press, 1952–83), 18:453, n.32.
21 Gilles Veinstein, 'Jews and Muslims in Ottoman Territory before the Expulsion from Spain', in *A History of Jewish–Muslim Relations*, ed. Meddeb and Stora, 166.

22 Quoted in Lewis, *The Jews of Islam*, 135–6.
23 Yosef Hayim Yerushalmi, *Zakhor: Jewish History & Jewish Memory* (Seattle: University of Washington Press, 1982).
24 Güleryüz, *The History of the Turkish Jews*, 21.
25 Julia Philips Cohen, *Becoming Ottomans: Sephardi Jews and Imperial Citizenship in the Modern Era* (Oxford: Oxford University Press, 2014), Chapter 2.
26 Aryeh Shmuelevitz, 'Jewish–Muslim Relations in the Writings of Rabbi Eliyahu Capsali' [in Hebrew], *Pe'amim* 61 (1994), 81; Joseph Hacker, 'Ottoman Policy toward the Jews and Jewish Attitudes towards the Ottomans during the Fifteenth Century', in *Christians and Jews in the Ottoman Empire: The Functioning of a Plural Society*, 2 vols, ed. Benjamin Braude and Bernard Lewis (New York: Holmes & Meier, 1982), 1:118–19.
27 Meir Benayahu, *Rabi Eliyahu Kapsali, Ish Kandiah: Rav Manhig ve Historyon* (Tel Aviv: Tel Aviv University Press, 1983) [in Hebrew].
28 Rabbi Moses Capsali was brother of Rabbi David Capsali, the grandfather of Rabbi Elijah Capsali. Benayahu, *Rabi Eliyahu Kapsali*, 20; Martin Jacobs, *Islamische Geschichte in jüdischen Chroniken: Hebräische Historiographie des 16. und 17. Jahrhunderts* (Tübingen: Mohr Siebeck, 2004), 58, 61; Aleida Paudice, *Between Several Worlds: The Life and Writings of Elia Capsali: The Historical Works of a 16th-Century Cretan Rabbi* (Munich: Martin Meidenbauer, 2010), 60–3.
29 Eliyahu Capsali, *Seder Eliyahu zuta*, 3 vols (1975–83), ed. Aryeh Shmuelevitz, Shlomo Simonsohn, and Meier Benayahu (Jerusalem: Mekhon Ben-Tsvi, 1975).
30 Yerushalmi, *Zakhor*, 23, 34, 36–7.
31 Ibid., 65.
32 Capsali, *Seder Eliyahu zuta*, 1:240.
33 Joseph Ha-Kohen, *The Chronicles of Rabbi Joseph ben Joshua ben Meir the Sephardi*, trans. C.H.F. Bialloblotzky (London, 1835), 273, quoted in Paudice, *Between Several Worlds*, 141.
34 *Samuel Usque's Consolation for the Tribulations of Israel* (*Consolaçam às tribulaçoes de Israel*), trans. from Portuguese by Martin A. Cohen (Philadelphia, PA: Jewish Publication Society of America, 1964), 231.

Notes

35 Joseph Ha-Kohen, *Sefer divrei ha-yamim le-malkhei Tzarefat u-malkhei beit Otman ha-Togar* (Sabionetta, 1554), 113a, quoted in Yerushalmi, *Zakhor*, 64.
36 According to Christians, the Messiah had already come through this door in the person of Jesus.
37 Paudice, *Between Several Worlds*, 157.
38 Jan Schmidt, review of Martin Jacobs, *Islamische Geschichte in jüdischen Chroniken*, *Journal of Early Modern History* 8, nos 3–4 (2004), 447.
39 Immanuel Aboab, *Nomologia o discursos legales* (Amsterdam, 1629), 195; 'Aboab, Immanuel', *Encyclopaedia Judaica Jerusalem*, 16 vols (Jerusalem: Keter, 1971), 2:90; and 'Ottoman Empire', *Encyclopaedia Judaica Jerusalem*, 16:1532–3.
40 Baer, 'Islamic Conversion Narratives of Women'.
41 Marc David Baer, *Honored by the Glory of Islam: Conversion and Conquest in Ottoman Europe* (Oxford: Oxford University Press, 2008), 23.
42 Halil Inalcik, 'Ahmed 'Âşıkî ('Âşık Paşa-zâde) on the Conqueror's Policy to Repopulate Istanbul', in Halil Inalcik, *The Survey of Istanbul, 1455: The Text, English Translation, Analysis of the Text, Documents* (Istanbul: Türkiye İş Bankası Kültür Yayınları, 2010), 581–7; and Cemal Kafadar, *Between Two Worlds: The Construction of the Ottoman State* (Berkeley: University of California Press, 1995), 138–54.
43 *Âşıkpaşazade, Osmanoğulları'nın Tarihi*, ed. Kemal Yavuz and M.A. Yekta Saraç (Istanbul: K, 2003); Lale Özdemir, *Ottoman History through the Eyes of Âşıkpaşazade* (Istanbul: Isis, 2013); Halil Inalcik, 'How to Read 'Ashık Pasha-zade's History', in *Studies in Ottoman History in Honour of Professor V.L. Ménage*, ed. C. Heywood and C. Imber (Istanbul, 1994), 139–56; V.L. Ménage, *Neshrī's History of the Ottomans: The Sources and Development of the Text* (London: Oxford University Press, 1964), 6–8.
44 Halil Inalcik, 'The Policy of Mehmed II toward the Greek Population of Istanbul', *Dumbarton Oaks Papers* 23 (1970), 242–5.
45 *Âşıkpaşaoğlu Tarihi*, ed. H. Nihal Atsız (Istanbul: Milli Eğitim Basımevi, 1970), 229; *Âşıkpaşazâde Tarihi (Osmanlı Tarihi 1285–1502)*, ed. Necdet Öztürk (Istanbul: Bilge, 2013), 297–8.
46 The text which includes this line is cited in Öztürk, *Âşıkpaşazâde Tarihi*,

298, n.5512. Lewis refers to 'the Istanbul edition, (1332), 192', quoted in Bernard Lewis, 'The Privilege Granted by Mehmed II to His Physician', *Bulletin of the School of Oriental and African Studies* 14, no. 3 (1952), 550–63, at 562, n.5, which also refers to a citation of the line in M. Tayyib Gökbilgin, *XV–XVI Asırlarda Edirne ve Paşa Livası* (Istanbul, 1952), 148.

47   Mehmed Neşri, *Kitâb-ı Cihan-Nümâ*, ed. Faik Reşat Unat and Mehmed A. Köymen, 2 vols (Ankara: Türk Tarih Kurumu, 2014), 2:687–713; Tursun Bey, *Târih-i Ebü'l-Feth*; *The History of Mehmed the Conqueror by Tursun Beg*, ed. Halil Inalcik and Rhoads Murphey (Minneapolis and Chicago: Bibliotheca Islamica, 1978), 65–76; *Rûhî Târîhî*, ed. Yaşar Yücel and Halil Engin Cengiz (Ankara: Türk Tarih Kurumu,1992); Kemalpaşazade, *Tevarih-i Al-i Osman*, ed. Şerafettin Turan, 2 vols (Ankara: Türk Tarihi Kurumu Basımevi, 1970–83), 7:28–105; Lutfi Pasha, *Tevarih-i Al-i Osman* (Istanbul: Matbaa-i Amire, 1341/1922–3), 174; and Müneccimbaşı Ahmed b. Lütfullah, *Camiü'D-Düvel: Osmanlı Tarihi* (1299–1481), ed. Ahmet Ağırakça (Istanbul: Insan Yayınları, 1995), 237–48.

48   *Heşt Bihişt*, folio 589a, quoted in Aikaterini Dimitriadou, 'The *Heşt Bihişt* of Idris Bidlisi: The Reign of Bayezid II (1481–1512)' (PhD diss., University of Edinburgh, 2000), 145–6, 212.

49   Halil Inalcik, 'Foundations of Ottoman–Jewish Cooperation', in *Jews, Turks, Ottomans: A Shared History, Fifteenth through the Twentieth Century*, ed. Avigdor Levy (Syracuse, NY: Syracuse University Press, 2002), 4.

50   Johannes H. Mordtmann, 'Die jüdischen Kira im Serai der Sultane', *Mitteilungen des Seminars für orientalische Sprachen: Westasiatische Studien* 32, no. 2 (1929), 2; Abraham Galanté, *Esther Kyra d'après de nouveaux documents: Contribution à l'Histoire des Juifs de Turquie* (Istanbul: l'Imprimerie Société Anonyme de Papeterie et d'Imprimerie (Fr. Haim), 1926), 3–7.

51   Murad III employed a Ragusan Jew, David Passi, as his advisor on finance, as well as domestic and foreign affairs. But his role was opposed by Grand Vizier Koca Sinan Pasha, who 'launched a violent campaign of defamation against Passi', and 'fulminated against all Jews and declared them unsuitable to hold positions of influence in an Islamic state; he

Notes

blamed the economic problems of the time on Passi, and sought to have him executed'. Instead in 1591 he was exiled to Rhodes. Caroline Finkel, *Osman's Dream: The History of the Ottoman Empire* (London: John Murray, 2007), 192; Pál Fodor, 'An Anti-Semite Grand Vizier? The Crisis in Ottoman–Jewish Relations, 1589–1591 and Its Consequences', in Pál Fodor, *In Quest of the Golden Apple: Imperial Ideology, Politics, and Military Administration in the Ottoman Empire* (Istanbul: Isis, 2000), 196–9.

52 Mehmed İpşirli, 'Giriş', in Selânikî Mustafa Efendi, *Tarih-i Selânikî*, ed. Mehmed İpşirli, 2 vols (Istanbul: Istanbul Üniversitesi Edebiyat Fakültesi, 1989), 1:xvii. See Mordtmann, 'Die jüdischen Kira im Serai der Sultane', 16–17.

53 Mehmed İpşirli, 'Mustafa Selaniki's History of the Ottomans' (PhD diss., Edinburgh University, 1976), xi–xviii.

54 Selânikî Mustafa Efendi, *Tarih-i Selânikî*, ed. İpşirli, 2:854. See also Mehmed İpşirli, 'Mustafa Selânikî and His History', *Tarih Enstitüsü Dergisi* 9 (January 1978), 417–72.

55 Selânikî Mustafa Efendi, *Tarih-i Selânikî*, 2:854.

56 Ibid., 2:855.

57 Ibid., 2:856.

58 Ibid., 2:856–7.

59 Ibid., 2:864.

60 Mordtmann, 'Die jüdischen Kira im Serai der Sultane', 17.

61 Selânikî Mustafa Efendi, *Tarih-i Selânikî*, 2:856. Hezarfen Hüseyin Efendi also mentions the subsequent imposition of sumptuary restrictions following the killing of the kira in his work completed in 1672/3, *Telhîsü'l-Beyân fî Kavânîn-i Âl-i Osmân*, ed. Sevim İlgürel (Ankara: Türk Tarih Kurumu, 1998), 55.

62 Selânikî, *Tarih-i Selânikî*.

63 This narrative is similar to another recorded by Selaniki in which 'an impure woman' (a Muslim prostitute) and a Jew were seized and lynched by a crowd near the ancient Egyptian obelisk erected by Pharaoh Thutmose III (1479–1425 BCE) re-erected by Emperor Theodosius I (r. 378–92 CE) in the Hippodrome, Istanbul. When Jews came to take the man's corpse, the *Acemi oğlanları* (Janissary recruits) crowded around them, and beat one of the Jews to death. They thrashed the woman's

corpse, tearing it from limb to limb, stuffed it in a sack, and paraded it around. Selânikî, *Tarih-i Selânikî*, 2:715.

64 Nevzat Kaya, 'Kara Çelebi-zâde Abdülaziz Efendi'nin Hayatı', in Kara Çelebi-zâde Abdülaziz Efendi, *Ravzatü'l-Ebrâr Zeyli* (Tahlîl ve Metin), 1732, ed. Nevzat Kaya (Ankara: Türk Tarihi Kurumu Basımevi, 2003), xiii–xxviii.

65 Kara Çelebi-zâde Abdülaziz Efendi, *Ravzatü'l-Ebrâr Zeyli*, 211–12.

66 Ibid., 213, 215.

67 Solakzâde Mehmed Hemdemî Çelebi, *Solakzâde Tarihi*, ed. Vahid Çabuk, 2 vols (Ankara: Türk Kültür Bakanlığı Yayınları, 1989), 2:406; Katip Çelebi, *Fezleke*, 2 vols (Istanbul: Ceride-i Havadis Matbaasi, 1286/1869), 1:128; quoted in Galanté, *Esther Kyra, d'après de nouveaux documents*, 11. Fezleke is the author's Turkish version of his original Arabic text entitled *Fezleket akvâl'l-ahyâr fi ilmi't-târîh ve'l-ahbâr*.

68 Moïse Franco, *Essai sur l'histoire des Israélites de l'Empire ottoman depuis les origines jusqu'à nos jours* (Paris: A. Durlacher, 1897), 73.

69 There is much confusion about the identity of three sixteenth-century kiras who are merged into one long-lived character. In the early sixteenth century Strongilah, a Karaite, served Hafsa Sultan, Suleiman I's mother. She converted at the end of her life, in Suleiman I's reign, becoming Fatma. Around the time of her death a Sephardic kira named Esther, widow of Eliyah Handali, began to serve the harem. She served Nurbanu the favourite of Selim II and then valide sultan of Murad III from 1566 to 1595. Esther was followed by several others including Esperanza Malki, who served Safiye Sultan, the favourite of Murad III, and then queen mother to Mehmed III until she was murdered in 1600. Minna Rozen, *A History of the Jewish Community in Istanbul: The Formative Years, 1453–1566* (Leiden: Brill, 2002), 206–7.

70 Selânikî, *Tarih-i Selânikî*, 2:723; Marc David Baer, 'The Great Fire of 1660 and the Islamization of Christian and Jewish Space in Istanbul', *International Journal of Middle East Studies* 36, no. 2 (2004), 159–81.

71 Kürd Hatib Mustafa, *Risāle-i Kürd Hatib*, Eski Hazine 1400, Topkapı Palace Museum Library, Istanbul, fol. 27a, 40a.

72 Baer, *Honored by the Glory of Islam*, 132–8.

73 Kürd Hatib Mustafa, *Risāle-i Kürd Hatib*, fol. 18a, quoted in ibid., 135.

74 Jews also remarked upon her power. In the responsa of Rabbi Shlomo

Notes

ben Avraham HaKohen we find 'The frightening and menacing lady, she has the power and the name in kings, courts, and castles, and her small word is enough to cause damage in anything she wishes, to his body or his capital'. Rozen, *A History of the Jewish Community in Istanbul*, 206, n.36.

75 This is corroborated by Silahdar, *Tarih-i Silahdar*, 2:578.
76 Kürd Hatib, *Risāle,* fols 18b–19b, quoted in Baer, *Honored by the Glory of Islam*, 136.
77 Kürd Hatib, *Risāle,* fol. 20a.
78 *A Study of Naima by Lewis V. Thomas*, ed. Norman Itzkowitz (New York: New York University Press, 1972), 1–2; Halide Edip, *Memoirs*, 232, quoted in *A Study of Naima*, 3.
79 Na'ima, *Tarîh-i Naîmâ*, 6 vols (Istanbul, 1281–3/1864–7), 1:231, 247; Naîmâ Mustafa Efendi, *Târih-i Na'îmâ (Ravzatü'l-Hüseyn Fî Hulâsati Ahbâri'l-Hâfikayn)*, ed. Mehmed İpşirli, 4 vols (Ankara: Türk Tarih Kurumu, 2007), 1:162–3.
80 Naîmâ Mustafa Efendi, *Târih-i Na'îmâ* 1:163.
81 *Seyahatname* II, 253b13, quoted in Robert Dankoff, *An Ottoman Mentality: The World of Evliya Çelebi* (Leiden: Brill, 2006), 68–9.
82 Dankoff, *An Ottoman Mentality*, 7.
83 *Seyahatname* I, 215a35, quoted in ibid., 68.
84 *Evliya Çelebi Seyahatnâmesi*, ed. Orhan Şaik Gökyay, Topkapı Sarayı Bağdat 304 Yazmasının Transkripsiyonu-Dizini, 1. Kitap: İstanbul (Istanbul: Yapı Kredi, 1996), 68–9. The citation in the original is 1:47b20.
85 Baer, *Honored by the Glory of Islam*, 121–32, 255–6.
86 Marc David Baer, *The Dönme: Jewish Converts, Muslim Revolutionaries, and Secular Turks* (Stanford, CA: Stanford University Press, 2010), 1–5.
87 Ibid., 3.
88 Quoted in *Sabbatian Heresy: Writings on Mysticism, Messianism, and the Origins of Jewish Modernity*, ed. Paweł Maciejko (Waltham, MA: Brandeis University Press, 2017), 36–7.
89 Baer, *The Dönme: Jewish Converts, Muslim Revolutionaries, and Secular Turks*, 25–55.
90 'Abdi Paşa, *Vekāyi'nāme*, Köprülü Library, 216, 224 a–b, quoted in Baer, *Honored by the Glory of Islam*, 127.

91 Râşid, *Tarih-i Râşid* 1:133, quoted in Baer, *Honored by the Glory of Islam*, 128.
92 Baer, *Honored by the Glory of Islam*, Chapters 4, 6.
93 Ibid., 137.
94 Marc David Baer, 'Death in the Hippodrome: Sexual Politics and Legal Culture in the Reign of Mehmed IV', *Past & Present* 210, no. 1 (2011), 61–91.
95 Silahdar Fındıklılı Mehmed Ağa, *Silahdar Tarihi*, 2 vols (Istanbul: Devlet, 1928), 1:731–2.
96 He is referring to a spiral column topped by three intertwined serpents' heads, which had been made to commemorate the Greek victory over the Persians at the battle of Platea in 479 BCE and dedicated as a votive offering to Apollo at Delphi. In the fourth century, Emperor Constantine brought this pillar to Constantinople. Thomas F. Madden, 'The Serpent Column of Delphi in Constantinople: Placement, Purposes, and Mutilations,' *Byzantine and Modern Greek Studies* 16 (1992), 111–45.
97 Lewis, *The Jews of Islam*, 67–106.
98 Nev'izade 'Ata'i, *Hada'iku'l-haka'ik fi tekmileti'ş-şaka'ik*, in *Şakaik-ı Nu'maniye ve Zeyilleri*, ed. Abdülkadir Özcan, 5 vols (Istanbul, 1989), 2:197.
99 Aslı Niyazioğlu, *Dreams and Lives in Ottoman Istanbul: A Seventeenth-Century Biographer's Perspective* (London and New York: Routledge, 2017), 61.
100 Silahdar, *Tarih-i Silahdar*, 2:578–9, quoted in Baer, *Honored by the Glory of Islam*, 137.
101 Lewis, *The Jews of Islam*, 148.
102 Kenbib, *Juifs et musulmans au Maroc*, 25.
103 Zafrani, *Two Thousand Years of Jewish Life in Morocco*, 140–5.
104 Kenbib, *Juifs et musulmans au Maroc*, 26.
105 Zafrani, *Two Thousand Years of Jewish Life in Morocco*, 140–1.
106 Kenbib, *Juifs et musulmans au Maroc*, 29–30.
107 Ibid., 30.
108 Ibid., 31;. Schroeter, *The Sultan's Jew*, 27.
109 Zafrani, *Two Thousand Years of Jewish Life in Morocco*, 8.
110 Kenbib, *Juifs et musulmans au Maroc*, 31.

Notes

111 Zafrani, *Two Thousand Years of Jewish Life in Morocco*, 265.
112 Kenbib, *Juifs et musulmans au Maroc*, 32.
113 Schroeter, *The Sultan's Jew*, 3.
114 Kenbib, *Juifs et musulmans au Maroc*, 34.
115 Sebag-Sarfaty, 'Notables juifs à la cour des sultans marocains', 35.
116 Daniel J. Schroeter, *Merchants of Essaouira: Urban Society and Imperialism in Southwestern Morocco, 1844–1886* (Cambridge: Cambridge University Press, 1988), 18.
117 Michel Abitbol, *Les commerçants du roi. Tujjār al Sultān. Une élite économique judéo-marocaine au XIXème siècle* (Paris: Maisonneuve & Larose, 1999).
118 Schroeter, *Merchants of Essaouira*, 7.
119 Kenbib, *Juifs et musulmans au Maroc*, 47.
120 Ibid., 48.
121 Schroeter, *Merchants of Essaouira*, 35.
122 Ibid., 36, 40.
123 Ibid., 42.
124 Ibid., 46–8.
125 Ibid., 21.
126 Ibid., 18–19.
127 Ibid.
128 Ibid., 21.
129 Ibid., 24.
130 Ibid., 2, 19.
131 García-Arenal and Wiegers, *A Man of Three Worlds*, 130.
132 Schroeter, *The Sultan's Jew*, 20, 22.
133 Ibid., 34.
134 Ibid., 88–90.
135 Ibid., xii.
136 Ibid., xiii. By 1815 the complete list of goods traded included manufactured textiles, sugar, coffee, pepper, iron bars, steel, tin, alum, paper, knives, manufactured goods, and green tea from China exported from England to Morocco, and animal skins, almonds, dates, gum Arabic, ostrich feathers, and wax exported to England from Morocco. Ibid., 82–3.
137 Ibid., 56.

138 He held that office again in 1829. Schroeter, *The Sultan's Jew*,138.
139 Yaacob Dweck, *Dissident Rabbi: The Life of Jacob Sasportas* (Princeton, NJ: Princeton University Press, 2019).
140 Schroeter, *The Sultan's Jew*, 46.
141 Ibid., 44.
142 Ibid., 75.
143 Daniel J. Schroeter, 'Morocco, England, and the End of the Sephardic World Order (The Sultan's Jew, Meir Macnin)', in *From Iberia to Diaspora: Studies in Sephardic History and* Culture, ed. Yedida Kalfon Stillman and Norman A. Stillman (Leiden: Brill, 1999), 86–9.
144 Ibid., 90.
145 Ibid., 90–1.
146 Schroeter, *The Sultan's Jew*, 70.
147 Schroeter, 'Morocco, England, and the End of the Sephardic World Order', 97.
148 Schroeter, *The Sultan's Jew*, 105.
149 Ibid., 106–7, 119, 120–1, 124–5, 128.
150 Schroeter, 'Morocco, England, and the End of the Sephardic World Order', 100.
151 Her tomb at the centre of the 15,000 white cylindrical graves of Fez's Jewish cemetery bordered by orange trees within the mellah is a pilgrimage site for Jews. She is the subject of Alfred Dehodencq's *Décapitation de Sol Hachuel à Fès* (1860), which depicts a kneeling, beautiful, young woman with long black hair, her hands bound behind her back, as a tall, muscular Black executioner stands over her, pointing his sword at her neck, while a crowd of Muslims and Jews, including a praying rabbi, gathers to watch.
152 Yaëlle Azagury, 'Sol Hachuel in the Collective Memory and Folktales of Moroccan Jews', in *Jewish Culture and Society in North Africa*, ed. Emily Benichou Gottreich and Daniel J. Schroeter (Bloomington: Indiana University Press, 2011), 191.

5. Severed Symbiosis and New Saviours: Colonialism and New Alliances in the Long Nineteenth Century, 1789–1914
1 Laskier, *Juifs et Musulmans en Égypte*, 80.
2 Ibid., 81.

Notes

3 Ibid., 82.
4 Napoleon Bonaparte, 'A L'intendant General de l'Egypte', in *Correspondance de Napoléon 1er*, vol. 5, 184.
5 Anouar Louca, 'Ya'qub et les lumières', *Revue des Mondes Musulmans et de la Méditerranée* 52–3 (1989), 63–76.
6 Abitbol and Filali-Ansary, 'Préface', in Laskier, *Juifs et Musulmans en Égypte*, 9.
7 Laskier, *Juifs et Musulmans en Égypte*, 85.
8 Ibid., 86.
9 Ibid., 86.
10 Ibid., 87.
11 Amnon Cohen, *Juifs et musulmans en Palestine et en Israël. Des origines à nos jours* (Paris: Tallandier, 2021), 72.
12 Ibid., 73.
13 Benjamin Stora, *Les trois exils: Juifs d'Algérie* (Paris: Stock, 2006), 40–1.
14 Ibid., 27.
15 Ibid., 28.
16 Ibid., 29.
17 Ibid., 30.
18 Ibid., 34.
19 Ibid., 35.
20 Ibid., 36.
21 Baer, *The Ottomans*, 344.
22 Ibid., 346.
23 Ibid., 347.
24 Abraham Galanté, *Histoire des Juifs d'Istanbul depuis la prise de cette ville, en 1453, par Fatih Mehmed II, jusqu'à nos jours* (Istanbul: Hüsnütabiat, 1941), 26.
25 Baer, *The Ottomans*, 347.
26 Ibid., 348.
27 Ibid., 349.
28 Ibid., 352.
29 (Ahmed) Cevdet Paşa, *Tezâkir*, ed. Cavid Baysun, 4 vols (Ankara: Türk Tarih Kurumu, 1953–67), 1:68.
30 The Pact appears in Armand Maarek, 'Le Pacte fundamental et les réformes à travers les archives diplomatiques françaises', in *Entre orient et*

occident. Juifs et Musulmans en Tunisie, ed. Denis Cohen-Tannoudji (Paris: Éditions de l'Éclat, 2007), 133.
31 Ibid., 137–8.
32 Quoted in Khlifa Chater, 'Ben Dhiaf et l'idéaltype des Lumières dans la Régence de Tunis au XIXe siècle', in *Entre orient et occident*, ed. Cohen-Tannoudji, 125.
33 Laskier, *Juifs et Musulmans en Égypte*, 88.
34 Jacqueline Kahanoff, 'A Culture Stillborn' [1973], in *Mongrels or Marvels: The Levantine Writings of Jacqueline Shohet Kahanoff*, ed. Deborah A. Starr and Sasson Somekh (Stanford, CA: Stanford University Press, 2011), 120.
35 Laskier, *Juifs et Musulmans en Égypte*, 89.
36 Abigail Green, 'Nationalism and the "Jewish International": Religious Internationalism in Europe and the Middle East *c*.1840–*c*.1880', *Comparative Studies in Society & History* 50, no. 2 (2008), 535–58.
37 Güleryüz, *The History of the Turkish Jews*, 12.
38 'A Blood Libel in Rhodes (1840)', translated in *Sephardi Lives: A Documentary History, 1700–1950*, ed. Julia Philips Cohen and Sarah Abrevaya Stein (Stanford, CA: Stanford University Press, 2014), 112.
39 Ibid., 115.
40 Quoted on the Quincentennial Foundation/500 Yıl Vakfı website, www.sephardichouse.org/Quincentennial-Foundation.html
41 The Montefiore Endowment, https://www.montefioreendowment.org.uk/sirmoses/about/, and Alain Amiel, 'Les Cent vies de Moïse Montefiore', *L'Arche*, special issue, 'les juifs du maroc', no. 700 (Sept.–Oct. 2023), 36–7.
42 Ivan Davidson Kalmar, 'Benjamin Disraeli, Romantic Orientalist', *Comparative Studies in Society & History* 47, no. 2 (April 2005), 348.
43 Quoted in ibid., 353.
44 Ibid., 361.
45 Bernard Lewis, 'The Pro-Islamic Jews', *Judaism* 17, no. 4 (1968), 391–2.
46 W.E. Gladstone, *Bulgarian Horrors and the Question of the East* (London: John Murray, 1876), 12–13.
47 Kalmar, 'Benjamin Disraeli, Romantic Orientalist', 348.
48 Ibid., 366.
49 Stora, *Les trois exils*, 39.

Notes

50 Malika Ziane, 'L'interprète, l'Algérie et la France', in *Juifs et musulmans de la France colonial à nos jours*, ed. Karima Dirèche, Mathias Dreyfuss, and Benjamin Stora (Paris: Seuil, 2022), 38.
51 Phillipe Danan, 'Les Juifs de Constantine au début de la presence française', in *Les Juifs d'Algérie. Une histoire de ruptures*, ed. Allouche-Benayoun and Dermenjian, 75–82.
52 Sabrina Dufourmont, 'Une facette méconnue. Les interprètes juifs de l'armée française lors de la conquête de l'Algérie (1830–1870)', in *Les Juifs d'Algérie. Une histoire de ruptures*, ed. Allouche-Benayoun and Dermenjian, 83–92.
53 Stora, *Les trois exils*, 84.
54 Dufourmont, 'Une facette méconnue', 85.
55 Ibid., 86.
56 Ibid., 87.
57 Ibid., 89.
58 Ibid., 91–2.
59 Stora, *Les trois exils*, 50.
60 Malika Ziane, 'L'interprète, l'Algérie et la France', 36, 38.
61 Stora, *Les trois exils*, 41.
62 Ibid., 43.
63 Ibid., 45–6.
64 Ibid., 46.
65 Ibid., 48.
66 Ibid., 51.
67 Allouche-Benayoun, 'Les juifs d'Algérie. Du *dhimmi* au citoyen français', 35.
68 Stora, *Les trois exils*, 52.
69 Sarah Stein, *Saharan Jews and the Fate of French Algeria* (Chicago: University of Chicago Press, 2014).
70 Stora, *Les trois exils*, 54.
71 Ibid., 55.
72 Allouche-Benayoun, 'Les juifs d'Algérie. Du *dhimmi* au citoyen français', 38.
73 Ibid., 40.
74 Stora, *Les trois exils*, 57.
75 Ibid., 58.

76 Ibid., 59.
77 Kenbib, *Juifs et musulmans au Maroc*, 62.
78 Ibid., 63.
79 Ibid., 65.
80 Ibid., 66.
81 Ibid., 67.
82 Ibid., 68.
83 Ibid., 69–70.
84 Schroeter, *The Sultan's Jew*, 153.
85 Kenbib, *Juifs et musulmans au Maroc*, 71.
86 Daniel J. Schroeter and Joseph Chetrit, 'Emancipation and Its Discontents: Jews at the Formative Period of Colonial Rule in Morocco', *Jewish Social Studies*, New Series 13, no. 1 (2006), 175–6.
87 Jessica Marglin, *Across Legal Lines: Jews and Muslims in Modern Morocco* (New Haven, CT: Yale University Press, 2016).
88 Georges Bensoussan, *Juifs en pays arabes. Le grand déracinement 1850–1975* (Paris: Tallandier, 2021), 306.
89 Michael M. Laskier, *The Alliance Israélite Universelle and the Jewish Communities of Morocco: 1862–1962* (Albany: State University of New York Press, 1983), 33–4.
90 Joy A. Land, 'Corresponding Women: Female Educators and the Alliance Israélite Universelle in Tunisia, 1882–1914', in *Jewish Culture and Society in North Africa*, ed. Gottreich and Schroeter, 240.
91 Frédéric Abécassis, 'Destins scolaires croisés. Le role de l'éducation dans l'évolution séparée des populations juives et musulmanes du maghreb', in *Juifs et musulmans de la France colonial à nos jours*, ed. Dirèche et al., 52.
92 Ibid., 54.
93 Ibid., 55.
94 Bensoussan, *Juifs en pays arabes*, 556.
95 Ibid., 30.
96 Ibid., 33.
97 Ibid., 36.
98 Ibid., 87.
99 Ibid., 320.
100 Laskier, *The Alliance Israélite Universelle and the Jewish Communities of Morocco*.

Notes

101 Kenbib, *Juifs et musulmans au Maroc*, 59.
102 Ibid., 60.
103 Bensoussan, *Juifs en pays arabes*, 392.
104 Benjamin Stora, *L'Arrivée: De Constantine à Paris, 1962–1972* (Paris: Tallandier, 2023), 81.
105 Sarah Abrevaya Stein, *Plumes: Ostrich Feathers, Jews, and a Lost World of Global Commerce* (New Haven, CT: Yale University Press, 2010).
106 Meir-Glitzenstein, *Juifs et musulmans en Irak*, 70.
107 Joseph Sassoon, *The Global Merchants: The Enterprise and Extravagance of the Sassoon Dynasty* (London: Allen Lane, 2022), 5–6.
108 Baer, *The Ottomans: Khans, Caesars and Caliphs*, 339–40.
109 Sassoon, *The Global Merchants*, 10.
110 Ibid., 19.
111 Ibid., xxxii.
112 Ibid., 20–1.
113 Ibid., 23–4.
114 Ibid., 50–1.
115 Ibid., 69.
116 Ibid., 122.
117 Ibid., 87.
118 Ibid., 172–3, 186.
119 Ibid., 182.
120 Ibid., 217, 220.
121 Ibid., 34.
122 Ibid., 47, 49.
123 Ibid., 102, 115–16.
124 Ibid., 131.
125 Ibid., 148, 156.
126 Ibid., 209, 211.
127 Ibid., 154–5.
128 Ibid., 148.
129 Ibid., 192–3.
130 Ibid., 199.
131 Ibid., 125–6.
132 Ibid., 136–7.
133 Ibid., 41.

134 Ibid., 48–9.
135 Ibid., 49, 69.
136 Ibid., 74–5, 103, 111.
137 Shimon Shamir, 'Preface', in *The Jews of Egypt*, ed. Shamir, xiv.
138 Ibid., xv.
139 Joel Beinin, *The Dispersion of Egyptian Jewry: Culture, Politics, and the Formation of a Modern Diaspora* (Berkeley: University of California Press, 1998), 207.
140 Laskier, *Juifs et Musulmans en Égypte*, 110.
141 Gudrun Krämer, *The Jews in Modern Egypt, 1914–1952* (Seattle: University of Washington Press, 1989), 36.
142 Ibid., 76–8.
143 Ibid., 88.
144 Ibid., 89, 102.
145 Ibid., 51.
146 Ibid., 55.
147 Shimon Shamir, 'The Evolution of the Egyptian Nationality Laws and Their Application to the Jews in the Monarchy Period', in *The Jews of Egypt*, ed. Shamir, 33.
148 Laskier, *Juifs et Musulmans en Égypte*, 114–15.
149 Krämer, *The Jews in Modern Egypt*, 17; Shamir, 'The Evolution of the Egyptian Nationality Laws', 38.
150 Krämer, *The Jews in Modern Egypt*, 15.
151 Ibid., 19.
152 Ibid., 24.
153 Ibid., 172.
154 Sarah Abrevaya Stein, 'Protected Persons? The Baghdadi Jewish Diaspora, the British State, and the Persistence of Empire', *American Historical Review* 116, no. 1 (2011), 80–1.
155 Meir-Glitzenstein, *Juifs et musulmans en Irak*, 71.
156 Ibid., 72.
157 Ethan B. Katz, *The Burdens of Brotherhood: Jews and Muslims from North Africa to France* (Cambridge, MA: Harvard University Press, 2015).
158 Rejwan, *Israel's Place in the Middle East*, 31.
159 Ibid., 33.

160 Ebüziya, *Millet-i Isra'iliye* (Kostantiniye: Kitabhane-i Ebüziya, 1305 AH/1887–8 CE).

161 Arthur de Gobineau, *Essai sur l'inégalité des races humaines*, 4 vols (Paris: Firmin Didot, 1853–5); Édouard Drumont, *La France juive: Essai d'histoire contemporaine*, 2 vols (Paris: Flammarion, 1886); Ernest Renan, *Histoire générale et système comparé des langues sémitiques* (Paris, 1855); Ernest Renan, *Le judaïsme comme race et comme religion* (Paris: Michel Lévy Frères, 1883).

162 Özgür Türesay, 'Antisionisme et Antisemitisme dans la Presse ottoman d'Istanbul à l'Époque jeune Turque (1909–1912): L'exemple d'Ebüzziya Tevfik', *Turcica* 41 (2009), 152.

163 Lewis, *The Jews of Islam*, 188.

164 Matti Bunzl, 'Between Anti-Semitism and Islamophobia: Some Thoughts on the New Europe', *American Ethnologist* 32, no. 4 (2005), 502.

165 Ebüziya, *Millet-i Isra'iliye*, 55.

166 Ibid., 3–4, 51.

167 Michael L. Miller, 'European Judaism and Islam: The Contribution of Jewish Orientalists', in *A History of Jewish–Muslim Relations*, ed. Meddeb and Stora, 833.

6. Enemies and Allies, Persecutors and Protectors: Jews, Muslims, and Nazism in Europe and the Middle East, 1933–45

1 'Netanyahu Holocaust Remarks: Israeli Prime Minister Criticised', BBC News, 21 October 2015, https://www.bbc.co.uk/news/world-middle-east-34594563.

2 Marc David Baer, 'Muslim Encounters with Nazism and the Holocaust: The Ahmadi of Berlin and Jewish Convert to Islam Hugo Marcus', *American Historical Review* 120, no. 1 (2015), 140.

3 *Mufti-Papiere: Briefe, Memoranden, Reden und Aufrufe Amin al-Husainis aus dem Exil, 1940–1945*, ed. Gerhard Höpp (Berlin: Klaus Schwarz, 2001); Bernd Bauknecht, *Muslime in Deutschland von 1920 bis 1945* (Cologne: Teiresias, 2001), 117–26; René Wildangel, *Zwischen Achse und Mandatsmacht: Palästina und der Nationalsozialismus* (Berlin: Klaus Schwarz, 2007), 331–2, 336–43; Gilbert Achcar, *The Arabs and the Holocaust: The Arab–Israeli War of Narratives* (London: Saqi,

2010), 150–8. As Philip Mattar has observed, most accounts of al-Husseini either vilify or glorify him, which tells us more about the politics of the biographers than about the Palestinian leader. Mattar, *The Mufti of Jerusalem: Al-Hajj Amin Al-Husayni and the Palestinian National Movement*, rev. ed. (New York: Columbia University Press, 1988), xiii–xiv.

4   Henry Laurens, 'The Mufti of Jerusalem, Opportunism and Anti-Semitism', in *A History of Jewish–Muslim Relations*, ed. Meddeb and Stora, 360.

5   Ronen Steinke, *Der Muslim und die Jüdin. Die Geschichte einer Rettung in Berlin* (Munich: Berlin Verlag, 2017), 104–5.

6   Ibid., 103.

7   *Mudhakkirāt al-Hāj Amīn al-Husayni*, ed. 'AbdulKarīm al-'Umar (Damascus, 1999), 128, quoted in Achcar, *The Arabs and the Holocaust*, 235.

8   Ibid., 238.

9   Ibid., 238.

10 Ibid., 239.

11 The first biography, *The Grand Mufti: Grand Agent of the Axis*, was written by Nazi hunter Simon Wiesenthal. Simon Wiesenthal, *Grossmufti: Grossagent der Achse* (Vienna, 1947).

12 Peter Novick, *The Holocaust in American Life* (Boston: Houghton Mifflin, 1999), 158.

13 Wildangel, *Zwischen Achse und Mandatsmacht*, 143–57, 181–9; Israel Gershoni and James Jankowski, *Confronting Fascism in Egypt: Dictatorship versus Democracy in the 1930s* (Stanford, CA: Stanford University Press, 2009), 281–2; Israel Gershoni and Götz Nordbruch, *Sympathie und Schrecken: Begegnungen mit Faschismus und Nationalsozialismus in Ägypten, 1922–1937* (Berlin: Klaus Schwarz, 2011); Götz Nordbruch, *Nazism in Syria and Lebanon: The Ambivalence of the German Option, 1933–1945* (New York: Routledge, 2009), 135–6; Orit Bashkin, *New Babylonians: A History of Jews in Modern Iraq* (Stanford, CA: Stanford University Press, 2012), Chapter 5; Israel Gershoni, 'Confronting Nazism in Egypt: Tawfiq al-Hakim's Anti-Totalitarianism, 1938–1945', *Deutschlandbilder: Tel Aviver Jahrbuch für deutsche Geschichte* 26 (1997), 121–50; Israel Gershoni, 'Egyptian

Notes

Liberalism in an Age of "Crisis of Orientation": Al-Risāla's Reaction to Fascism and Nazism, 1933–39', *International Journal of Middle East Studies* 31 (1999), 551–76; Israel Gershoni, '"Der verfolgte Jude": Al-Hilals Reaktionen auf den Antisemitismus in Europa und Hitlers Machtergreifung', in *Blind für die Geschichte? Arabische Begegnungen mit dem Nationalsozialismus*, ed. Gerhard Höpp et al. (Berlin: Klaus Schwarz, 2004), 39–72; René Wildangel, '"Der größte Feind der Menschheit": Der Nationalsozialismus in der arabischen öffentlichen Meinung in Palästina während des Zweiten Weltkrieges', in ibid., 115–54; Peter Wien, *Iraqi Arab Nationalism: Authoritarian, Totalitarian, and Pro-Fascist Inclinations, 1932–1941* (New York: Routledge, 2006); Orit Bashkin, *The Other Iraq: Pluralism and Culture in Hashemite Iraq* (Stanford, CA: Stanford University Press, 2008).

14 Abdelwahab Meddeb, 'Taha Hussein: An Arab Writer Denounces Nazi Barbarism', in *A History of Jewish–Muslim Relations*, ed. Meddeb and Stora, 371.

15 Gershoni, 'Egyptian Liberalism in an Age of "Crisis of Orientation"', 555.

16 Michel Abitbol, 'The Diverse Reactions to Nazism by Leaders in the Muslim Countries', in *A History of Jewish–Muslim Relations*, ed. Meddeb and Stora, 349.

17 David Motadel, *Islam and Nazi Germany's War* (London: Belknap Press, 2014), 56.

18 Ibid., 58–9, 65.

19 Ibid., 1.

20 Ibid., 196.

21 Ibid., 234.

22 Gudrun Krämer, 'Anti-Semitism in the Muslim World: A Critical Review', *Die Welt des Islams: International Journal for the Study of Modern Islam*, New Series, 46, no. 3 (2006), 260.

23 Gerhard Höpp, 'The Suppressed Discourse', in *The World in World Wars: Experiences, Perceptions and Perspectives from Africa and Asia*, ed. Heike Liebau et al. (Leiden: Brill, 2010), 167–216, at 170; Peter Wien, 'The Culpability of Exile: Arabs in Nazi Germany', *Geschichte und Gesellschaft* 37 (2011), 332.

24 Baer, 'Muslim Encounters with Nazism and the Holocaust', 140–1; Marc

David Baer, *German, Jew, Muslim, Gay: The Life and Times of Hugo Marcus* (New York: Columbia University Press, 2020).
25   Steinke, *Der Muslim und die Jüdin*, 33.
26   Ibid., 41.
27   Ibid., 57.
28   Ibid., 9.
29   Ibid., 10.
30   Ibid., 92, 93.
31   Ibid., 104.
32   Ibid., 97–8.
33   Ibid., 156.
34   'Dr Mohamed Helmy and Frieda Szturmann', Yad Vashem, https://www.yadvashem.org/righteous/stories/helmy-szturmann.html.
35   Kirsten Grieshaber and Mariam Rizk, 'Family of First Arab to Get Yad Vashem Recognition Rejects Award', *Times of Israel*, 20 October 2013, https://www.timesofisrael.com/family-of-first-arab-to-get-yad-vashem-recognition-rejects-award.
36   'Arab to Finally Receive Israeli Honor as Holocaust Hero', France24, 25 October 2017, https://www.france24.com/en/20171025-arab-finally-receive-israeli-honor-holocaust-hero.
37   Steinke, *Der Muslim und die Jüdin*, 146.
38   Daniel J. Schroeter, 'Between Metropole and French North Africa: Vichy's Anti-Semitic Legislation and Colonialism's Racial Hierarchies', in *The Holocaust and North Africa*, ed. Aomar Boum and Sarah Abrevaya Stein (Stanford, CA: Stanford University Press, 2019), 19–49.
39   Tartakowsky, *Les juifs et le maghreb*, 169.
40   'Abdelwahab: The Full Picture', Yad Vashem, https://www.yadvashem.org/blog/abdelwahab-the-full-picture.html.
41   Habib Kazdaghli, 'The Tunisian Jews in the German Occupation', in *A History of Jewish–Muslim Relations*, ed. Meddeb and Stora, 368.
42   Abitbol, 'The Diverse Reactions to Nazism', 351.
43   Tartakowsky, *Les juifs et le maghreb*, 168.
44   Comité Algérien d'Études Sociales, *Le Livre d'or du judaïsme algérien (1914–1918)* (Algiers, 1919), cited in Geneviève Dermenjian, 'Les juifs d'Algérie entre deux hostilités (1830–1943)', in *Les Juifs d'Algérie. Une*

histoire de ruptures, ed. Allouche-Benayoun and Dermenjian, 105–33, at 113.
45 Jacob Oliel, 'Les camps d'internement en Algérie (1941–1944)', in *Les Juifs d'Algérie. Une histoire de ruptures*, ed. Allouche-Benayoun and Dermenjian, 153–66, at 156.
46 Ibid., 160.
47 Ibid., 161.
48 Ibid., 163.
49 Ibid., 166.
50 Renée Dray-Bensousan, 'Les juifs d'Algérie à Marseille pendant la Second Guerre mondiale', in *Les Juifs d'Algérie. Une histoire de ruptures*, ed. Allouche-Benayoun and Dermenjian, 167–75, at 167.
51 Ibid., 171.
52 Maud S. Mandel, *Muslims and Jews in France: History of a Conflict* (Princeton, NJ: Princeton University Press, 2014), 24.
53 Dray-Bensousan, 'Les juifs d'Algérie à Marseille pendant la Second Guerre mondiale', 174.
54 Ethan B. Katz, 'In the Shadow of the Republic: A Century of Coexistence and Conflict', in *A History of Jewish–Muslim Relations*, ed. Meddeb and Stora, 505.
55 Ethan Katz, 'Soldats juifs, soldats musulmans à l'épreuve du feu pendant la première guerre mondiale', in *Juifs et musulmans de la France colonial à nos jours*, ed. Dirèche et al., 72.
56 Ibid., 75; Katz, 'In the Shadow of the Republic', 503.
57 Karima Dirèche, 'Ouverture. 1914–1939. Engagés dans le projet imperial français', in *Juifs et musulmans de la France colonial à nos jours*, ed. Dirèche et al., 69.
58 Katz, 'Soldats juifs, soldats musulmans à l'épreuve du feu', 75.
59 Katz, 'In the Shadow of the Republic', 502.
60 Jalila Sbai, 'The Mosque of Paris and the Saving of the Jews: An Unresolved Question', in *A History of Jewish–Muslim Relations*, ed. Meddeb and Stora, 516.
61 'La Mosquée de Paris: une résistance oubliée' (FR3, 1991, Derri Berkani), Mohamed Fekrane, 'Ensemble' (2009), and Ismaël Ferroukhi, 'Les hommes libres' (2011).

62 Mohammed Aïssaoui, *L'Étoile jaune et le croissant* (Paris: Gallimard, 2012), 43–5.
63 Ibid., 47.
64 Ibid., 94.
65 Ibid., 95.
66 Ibid., 96.
67 Ibid., 101.
68 Ibid., 105–6.
69 Ibid., 107.
70 Mathias Dreyfuss, 'Ouverture. 1939–1945. Le chaos de la guerre', in *Juifs et musulmans de la France colonial à nos jours*, ed. Dirèche et al., 114.
71 Jean Laloum, 'Les juifs d'Algérie à Paris au temps des années noires', in *Juifs et musulmans de la France colonial à nos jours*, ed. Dirèche et al., 125.
72 Motadel, *Islam and Nazi Germany's War*, 318.
73 Ethan Katz, 'Between Emancipation and Persecution: Algerian Jewish Memory in the *Longue durée* (1930–1970)', *Journal of North African Studies*, 17, no. 5 (2012), 793–820.
74 Ibid., 801.
75 Joshua Cole, *Lethal Provocation: The Constantine Murders and the Politics of French Algeria* (Ithaca: Cornell University Press, 2019), 116–19.
76 Ibid., 255–7.
77 Stora, *Les trois exils*, 62.
78 Cole, *Lethal Provocation*, 75.
79 Joshua Cole, 'De Constantine à Vichy', in *Juifs et musulmans de la France colonial à nos jours*, ed. Dirèche et al., 96.
80 Ibid., 100.
81 Stora, *Les trois exils*, 64.
82 Ibid., 65–6.
83 Ibid., 67.
84 Ibid., 76.
85 Ibid., 78.
86 Ibid., 79.
87 Ibid., 81.
88 Ibid., 84.
89 Ibid., 85.

90 Ibid., 86.
91 Quoted in Abitbol, 'The Diverse Reactions to Nazism', 350.
92 Stora, *Les trois exils*, 94.
93 Ibid., 95.
94 Ibid., 97.
95 Schroeter, 'Between Metropole and French North Africa', 19–22.
96 Stora, *Les trois exils*, 99.
97 Ibid., 100.
98 Ibid., 102.
99 Ibid., 104.
100 Ibid., 107.
101 Ibid., 111.
102 Ibid., 112.
103 Ibid., 113.
104 Ibid., 114–15.
105 Ibid., 116.
106 Ibid., 117.
107 Ibid., 119.
108 Ibid., 120.
109 Ibid., 122.
110 Ibid., 123.
111 Ibid., 125–6.
112 Kenbib, *Juifs et musulmans au Maroc*, 149.
113 Ibid., 150.
114 Ibid., 151.
115 Ibid., 156.
116 Ibid., 157.
117 Ibid., 158, 159.
118 Ibid., 162.
119 Archives of Foreign Relations, Paris, Quai d'Orsay, 1939/1945 War Series, Vichy-Morocco, File 18, Jews (general), Binder 665, Diplomatic Corps Series (Annex 1), quoted in Zafrani, *Two Thousand Years of Jewish Life in Morocco*, 294–5.
120 Daniel Schroeter, 'Vichy in Morocco: The Residency, Mohammed V, and His Indigenous Jewish Subjects', in *Colonialism and the Jews*, ed.

Ethan B. Katz, Lisa Moses Leff and Maud S. Mandel (Bloomington: Indiana University Press, 2017), 215–17.
121 Kenbib, *Juifs et musulmans au Maroc*, 165.
122 Ibid., 166.
123 Schroeter, 'Vichy in Morocco', 215–50.
124 Kenbib, *Juifs et musulmans au Maroc*, 167.
125 Aïssaoui, *L'Étoile jaune et le croissant*, 54. The story is told by Serge Berdugo, former Moroccan minister of tourism (1993–5) and ambassador at large to HM Mohammed VI, president of the Council of the Jewish Community of Casablanca, and secretary general of the Committee of the Jewish Community of Morocco.
126 Kenbib, *Juifs et musulmans au Maroc*, 168.
127 Ibid., 171.
128 Ibid., 172.
129 Ibid., 173.
130 Quoted in ibid., 176.
131 Xavier Bougarel, *La division Handschar: Waffen-SS de Bosnie, 1943–1945* (Paris: Passés/Composés, 2020).
132 Exhibition, Jewish Museum of Sarajevo.
133 'Sarajevo Haggadah', Zemaljski Muzej, https://zemaljskimuzej.ba/en/item/sarajevo-haggadah.
134 'Korkut Dervis & Servet', Yad Vashem, https://collections.yadvashem.org/en/righteous/4021797?fbclid=IwAR0zfVApT9vVkJViyLqxDl29tH9kVQP7d9dI18aFECGnCJ0gprzb7hcQoZY.
135 Norman H. Gershman, *Besa: Muslims Who Saved Jews in World War Two* (Syracuse, NY: Syracuse University Press, 2008), 4.
136 Irena Steinfeldt, 'Muslim Righteous among the Nations', in *A History of Jewish–Muslim Relations*, ed. Meddeb and Stora, 373.
137 'Brothers Hamid and Xhemal Veseli', Yad Vashem, https://www.yadvashem.org/yv/en/exhibitions/besa/veseli.asp.
138 Laskier, *Juifs et Musulmans en Égypte*, 138.
139 Krämer, *The Jews in Modern Egypt*, 189.
140 Ibid., 116.
141 Ibid., 146.
142 Laskier, *Juifs et Musulmans en Égypte*, 147–9.
143 Krämer, *The Jews in Modern Egypt*, 130.

144 Ibid., 135.
145 Krämer, *The Jews in Modern Egypt*, 96–7, 136; Alcalay, *After Jews and Arabs*, 202. Krämer, *The Jews in Modern Egypt*, 136.
146 Ibid., 138–9.
147 Ibid., 150.
148 Ibid., 150.
149 Laskier, *Juifs et Musulmans en Égypte*, 155.
150 Krämer, *The Jews in Modern Egypt*, 156.
151 Laskier, *Juifs et Musulmans en Égypte*, 157.
152 Ibid., 156.
153 Ibid., 159.
154 Ibid., 160.
155 Ibid., 162–3.
156 Krämer, *The Jews in Modern Egypt*, 142.
157 Laskier, *Juifs et Musulmans en Égypte*, 163–4.
158 Ibid., 165, 167.
159 Ibid., 170.
160 Ibid., 171.
161 Krämer, *The Jews in Modern Egypt*, 164.
162 Laskier, *Juifs et Musulmans en Égypte*, 172.
163 Ibid., 175.
164 Ibid., 178.
165 Gudrun Krämer, 'Political Participation of the Jews in Egypt between World War I and the 1952 Revolution', in *The Jews of Egypt*, ed. Shamir, 71.
166 Ibid., 72.
167 Ibid., 74.
168 Krämer, *The Jews in Modern Egypt*, 174.
169 Krämer, 'Political Participation of the Jews in Egypt', 76.
170 Ibid., 77.
171 Krämer, *The Jews in Modern Egypt*, 180.
172 Meir-Glitzenstein, *Juifs et musulmans en Irak*, 106.
173 Ibid., 100.
174 Ibid., 101–2.
175 Ibid., 125, 134.
176 Ibid., 136.

177 Ibid., 137.
178 Bashkin, *New Babylonians*, 117.
179 Ibid., 126.
180 Ibid., 129.
181 Ibid., 122.
182 Ibid., 139–40.
183 Meir-Glitzenstein, *Juifs et musulmans en Irak*, 142.
184 Bashkin, *New Babylonians*, 104.
185 Ibid., 131–2.
186 Ibid., 133.
187 Meir-Glitzenstein, *Juifs et musulmans en Irak*, 142–3.
188 Bashkin, *New Babylonians*, 139.
189 Meir-Glitzenstein, *Juifs et musulmans en Irak*, 144.
190 Laurent Mallet, 'Karikatür dergisinde yahudilerle ilgili karikatürler, 1936–1948', *Toplumsal Tarih* 34 (Oct. 1996), 19–36; Hatice Bayraktar, *Salamon und Rabeka: Judenstereotype in Karikaturen der türkischen Zeitschriften 'Akbaba', 'Karikatür' und 'Milli Inkilap', 1933–1945* (Berlin: Klaus Schwarz, 2006); and Hatice Bayraktar, 'Stereotypes of Jews in Turkish Caricatures, 1933–1945', in *Jewish Images in the Media*, ed. Martin Liepach et al. (Vienna: Austrian Academy of Sciences, 2007), 85–104.
191 'Haim Bejarano Viaja a Béjar', Museo Judío David Melul, Béjar, https://www.museojudiobejar.com/2020/05/haim-bejarano-viaja-bejar.
192 Quoted in Jacob M. Landau, *Tekinalp, Turkish Patriot, 1883–1961* (Istanbul: Nederlands Historisch-Archaeologisch Instituut, 1984), 284.
193 Baer, *Sultanic Saviors and Tolerant Turks*, 247.
194 Rıfat N. Bali, *Cumhuriyet Yıllarında Türkiye Yahudileri: Bir Türkleştirme Serüveni, 1923–1945* (Istanbul: Iletişim, 1999), 246.
195 Hatice Bayraktar, 'The Anti-Jewish Pogrom in Eastern Thrace in 1934: New Evidence for the Responsibility of the Turkish Government', *Patterns of Prejudice* 40, no. 2 (2006), 104–5.
196 Quoted in Avigdor Levi, *Türkiye Cumhuriyetinde Yahudiler: Hukukî ve Siyasî Durumları*, ed. Rıfat N. Bali (Istanbul: Iletişim, 1996), 110.
197 Bali, *Cumhuriyet Yıllarında Türkiye Yahudileri*, 332–3.
198 Corroborating evidence is provided by Ayhan Aktar, *Varlık Vergisi ve Türkleştirme Politikaları* (Istanbul: Iletişim, 2000).

Notes

199 Levi, *Türkiye Cumhuriyetinde Yahudiler: Hukukî ve Siyasî Durumları*, ed. Bali, 142.
200 Rıdvan Akar, *Aşkale Yolcuları: Varlık Vergisi ve Çalışma Kampları* (Istanbul: Belge, 1999); Eli Şaul, *Balat'tan Bat-Yam'a*, ed. Rıfat N. Bali (Istanbul: Iletişim, 1999), 89.
201 Bali, *Cumhuriyet Yıllarında Türkiye Yahudileri*, 464.
202 Ibid., 426.
203 Ibid., 445.
204 Ibid., 482.
205 Ibid., 478.
206 Ibid., 447–8.
207 Rıfat N. Bali, *Yirmi Kur'a Nafia Askerleri: Gayrimüslimlerin Askerlik Serüveni (Mayis 1941–Temmuz 1942)*, 2nd ed. (Istanbul: Kitabevi, 2022).
208 Selim Deringil, *Turkish Foreign Policy during the Second World War: An 'Active' Neutrality* (Cambridge: Cambridge University Press, 1989).
209 Cevat Rıfat Atilhan, *Yahudi casusu Suzy Liberman* (Istanbul: Türkiye, 1935); and Rıfat Bali, 'Cevat Rıfat Atilhan', *Modern Türkiye'de siyasî düşünce* (Istanbul: İletişim, 2003), 404–7.
210 Corry Guttstadt, *Turkey, the Jews, and the Holocaust*, trans. Kathleen M. Dell'Orto, Sabine Bartel, and Michelle Miles (Cambridge: Cambridge University Press, 2013), 33–4; Motadel, *Islam and Nazi Germany's War*, 234–5.
211 Hüsrev Gerede, *Harb içinde Almanya (1939–1942)*, ed. Hulûsi Turgut ve Sırrı Yüksel Cebeci (Istanbul: ABC Ajansı, 1994), 250.
212 Ibid., 251.
213 Motadel, *Islam and Nazi Germany's War*, 170.
214 Kansu Şarman, *Türk Promethe'ler: Cumhuriyet'in öğrencileri Avrupa'da (1925–1945)* (Istanbul: Türkiye İş Bankası, 2005), 172.
215 Marc David Baer, 'Mistaken for Jews: Turkish PhD Students in Nazi Germany', *German Studies Review* 41, no. 1 (2018), 19–39.
216 Şefik Okday, *Der letzte Grosswesir und seine preußischen Söhne* (Göttingen: Muster-Schmidt, 1991), 142.
217 Corry Guttstadt, *Die Türkei, die Juden und der Holocaust* (Hamburg: Assoziation A, 2008), 145.
218 Marc David Baer, 'Turk and Jew in Berlin: The First Turkish Migration

to Germany and the Shoah', *Comparative Studies in Society & History* 55, no. 2 (2013), 330–55.
219 Isaak Behar, *'Versprich mir, dass du am Leben bleibst': Ein jüdische Schicksal*, 2nd ed. (Munich: List, 2009), 59.
220 Ibid., 68–70.
221 Ibid., 70.
222 Ibid., 71.
223 Ibid., 72.
224 Guttstadt, *Die Türkei, die Juden und der Holocaust*, 268.
225 Corinna Guttstadt, 'Sepharden an der Spree: Türkische Juden im Berlin der 20er- und 30er-Jahre und ihr Schicksal während der Schoah', in *Berlin in Geschichte und Gegenwart: Jahrbuch des Landesarchivs Berlin 2008* (2009), 223.
226 Behar, *'Versprich mir, dass du am Leben bleibst'*, 73–4.
227 Guttstadt, 'Sepharden an der Spree', 224–5.
228 Türkiye Cumhuriyet Dışişleri Bakanlığı Arşivleri, İkinci Dünya Harbinde Yahudiler Fonları, K.9, D.1: T. C. Berlin Büyükelçiliğinden Dışişleri Bakanlığına rapor, 'Zata mahsus', 3 Dec. 1941, no. 1557/671. The document was published in Bilâl N. Şimşir, *Türk Yahudiler II: Avrupa ırkçılarına karşı Türkiye' nin mücadelesi* (Ankara: Bilgi, 2010), 293–4.
229 Auswärtiges Amt-Politisches Archiv, R 100889, Vortragsnotiz zu Inland II 1947g, 12 July 1943.
230 Guttstadt, 'Sepharden an der Spree', 231.
231 Ibid., 226–7.
232 Rıfat Bali, 'Sachsenhausen Temerküz Kampı'nın Türk Ziyaretçileri', *Toplumsal Tarih* 151 (July 2006), 43.
233 On Sachsenhausen, see Gedenkstätte und Museum Sachsenhausen, sachsenhausen-sbg.de.
234 *Sachsenhausen Concentration Camp, 1936–1945: Events and Developments*, ed. Günter Morsch and Astrid Ley (Berlin: Metropol, 2011), 79, 182.
235 These are the words of the Dutch camp survivor Ab Nikolaas. Quoted in ibid., 12.
236 The Istanbul chief of police and the police official in charge of the office of foreigners and minorities travelled to Germany in January and February 1943, ostensibly to bring back to Turkey the remains of Talat

Pasha, assassinated by Armenians in Berlin in 1921 in retaliation for his role in the Armenian genocide. See Rıfat Bali, 'Talat Paşa'nın Kemiklerini Mi? Nazi Fırınları Mı?', *Toplumsal Tarih* 150 (June 2006), 42–7; and Bali, 'Sachsenhausen Temerküz Kampı'nın Türk Ziyaretçileri', 38–43.

237 Rıfat Bali, 'Hitler ile Görüşme: Ordu Komutanı Orgeneral Cemil Cahit Toydemir'in Almanya Gezisi' , *Toplumsal Tarih* 165 (Sept. 2007), 38–42.
238 Bundesarchiv Berlin, Lichterfelde, Reichssippenamt R39/152, 'Karaim'.
239 Kader Konuk, *East West Mimesis: Auerbach in Turkey* (Stanford, CA: Stanford University Press, 2010), 49.
240 İzzet Bahar, 'German or Jewish, Humanity or Raison d'Etat: The German Scholars in Turkey, 1933–1952', *Shofar* 29, no. 1 (2010), 48–72.
241 Guttstadt, *Die Türkei, die Juden und der Holocaust*, 365.
242 Şimşir, *Türk Yahudiler II*, 12–13.
243 Guttstadt, *Die Türkei, die Juden und der Holocaust*, 402–7.
244 Ibid., 375–6.
245 Ibid., 465–6.
246 'Abdol Hossein Sardari', United States Holocaust Memorial Museum, https://encyclopedia.ushmm.org/content/en/article/abdol-hossein-sardari-1895-1981. His actions were celebrated in a series shown on Iranian state television in 2007, *Zero Degree Turn*.
247 Guttstadt, 'Sepharden an der Spree', 229.
248 Guttstadt, *Die Türkei, die Juden und der Holocaust*, 312–13.
249 Atina Grossmann, *Jews, Germans, and Allies: Close Encounters in Occupied Germany* (Princeton, NJ: Princeton University Press, 2007), 88–129.
250 Behar, *'Versprich mir, dass du am Leben bleibst'*, 211. Behar passed away in Berlin at the age of eighty-seven, on 22 April 2011, not long after I met him at an open house for the Sephardic synagogue in Berlin, used mainly by Azerbaijani Jews. Detlef David Kauschke, 'Isaak Behar ist tot: Nachruf auf den Gemeindeältesten', *Jüdische Allgemeine*, 27 April 2011, http://www.juedischeallgemeine.de/article/view/id/10259.
251 Bali, *Cumhuriyet Yıllarında Türkiye Yahudileri*, 538–41.
252 Brink-Danan, *Jewish Life in 21st-Century Turkey*, 63–82.

7. Transforming Jewish–Muslim Relations: Jewish Nationalism and the Establishment of Israel

1. Menachem Klein, 'Arab Jew in Palestine', *Israel Studies* 19, no. 3 (2014), 143.
2. Ibid., 142.
3. Ya'akov Yehoshua, *Childhood in Old Jerusalem* [in Hebrew], 2 vols (Jerusalem, 1979), 2:66–71, quoted in Klein, 'Arab Jew in Palestine', 141.
4. Ezra Menachem, *From the Tales of a Jerusalem Boy* [in Hebrew] (Tel Aviv, 1988), 49, 51, quoted in Klein, 'Arab Jew in Palestine', 141.
5. Menashe Mani, *Hebron and Its Heroes* (Tel Aviv, 1963) [in Hebrew], 74, quoted in Klein, 'Arab Jew in Palestine', 142.
6. Mani, *Hebron and Its Heroes*, 33, quoted in Klein, 'Arab Jew in Palestine', 142.
7. Klein, 'Arab Jew in Palestine', 135.
8. Abigail Jacobson and Moshe Naor, *Oriental Neighbors: Middle Eastern Jews and Arabs in Mandatory Palestine* (Waltham, MA: Brandeis University Press, 2016), Chapter 4.
9. His son, my great-grandfather Be'er, migrated to the United States the same year.
10. Cohen, *Juifs et musulmans en Palestine et en Israël*, 81.
11. Ibid., 20.
12. Ibid., 85, 251.
13. Ibid., 31.
14. Ibid., 32, 34–5.
15. Ibid., 36, 53, 55, 66.
16. Ibid., 15.
17. Ibid., 79.
18. Ibid., 64–5.
19. Ibid., 68–9.
20. Ibid., 71.
21. Shmuel Moreh, 'Ya'qūb Sanū': His Religious Identity and Work in the Theater and Journalism, According to the Family Archive', in *The Jews of Egypt*, ed. Shamir, 111.
22. Ibid., 122.
23. Ibid., 126.
24. Michel Abitbol, *Juifs et arabes au xxe siècle* (Paris: Perrin, 2006), 342.

Notes

25 Moreh, 'Ya'qūb Sanū': His Religious Identity and Work in the Theater and Journalism', 115.
26 Cohen, *Juifs et musulmans en Palestine et en Israël*, 94.
27 The Bilu, 'Manifesto', in *The Jew in the Modern World: A Documentary History*, ed. Paul R. Mendes-Flohr and Jehuda Reinharz (Oxford: Oxford University Press, 1980), 421.
28 Theodor Herzl, 'A Solution to the Jewish Question', *Jewish Chronicle*, 17 January 1896, 12–13, in *The Jew in the Modern World: A Documentary History*, ed. Mendes-Flohr and Reinharz, 422–6.
29 The First Zionist Congress, 'The Basel Programme', in *The Jew in the Modern World: A Documentary History*, ed. Mendes-Flohr and Reinharz, 429.
30 Herzl, 'A Solution to the Jewish Question', in *The Jew in the Modern World: A Documentary History*, ed. Mendes-Flohr and Reinharz, 425.
31 Quoted in Baer, *Sultanic Saviors and Tolerant Turks*, 61.
32 Ibid., 61–2.
33 Ibid., 62.
34 Ibid.
35 Michael L. Miller, 'European Judaism and Islam: The Contribution of Jewish Orientalists', in *A History of Jewish–Muslim Relations*, ed. Meddeb and Stora, 833.
36 *Haim Nahum: A Sephardic Chief Rabbi in Politics, 1892–1923*, ed. and intro. Esther Benbassa, trans. Miriam Kochan (Tuscaloosa: University of Alabama Press, 1995), 15.
37 Ibid., 17.
38 Ibid., 19, 162.
39 Quoted in Michelle U. Campos, *Ottoman Brothers: Muslims, Christians, and Jews in Early Twentieth-Century Palestine* (Stanford, CA: Stanford University Press, 2011), 213.
40 Ibid., 214.
41 *Haim Nahum: A Sephardic Chief Rabbi in Politics*, 161.
42 Landau, *Tekinalp: Turkish Patriot*, 21. The original speech in German appears on 45–6.
43 Ibid., 46.
44 Ibid., 21.
45 Ibid., 54.

46 Tekinalp, 'Die Juden in den Balkanländern', *Monatsschrift der österreichisch-israelitischen Union* 25, nos 9–10 (1913), 17.
47 Quoted in Campos, *Ottoman Brothers*, 216.
48 Ibid., 218–19.
49 Cohen, *Juifs et musulmans en Palestine et en Israël*, 96.
50 Ibid., 97.
51 Ibid., 98.
52 Ibid., 98–9.
53 Ibid., 99.
54 Ibid., 102.
55 Ibid., 103.
56 Quoted in Rashid Khalidi, *The Hundred Years' War on Palestine: A History of Settler Colonial Conquest and Resistance* (London: Profile, 2020), 26.
57 Ibid., 29.
58 Bensoussan, *Juifs en pays arabes*, 486.
59 Ibid., 506.
60 Cohen, *Juifs et musulmans en Palestine et en Israël*, 87.
61 Joanna Paraszczuk, 'The "Arab Jew" from Algeria', *Jerusalem Post*, 15 October 2010, https://www.jpost.com/local-israel/tel-aviv-and-center/the-arab-jew-from-algeria.
62 Cohen, *Juifs et musulmans en Palestine et en Israël*, 90.
63 Johann Büssow, *Hamidian Palestine: Politics and Society in the District of Jerusalem, 1872–1908* (Leiden: Brill, 2011), 193–4.
64 Paraszczuk, 'The "Arab Jew" from Algeria'.
65 Louis Fishman, *Claiming the Homeland: Jews and Palestinians in the Late Ottoman Era, 1908–1914* (Edinburgh: Edinburgh University Press, 2019), 49.
66 Cohen, *Juifs et musulmans en Palestine et en Israël*, 92.
67 Louis Fishman, 'Palestine and Zionism during the Period of Abdülhamid II and the Young Turks', in *The I.B. Tauris Handbook of the Late Ottoman Empire: History and Legacy*, ed. Hans Lukas Kieser and Khatchig Mouradian (London: I.B. Tauris, 2025), 7–8.
68 Campos, *Ottoman Brothers*.
69 Fishman, 'Palestine and Zionism during the Period of Abdülhamid II and the Young Turks', 1–2.

Notes

70 Quoted in *Campos, Ottoman Brothers*, 2.
71 Quoted in Fishman, 'Palestine and Zionism during the Period of Abdülhamid II and the Young Turks', 14.
72 'The Balfour Declaration', in *The Jew in the Modern World: A Documentary History*, ed. Mendes-Flohr and Reinharz, 458.
73 Khalidi, *The Hundred Years' War on Palestine*, 37.
74 Sassoon, *The Global Merchants*, 285.
75 Ibid., 236, 239.
76 Khalidi, *The Hundred Years' War on Palestine*, 25.
77 James Renton, 'The End of the Semites', in *Antisemitism and Islamophobia in Europe: A Shared Story?*, ed. James Renton and Ben Gidley (London: Palgrave Macmillan, 2017), 109.
78 Quoted in Renton, 'The End of the Semites', 110.
79 Poster, 'To the Inhabitants of Jerusalem the Blessed', Art.IWM PST 12511, Imperial War Museum, London, https://www.iwm.org.uk/collections/item/object/31071.
80 World Zionist Organisation, London Bureau, 'Zionist Manifesto Issued after the Balfour Declaration', *Jewish Chronicle*, 21 December 1917, 16, in *The Jew in the Modern World: A Documentary History*, ed. Mendes-Flohr and Reinharz, 459.
81 Bensoussan, *Juifs en pays arabes*, 261.
82 Quoted in Michel Abitbol, *Juifs et arabes au XXe siècle*, 55, 341–2.
83 Ibid., 21.
84 Khalidi, *The Hundred Years' War on Palestine*, 17.
85 Quoted in ibid., 38.
86 Renton, 'The End of the Semites', 113.
87 Quoted in ibid., 114.
88 Ibid., 114–15.
89 Quoted in ibid., 116.
90 The Council of the League of Nations, 'Mandate for Palestine', in *The Jew in the Modern World: A Documentary History*, ed. Mendes-Flohr and Reinharz, 461.
91 Cohen, *Juifs et musulmans en Palestine et en Israël*, 111.
92 Khalidi, *The Hundred Years' War on Palestine*, 35.
93 Cohen, *Juifs et musulmans en Palestine et en Israël*, 113.
94 Ibid., 120.

95 Ibid., 114.
96 Ibid., 122.
97 Ibid., 118–19.
98 Ibid., 120.
99 Jacobson and Naor, *Oriental Neighbors*, Chapter 5.
100 Cohen, *Juifs et musulmans en Palestine et en Israël*, 128.
101 Quoted in Renton, 'The End of the Semites', 125.
102 Cohen, *Juifs et musulmans en Palestine et en Israël*, 125.
103 Ibid., 126.
104 Ibid., 127.
105 Ibid., 129.
106 Ibid., 130.
107 Ibid., 131.
108 Ibid., 134.
109 Ibid., 136.
110 Ibid., 137; Khalidi, *The Hundred Years' War on Palestine*, 44.
111 Cohen, *Juifs et musulmans en Palestine et en Israël*, 138.
112 Ibid., 139.
113 Malcolm Macdonald, 'White Paper of 1939', in *The Jew in the Modern World: A Documentary History*, ed. Mendes-Flohr and Reinharz, 466–9.
114 Ibid., 466.
115 Cohen, *Juifs et musulmans en Palestine et en Israël*, 145.
116 Ibid., 726.
117 Ibid., 734–5.
118 Ibid., 712.
119 Ibid., 727.
120 Ibid., 1026, n.82.
121 Cohen, *Juifs et musulmans en Palestine et en Israël*, 148.
122 Ibid., 149.
123 Avi Shlaim, *Collusion across the Jordan: King Abdullah, the Zionist Movement, and the Partition of Palestine* (New York: Columbia University Press, 1988).
124 Khalidi, *The Hundred Years' War on Palestine*, 66.
125 Cohen, *Juifs et musulmans en Palestine et en Israël*, 151.
126 Ibid., 153.
127 Ibid., 154.

128 Ibid., 156.
129 Ibid., 159.
130 Ibid., 161.
131 Ibid., 163.
132 Ibid., 164.
133 Ibid., 165.
134 Abitbol, *Juifs et arabes au XXe siècle*, 31.
135 Ibid., 104.
136 Cohen, *Juifs et musulmans en Palestine et en Israël*, 166.
137 Ibid., 167.
138 Ibid., 168.
139 Ibid., 169.
140 Ibid., 170.
141 Ibid., 172.
142 Ibid., 174.
143 Ibid., 173.
144 Ibid., 179.
145 Ibid., 181.
146 Ibid., 182; Ari Shavit, 'Lydda, 1948', *New Yorker* (14 October 2013), https://www.newyorker.com/magazine/2013/10/21/lydda-1948.
147 Cohen, *Juifs et musulmans en Palestine et en Israël*, 183.
148 Ibid., 184.
149 Ibid., 185.
150 Ibid., 186.
151 Ibid., 187.
152 Ibid., 188.
153 'Proclamation of the State of Israel', in *The Jew in the Modern World: A Documentary History*, ed. Mendes-Flohr and Reinharz, 477–9.
154 Constantine Zureiq, *Ma'na al-Nakba* (1948), first appeared in English as *Palestine: The Meaning of the Disaster*, trans. R. Bayly Winder (London, 1956).
155 'The Question of Palestine', United Nations, https://www.un.org/unispal/about-the-nakba.
156 'The Law of Return', in *The Jew in the Modern World: A Documentary History*, ed. Mendes-Flohr and Reinharz, 481.
157 Cohen, *Juifs et musulmans en Palestine et en Israël*, 194.

158 Ibid., 195.
159 Ibid., 202–3.
160 Quoted in Abitbol, *Juifs et arabes au XXe siècle*, 175.
161 Ibid., 182.
162 Ibid., 176.
163 Khalidi, *The Hundred Years' War on Palestine*, 114.
164 Ibid., 123.
165 Ibid., 124.
166 'Munich Massacre', Britannica, https://www.britannica.com/event/Munich-Massacre.
167 'Palestine at the United Nations: 1. The Speech of Yasser Arafat', *Journal of Palestine Studies* 4, no. 2 (1975), 192.
168 Ibid., 184.
169 Ibid., 185.
170 Ibid., 186.
171 Ibid., 187.
172 Ibid., 188.
173 Ibid., 185.
174 Ibid., 189.
175 Ibid., 190.
176 Ibid., 191.
177 Khalidi, *The Hundred Years' War on Palestine*, 152.
178 'Elimination of All Forms of Racial Discrimination: Zionism as Racism – GA Resolution', United Nations, https://www.un.org/unispal/document/auto-insert-181963.
179 Cohen, *Juifs et musulmans en Palestine et en Israël*, 210.
180 'Resolution 242 (1967)', United Nations, https://digitallibrary.un.org/record/90717?ln=en&v=pdf.
181 Khalidi, *The Hundred Years' War on Palestine*, 178.
182 Ibid., 186.
183 Cohen, *Juifs et musulmans en Palestine et en Israël*, 238.
184 Ibid., 206–7.
185 Ibid., 211.
186 'Rioting as Sharon Visits Islam Holy Site', *Guardian*, 29 September 2000, https://www.theguardian.com/world/2000/sep/29/israel.
187 Cohen, *Juifs et musulmans en Palestine et en Israël*, 212.

188 Khalidi, *The Hundred Years' War on Palestine*, 213–14.
189 Ibid., 258–9.
190 Abitbol, *Juifs et arabes au XXe siècle*, 344.
191 Ibid., 182.
192 Ibid., 183.
193 Ibid., 183, 230.
194 Cohen, *Juifs et musulmans en Palestine et en Israël*, 242.
195 Ibid., 235.
196 Abitbol, *Juifs et arabes au XXe siècle*, 240.
197 'Who We Are', Peace Now, https://peacenow.org.il/en/about-us/who-are-we.
198 Quoted in Abitbol, *Juifs et arabes au XXe siècle*, 184–5.
199 Ibid., 189–90.
200 Ibid., 18, 343.
201 Daniel J. Schroeter, 'AHR Roundtable: "Islamic Anti-Semitism" in Historical Discourse', *American Historical Review* 123 (2018), 1184.
202 Ruhollah Khomeini, *Islam and Revolution: Writings and Declarations of Imam Khomeini*, trans. Hamid Algar (Berkeley, CA: Mizan Press, 1981); 'Osama bin Laden v. the US: Edicts and Statements', *Frontline*, PBS, https://www.pbs.org/wgbh/pages/frontline/shows/binladen/who/edicts.html.
203 Ronald L. Nettler, *Past Trials & Present Tribulations: A Muslim Fundamentalist's View of the Jews* (Oxford: Pergamon Press, 1987), 75.
204 Ibid., 77.
205 Ibid., 78, 79.
206 Ibid., 83, 80, 84, 81.
207 Ibid., 81–7.

8. The Arab Jew in the Middle East and Europe after 1948

1   Stora, *L'Arrivée*, 34.
2   Albert Memmi in *L'Arche*, February 1962, cited in Memmi, *Juifs et arabes* (Paris: Gallimard, 1974), 94.
3   Philippe Barbé, 'Jewish–Muslim Syncretism and Intercommunity Cohabitation in the Writings of Albert Memmi: The *Partage* of Tunis', trans. Allan MacVicar, in *Jewish Culture and Society in North Africa*, ed. Gottreich and Schroeter, 117.

4   Ella Shohat, *Taboo Memories, Diasporic Voices* (Durham, NC: Duke University Press, 2006), 205.
5   Abitbol, *Juifs et arabes au XXe siècle*, 14.
6   Ibid., 343.
7   Ibid., 199 and map 12 following 384; Sergio Della Pergola, 'World Jewish Population, 2021', in *The American Jewish Year Book 2021*, ed. Arnold Dashefsky and Ira M. Sheskin, 313–412.
8   Joëlle Allouche-Benayoun and Geneviève Dermenjian, 'Introduction', in *Les Juifs d'Algérie. Une histoire de ruptures*, ed. Allouche-Benayoun and Dermenjian, 17.
9   Stora, *Les trois exils*, 13–15.
10 'New French Premier Is Son of Sephardic Jewish Family', *Jewish Telegraph Agency, Daily News Bulletin*, 21 June 1954.
11 Beinin, *The Dispersion of Egyptian Jewry*, 165.
12 Stora, *Les trois exils*, 144–5.
13 Ibid., 146–7.
14 Ibid., 147.
15 Ibid., 148–9.
16 Ibid., 155–6.
17 Ibid., 156–7.
18 Bertrand Dicale, *Cheikh Raymond. Une histoire algérienne* (Paris: First, 2011).
19 'Cheikh Raymond', Institut Européen des Musiques Juives, https://www.iemj.org/en/cheikh-raymond-1912-1961.
20 Stora, *Les trois exils*, 160.
21 Ibid., 161.
22 Ibid., 162.
23 Ibid., 163.
24 Ibid., 164.
25 Ibid., 165.
26 Ibid., 70.
27 Eliezer Ben-Rafael, 'Juifs d'Algérie en Israël', in *Les Juifs d'Algérie. Une histoire de ruptures*, ed. Allouche-Benayoun and Dermenjian, 272.
28 Stora, *Les trois exils*, 171.
29 Ibid., 172–3.
30 Stora, *L'Arrivée*, 65.

Notes

31 Bensoussan, *Juifs en pays arabes*, 842–3.
32 Kenbib, *Juifs et musulmans au Maroc*, 177.
33 Ibid., 178–9.
34 Ibid., 180.
35 Ibid., 181.
36 Ibid., 182.
37 Marcel Amsellem, 'Témoignage: Une harmonie qui ne résista pas à l'historie', *L'Arche*, special issue, 'les juifs du maroc', no. 700 (Sept.–Oct. 2023), 81.
38 Kenbib, *Juifs et musulmans au Maroc*, 184–5.
39 Ibid., 186.
40 Ibid., 187.
41 Ibid., 188.
42 Ibid., 189.
43 Ibid., 190.
44 Bensoussan, *Juifs en pays arabes*, 845.
45 From the French Mandate in the 1920s to the mid-1970s, the Jews of Lebanon were fully integrated into society and defined themselves as Lebanese. In 1951 the Sunni Muslim prime minister and heads of other religious communities participated in a communal Passover Seder. Lebanese Jews 'unequivocally considered their home to be Lebanon, defined themselves as Lebanese nationals of Jewish religion'. Kirsten E. Schulze, *The Jews of Lebanon: Between Coexistence and Conflict*, 2nd ed. (Brighton: Sussex Academic Press, 2008), 181.
46 Kenbib, *Juifs et musulmans au Maroc*, 191.
47 Michel Toledano, 'Quand le Dr Léon Benzaquen deviant ministre des Postes', *L'Arche*, special issue, 'les juifs du maroc', no. 700 (Sept.–Oct. 2023), 62.
48 Perrine Simon-Nahum, 'Mohammed V', *L'Arche*, special issue, 'les juifs du maroc', no. 700 (Sept.–Oct. 2023), 62.
49 Kenbib, *Juifs et musulmans au Maroc*, 192.
50 Ibid., 193.
51 Ibid., 197.
52 Ibid., 198.
53 Ibid., 199.
54 Ibid., 200.

55 Simon-Nahum, 'Mohammed V', 62.
56 Valentine Rozenblat-Fellous, 'Rav Chalom Messas', *l'Arche*, special issue, 'les juifs du maroc', no. 700 (Sept.–Oct. 2023), 119.
57 Kenbib, *Juifs et musulmans au Maroc*, 200.
58 Ibid., 201.
59 Ibid., 202.
60 Ibid., 203.
61 Bensoussan, *Juifs en pays arabes*, 903, 907.
62 Laskier, *Juifs et Musulmans en Égypte*, 184.
63 Ibid., 192.
64 Krämer, 'Political Participation of the Jews in Egypt', 78.
65 Beinin, *The Dispersion of Egyptian Jewry*, 145–6.
66 Shamir, 'The Evolution of the Egyptian Nationality Laws', 34, 59.
67 Ibid., 60, 62.
68 Laskier, *Juifs et Musulmans en Égypte*, 200.
69 Krämer, *The Jews in Modern Egypt*, 213.
70 Laskier, *Juifs et Musulmans en Égypte*, 208–11.
71 Ibid., 201–2.
72 Ibid., 203–4.
73 Ibid., 205.
74 Ibid., 206.
75 Krämer, *The Jews in Modern Egypt*, 106.
76 Laskier, *Juifs et Musulmans en Égypte*, 207.
77 Krämer, 'Political Participation of the Jews in Egypt', 75.
78 Laskier, *Juifs et Musulmans en Égypte*, 213.
79 Krämer, *The Jews in Modern Egypt*, 205.
80 Beinin, *The Dispersion of Egyptian Jewry*, 147.
81 Laskier, *Juifs et Musulmans en Égypte*, 214.
82 Krämer, *The Jews in Modern Egypt*, 73.
83 Laskier, *Juifs et Musulmans en Égypte*, 250–2.
84 Ibid., 253–4.
85 Ibid., 255.
86 Ibid., 256.
87 Ibid., 257.
88 Beinin, *The Dispersion of Egyptian Jewry*, 91–5.
89 Ibid., 105–7.

Notes

90 Laskier, *Juifs et Musulmans en Égypte*, 258.
91 Ibid., 259.
92 Marzuq's brother Yosef, who migrated to Israel, was not allowed to marry a rabbinic Jewish woman by the Tel Aviv rabbinic court in 1961 on account of his being a Karaite. He was allowed to marry by the Haifa rabbinic court. But his experience is an example of the difficulties Karaites face in the Jewish state, where their Jewishness is doubted by the Orthodox Rabbinate, where they are seen as Arabs and Arabic speakers overly influenced by Islam. Beinin, *The Dispersion of Egyptian Jewry*, 181–5.
93 Beinin, *The Dispersion of Egyptian Jewry*, 19.
94 Laskier, *Juifs et Musulmans en Égypte*, 268.
95 Ibid., 269.
96 Ibid., 270.
97 Ibid., 270–1.
98 Ibid., 272.
99 Ibid., 242.
100 Ibid., 273.
101 Ibid., 274.
102 Ibid., 275.
103 Ibid., 275–6.
104 *Al-Ahram*, 29 September 1958, English translation in *President Gamal Abdel Nasser's Speeches and Press Interviews, 1958* (Cairo, 1959), 402, cited in Lewis, *The Jews of Islam*, 186.
105 Kahanoff, *Mongrels or Marvels*, xi.
106 Ibid., 179–82.
107 Ibid., 185–6.
108 Ibid., 189–90.
109 Laskier, *Juifs et Musulmans en Égypte*, 279.
110 Krämer, *The Jews in Modern Egypt*, 182; Beinin, *The Dispersion of Egyptian Jewry*, 156–7.
111 Beinin, *The Dispersion of Egyptian Jewry*, 158.
112 Ibid., 160.
113 Ibid., 161.
114 Ibid., 167–78.
115 Ibid., 178.

116 Krämer, *The Jews in Modern Egypt*, 97.
117 Ibid., 71.
118 Laskier, *Juifs et Musulmans en Égypte*, 295.
119 Beinin, *The Dispersion of Egyptian Jewry*, 110.
120 Laskier, *Juifs et Musulmans en Égypte*, 296, 298.
121 Ibid., 297.
122 Ibid., 299.
123 Bensoussan, *Juifs en pays arabes*, 507.
124 Meir-Glitzenstein, *Juifs et musulmans en Irak*, 116.
125 Ibid., 118–19.
126 Ibid., 120.
127 Ibid., 121.
128 Ibid., 159.
129 Ibid., 160.
130 Ibid., 161.
131 Ibid., 165.
132 Ibid., 155.
133 Ibid., 176.
134 Ibid., 188–9.
135 Ibid., 198.
136 Ibid., 198–200.
137 Ibid., 178.
138 Ibid., 172.
139 Ibid., 204–5.
140 Ibid., 208.
141 Sami Michael, *Gvoulot harouah* (Tel Aviv: Hakibbutz Hameouhad, 2000), 46.
142 *Iraq's Last Jews: Stories of Daily Life, Upheaval, and Escape from Modern Babylon*, ed. Tamar Morad, Dennis Shasha, and Robert Shasha (London: Palgrave Macmillan, 2008), 80.
143 Naïm Kattan, *Adieu Babylone: Mémoires d'un Juif d'Irak* (Paris: Albin Michel, 2003), 132.
144 *Iraq's Last Jews*, ed. Morad et al., 83.
145 Bashkin, *New Babylonians*, 154.
146 Ibid., 162.
147 Bensoussan, *Juifs en pays arabes*, 514.

148 Bashkin, *New Babylonians*, 166.
149 Quoted in ibid., 169.
150 Ibid., 171, 177.
151 Ibid., 173.
152 Ibid., 161.
153 *Iraq's Last Jews*, ed. Morad et al., 84.
154 Ibid., 85.
155 Ibid., 86.
156 Ella Shohat, 'Rupture and Return: Zionist Discourse and the Study of Arab Jews', *Social Text* 21, no. 2 (2003), 56–7.
157 Meir-Glitzenstein, *Juifs et musulmans en Irak*, 213.
158 Bashkin, *New Babylonians*.
159 *Iraq's Last Jews*, ed. Morad et al., 82.
160 Meir-Glitzenstein, *Juifs et musulmans en Irak*, 214.
161 Ibid., 217.
162 Ibid., 218.
163 Ibid., 219–21.
164 Ibid., 221.
165 Ibid., 222.
166 Ibid., 223.
167 Ibid., 242.
168 Ibid.
169 Ibid., 243.
170 Ibid., 245–6, 251.
171 Ibid., 256.
172 Ibid., 257.
173 Ibid., 258–9.
174 Ibid., 260.
175 Ibid., 273.
176 Ibid., 275–6.
177 Ibid., 276.
178 Ibid., 271.
179 Ibid., 278.
180 Avi Shlaim, *Three Worlds: Memoirs of an Arab-Jew* (London: Oneworld, 2023), chapter 7.
181 Meir-Glitzenstein, *Juifs et musulmans en Irak*, 214.

182 Ibid., 281.
183 Ibid., 282.
184 Ibid., 283.
185 Ibid., 285.
186 Bensoussan, *Juifs en pays arabes*, 904–5.
187 Meir-Glitzenstein, *Juifs et musulmans en Irak*, 286.
188 Sabar, *My Father's Paradise*, 15.
189 Ibid., 83–4.
190 Ibid., 36.
191 Ibid., 69.
192 Ibid., 43.
193 Ibid., 80.
194 Ibid., 81.
195 Ibid., 82.
196 Ibid., 87.
197 Ibid., 93.
198 Ibid., 94.
199 Ibid., 95–6.
200 Ibid., 97.
201 Ibid., 100.
202 Ibid., 101.
203 Ibid., 98.
204 Ibid., 104–5.
205 Ibid., 105–6.
206 Bensoussan, *Juifs en pays arabes*, 870.
207 Quoted in Alcalay, *After Jews and Arabs*, 220.
208 *Iraq's Last Jews*, ed. Morad et al., 60.
209 Ibid., 65–6.
210 Quoted by G.N. Giladi in *Discord in Zion: Conflict Between Ashkenazi and Sephardi Jews in Israel* (London: Scorpion, 1990), 103–4.
211 Mickaël Parienté, *A l'Ombre des murailles: Souvenirs d'enfance, mémoire d'une communauté disparue* (Montrouge: StavNet Book, 2015), 163.
212 Ibid., 19.
213 Alcalay, *After Jews and Arabs*, 51.
214 Cited in Ella Shohat, *Israeli Cinema: East–West and the Politics of Representation* (London: I.B. Tauris, 2010), 116–18.

215 Kenbib, *Juifs et musulmans au Maroc*, 204.
216 Ibid., 205.
217 Shlaim, *Three Worlds*, 170.
218 Abitbol, *Juifs et arabes au XXe siècle*, 343.
219 Mark R. Cohen, 'The Neo-Lachrymose Conception of Jewish-Arab History', *Tikkun* 6, no. 3 (1991), 55–64.
220 Jean-Pierre Allali, *Séfarades-Palestiniens. Les réfugiés échangés* (Paris: Safed, 2005), 153.
221 Shohat, 'Rupture and Return', 62.
222 Ibid., 63.
223 Ella Shohat, *On the Arab-Jew, Palestine, and Other Displacements: Selected Writings* (London: Pluto Press, 2017), 6.
224 'Three Worlds: Avi Shlaim and Marc David Baer in Conversation', Bradford Literature Festival, Bradford, England, 27 June 2023, https://rss.com/podcasts/bradfordlitfest/1094146.
225 Tartakowsky, *Les juifs et le maghreb*, 159–60.

9. Duelling Myths, Divided Histories, and Promoting Symbiosis Today

1 Laskier, *Juifs et Musulmans en Égypte*, 299.
2 Ibid., 300–1, 304–5.
3 Ibid., 301.
4 'Egypt's Jewish Community Buries Deputy Leader', A; Jazeera, 12 March 2014, https://www.aljazeera.com/features/2014/3/12/egypts-jewish-community-buries-deputy-leader.
5 Laskier, *Juifs et Musulmans en Égypte*, 300.
6 Ibid., 302–3.
7 Ibid., 303–4.
8 Brink-Danan, *Jewish Life in 21st-Century Turkey*, 35–55.
9 Interfilm Istanbul, 2011. 'Mutlulukla biten tek soykırım filmi: Türk Pasaportu', 1 Aug. 2011, euronewstr.
10 Baer, *Sultanic Saviors and Tolerant Turks*, 269–70.
11 Yusuf Ziya Durmuş, 'Edirne Synagogue Reopens its Doors After Restoration', *Daily Sabah*, 27 March 2015.
12 Recep Tayyip Erdoğan, Address to the Council of Foreign Relations, New York, 23 September 2014, Presidency of the Republic of Turkey,

13 'Erdoğan Lashes Out at Foreign Media Ahead of Turkey Polls', AFP (Agence France-Presse), 6 June 2015.

14 'Erdoğan'dan Yahudi açılımı', *Hürriyet*, 7 Oct. 2009; Joe Parkinson, 'Dismay over Turkish Rates', *Wall Street Journal*, 12 Jan. 2012.

15 Mustafa Akyol, 'Unraveling the AKP's "Mastermind" Conspiracy Theory', *Al-Monitor*, 19 March 2015, http://www.al-monitor.com/pulse/originals/2015/03/turkey-zion-protocols-akp-version.html. The two-hour 'Mastermind' documentary which was shown on Turkish television channel A Haber on 15 March 2015 can be viewed on YouTube: https://www.youtube.com/watch?v=Zqw2eZ1K6Uw.

16 'Cumhurbaşkanı Erdoğan: FETÖ tam bir maşa, onun üstünde üst akıl var', Haber 10, 31 July 2016; 'Erdoğan: Üst akıl Fethullah Gülen değil', Timeturk, 31 July 2016. According to Erdoğan, 'Today very insidious, very vile, and very bloody tricks are being played both on our region and on our country. The thing I call the Mastermind appears before us every day with new deviltry, trying to sow new seeds of enmity and discord in our region. He is trying to blacken the future of our region with bloody tears, civil war, and sectarian wars. We are aware of this reality, that this is a power struggle.' 'Cumhurbaşkanı Erdoğan: Milli seferberlik ilan ediyorum', CNNTurk, 14 Dec. 2016.

17 Ersin Ramoğlu (Güney), 'Karay Yahudisi Fethullah Gülen', *Sabah*, 28 Dec. 2016; 'Bakan Eroğlu: Gülen, Yahudi mezarlığına gömülecek', siyasihaber3.org, 9 Dec. 2016; 'Pis bir Yahudi mahallesi idi', *Şalom*, 9 Dec. 2016; 'Fethullah Gülen Sabetayist mi?', Odatv, 23 Aug. 2016; Tamer Korkmaz, 'Sakladım, gizli tuttum, söylemedim, uyuttum!', *Yeni Şafak*, 23 Aug. 2016; 'Gülen babadan Ermeni anadan Yahudi'dir!', *Yeni Akit*, 16 Aug. 2016; Tamer Korkmaz, 'Rabin'in oğlu Fetullah bunalımda!', *Yeni Şafak*, 12 Aug. 2016; Pinar Tremblay, 'Is Gulen an Armenian?' *Al-Monitor*, 12 Aug. 2016.

18 Marc David Baer, 'An Enemy Old and New: The Dönme, Anti-Semitism, and Conspiracy Theories in the Ottoman Empire and Turkish Republic', *Jewish Quarterly Review* 103, no. 4 (2013), 528–9.

19 Ibid., 530.

20 'President Erdoğan not Anti-Semitic, Turkey's Jewish Community Says',

Notes

      Daily Sabah (Istanbul), 19 May 2021, https://www.dailysabah.com/politics/diplomacy/president-erdogan-not-anti-semitic-turkeys-jewish-community-says.
21 Emily Benichou Gottreich and Daniel J. Schroeter, 'Introduction', in *Jewish Culture and Society in North Africa*, ed. Gottreich and Schroeter, 5.
22 Ibid., 4.
23 Aomar Boum, 'The Performance of Convivencia: Communities of Tolerance and the Reification of Toleration', *Religion Compass* 6, no. 3 (2012), 180.
24 Jonathan Glasser, *The Lost Paradise: Andalusi Music in Urban North Africa* (Chicago: University of Chicago Press, 2016); Christopher Silver, *Recording History: Jews, Muslims and Music across Twentieth-Century North Africa* (Stanford, CA: Stanford University Press, 2022).
25 Irina Tsukerman, 'Inauguration of Beit Dakira Marks Renaissance of Jewish Life in Morocco', *Jerusalem Post*, 30 January 2020, https://www.jpost.com/opinion/inauguration-of-beit-dakira-marks-renaissance-of-jewish-life-in-morocco-616016.
26 Kenbib, *Juifs et musulmans au Maroc*, 209–10.
27 Ibid., 210–11.
28 Ibid., 213.
29 Ibid., 215.
30 Ibid., 224.
31 Ibid., 216.
32 Regina Keil-Sagawe, 'The Writer Edmond Amran El Maleh: A Moroccan Jew with Arab-Berber Roots', Qantara.de, 31 March 2011, https://qantara.de/en/article/writer-edmond-amran-el-maleh-moroccan-jew-arabo-berber-roots; Alfred Hackensberger, 'Interview with Simon Levi: "A Culture Is Never Lost"', Qantara.de, 17 January 2011, https://qantara.de/en/article/interview-simon-levi-culture-never-lost.
33 Bensoussan, *Juifs en pays arabes*, 356–7.
34 'Jewish Community Shrinks in Morocco', PBS Newshour, 27 July 2015, https://www.youtube.com/live/R6uB3KfTaJg?app=desktop.
35 Aomar Boum, *Memories of Absence: How Muslims Remember Jews in Morocco* (Stanford, CA: Stanford University Press, 2013), 4.

36 Karima Dirèche, 'Ouverture. 1967 à nos jours. Éloignement et oubli. Vers d'autres destins?', in *Juifs et musulmans de la France colonial à nos jours*, ed. Dirèche et al., 182.
37 Mandel, *Muslims and Jews in France*, 11.
38 Ibid., 7.
39 Ibid., 71.
40 Ibid., 77–8.
41 Ibid., 72.
42 Ibid., 73.
43 Yann Scioldo-Zürcher Lévi and Marc André, 'Rapatriements et immigration: Deux ingénieries d'état opposées', in *Juifs et musulmans de la France colonial à nos jours*, ed. Dirèche et al., 146, 149.
44 Martin Messika and Aliénor Cadiot, 'Migrations juives et musulmanes en metropole: acteurs publics et privés reflets d'histoires séparées', in *Juifs et musulmans de la France colonial à nos jours*, ed. Dirèche et al., 164.
45 Colette Zytnicki, 'L'invention du juif séfarade et de l'immigré maghrébin: Des representations toujours mouvantes', in *Juifs et musulmans de la France colonial à nos jours*, ed. Dirèche et al., 186.
46 Ibid., 189.
47 Mandel, *Muslims and Jews in France*, 67.
48 Ibid., 35–7.
49 Ibid., 39–41.
50 Ibid., 41.
51 Mandel, *Muslims and Jews in France*, 92.
52 Ibid., 99.
53 Dirèche, 'Ouverture. 1967 à nos jours', 183.
54 Pierre Mendès-France, 'Au Moyen-Orient, comme au Viêt-nam, la paix est un devoir', *Nouvel observateur*, 24–30 April 1968, 24.
55 Katz, 'In the Shadow of the Republic', 508–9.
56 Mandel, *Muslims and Jews in France*, 100.
57 Ibid., 101.
58 Ibid., 102.
59 Ibid., 107.
60 His books include *Israel: A Colonial-Settler State?* (1973). See Douglas Johnson, 'Obituary: Maxime Rodinson', *Guardian*, 3 June 2004,

https://www.theguardian.com/news/2004/jun/03/guardianobituaries.france.

61 Mandel, *Muslims and Jews in France*, 108.
62 Ibid., 108.
63 Ibid., 109.
64 Ibid., 116.
65 Ibid., 117.
66 Ibid., 118.
67 Beinin, *The Dispersion of Egyptian Jewry*, 176.
68 Mandel, *Muslims and Jews in France*, 132–3.
69 Ibid., 133.
70 Ibid., 134.
71 Ibid., 128.
72 Ibid., 144, 140.
73 Ibid., 142.
74 Ibid., 147.
75 Ibid., 149–1.
76 Esther Benbassa, *La République face à ses minorités: Les Juifs hier, les Musulmans aujourd'hui* (Paris: Mille et une nuits, 2004).
77 'Toulouse Shootings: A Decade On, Locals Remember Horror of Jewish School Attack', France24, 11 March 2022, https://www.france24.com/en/tv-shows/focus/20220311-toulouse-shootings-a-decade-on-locals-remember-horror-of-jewish-school-attack.
78 'Charlie Hebdo Attack: Three Days of Terror', BBC News, 14 January 2015, https://www.bbc.co.uk/news/world-europe-30708237.
79 James McAuley, 'How the Murders of Two Elderly Jewish Women Shook France', *Guardian*, 27 November 2018, https://www.theguardian.com/world/2018/nov/27/how-the-murders-of-two-elderly-jewish-women-shook-france-antisemitism-mireille-knoll-sarah-halimi.
80 'French President Condemns Antisemitism after Attack on Orleans' Chief Rabbi', CNN, 23 March 2025, https://edition.cnn.com/2025/03/23/europe/macron-orleans-rabbi-attack-arie-engelberg-intl/index.html.
81 Katz, 'In the Shadow of the Republic', 510.
82 'Swords of Iron: Civilian Casualties', Ministry of Foreign Affairs, 26 November 2025, https://www.gov.il/en/pages/swords-of-iron-civilian-casualties.

83 'Revealed: Israeli military's own data indicates civilian death rate of 83% in Gaza war', *Guardian*, 21 August 2025, https://www.theguardian.com/world/ng-interactive/2025/aug/21/revealed-israeli-militarys-own-data-indicates-civilian-death-rate-of-83-in-gaza-war.

84 'Hamas in 2017: The Document in Full', *Middle East Eye*, 2 May 2017, https://www.middleeasteye.net/news/hamas-2017-document-full.

85 Quoted in Abitbol, *Juifs et arabes au XXe siècle*, 310.

86 Quoted in ibid., 294.

87 'Statement by PM Netanyahu', Ministry of Foreign Affairs (Israel), 28 October 2023, https://www.gov.il/en/pages/statement-by-pm-netanyahu-28-oct-2023.

88 Avram Galanti, *Türkler ve Yahudiler: Tarihî, Siyasî Tetkik*, 2nd ed. (Istanbul: Tan, 1947), 23.

89 *Antisemitic Incidents Report 2015* (London: Community Security Trust, 2016), 9.

90 Ibid., 4.

91 Neha Gohil, 'A Year On, How the Hamas Attack Has Profoundly Affected UK Political Life', *Guardian*, 4 October 2024, https://www.theguardian.com/world/2024/oct/04/leicester-south-reveals-the-gaza-wars-impact-on-british-life.

92 'What We Know about Manchester Synagogue Attack', BBC News, 2 October 2025, https://www.bbc.co.uk/news/articles/cd63p1djgd70.

93 'We Stand Together on the Middle East Crisis, United in Grief', *Observer*, 6 October 2024, https://www.theguardian.com/theobserver/2024/oct/06/we-stand-together-on-the-middle-east-crisis-united-in-grief.

Conclusion: Abraham's Inheritance: Ishmael and Isaac, Hagar and Sarah Today

1 Kahanoff, *Mongrels or Marvels*, 235.

2 Ibid., 238.

3 'From East the Sun' (1968), cited in Kahanoff, *Mongrels or Marvels*, 256.

4 Kahanoff, *Mongrels or Marvels*, 247, 251, 255.

5 L'Amitié Judéo-Musulmane de France (Antenne de Paris) website, https://ajmfparis1.com.

Notes

6   Shirli Sitbon, '"We All Have to Eat, Don't We?": An Israeli–Palestinian Pop-up Eatery Takes Paris by Storm', *Haaretz*, 29 June 2025.

7   Joseph Interfaith Foundation, www.josephinterfaithfoundation.org.

8   Nisa-Nashim, https://www.nisanashim.com.

9   Maimonides Foundation, https://www.maimonides-foundation.org.

10   'Tunisie: René Trabelsi, Voyagiste de Confession Juive, Nommé Ministre du Tourisme', *Le Point*, 6 November 2018, https://www.lepoint.fr/afrique/tunisie-rene-trabelsi-voyagiste-de-confession-juive-nomme-ministre-du-tourisme-06-11-2018-2269024_3826.php#xtmc=trabelsi&xtnp=1&xtcr=9.

11   'Tunisia Police Officer Kills Five in Shooting near Africa's Oldest Synagogue', *Guardian*, 10 May 2023, https://www.theguardian.com/world/2023/may/10/tunisia-police-officer-kills-four-in-shooting-near-africas-oldest-synagogue.

12   Li'or Ben Ari, 'Niftar Ehad Me'ahronei Hayehudim Be'teman, Shenav Hamuslemim Kavru Oto', *Ynet*, 16 June 2024, https://www.ynet.co.il/judaism/article/s1u111mshsc.

13   Nancy A. Moran, *Symbiosis: A Very Short Introduction* (Oxford: Oxford University Press, 2025), 125, 140.

14   Hugh Goddard, *A History of Christian–Muslim Relations* (Chicago: New Amsterdam Books, 2000), 4.

15   André Aciman, *Alibis: Essays on Elsewhere* (New York: Farrar, Straus and Giroux, 2011), 81.

INDEX

A

Aaron (biblical figure) 54
Abbas I, Khedive of Egypt 185
Abbas, Ferhat 211, 212, 307
Abbasid caliphate/Empire 47–9, 51, 52, 56, 63, 64, 65, 66, 70, 76
Abd Allah ibn Buluggin, Sultan of Taifa of Granada: *Tibyan* 84
Abd al-Malik ibn Marwan, Umayyad Caliph 40–41
Abd al-Rahman, Sultan of Morocco 149, 153, 170
Abd al-Rahman I, Umayyad prince of Damascus 74–5
Abd al-Rahman II, Emir of Córdoba 81
Abd al-Rahman III, Emir of Córdoba 53, 63–4, 75, 76
Abd el-Kader, Emir of Algeria 168, 169
Abdelwahab, Khaled 201
Abdi Pasha, Abd al-Rahman 138–9
Abdülaziz, Sultan of the Ottoman Empire 166
Abdülhamid II, Sultan of the Ottoman Empire 257, 258, 262, 300, 354, 355
Abdullah I, King of Transjordan 281
Abdülmecid I, Sultan of the Ottoman Empire 161–3, 165
Aboab, Immanuel 122
Aboudagga, Radjaa 378
Aboulker, José 212–13

Abraham (biblical figure) 2, 3, 11, 17–18, 33, 35, 36, 37, 39–40, 42, 54, 250, 377
Abrahamic religions 89, 377, 379
Abraham Accords (2020) 358
Abraham ben Ezra 58–9
Abrahamic Family House, Abu Dhabi 379
Abravanel, Moses 132, 133
Abravanel, Raphael 132, 133
Abu 'Isa al-Isfahani 43
Abulfacem (Jewish man arrested for living with his Muslim concubine Axona) (1298) 102
Achaemenid dynasty 131
Aciman, André 383
Acre, Palestine 56, 251, 265, 285
Ades, Shafiq 336, 342
Adhri'at, Syria 25
Adiabene, Mesopotamia 62
Afghanistan 304
Afriat family 148, 151
Ahasueras, King (Xerxes I) of Persia 131
Ahbar, Ka'b al- 24
Ahmad al-Mansur, Sultan of Morocco 108–9
Ahmadiyya 197, 198
Ahmed Cevdet Pasha 163
Ahmed Pasha Bey, Bey of Tunis 201
Akka, Morocco 360
AKP (Justice and Development Party) 355

Index

Akyıldız, Mevlut: *The Embrace of Freedom* 117
Al-Ahram 317
Al-Andalus
  Almohad kingdom collapses (1269) 99
  Arab conquest of 28, 74–5, 112, 383
  Christians in 74–6, 87, 89, 90, 95, 97–8
  convivencia (idealised inter-faith relations) 75, 76, 84, 86, 104, 117
  dhimmi and 74, 75, 79, 83, 84, 86, 87, 99
  emergence of 74–5
  Jews and Muslims share secular culture in 45, 74–99, 115, 117, 149, 182, 183, 189, 209, 249, 306, 357–8, 379
  music in 81, 249, 306, 357–8
  Nasrids and 98–9, 103, 106
  Ottoman Empire and 106, 125, 126
al-aqsa (furthest point Muhammad reached during his night journey) 40
'Alawi dynasty 146, 147
Al-Azhar University, Cairo 222
Al-Balagh 223
Al-Farabi 88–9, 91
Al-Futuwwa 196, 229
Al-Hakam II, Umayyad Caliph of Córdoba 76, 81
al-Idrisi 27
Al-Karmil 263
Al-Ksar Kebir (Alcazarquivir) 145
Al-Ma'mun, Abbasid Caliph 49
al-Mahdiyya, Tunisia 58
Al-Mansur, Abbasid Caliph 48
Al-Mas'udi 67–8, 69, 71
Al-Muqaddasi 72
Al-Muqtadir, Abbasid Caliph 66
Al-Qaeda 296, 380
Al-Qassam Brigades 296
Al-Wifaq (Entente) 313
Albania 62, 137, 200, 220, 221
Albert, Prince of Saxe-Coburg and Gotha 182

Alexandria, Egypt 157, 158, 165, 185, 222–4, 226, 227, 316, 320, 322, 326, 350, 352, 383
Alfonso X, King of Castile and León 99–100
Algeria 28, 29, 151, 205, 264, 302, 311, 331, 357, 360, 378
  Algerian Communist Party 213, 308
  Arab-Israeli conflict and 363
  coloniser (France) aligns itself with Jews in 183, 184, 188, 275
  Crémieux Decree (1870) 171–3, 175, 201, 203, 209, 210, 211–12, 230–31, 304 education of Jews in 176–7
  First World War and 202, 204
  France conquers (1830) and makes department of 160–61, 169, 207, 255, 304, 366
  France grants citizenship to Jews in 173, 201, 209
  France intervenes on behalf of Jews following famine (1805) 159
  Jewish population (2021) 303
  Jewish refugees from Spain in 104, 106
  Jews commemorate centenary of French conquest (1930) 207
  Jews emigrate to France 304
  Jews emigrate to Palestine 213
  Jews play diplomatic role as intermediaries in 168–77
  Second World War and 201, 203, 209–13, 224, 304
  War of Independence (1954–62) 303–9, 314, 321, 323, 324, 325, 362, 364, 368
  See also individual place name
Algiers, Algeria 159–61, 168–9, 173, 174, 176, 202–3, 210, 213, 217, 307
  French occupation of (1830) 169, 304, 305
  Great Synagogue, Muslim rioters sack (1960) 306
Alhambra, Granada 98–9, 103

Ali (Muhammad's cousin) 24, 42, 43, 44
Ali ben Baza, shaykh 169–70
Ali of Kavala, Muhammad 158
Ali, Mothin 374
aljama (Muslim councils) 101
Alkabetz, Shlomo ha-Levi: 'Lekha Dodi' ('Come My Beloved') 116
Al-Hakim bi-Amr Allah, Fatimid Caliph 54
Allenby, Field Marshal Edmund 270
Alliance Israélite Universelle (AIU) 171–2, 175–9, 194, 216, 233–4, 249, 261, 263, 266, 280, 309, 346, 358–9
Almohad dynasty 75, 97, 98
Alp, Tekin (Moiz Kohen) 234, 260
Altara family 180–81
Amalekites 77, 372
Amazigh 29, 74, 77, 160, 356
American University of Beirut 287
Amitié Judéo-Musulmane de France 378
Amsellem, Marcel 311
Amsellem, Rabbi Salomon 311
Amsterdam, Netherlands 108, 109, 110, 148, 150–51
Anatolia 98, 232, 266, 268
Ancona, Italy 116
Anan ben David 48–9
Antébi, Albert 261, 266
Anti-Jewish League of Algiers 173
Anti-Semitic League of France 191
anti-Semitism
    antagonistic view of Jewish-Muslim relations, myth of and *see* myths
    anti-Judaism and 110, 189–90, 196
    Balfour Declaration and 269–70, 272
    conflicts/wars and *see individual conflict name*
    definitions of 190–92, 373
    fascism and *see* fascism
    Islamophobia and 9
    Nazism/Second World War and 194–8, 201, 207–11, 213–15, 217, 222–4, 233, 235–6, 238–9, 241, 247, 280
    origins of 189–92
    persecution of Jews *see individual nation and incident name*
    pogroms *see* pogroms
    political parties founded on emerge 191
    riots and *see* riots
    term/idea of eternal Jewish type and 190–92
    The Protocols of the Elders of Zion and *see Protocols of the Elders of Zion, The*
    See also individual nation name
Arab
    Arab-Israeli conflict/wars *see* Israel and *individual war and conflict name*
    Arab Jews *see* Arab Jews
    Arabic and 15 *see also* Arabic
    conquest, era of 10, 11, 26–8, 30–31, 48, 53, 62–3, 79–80, 112–13
    fascist Arab movements 196–7
    first pogrom against Jews in modern Arab state 230
    Israel, origins of and 274, 275–82
    nationalism 228, 255–6, 274, 276, 281–3, 301, 333
Arab High Committee 278, 279, 282
Arab Jews 24, 165, 197, 381
    Arabia and Yemen, in seventh-century 15–26
    end of era of 301
    Holocaust and 280, 362
    Israel and 283, 291–2, 301, 302, 343–9, 362
    in Middle East and Europe after 1948 302–49
    Muhammad first meets in Arabia 12, 16–17
    Palestine and 250–52, 264, 266, 267, 276, 280, 291
    See also individual nation name
Arab League 283, 290, 314, 332, 339
Arab Spring (2011) 351
Arabia 12, 15–26, 61, 270, 303
Arabic 74, 143, 144
    Arab defined as speaker of 15–16

Index

Beyt al-Hikma (House of Wisdom)
  translates ancient Greek philosophy
  and science into *see* Baghdad
burning of Arabic-language books 104
Greco-Arabic thought, emergence of
  51–2
Israel and 275, 345
Jews, adoption of/Arabic-speaking 15,
  20, 29–30, 35–6, 38, 42–4, 46,
  49–54, 56, 60, 65, 73, 76–8, 80–82,
  88–96, 99, 149, 150, 152, 160, 169,
  171, 173, 180, 183, 186–8, 200, 214,
  249, 319, 330, 345, 348, 383
Judeo-Arabic 15, 51, 53–4, 96, 149, 152,
  173, 180, 186–7, 188, 214, 345
Maimonides writes in 92, 93, 200
poetry 44, 78, 80–82, 88, 94–5, 99,
  330–31, 383
Qur'an and 17
Second World War, Arabic-speaking
  Jews in 203–5
Shaykh Raymond and 306
Torah and 29, 42, 51–4, 56, 60
Arafat, Yasser 290–92, 294, 295
Aragon, Spain 100, 101, 103, 104, 113
Aramaic 15, 190
Ard al-Khazar (Land of the Khazars). *See*
  Khazar kingdom/Empire
Ardabil, Kurdistan 62
Aristotelian philosophy 73, 87–91, 96
Arliel, Burak Cem 353
Armenia 25, 106, 257–8, 266, 267, 319, 361
  genocide (1915) 117, 266, 268, 354
Arsiyya 68–70
Aryanisation 210, 214
As, Amr ibn al- 26
Ashkenazi Jews 165, 184
  Albania and 220
  Arab Jews and 348
  Egypt and 158, 165, 184, 187, 225, 227,
    316, 352
  France and 362, 364
  Holocaust and 280, 349
  Iraq and 227
  Israel and 302, 346
  Jerusalem and 159, 254–5
  London and 167
  origins of 71–3
  Palestine and 254–5, 261, 264, 267, 280,
    283, 302
  Sarajevo and 218, 219
Ashley Park, Surrey 183
Asim, Imam Qari Muhammad 375
Aşıkpaşazade: *Tevārīḫ-i Āl-i ʿOsmān*
  124–5
Asriël, Davisco 246
Assouline, Albert 206
Assus, Salomon 168
Assyria 62, 268
Ata'i, Nev'izade 142
Atılhan, Cevat Rifat 236
Atsız, Nihal 236
Attal, Jacob 144, 147
Attal, Lucie 368
Attlee, Clement 281
Auerbach, Erich 245
Auschwitz death camp, Poland 10, 199,
  211, 241, 242, 243, 246, 247, 364
Austria-Hungary 191, 218, 267
Axona, concubine 102
Ayyashi, Muhammad al- 110
Ayyubid sultans 54
Azar, Shmuel 321
Azerbaijani Legion of the Wehrmacht
  197
Azoulay, André 309, 357, 359, 366
Azoulay, Audrey 357
Azoury, Najib: *The Awakening of the Arab
  Nation in Turkish Asia* 272

B

Baath Party 340
Babylon/Babylonia 16, 38, 47, 50, 121, 183,
  380
Bacri family 159–61
Bacri, Jacob 161

Badis, Buluggin ibn 84
Badis ibn Habbus, Zirid Sultan 77, 84–5
Badr, Battle of (624) 21–2
Badr, Operation (1973) 297
Baghdad
  Beyt al-Hikma (House of Wisdom) 49, 51
  exodus of Jews from (to Israel) 339–45
  Farhud (1941) and 228–32, 329–30, 342
  Jerusalem, Jews from in 264, 289
  Mandate of Iraq and 227–30
  pre-modern symbiosis in 45, 46–8, 51–3, 55–6, 62, 63, 81, 88
  Sassoon family and 179–81, 183, 187–8, 270
Balfour Declaration (1917) 268–74, 279, 282, 290
Balkan Wars (1912–13) 268
Bank of England 152, 167
Banna, Hasan al- 224, 319
Banu 'Awf 19, 21
Banu 'Aws 19, 21, 22–3
Banu al-Nadir 19, 20, 22
Banu Khazraj 19, 23
Banu Qaynuqa 19, 20–23, 25
Banu Qurayza 19, 20, 22–3, 25
Barak, Ehud 295
Bardhi, Haxhi Dede Reshat 220
Baruch, André 312
Bash-A'yan, Shaykh Ahmad 230
Basra, Iraq 44, 179, 227, 228, 229, 230, 336, 340
Bassatine Cemetery, Cairo 351
Batsri, Yossef 338–9
Bayezid II, Sultan of the Ottoman Empire 117, 119, 120, 122, 124, 125, 126, 260
Becerano, Chief Rabbi Haim 233–4
Begin, Menachem 296, 297; *The Revolt* 324
Behar, Isaak 240–42, 245, 247
Beirut, Lebanon 226, 267, 287, 295, 316

Believers (*mu'minun*) 17, 19–21, 30–31, 36, 40, 138, 299
Ben Bella, Ahmed 323–4
Ben Diaf, Ahmed 164
Ben Gurion, David 278, 279, 280, 283, 286, 343
Ben Jelloun, Tahar 366
Ben Porat, Mordechai 338–9
Ben Yossef, Yahya 381–2
Benchimol, Abraham 170
Bendjelloul, Mohamed Salah 208–9
Benghabrit, Si Kaddour 203–7
Benjamin of Tudela 47
Benjamin, Abraham 152
Benoliel, Judah 147, 153
Benyahia, Mohamed 307
Benzaken, Dr Léon 313
Benzouaou, Mohammed 206
Berber Muslims 11, 27–30, 53, 74, 75, 77, 84, 108, 112, 160, 304
Berlin, Germany 193–4, 197–200, 209, 239, 240–44, 246–7, 257
besa ('to keep the promise') 220
Bessis, André 312
Bevin, Ernest 281
Bey, Cevat 240
Bibas, Ariel 375
Bibas, Kfar 375
Bigart, Jacques 263
Bilu group 256
bin Laden, Osama 296, 299
Binnet, Meir (Max) 320–21
Bismillahirahim (in the name of the merciful, the compassionate) 54
Blum, Léon 305
Boabdil (Abu Abd Allah Muhammad) 103
Boganim, Oro 205
Bombay (Mumbai), India 160, 180–84
Bonaparte, Napoleon 157–8, 169
Book of Daniel 120
Book of Esther 130–31
Boros, Anna 197, 198–9

Index

Boros, Carla 199
Bosnia and Herzegovina 194, 218–19, 221
Boubakeur, Dalil 206
Boukris family 201
Boumendjel, Ahmed 210–11, 307
Bourguiba, Habib 323
Bourmont, Count de 161
Brethren of Purity (*Ikhwan al-Safa'*) 96
Britain
  Aliens Act (1905) 270
  Arab-Israeli war (1948) and 284–5, 286
  Balfour Declaration (1917) *see* Balfour Declaration
  Board of Deputies of British Jews 167, 174
  British Jews, attacks on 374–5
  British Mandate of Palestine/establishment of Israel and 194, 217–18, 231, 268–84, 324, 332, 342
  Court of St James 147, 153
  Empire 9, 157, 158, 163, 165, 167, 168, 179–83, 186, 187–8, 194, 197, 198, 217–18, 223–5, 227–31, 252, 255, 263, 265, 268–87, 319, 320, 324, 328, 332, 336, 342
  interfaith efforts in 378–9
  Islamophobia in 374
  Israeli-Palestinian conflict and 373–5
  Mandate of Iraq 227–31, 328, 331, 336
  readmission of Jews (1656) 150, 151
  Second World War and 214, 229–30, 238, 279–80, 305
  Suez Crisis and 312, 321–2
  synagogues in 150, 151–2, 166–7, 374
  terrorist attacks by Muslims in 8
Buchenwald concentration camp, Germany 241, 243
Buhillal, Al-Haj Abd al-Salam 152
Buhlul, Abu al-Nasr al-Mansur Abu al- 81
Bulan I, Khazar King 63
Bursa, Turkey 11, 112
Busnach (Livornese Jew) 159–60

Byzantine Empire 11, 25–8, 40, 61–5, 67–8, 72, 75, 76, 112–13, 119, 126

C

Cabessa, Abraham and Isaac 146
Cairo, Egypt 45, 64, 93, 116, 146, 164, 180–81, 185–6, 191, 290, 305, 316, 318, 320, 325–6, 377
  Arab League founded in 283, 290
  French first enter (1798) 157–8
  Jews arrested in 323, 326
  Jews remaining in 350–52
  origins 53–8
  Second World War and 196, 200, 209, 221, 222, 224–7
Camp David Accords (2000) 295
Canary Islands 110
Candia (Heraklion) 120
Capsali, Rabbi Elijah ben Elkanah 120
  Seder Eliyahu zuta: Toldot ha-'Ot'omanim u-Venitsi'ah ve korot 'am Yisrael be-mamlekhot Turki'yah, Sefarad u-Venitsi'ah (Minor Order of Elijah: History of the Ottomans and Venice and the People of Israel in Turkey, Spain, and Venice) 120–22
Capsali, Moses 120, 126
Caro, Joseph: *Shulkhan Aruch (The Set Table)* 116
Carpentras, Jewish cemetery at, France 366
Carsinet, Aaron 144
Casablanca, Morocco 177, 205, 215, 216, 313, 358
  Anglo-American landing in (1942) 202, 217
  Hassan II attends Yom Kippur services in 314–15
  Jewish Museum 359
  riots/massacre (1952) 310
casbah (fortified centre of the city) 149
Castile, Spain 97, 99, 103, 104
Castro, Américo 75

Castro, Léon 222, 226
Catholicism 6, 103–4, 106, 108, 109, 115, 165, 194
Cattaoui (Qattawi) family 158, 185–6, 221, 222, 224, 317
Cattaoui, Joseph Aslan 186, 221, 222, 317
Cattaoui, Moise de 186
Cattaoui, René 224, 226, 317
Cattoui, Joseph 164
Caucasus 60–62, 73, 244, 245
Cave of Machpelah, Hebron 11, 250
Çelebi, Evliya: *Seyahatname (Book of Travels)* 134–6
Çelebi, Solakzâde Mehmed Hemdemî 130
Central Consistory of the Jews of France 171
Ceuta, Spain 107, 108
Chamberlain, Neville 279
Charles II, King of England 180
Charlie Hebdo attacks (2015) 367
Chelmno death camp, Poland 242
Chelouches, Aharon 264–5
Chelouches, Avraham 264
Chelouches, Yosef Eliahu 265
Chenik, Mohammed 201
China 48, 49, 61, 65, 180, 181–2, 187–8
Chouraqui, André 29
CHP (Cumhuriyet Halk Partisi, the Republican People's Party) 236, 238, 248
Christianity
  Abraham and 3, 17, 18, 34
  Al-Andalus and 74–6, 87, 89, 90, 95, 97–8, 114, 189
  anti-Judaism and 110–11, 252–4
  anti-Semitism and 189, 190–91
  Arab nationalism and 228, 255
  Christian involvement causes relations between Jews and Muslims to worsen 3, 4, 189, 272–3
  converts to Islam 24, 102, 103, 105–9, 113–16, 121–2, 124, 125, 129, 137, 142, 150, 299, 355, 356
  Crusades *see* Crusades
  Conversos (New Christians) (converted Jews) *see* Conversos
  Egypt and 56, 158, 351
  Fascist Arab movements and 196
  Fourth Lateran Council (1215) 252
  Israel and 5, 303
  Jews convert to 6–7, 28, 61, 99, 102–9, 113–16, 121–3, 131, 132, 133, 136, 137, 138, 142, 150, 171, 190, 299, 355, 356
  Judeo-Christian culture, myth of a 8, 9
  kahina and 28
  Khazars and 64, 65, 68, 69, 70, 71, 72, 73
  Lebanon and 315–16
  Muslim-majority pre-modern societies treat Jews better than contemporary Christendom 33–5
  Ottoman Empire and 118–19, 120, 123, 124, 163, 165, 168, 254, 258, 260, 261, 262, 265–8, 354
  Pact of Umar and 30–33
  Palestine and 251–4, 258, 260, 261, 262, 263, 264, 265–6, 266, 268, 272–3, 275, 276, 277, 278, 279, 282, 283, 284, 285–6, 287, 288, 290, 291, 295, 297
  Spanish Christian kingdoms 99–107, 113
  translation of ancient Greek texts in Baghdad by Christian Arabs 51
  Turkey and 352, 354, 355, 356
  Zionism and 269–77, 278, 279, 282, 283, 284, 285–6, 287, 288, 290, 291, 295, 297
Çiçek, Princess 62
Cicurel, Salvator 305, 318
circumcision 2, 18, 37, 38, 61, 64, 65, 110, 114, 121, 239, 361
Cohen, Benjamin 110
Cohen, Shimon 359, 360
Cohn-Bendit, Daniel 363, 364
colonialism 4, 9, 29, 58, 157–92, 196, 197, 203, 205, 207, 210, 212, 221, 231, 232,

273, 296, 302, 305, 309, 324–5, 327, 329, 331–2, 356, 360–62, 364, 366, 383. *See also individual nation name*
Columbus, Christopher 98
Comités Palestine 365
Committee of Union and Progress (CUP) 258–9, 267
communism 3, 202, 208, 213, 219, 226–7, 232, 236, 282, 288, 300, 308, 310, 316–19, 321, 324–6, 329–35, 337, 340, 359, 364
Community Security Trust (CST) 373–4
comparative religion 52
Compiègne, camp of, France 203
Constantine V, Emperor of Byzantium 62
Constantine, capture of (1837) 169
Constantinople 113, 126
　Ottoman conquest (1453) 118, 124, 125
Conversos (New Christians) (converted Jews) 103, 105–9, 113–16, 121–2, 137, 142, 150, 299, 355, 356
Converts (*Dönmeler*, Turkish) 138
Coptic churches 59
Corcos family 147, 148
Corcos, Jacob 148
Corcos, Solomon 148
Córdoba, Spain 11, 53, 63, 75–7, 79, 81, 86, 87, 89, 90, 92, 97, 107
Cordovero, Moses 116
corsairs 106, 110, 147–8
Crémieux, Adolphe/Crémieux Decree 171–3, 175, 201, 203, 209, 210, 211, 230–31, 304
Créteil, France, rape of the woman in (2014) 367
Crimea 61, 63, 65, 163, 243, 244
　Crimean War (1853–6) 163
Cromwell, Oliver 150, 151
Crusades 4, 6, 56, 110–11, 251, 296, 300
Cumhuriyet (*Republic*) 247
Curiel, Henri 226, 318, 319, 325
Curiel, Raoul 226
Cyprus 115, 281
Cyrus II 'the Great' of Persia 121

D
D'ror Yiqra ('Freedom shall He proclaim') 53
Da'ud, Abraham ibn
　Ha-Emunah ha-Ramah (*Exalted Faith*) 89
　Sefer ha-Kabbalah 89, 90
Dahmani, Arezki 366
Dajjal, or Anti-Messiah 43
Dallal, Sasson 330, 332, 335
Daloya, Rabbi Yitzhak 145
Damascus, Syria 96, 121, 167, 191, 261, 263
　Damascus Affair of (1840) 165, 171
Daniel, Ezra 328
Daniel, Menahem 327
Darmon, Amram 169
Daroca, Spain 101, 102
Darwish, Shalom 328, 330–31
Daud, Abraham ibn 76; *Sefer ha-Kabbalah* (*Book of Tradition*) 83–4
David, King (biblical figure) 19, 44, 47, 76, 77, 95–6
David Sassoon Library, Mumbai 184
Davud Pasha, governor of Baghdad 180
Deir Yassin massacre (1948), Palestine 284–5
Delacroix, Eugène 170
Derbend 61, 68, 69
dhimma, laws of (pact of protection granted to Jews) 4, 10, 68
　Abu Ishaq and 85
　Al-Andalus and 74, 75, 79, 83, 84, 86, 87, 99
　Albania and 220
　Algeria and 160, 161, 173, 201, 304, 307
　Egypt and 224
　Iraq and 227, 230, 231
　Israel and 4, 270–71, 288, 291, 299, 358
　jizya and 7
　Judah Halevi offers dream-fantasy of Muslims as 83
　Morocco and 107, 144, 148, 150, 153, 174, 175, 177, 215, 356

origins 30–33
Ottoman Empire and 116, 117, 119, 122–3, 139, 140, 142, 161, 163, 164, 165, 218, 227, 255
Palestine and 252, 270–71
Shi'i Fatimid dynasty and 54
Sunni Mamluks and 56
Turkey and 232, 234
Dihya statue, Khenchela, Algeria 29
discrimination
　discriminatory laws, Jews targeted by 25, 164, 172, 214–15, 230, 232, 252, 287–8, 335, 353, 362
　Jews face from other types of Jews 291, 293, 302, 346
　tolerance and 7
Disraeli, Benjamin 167–8, 182
Djerawa 28
Djerid, nomad Jews living in 27
Dönme (Converso fulfilling world Jewry's alleged secret agenda) 355, 356
Draâ, Morocco 29, 30
Dray, Julien 366
Drumont, Édouard 173, 191
Druze 285–6, 288
Dugali, Said ibn Faraj al- 110
Dunash ben Labrat 52–3; *D'ror Yiqra* ('Freedom shall He proclaim') 53
Duval, General 212
Dwek, Haim 325

E
East India Company 180, 182
Easter 102, 251
Eastern Europe 60–61, 62, 158. *See also individual nation name*
Eastern Turkic SS Corps 197
Eban, Abba 345–6
Edirne, Turkey 118, 235, 354
Edward VII, King of the United Kingdom 182

Egypt 30, 44, 58, 59–60, 61, 80, 87, 92, 132, 136, 199, 200, 207, 232, 253, 372, 379, 383
　Arab conquest of 26–8, 53
　Arab nationalism and 255, 283
　British occupation/protectorate 165, 168, 186–7, 270, 319
　Cairo *see* Cairo
　coup (1952) 319
　Egyptian League against German Anti-Semitism (LICA) 222
　Egyptian Socialist Party 226
　fascist Arab movements and 196, 221–3
　Fatimids accelerate immigration of Jews to 55–6
　French colonial rule 157–9, 164, 165, 188–9, 255, 303, 321–2
　Iraqi Jews settle in 53–4
　Isma'il and 164–5, 185, 255
　Israel, 1948 war with 283, 286, 287, 317
　Israel, 1967 war with 288, 290, 296, 326–7
　Jewish nostalgia for 350
　Jewish population (2021) 303
　Jewish emigration from 319–26, 350–52
　Karaites establish themselves in 53
　khedives and kings period (1860–1950), Jews prosper in 184–6
　monarchy abolished (1953) 319
　Morocco and 311, 314
　Moses and 16, 143, 219
　Muhammad Ali and 158–9, 164, 165, 319
　Muslim Brotherhood and *see* Muslim Brotherhood
　Napoleon in 157–8, 169, 188
　Operation Susannah (1954) and 319–21
　relations between Jews and Muslims begin to deteriorate (1930s) 221–3
　Sadat assassinated (1981) 298
　Sadat visits Jerusalem (1977) 350, 377
　Sayyid Qutb and 299
　Second World War and 223–5

Index

Suez Canal/Crisis 164, 312, 321–2, 324, 325
   United Arab Republic and 324
   Zionism and 221–7, 302, 315, 316–23
   See also individual place name
Eichmann, Adolf 196, 243
El Alamein, battle of (1942) 224
El Badi Palace, Morocco 145
El Maghribi, Samy 313
El Maleh, Edmond Amran 359
El Tiempo: 'Is Zionism Compatible with Ottomanism?' 259
El-Sisi, Abdel Fattah 351
Elmaleh family 148
Elohim, Eved 43
Erbil, Kurdish kingdom in 62
Erdoğan, Receb Tayyib 299, 354–6
Esperança de Israel (*Hope of Israel*) 151
Essaouira, Morocco 146, 147, 148, 149, 150, 152, 205, 213, 358
   Beyt Dakira (House of Memory) 357–8
   Festival of Atlantic Andalusias 357
   Jewish Museum 357
Esther (biblical figure) 130–31
Étoile nord-africaine (North African Star) 212
Etzel and Lehi paramilitaries 284–5
Eugenie, Empress of France 164
Euryalus, HMS 283

F

fascism 193, 208, 209, 212, 214, 218, 221, 222, 226, 228, 231, 236, 238, 304, 329
   fascist Arab movements 196–7
   See also Nazism
Fadlan, Ahmad ibn 63, 66, 68, 70
Farouk, King of Egypt 223, 317, 319
Fassiya, Zohra 313–14
fasting 1, 2, 17, 37, 38, 40, 94, 137
Fatah 290, 296
Fatiha, the 60
Fatima (daughter of Muhammad) 146
Fatimid dynasty (909–1171) 54, 55–6, 185
fatwa (question and response) 39, 42, 48, 128, 231
Faysal I, King of Iraq 228, 274
Ferdinand II, King of Aragon 103, 104, 132
Ferrara, Italy 115
Fez, Morocco 30, 52–3, 91, 92, 103, 108, 109, 143–5, 153, 163, 203, 216, 358, 359
Filastin 263
First Eastern Muslim SS Regiment 197
First Gulf War (1991) 366
First World War (1914–18) 181, 183, 194, 198, 202–4, 213, 232, 236, 240, 243, 252, 255, 263, 266–9, 272, 306
Foundation of Judeo-Moroccan Cultural Patrimony (FPCJM) 358, 359
France
   abolition of last discriminatory laws against Jews in 172
   Algeria, colonial rule of 159–61, 168–73, 177, 183, 184, 188–9, 201–13, 255, 275, 304–9, 321, 362, 364
   anti-Jewish violence committed by Muslims in (2000–2020) 8, 367–8
   anti-Semitism and 9, 189–91, 365–8
   Arab-Israeli war (1967) and 362–4
   citizenship granted to Maghrebi Jews 170, 173, 178–9, 201, 204, 208, 209, 211, 213, 237, 304, 305, 322, 323, 361, 362
   colonial empire launched in Middle East and North Africa under Bonaparte 157–9 colonialism renders continued Jewish-Muslim intimacy dead end 188–9
   Damascus Affair (1840) and 165
   education turns Jews of Maghreb and Middle East culturally towards 175–9, 280
   Egypt, colonial rule of 157–9, 164, 165, 188–9, 255, 303, 321–2
   Gibraltar, siege of (1781) 152

Jewish population (2021) 303
Jewish-Muslim cooperation collapses within 360–67
Jews fight for in world wars 202–4, 209–10, 213
Jews flee Spain for 109
largest Muslim and Jewish population in Europe 360–61
Morocco and 174–5, 178–80, 188–9, 213–15, 303, 309, 310, 311, 312, 359
multiculturalism in 365–6
relations between Muslims and Jews in worsen/attacks against Jewish targets in 365, 367–8, 378
Revolution (1789) 157, 161, 170, 171, 172, 178, 255
Revolution (1848) 172
Second World War and 200–204, 206–17, 224, 228, 237, 243, 246, 280, 304–5, 314, 364
Shanghai Municipality, French Concession 188
Suez Crisis and 312, 321–2
Syria, mandate over 273
Vichy 200–202, 206–17, 224, 228, 237, 304–5, 314
See also individual place name
France Plus 366
Franco, Moïse 130
Francos, Ania 364
Franks 62
Frasheri, Mehdi 220
Fresco, David 233, 259, 260, 261
Fresco, chief rabbi, Haim Moses 166
Front de Libération Nationale (FLN) 304–8, 314, 321, 323, 325, 362, 364
Front National 365
Fustat, Egypt 53, 58–9, 92, 352

G
Gabbay, Ezekiel 180
Gabbay, Farha 181
Gabbay, Moshe 343

Gabriel, angel (biblical figure) 16, 22
Galanti, Professor Avram: *Türkler ve Yahudiler (Turks and Jews)* 233–4, 372–3
Galilee, Palestine/Israel 25, 277–8, 282–3, 285–6, 289, 293
Gaon, Sa'adia 52, 53, 97, 351; *Book of Beliefs and Opinions* 56
Ghassani, General Hassan ibn al-Nu'man al- 28
Gaza, Palestine/Israel 136, 137, 265, 282, 286–90, 321, 322
Arab-Israeli War (1967) and 288, 290
Israel evacuates its military and civilians from (2005) 296
Jewish settlements in 297
October 7 attacks (2023) and 368–9
Palestinian uprising (intifada), outbreak of, Jabaliya refugee camp (1987) 293
War in (2023–) 368–71, 373–5
Geismar, Alain 364–5
General Commission on Jewish Questions 207
geniza (chamber connected to the synagogue) 59, 64, 180, 181, 351, 352
geonim (heads of the yeshivot) 47–8, 53
George V, King of United Kingdom 183
Gerede, Hüsrev 239, 242
Germany
anti-Semitic political parties emerge in 191
anti-Semitism and Islamophobia in, battle against 9
German Jews migrate to Poland in medieval times 71, 73
Nazi 4, 6–8, 10, 193–203, 205, 207, 209–10, 214, 217–25, 228–9, 231, 235–45, 270, 277, 279–81, 321, 329, 347, 349, 363, 364
terrorist attacks by Muslims in 8
Gestapo 199, 200, 203, 209, 241, 242, 243, 244

Index

Gharnati, Abu Hamid al-Andalusi al- ('the Granadan') 112
Ghébali, Eric 366
Giacomo of Gaeta (Hekim Yakub Pasha) 124
Gibraltar 74, 81, 107, 147, 151–3, 169, 174, 175, 314
Giraud, General 211
Gladstone, William 168
Goar, Edwin 224
God 44, 48, 52, 64–5, 77, 79, 83, 93–8, 114, 119, 120–22, 130, 135, 136, 191, 220, 250, 256, 298, 300
   Ibn Paquda and 96–7
   Jews use term Allah for 42
   Muhammad and 16–18, 21, 93
   Muslims as saviours of Jews and 26
   names for 54, 59, 60
   neo-Platonists and 88, 94, 95
   Pact of Medina/Pact of Umar and 32
   Qur'an and 33, 34, 37, 40–42, 49, 59, 60, 301, 370
   similarities between Islam and Judaism and 1–2, 35–7, 44
   Torah and 37, 371–2
Gog and Magog 120–21
Goitein, Shelomo Dov: *Jews and Arabs: Their Contacts through the Ages* 36–7, 184
Goldstein, Baruch 298
Goldziher, Ignaz 191
Goren, Rabbi Shlomo 288
Gozlan, Élie 209, 212, 308
Granada, Spain 11, 50, 74, 77, 80, 84–7, 98, 103–6, 110, 112
   Jews massacred by mobs in (1066) 86
Greater Syria 327
Greece 237, 347
   ancient 6, 26, 49, 51–2, 76, 90
   Greco-Arabic thought, emergence of 49, 51–2, 90, 92
   Ottoman Empire and 113, 120, 124, 136, 159, 218, 263, 266, 268

Orthodox Church 218, 255, 263, 266
Green Shirts 222
Guelma, massacre (1945) 212
Guessous, Said 175
Gülen, Fethullah 355
Gush Emunim (Bloc of the Faithful) 297

H

ha-Kohen, Joseph ben Joshua: *Sefer divre ha-yamim le-malkhey Tzarefat u-malkhey beyt*
   Ottoman ha-Togar (*History of the Kings of France and the Kings of the Dynasty of Othman, the Turk*) 121
Habsburg dynasty 115, 119
Hadi, Awni Abd al- 276
Hadj, Messali 210, 212
Haganah 278, 284
Hagar (biblical figure, concubine of Abraham) 2, 38, 83, 377
Haggadah 29
Haifa, Palestine/Israel 263, 264, 265, 275, 277, 278, 282, 283, 284, 285, 333, 335, 346
Haj, Mohamed el- 144
Halahmy, Oded 344–5
Halali, Salim 313–14
Halevi, Judah (Abu al-Hassan) 89, 94–5, 97, 256
   Kitab al-Khazari (*Book of the Khazar*) 73, 78, 80, 83
Halimi, Ilan 367
Haman, grand vizier 131, 372
Hamas (Islamic Resistance Movement) 294–6, 299, 368–75
Hamchari, Mahmoud 365
Handžar 218
Hanifa, Abu 49
Hanoun, Lucien 308
hara (special quarter) 160
Harari, Ezra 227
Hardaga, Zeyneba and Mustafa 219
Hardoon, Silas Aaron 187–8

harem 122, 123, 126, 127, 128
Haroun al-Rashid, Abbasid Caliph 48, 67
Haroun, Magda Shehata 351
Haroun, Nadia 351
Hasan, Sayyid ibn 56
hasidim (pietists) 44
Hassan, Joshua 314
Hassan II, King of Morocco 313, 314–15, 357
Hatchuel, Sol (Lalla Suleika) 153
hate crimes 368
Hayatizade, Mustafa Fevzi Efendi 132, 133, 142
Haykal, Muhammad Hussein 317
Hazan, Chief Rabbi Avraham 211
Hebrew 143, 144, 160, 161, 171, 178, 182, 183, 190, 216, 234, 249, 255, 256, 280, 309, 314,
329, 346, 357, 359, 377, 381
  Al-Andalus and 76–9, 81, 82, 90, 91, 94–8
  Arab Jews and 15–17, 26–7, 29, 30, 36–8, 42–4, 50–54, 60, 62–4, 76–9, 81–2, 90, 91, 94–8
  Israel and 275, 348
  Judeo-Arabic and 15–16
Hebron, Palestine/Israel 10, 26, 39, 113, 167, 249, 250, 251, 264, 265, 276, 288–9, 297, 298
Helen, Queen of Parthia 62
Helmy, Dr Mohammed 197, 199–200
Heraclius, Emperor of Byzantium 25, 26
Herzl, Theodor 256–8, 283; *Der Judenstaat* (*The Jews' State*) 256, 283
Heydrich, Reinhard 196, 239
Hijaz 16, 274
Himmler, Heinrich 194–6, 200, 243
Himyar, Yemen 16, 24
Hispanophobia 108
Hitler, Adolf 10, 193–6, 199, 214, 223, 239, 240, 244, 276, 279–80, 301, 363
Hofjuden (court Jews) 149

Holocaust 5, 6, 8, 9, 193–6, 199, 203, 244, 246, 280, 281, 362, 364, 366, 368, 372, 373
Holy of Holies 40
Holy Roman Empire 76
Homs, Syria 11
Höss, Rudolf 243
Husayni, Hussein al- 266
Hussein, Saddam 340
Hussein, Taha 196
Husseini, Grand Mufti of Jerusalem, Al-Hajj Amin al- 193–7, 200, 207, 209, 228, 229, 275–6
Husrev, Gazi 218

I

Ibn Arabi 96; *The Meccan Openings and Fusus al-Hikam* (*The Bezels of Wisdom*) 96–7
Ibn Bajja 88–9
Ibn Ezra, Abraham 77
Ibn Ezra, Moses 78, 88: *Kitab al-Muhadara wa'l-Mudhakara* (*Conversations and Recollections*) (*Shirat Yisrael*) 79–80
Ibn Gabirol, Solomon 77; *The Fountain of Life* 94
Ibn Hawqal 71
Ibn Hazm: *Radd ala ibn al-Nagrila* (*Refutation of Ibn Naghrela*) 78
Ibn Hisham 20
Ibn Khaldun 27, 28
Ibn Rushd (Averroes) 88–92; *Tahafut al-Tahafut* (*The Incoherence of the Incoherence*) 91
Ibn Rusta 65–6
Ibn Taymiyya 56; *Minhaj al-Sunna* 44
Ibrahim Edhem Pasha, Grand Vizier 119
Ibrahim Pasha, Grand Vizier 128, 129, 140
Identité et Dialogue 366
Idris I, King of Morocco 30
Idris II, King of Morocco 30

Index

IG Farben 243
Ila al Amam (Forward) 315
Independence Party 276
India 30, 55, 56, 58, 157, 180–83, 187–8, 198, 229, 270, 279, 281, 282, 347
Innocent III, Pope 252
International Brigades 202
Interpreter Corps (Arab Bureau) 169
Iran 43, 62, 65–6, 142, 176, 181–2, 246, 281–2, 296, 299, 304, 321, 330, 334, 337, 340, 378–9
Iraq 47, 96, 177, 194, 277, 279, 283, 286, 320, 321, 326–45, 348, 367, 383
    Arab-Israeli War (1948) and 329, 335–45
    coup (1963) 340
    Egyptian cities, Iraqi Jews settle in 53
    exodus of Jews to Israel 336–48
    Farhud (looting, robbing) pogrom (1941) 228–32, 329–30, 342
    Fascist Arab movements in 196
    First Shi'i or pro-Ali group emerges in 43
    Iraqi Communist Party (ICP)/Jews' participation in centrist and leftist political parties 326, 329–35
    Jewish militant reaction to Islamification in 43
    Jewish population (2021) 303
    Jews of Abbasid Iraq divided by class 49
    Jews split into sectarian groups of rabbinic Jews and Karaites in 39
    literature, Jews' participation in birth of modern Iraqi 326–7
    Mandate of Iraq 227–32
    revolution (1958) 339–40
    Sassoon family and *see* Sassoon family
    Sufi ascetics in 44
    Zionism and 302, 315, 327–37, 339, 341, 342
    See also individual place name
Isa, Isa al- 263
'Isawiyya 43
Isaac (biblical figure) 2, 11, 18, 37, 39, 40, 250, 377
Isaac, Israel 252
Isabella, Queen of Castile 103, 104
Isfahan 43, 65
Ishaq, Abu 84–7, 99
Ishaq, Muhammad Ibn 20
Ishmael (biblical figure) 2, 18, 26, 38, 63, 256, 377
Islam
    birth and rise of, seventh century 8, 15–30, 61, 300
    festivals and feast days *see individual name*
    fundamentalist 146, 298–9
    Islamism 8, 29, 294–6, 298, 299, 300, 355, 367, 368–9
    Islamophobia 9, 365, 368–70, 374
    Jews convert to 7, 17, 20, 24, 28, 42, 43, 54–6, 61, 63, 72–3, 75, 93–4, 102, 122, 123, 124, 125, 137, 138, 139, 140, 143–4, 158, 175, 197, 198, 255, 256, 350
    Judeo-Islamic religious symbiosis *see* symbiosis, Judeo-Islamic
    law and 20–21, 25, 30–33, 140, 161, 254, 267
    munafiqun (hypocrites, false converts) 20
    Muslims convert to Christianity 105–7, 109–10, 115
    Nazi regime promotes itself as defender of 196–7
    Pact of Medina/Pact of Umar and 30–33
    philosophy, development of 46, 49, 51–2, 87–97
    Qur'an and *see* Qur'an
    Shi'i 24, 39, 42–4, 54, 230, 299, 328, 330
    similarities with Judaism 1–2, 37–45, 110–11
    Sunni 2, 39, 43–4, 49, 56, 328, 334–5, 355

terrorism/terrorist attacks and *see* terrorism/terrorist attacks
See also Muslims
Islamic Jihad 294–6, 299, 368
Isma'il Ali, Khedive (viceroy) of Egypt 164–5, 185, 255
Isma'ilis 43, 44
Isra'iliyyat 24, 42
Israel
  Abraham Accords 358
  ancient 16, 19, 25, 26, 27, 28, 41, 62, 71–2, 77, 99, 121, 125, 151, 251–3, 350, 380–81
  antagonistic view of Jewish-Muslim relations codified recently in 7–8, 348–9
  Arab-Israeli War (1948) 283–8, 296, 299, 317, 329, 335, 336, 371
  Arab-Israeli War (1967) 288–9, 290, 293–4, 296, 298–9, 308, 315, 326, 340, 351, 362–3
  Arab Jews in 291–2, 302, 343–9, 362
  Camp David Summit (2000) 295
  Declaration of Principles (1993) 294
  establishment of (1948) 5, 248, 249–88, 300, 302, 309, 310, 317, 319, 333, 335, 351, 353, 383
  European states support for 9
  Galut (exile from the Land of Israel) 256
  Hamas, wars with 296, 368–75
  Israel Defense Forces (IDF) 284–5, 293, 297
  Jews and Israelis, distinction between dissolved in 302–3
  Law of Return (1950) 287
  Lebanon, invasion of (1982) 293, 295, 297, 316
  messianism in 297
  migration to 24, 36, 171, 220, 227, 287, 303, 304, 308–12, 314–15, 316, 317, 318, 319, 322, 324, 330, 333, 334, 336, 338–9, 343–9, 353, 362
  Munich Olympics terror attacks (1972) 290, 365
  Muslim (and Christian) presence not desired in 303
  Muslims treated as second-class citizens in 287–8
  October 7 terrorist attacks on (2023) 296, 368–9, 370, 373, 375
  Operation Badr (1973) and 297
  Oslo Accords (1993) 294, 298, 357
  Palestinian conflict 2, 7, 12, 193, 227, 228, 229, 231, 251–8, 260, 289–300, 301, 310, 313, 315, 316, 317, 324, 327–37, 339, 341–2, 346, 347, 349, 357, 359, 360, 363–75, 377, 381 *see also* Palestine
  settlement schemes in Israel-Palestine 291, 293, 295–7
  Suez Crisis and 312, 321–2, 324
  Susannah, Operation (1954) 320–21
  Zionism and *see* Zionism
Israel, Marcel 319
Israel, Menasseh ben 150–51
Israeli, Isaac d' 167
Istakhri 66–70
Istanbul 11, 218, 238, 243, 244, 254, 258, 259, 292
  Istanbul University 235
  Jewish Museum 122, 353
  Ottoman 114, 115, 117–20, 122, 125, 128, 134–7, 139, 140, 163, 165
  Spanish Muslims settle in Galata 106
  synagogues in 11, 112, 119
  Valide Sultan Mosque 132–3
Istiqlal (Independence) Party 312, 313, 362
Itil 61, 68, 69, 70, 72, 112
Izates 62
Izmir 136, 137, 244, 259

J

Jabiya-Yarmuk, battle of (636) 26
Jacob (biblical figure) 11, 18, 39, 148, 250
Jacob ben Idder 147

Index

Jaffa, Palestine/Israel 121, 249, 262, 263, 264, 265, 266, 275, 277, 278, 282–3, 285
Jaha, Lamija 220
Jamali, Fadhel al- 328
Janissaries 113
Jerusalem, Palestine/Israel 1, 17, 29, 37, 38, 62, 116, 119, 122, 136, 146, 159, 167, 213, 218, 249, 250, 257, 261, 262
  Allenby enters (1917) 270–71
  anti-Jewish riots in Jewish quarter (1920) 275
  Arab-Israeli War (1948) and 284–7
  Arab-Israeli War (1967) and 288–9, 298
  Ashkenazi and 255
  British in 270–71, 276, 278, 281–5
  Church of the Holy Sepulchre 251
  Crusaders take (1099) 110–11
  Dome of the Rock 40–41, 75, 276
  East Jerusalem 286–9, 297, 298
  Estambouli 254
  grand mufti of *see* Al-Hajj Amin al-Husseini
  Haram al-Sharif (Noble Sanctuary) 40, 168, 295
  Heraclius recovers (625) 25
  Hurva synagogue 159, 289
  Israeli citizens living in East Jerusalem 297
  King David Hotel 281
  Mount of Olives 252, 351
  Muslims attack Jews in (1929) 276
  Nebuchadnezzar II conquers (586) 47
  'next year in Jerusalem', Seder wish 251–2
  Old City 121, 159, 167, 264, 286, 298
  Ottoman 264, 265, 266
  Palestinian uprisings (intifadas) and 293, 294
  Persia conquers (614) 25
  Rabbi Zvi Yehuda Kook's yeshiva in 297
  Rishon LeZion 266
  Sadat visits (1977) 350, 377
  Saladin reconquers (1187) 251
  Second Temple 40, 41, 251, 252, 288, 301
  Suleiman I rebuilds walls of Old City 121
  Supreme Muslim Council 275–6
  Temple Mount 25, 39–41, 96, 121, 251, 254, 289, 295
  Temple of Solomon/First Temple 17, 25, 40, 41, 47, 95–6, 119, 121, 288, 301, 380 Western Wall 276, 295, 380
  Yad Vashem in 195–6
Jesus (biblical figure) 16, 18, 33, 40, 43, 102
Jewish Agency 275, 276, 278, 279, 280–83, 311
Jewish Brigade 280
Jewish Chronicle 174–5, 256
Jews
  Abraham and 2, 3, 11, 17–18, 33, 35, 36, 37, 39–40, 42, 54, 250, 377
  allies of Muslims/participation in battles against Christian oppressors 8, 11–12, 15, 20, 21, 22–3, 25, 27–8, 34, 42, 55–6, 74, 106, 113–15, 161, 168, 258
  antagonistic view of Jewish-Muslim relations, myth of *see* symbiosis, Judeo-Islamic
  anti-Semitism and *see* anti-Semitism
  Arab Jews *see* Arab Jews *and individual nation name*
  Arabic and *see* Arabic
  Ashkenazi *see* Ashkenazi Jews
  Believers (*mu'minun*) 17, 19–21, 30–31, 36, 40, 138, 299
  blood libel 116, 165–6, 356 Jewish-Muslim symbiosis *see* symbiosis, Judeo-Islamic
  Christianity and *see* Christianity
  colonialism and *see individual nation name*

converts to Christianity 61, 68, 99, 100, 103–9, 113–16, 121–2, 137, 142, 150, 190, 299, 355, 356
converts to Islam 17, 20, 24, 25, 42–3, 54, 55, 56, 72–3, 75, 92–3, 102, 122–5, 137–40, 143–4, 158, 175, 197–8, 255, 325, 350, 356, 363, 366
corrupters of morals, portrayed as 122–6, 133–7, 139, 140
dhimma, laws of (pact of protection granted to Jews) *see* dhimma, laws of (pact of protection granted to Jews)
education of in Maghreb and Middle East 175–9, 280
exilarchs (leaders of the exile) 44, 47–8, 52, 76, 183
geonim see geonim
halakhah (path to live a Jewish life) 38, 91
holy man (kabbalist, *tzaddik*) 38
Israel and *see* Israel
Jewish-Muslim symbiosis *see* symbiosis, Judeo-Islamic
Jewish population by country (2021) *303*
Jews in non-Arab Muslim-majority lands tend to fare better, except for Afghanistan *304*
Judaism and *see* Judaism
Karaite (who do not accept the Talmud) 39, 43, 48–9, 53–4, 92, 158, 184, 187, 244–5, 318, 321, 326
Khazar kingdom and rule over Muslims 60–73
Muhammad and *see* Muhammad
Nazism in Europe and the Middle East (1933–45) and 193–248
origins of relations between Muslims and, seventh-century Arabia 15–16
Ottoman Empire and *see* Ottoman Empire
philosophy, development of 46, 49, 51–2, 87–97

poverty of 38, 170, 176, 177, 186, 338, 348, 362
Qur'an and *see* Qur'an
rabbinic 39, 42, 47, 48, 50, 73, 76, 89, 93, 146, 158, 161, 179, 184, 326, 358
Sephardic *see* Sephardic Jews
sexual relations with Christian or Muslim women 3, 56, 100–102, 111, 123, 136, 139–40
stateless 186, 221, 227, 241, 242, 245, 246, 316–17, 322, 326, 342–3
tolerance, golden ages and interfaith utopias between Jews and Muslims, myth of *see* symbiosis, Judeo-Islamic
usury and 35, 101
yellow badges, required to wear 54, 252
yellow fabric on turbans, required to wear 56
yellow Star of David, required to wear 216–17
Zionism and *see* Zionism
jizya (poll tax) 7, 30, 32–3, 150, 159, 175
Jordan 26, 274, 277, 278, 281, 283, 286–90, 293, 294, 296, 342, 365
Joseph (biblical figure) 26, 77
Jacob ben Sasportas 151
Joseph Interfaith Foundation 378
Joseph, Khazar ruler 63–4
Juda ben Duran 168
Judaism
anti-Judaism 110, 189–90, 196
Christianity as divine fulfilment of 34
converts to 27–8, 62–5, 71, 102, 109, 131, 245
cremation and 129
festivals and feast days *see individual name*
Israel, centrality of in 252, 289, 295
Jew as someone who practices 15
Kabbalah (mysticism) *see* Kabbalah
Karaite 39, 43, 48–9, 53–4, 92, 158, 184, 187, 244–5, 318, 321, 326
messianism and *see* messianism

Index

Mishnah (oral law) 38, 53, 91
Muhammad and 17–18, 23
origins of 36–7
philosophy, development of 46, 49, 51–2, 87–97
rabbinic 39, 42, 47, 48, 50, 73, 76, 89, 93, 146, 158, 161, 179, 184, 326, 358
similarities with Islam 1–2, 37–45, 110–11
symbiosis with Islam *see* symbiosis, Judeo-Islamic
synagogue and *see* synagogue
Talmud and *see* Talmud
Torah and *see* Torah
See also individual nation name
Judeo-Arabic 15, 51, 53, 96, 152, 173, 180, 186, 188, 214, 345
Judeo-Persian 51
judezmo (a Jewish Spanish, mainly Castilian) 113

K
Ka'ba, Mecca 38
Kabbalah (mysticism) 96, 113, 116, 136
Kabilio, Joseph 219
Kabir, Ibrahim al- 328, 336
Kahanoff, Jacqueline 323
  'My Brother Ishmael' 377
  Rebel, My Brother 323–4
kahina (diviner, soothsayer) 28–9, 307
Kahn, Zadoc 207
kalam (defence apologetics, or the science of discourse) 88
Kara Mustafa Pasha, Grand Vizier 140
Karaçelebizade Abdül Aziz Efendi, Shaykh al-Islam: *Ravzatü'l-ebrâr fi'l Tarih* (*The Gardens of Fruit*) 130
kara'im or *bene mikra* (known as Karaites) 53
Karim, Agha Abd al- 342
Kassem, Abdel Karim 340
Kataeb (Phalange) 195
Kataeb al-Shabab 228, 229

Kattan, Naim 331
Kaylani, Rashid Ali al- 228–9, 231
Kedourie, Elie 229
Kedourie, Rabbi Sasson 231, 336–7
Kedourie family 188
Kemaleddin Sami Pasha 240
Kent, Necdet 246
Khalifa, Elie 207–8
Khalili, Professor Sir Nasser David 379
Khaybar 22, 23
Khazaria/Khazar kingdom 60–76, 112, 245, 283
Khomeini, Ayatollah Ruhollah 296, 299
kibbutzim 262, 284, 285, 329
Killis, Ya'kub ibn 55
kira (Greek: dame) 126–34, 139, 140–42
Kira, Esther 117
Kırklareli 235
Kléber, Jean-Baptiste 158
Knafo, M.I. 213–14; *Les Hitlériques* 213–14
Knolle, Mireille 368
Koç, Vehbi 238
Kook, Rabbi Zvi Yehuda 297
Korkud, Salahattin 243
Korkut, Derviš 219–20
Kotby, Dr Nasser 200
Krivine, Alain 364
Krupp 243
Kufa, Iraq 43
Kurdistan 62, 227, 340–42
Kurds 62, 132, 227, 328, 334–5, 339, 340–42
Kyiv 70, 71, 242

L
Laghouat 169
Laloum, Edgar 378
Lanzarote 110
Lausanne Peace Conference (1923) 232
Laylat al-Tawhid ('Unity of the Divine') 54
Le Pen, Jean-Marie 365

471

League against Zionism 227
League for Combating Zionism 331–2
League of Nations 227, 273, 274, 327
Lebanon 278, 286, 287, 293, 297, 303, 312, 315–16
Leo III, Emperor of Byzantium 62
Leo IV, 'Leo the Khazar' 62
León, Spain 97, 99, 103
León, Moses de: *Zohar (Book of Splendour)* 96
Léon Réne Sultan, of Algeria 331
Levantism 352
Leven, Narcisse 263
Lévy, Adolphe 307
Lévy, Benny (Pierre Victor) 325, 364
Lévy, Bernard-Henri 366
Lévy, Catherine 364
Levy, Eliaho 147
Lévy, Léo 364–5
Lévy, Simon 359
Lévy, William 307
Lévyne, Rabbi Emmanuel 364
Lewis, Bernard: *The Jews of Islam* 10, 37
Leyris, Raymond Raoul (Shaykh Raymond) 306–7
Liberal Party 276
Libya 27, 28, 57, 223, 303, 315
Likud Party 295, 296, 298
Lisbon, Portugal 108, 150
Livornese Jews 148, 159, 160, 161, 166
Lloyd George, David 269–70
Łódź, Poland 242
London
  Conference of St James (1939) 278–9
  Islamophobia incidents in 374, 378
  Jewish emigration to/life in 1, 147, 148–53, 166–7, 181, 182, 184, 256, 257, 261, 327, 378
  pro-Palestine marches in 373
  Stock Exchange 167
  synagogues 150–52, 166–7, 183
Lovers of Zion (Hovevei Zion) 256
Luria, Isaac ben Solomon 116
Lyautey, Louis-Hubert-Gonzalve 179, 205
Lydda, Israel 284, 285

M

Maadi, Mohammed el- 207, 208
Macnin, Meir 149–50, 152–3
Madrid Peace Conference (1991) 294
Maghreb 27, 34, 113, 143, 176, 179, 196, 207, 280, 360–63, 365, 366
Mahdi 42–3, 144
Mahdiyya, Abraham ben Yiju al- 58
Maimonides (Musa ibn Maimun, or Rambam) 57, 59, 87, 89, 90–97, 114, 200, 205, 379
  Mishneh Torah 91
  The Epistle on Yemen/Epistle on Martyrdom 93
  The Guide of the Perplexed 92
  Treatise on Logic 91
Maimonides, Abraham 93–5, 97
Maimonides Interfaith Foundation 379
Maimran, Abraham 146
majlis (gathering) 89
Makaci, Kaddour 209
Maksan, Sultan Habbus ibn 77
Málaga, Spain 84, 109
Mamluks 55, 56, 59, 253
Manuel I, King of Portugal 103, 107–8
Maoists 315, 325, 363–5
Mapai (Labour) party 298
maqama (rhymed prose and rhymed poetry) 80
marabout of Dila 144
Marcus, Hugo 197–8
Marrakesh, Morocco 75, 90, 98, 108, 144, 145, 149, 152, 179, 358
Marseille, France 148–9, 181, 203, 246, 319, 360, 361–5, 367
Marudes, Palomba 249
Marwan II, Umayyad Caliph 63
Marxism 262, 300, 315, 323, 325, 364
Mary, mother of Jesus (biblical figure) 16, 40

Index

Marzuq, Moshe 321
Mashallah 48
Masons 171, 267
Maurice of Nassau, Prince of Orange 108
Mecca 16, 19, 20, 21–2, 38, 40, 41, 96, 228, 299
Mecnin, Meir (Meyer Ouaknine) 147
Medina 19, 20, 21, 22, 23, 25, 40, 41, 42, 164, 283, 299
   Pact of Medina 20–21, 25, 30–33
Medina, Chief Rabbi Samuel 114
Mehdi Bey, Ottoman governor of Jerusalem 266
Mehmed II, Sultan of the Ottoman Empire 119, 120, 124–6
Mehmed III, Sultan of the Ottoman Empire 127
Mehmed IV, Sultan of the Ottoman Empire 130, 132, 137, 138–41
Mehmed VI, Sultan of the Ottoman Empire 232
Mehmed Agha, Silahdar Fındıklılı 140
Meknes, Morocco 146, 215, 313, 345, 358
Melilla, Spain 107
mellah (Moroccan term for walled Jewish quarter within or near the medina) 143–6, 187, 280, 311, 357
Memmi, Albert 302
Menasce family 158, 185, 186
Menasce, Ya'qub 185
Mendès-France, Pierre 305, 363
Mendes, Don Alvaro (Salomon ibn Yaesh) 115
Menemencioğlu, Numan 239
Menocal, María: *The Ornament of the World: How Muslims, Jews, and Christians Created a Culture of Tolerance in Medieval Spain* 86–7
Menou, General Abdallah Jacques 158
Merinid dynasty 143, 147
Mesopotamia 41, 227
Messas, Rabbi Shalom 314–15
messianism 89, 120, 137, 138, 296, 297, 298

Metatron 44
mezid (deliberate sinner) 144
Michael, Sami (Salah Mujalid) 330, 333–5, 345
migration. *See individual nation name*
mimuna (festival of good fortune) 143
Mirvis, Chief Rabbi Sir Ephraim 375, 379
Mishkenot Sha'ananim (Peaceful Habitation) 167
Mitterrand, François 365
Mizrahim 346
Mohammed V, Sultan of Morocco 314
Mohammed VI, Sultan of Morocco 358–99
Mohammed, Moulay 146
Moncef Bey, Bey of Tunis 201
Mongols 56
monotheism 16, 17, 27, 28, 34, 36, 41, 52, 64–5, 95, 98
Montefiore, Moses Haim 166–7, 174–5
Mordecai, Persian vizier 131
Morgenthau, Henry 217
Moriah, Mount 41
Morinaud, Émile 208
Moriscos (converted Muslims) 105–7, 109–10, 115
Morocco 44–5, 58, 65, 145, 147–53, 160, 169, 185, 188, 205, 289, 331, 362, 367, 368, 383
   Abraham Accords, signs (2020) 358
   AIU in 175–9, 309, 346, 358–60
   Arab League, joins (1958) 314
   Code of Nationality 358
   Communist Party (MCP) 310
   education in 176–7, 178–9
   First World War and 203–4
   Foundation of Judeo-Moroccan Cultural Patrimony (FPCJM) 358, 359
   independence (1956) 309, 312–13, 356
   Israel, migration of Jews to 309–15, 345, 346, 358
   Jewish kingdoms in 27

Jewish population (2021) 303
Jews bilingual in Arabic and Amazigh live in Atlas 29
Jews persecuted in Spain and Portugal take refuge in 6, 106–10, 115, 137
Maimonides in 91, 92
mellah in 143–6
persecution of Jews in 143, 144, 153, 174–5
rise of Jews in 106–10, 115, 137, 142–3
presence of Jews valued in 356–9
royal merchants, Jews as 147–53
Second World War and 203–6, 213–17, 224
Sephardic Jews emigrate to London from 151–2
support for Jews after independence within 312–14, 356
trade and 107–9, 141–53, 166, 383
Zionist movement in 309–10
See also individual place name
Morsi, Mohammed 351
Moses (biblical figure) 2, 16, 17, 18, 23, 36, 38, 42, 54, 59, 60, 87, 105, 131, 234, 250, 372, 379
Moses ben Joseph Hamon 117, 142
mosque 144, 146, 191, 220, 250, 375, 378, 380
    Abu Dhabi 379
    Al-Andalus 75, 98, 105, 106
    Al-Aqsa 40, 95
    Berlin 197–8
    Grand Mosque of Paris 203–7
    Khazar 68–70, 112
    Kutubiyya (Booksellers' Mosque), Seville 98
    Sarajevo 218
    Valide Sultan Mosque, Istanbul 132–3
Mosul, Iraq 62, 227, 342, 343
Moulay Abderrahmane, Sultan of Morocco 147
Moulay Ahmed al-Mansur, Sultan of Morocco 145–6

Moulay Ismail, Sultan of Morocco 146, 147
Moulay Rashid, Sultan of Morocco 144
Moulay Slimane, Sultan of Morocco 146
Moulay Sulayman, Sultan of Morocco 144, 150
Moulay Zaidan, Sultan of Morocco 108
Moulay Yazid, Sultan of Morocco 144
Mouthy, Nathan 169
Mu'adh, Sa'd ibn 22–3
Mu'tazilites 49, 53, 92
mufti 39, 93, 194, 195–6, 197, 200, 207, 228, 230, 275, 276, 278, 279, 281, 289–90
muhajirun (migrants) 19
Muhammad Abdullah, Dr Shaykh 198
Muhammad, Prophet 93, 111, 136, 146, 250, 283, 300, 303, 331, 347, 367, 370
    Abraham and 17–18
    death of 10, 25, 33
    hadith (oral tradition) 38, 370
    Haram al-Sharif and 40
    hijrah (migration) 19
    'Isawiyya and 43
    Jewish Arabs in Arabia, first meets 12
    Jewish tribes and 19–25, 41–2
    Jewish women and 23
    Jews assist armies of 25
    Jews believe is Messiah 24
    Jews to accept call, expects 16–17, 36
    jizya and 32–3
    merchant 35
    night journey 17, 40, 96
    Pact or Constitution of Medina/Pact of Medina and 20, 25, 32
    pray in direction of Jerusalem, instructs followers to 17
    Qur'an and 16–17, 34, 38, 41–2
    starts to preach 3, 16
Muhammad V, Sultan of Granada 99
Mulay Abd al-Malik, Sultan of Morocco 145
Munabbih, Wahb ibn 24
munafiqun (hypocrites, false converts) 20

Index

Munich Olympics terror attacks (1972) 290, 365
Murad III, Sultan of the Ottoman Empire 115, 127
Murad IV, Sultan of the Ottoman Empire 130
Murcia, Spain 96, 102
Musa, Nebi 250
music 11, 30, 45, 46, 148, 187
    Arabo-Andalusian 77, 78, 80–81, 249, 306–7, 357
    Jewish 254, 313, 343, 348
Muslim Brotherhood 143, 221–2, 224, 225, 299, 317–20, 351, 370
Muslims
    Al-Andalus and *see* Al-Andalus
    antagonistic view of Jewish-Muslim relations, myth of *see* symbiosis, Judeo-Islamic
    colonialism and *see individual nation name*
    conversion to Judaism 102
    holy man (Sufi, *marabout*) 38
    Israel and *see* Israel
    Jews as allies of/participation in battles against Christian oppressors 8, 11–12, 15, 20, 21, 22–3, 25, 27–8, 34, 42, 55–6, 74, 106, 113–15, 161, 168, 258
    Khazar kingdom/Jews ruling over 46–73
    mosque and *see* mosque
    Muhammad and *see* Muhammad
    Nazism and 193–248
    origins of 2–3, 15–45
    Ottoman Empire and *see* Ottoman Empire
    pacts of alliance and protection with Jews, seventh-thirteenth centuries 15–45
    Qur'an and *see* Qur'an
    as saviour of the Jew 4, 5, 6–7, 25, 26, 106, 116, 118, 121, 138, 141, 165, 235, 240, 254, 306, 352–3, 354, 356
    similarities with Judaism 1–2, 37–45, 110–11
    symbiosis, Judeo-Islamic *see* symbiosis, Judeo-Islamic
    term 17
    terrorism/terrorist attacks and *see* terrorism/terrorist attacks
    tolerance, golden ages and interfaith utopias between Jews and, myth of *see* symbiosis, Judeo-Islamic
    Zionism and *see* Zionism
    See also Islam *and individual nation name*
Mustafa Reşid Pasha, Ottoman Grand Vizier 161
mutakallimun (philosophers) 88, 92
muwashshah (poetry) 80–81
myths
    antagonistic view of Jewish-Muslim relations 5, 7–8, 10, 12, 25, 271, 300, 321, 331, 339, 346–9, 362, 370
    tolerance, golden ages and interfaith utopias between Jews and Muslims 4–5, 6–7, 10, 12, 25, 33, 75, 76, 86 118–19, 232, 260, 291, 300, 305, 353, 354
Mzab, Algeria 160, 172

N

Nablus, Israel 277
Naghrela ha-Nagid, Joseph ibn 84–5, 87, 99
Naghrela ha-Nagid, Samuel ibn 76, 77, 79, 83–4, 85–7, 99
nagid or *shaykh al-yahud* (leader of Jewry) 54, 76, 77, 144, 146
Nahhas Pasha, Mustafa 224
Nahum, Chief Rabbi of Egypt, Haim 222, 224, 225, 226, 232, 259–60, 325–6
Naima, Mustafa: *Tarih-i Naima or Ravdat-ül-Hüseyn fi Hülâsâ-i Ahbâr-il-Hâfikayn (Garden of al-Huseyin, or, Choicest News of East and West* 133–4, 139

Najara, Rabbi Jacob 137
Najd, Arabia 16
Napoleon III, Emperor of the French 164
Nashashibi family 159, 249, 275–6
nasi (prince, descendant of King David) 76–7, 180
Nasi (Mendes), Doña Gracia 115–16, 181
Nasi, Duke of Naxos, Don Joseph (João Migues) 115
Nasrid dynasty 98–9, 103, 106
Nassar, Najib 263
Nasser, Colonel Gamal Abdel 319, 321–4, 363
Natan of Gaza 137
nationalism/nationalist movements 3, 5, 29, 306
   anti-Semitism, emergence of and 191, 192, 194, 196, 197, 204, 215, 221, 228, 255–6
   Arab nationalism, emergence of 255–6, 283, 284, 301, 333
   drives Arab and Jewish peoples apart/ religious nationalism aggravates mutual alienation 383
   Egypt 196, 221, 223, 255–6, 321–6, 352
   Iraq 228, 229, 230, 231
   Maghrebi Jews' conflict with Muslims, myth of and 362
   Morocco 310, 311, 313, 314, 356
   Palestine 228, 229, 262–3, 268, 274, 276, 278, 281, 284, 291, 299, 301
   religious nationalist movements 297–9
   Turkish Republic 232, 266
   Zionism *see* Zionism
Navarino, battle of (1827) 159
Nawa, Syria 25
Nazareth, Palestine/Israel 278, 282, 285
Nazism 4, 6–8, 10, 193–248, 270, 277, 279–81, 304, 321, 329, 347, 349, 363, 364
   Al-Husseini and 193–7, 200, 207, 209, 228, 229, 275–6
   Albania and 220–21
   fascist Arab movements 196–7
   Germany, Muslims and Jews in and 197–200
   Iraq and 227–32
   North Africa/Vichy and 200–217, 221–4
   Sarajevo and 218–20
   Turkey and 232–48
   Zionism and 213, 222, 224–7, 229, 231, 232
Nebuchadnezzar II, King of Neo-Babylonian Empire 47
Negev Desert 278, 282–3, 346
Nelson, Lord 158
neo-Platonism 87–8, 94–6
Netanyahu, Benjamin 193, 296, 371, 372
Netherlands 108–10, 115, 145, 146, 150–51
Neve Tzedek 265
New York Times 354
Niknam, Mehri 379
Ninio, Marcelle 321
Nisa-Nashim 379
Niyego, Elza 233
Noah (biblical figure) 39–40
Noble Decree of the Rose Garden (1839) 162
Noguès, General 214, 216, 217
North Africa
   colonial powers alignment with Jews in 179, 183, 188–9, 272
   French launch colonial empire in 157–8
   Jews, origins of in 26–30
   Moriscos exile in 106
   poverty and destitution of Jews in 176, 177, 186
   Second World War and 203, 204–5, 207, 209, 212, 223, 224, 228
   synagogue and 59
   Vichy regime and 201, 209, 212, 228
   See also individual nation name
Nous Réconcilier (Let's Reconcile) 378
Novgorod, Russia 71
Nuqrashi, Fahmi al- 317–19

Index

O
Ohana, Jo (Joseph) 313
Ohana, Paul 313
Opium Wars
  First (1839–42) 181–2
  Second (1858) 182
Oppenheimer family 149
Oran, Algeria 151, 160, 169, 173, 176, 264, 306, 307, 366
Organisation armée secrète (Secret Army Organisation, OAS) 307–8
Orhan, Sultan of Ottoman Empire 11, 112
Orientalisation 273
Ottoman Empire 59, 149, 157, 164, 168, 174, 180, 181, 218, 227, 341, 355, 356
  anti-Semitism, origins of and 189–91
  Crimean War (1853–6) and 163, 168, 181
  falls (1922) 232
  First World War and 194, 232, 236, 243–4, 266, 268, 270
  great powers take territories from in North Africa 157–9, 161, 165, 186
  Jews help conquer Bursa 11
  Imperial Reform Edict (1856) 162–3
  Jews persecuted in Spain and Portugal find refuge in 6, 104, 106, 108–11, 112–13, 247
  Muhammad Ali's defeat of 157–9
  Muslim chronicles, Jewish characters/anti-Jewish sentiment expressed in 120–42
  Palestine and 252–62, 264–8, 270, 273–5, 284, 289, 317
  peaceful coexistence between Muslims and Jews in, myth of 6, 11, 112–42, 247, 254, 258, 352–3
  reform decrees make all subjects equal under law 161–3
  Sephardic elite become Ottoman dynasty's trusted allies 114–16
Oued Nini, Battle of (698) 28
Oujda, Morocco 27, 311

Outmezguine, Eliahu 146–7
Ouzzan family 201
Oz, Amos 298

P
Pact of Security 163
Pact or Constitution of Medina 20–21, 25, 30–33
Paquda, Bahya ibn 96
  Guidebook to the Duties of the Heart (al–Hidaya ila fara'id al-qulub) 96–7
Palace of the Lions, Granada 99
Palestine 2, 9, 27, 29, 38, 55, 57, 58, 185, 227, 238, 377–8, 381
  Arab-Israeli War (1948) and 283–8, 296, 317, 329, 335, 349
  Arab-Israeli War (1967) and 288–90, 293–4, 296, 326, 340, 362–3
  Al-Husseini and 193–6, 229
  Algerian Jews emigrate to 213
  Arab Jews and 251, 347
  Ashkenazi Jews and 72
  Balfour Declaration (1917) 268–74, 279, 282, 290
  British Mandate of Palestine 194, 217–18, 231, 270, 272–9, 282–5, 342–3
  Camp David Accords (2000) 294
  Declaration of Principles (1993) 294
  dhimma pact and 252
  Egypt and 53, 221–6, 317
  Jewish settlements in 293, 296–7
  faiths of inhabitants 284
  France and 363–5, 368
  Gaza War (2023–) 368–71, 373–5
  Hebron, Jews help Arabs conquer (638) 11
  Holocaust and 280, 281
  increasing conflict between Jews and Muslims in (1936–9) 228, 276–8
  interfaith utopia myth and 7
  Iraq and 327–36, 339, 341–2

Islamist groups and 294–6
Judah Halevi in 80
Law of Return (1950) 287
Lebanon, refugees in 294, 315
nakba (catastrophe), loss of as 287
Madrid Peace Conference (1991) 294
Mamluks and 56, 253
messianism of Jews and 296–7
Morocco and 310, 313, 359, 360
Muhammad's armies conquer 22, 25, 26
Muslim citizens ruled according to martial law (1948–66) 287–8
Muslim communities emerge in 61
Nasi and 115
October 7 terrorist attacks on Israel and (2023) 296, 368–71, 373, 375
Oslo Accords (1993) 294, 298, 357
Ottoman Empire and 116, 252–66, 270–71
Palestine Liberation Organisation (PLO) *see* Palestine Liberation Organisation
PLO/PFLP terror attacks 292–3, 299, 264–5, 367
refugees, most Muslims in become 287, 289
Sargon II exiles Jews from northern 62
UN and *see* United Nations
uprising (intifada), Jabaliya refugee camp (1987) 293
uprising (intifada), second (2000) 295–6
Zionism and 255–66, 291
Palestine Liberation Organisation (PLO) 290, 292–4, 297–9, 325, 357, 364–5, 371
Palestinian Arab National Party 276
Palestinian Authority 296
Palestinian Front for the Liberation of Palestine (PFLP) 292, 299, 264–5, 367
Pallache, Samuel 108–10
Papo, Donkica 219–20
Parienté family 174, 345, 381
Parienté, Moses 174

Paris, France 163, 176, 200, 209, 246, 255, 257, 261, 305, 311–12, 315, 360, 363, 365, 366
Grand Mosque of 203–7
Muslim terror attacks in 367–8
Sababa (Joy of Living) 378
synagogues 292, 367
Parti du peuple algérien (Algerian People's Party) 212
Passover (Pesach) 16, 29, 42, 54, 105, 143, 207, 219, 251, 254, 311, 341, 359, 374
Seder (ritual meal) 16, 219, 251
Patriarchs and Matriarchs 11, 39
Paul, St. 18
Pečenegs 66
Peel Commission 277–8
Peker, Recep 236
Pepeyi, Nihat Halûk 243
Period of Reforms (*Tanzimat*) 161
Persia 24, 25–6, 43, 48, 51, 58, 62, 65, 121, 131, 179, 181, 372
Pétain, Marshal 210, 211
Petrović, Jozo 219
Peyrouton, Marcel 210, 211
Philip II, King of Spain 115
Philip III, King of Spain 105
philosophy 35, 45, 46, 49, 51–2, 73, 77–9, 87–97, 191, 213, 364, 379
Phoenicians 26–7, 281
pilgrimage 16, 30, 38, 44, 80, 229, 250, 261, 270–71, 309, 350, 380, 381
Pisces 314
Plato: *Republic and Laws* 88
poetry 30, 44–5, 53, 54, 55, 77–8, 80–82, 84–5, 88, 90, 94–6, 98, 99, 383
pogroms 6, 201
Algeria (1870) 173
Farhud (1941), Iraq 228–32, 329–30, 342
Kristallnacht, Germany (9–10 November 1938) 239–40, 241
Oujda (1948) 311
Spain (1391) 103

Index

Turkey (1934) 230, 235, 236, 354
Poland 71–3, 115, 165, 194, 195, 197, 242, 243, 244, 255, 338
Polanski, Zack 374
poll tax 7, 25, 30, 32–3
polygamy 95, 176
Porat Yossef 264, 289
Portugal 6, 103–4, 107–8, 110, 114, 121, 137, 145, 146, 147, 150–52, 180, 292, 378, 381
prostitution 102, 136
Protocols of the Elders of Zion, The 323, 354–5, 371
Purim, festival of 130, 144, 145, 217, 249, 372
Purim de los Cristianos 145

Q

Qa'uqji, Fawzi al- 277, 283–6
Qaddah, Maymun ibn 44
qadi (Islamic judge) 39, 84–5, 900
Qarawiyine 144
qasida (poetry) 80
Qassam, Izz al-Din al- 276–7, 296
Qattawi, Aslan Bey 186
Qattawi, Ya'qub Menasce 185–6
Qissarya 144
Qur'an 16–18, 31–4, 38, 40–42, 49, 51, 54, 60, 68, 70, 77, 79, 96, 129, 131, 300, 301, 311, 370
Qurayshi tribe 19
Qutb, Sayyid 296; *Our Struggle with the Jews* 299–301

R

Rabat, Morocco 107, 312, 314, 357, 358
Rabin, Yitzhak 294, 295, 298
Radhaniya 65
Rajab, Hind 375
Ramadan 40, 137, 311, 341
Raşid Efendi, Mehmed: *Tarih-i Râşid* 139
Ravaya, Jucef 102

Ravensbrück concentration camp, Germany 243
Rebecca (biblical figure) 11, 39
Reconquista 4
Red Crescent 249
Red Palace ('al-Hamra'), Granada 99
Régis, Max 173
Rembrandt: 'Man in Oriental Costume' 110
Renaissance 52, 90, 98
Renan, Ernst 191
Reşid Pasha, Grand Vizier 166
Revolutionary Communist League 364
Rhodes, Greece 166, 246
Rifaat, Adil 325, 363–4
riots 56, 102, 159–60, 173, 208, 223, 224, 229, 251, 260, 275, 310, 312, 319, 328, 352, 362, 363
ritual sacrifice of animals 38
Rodinson, Maxime 364
Roland (née Marzouk), Germaine 206
Romania 165, 237–8, 260, 338
Roman Empire 25, 26, 27, 59, 61, 62, 71, 251
Rommel, Erwin 223–4
Rosenthal, Joseph 226
Rothschild family 167, 261, 269
Rothschild, 2nd Baron Rothschild, Lionel Walter 269
Rouleau, Eric 325
Rumi, Jalal al-Din 95–6
Russia 61, 65, 119, 159, 163, 165, 168, 226, 239, 244, 255, 257, 260, 264, 270

S

Sa'adian dynasty 108, 145, 146, 147, 351
Saba al-Himyari, Abdallah ibn 24, 42–4
Saba'iyya 43–4
Sabbagh, Colonel Salah al-Din al- 228
Sabra and Shatila refugee camps, Beirut 294
Sachsenhausen concentration camp, Germany 198, 243–4

479

Sadat, Anwar 298, 350, 377
Sadi, Abu Umar Ahmad ibn Muhammad ibn- 46
Sadiq, Yehuda 330, 332–3, 335
Sadok Bey, Bey of Tunis 164
Safed, Palestine 115, 116, 167, 251, 253–4, 264, 265, 276, 282–3, 285
Safi, Morocco 148, 174–5
Safiya (wife of Muhammad) 23
Safiye Sultan (mother of Mehmed III) 127, 132
Said, Nuri 231, 327–8, 336
Saint-Jean-de-Luz, France 109
Saladin 251
Salam, Abdullah ibn 17
Salé, Morocco 106, 107, 110, 146, 215
Salonica, Ottoman Empire 113, 115, 116, 136, 138, 211, 259, 264
Samandar (Khazar city) 68–9
Samkarsh (Khazar city) 65
San Remo Conference (1920) 273
Sanu, Yaqub 255
Saqaliba (Slavs) 68, 69
Saqsin 112
Saraçoğlu, Şükrü 237, 239
Sara (wife of Shabbatai Tzevi) 136
Sarah (biblical figure) 2, 11, 18, 37, 38, 39, 64, 83, 377
Sarajevo 218–19
Sardari, Abdol Hossein 246
Sargon II, King of Neo-Assyrian Empire 62
Sassoon, Abdallah/Sir Albert 181, 182, 183
Sassoon, David 180–84, 187, 188
Sassoon, Edward 183
Sassoon, Elias 181, 182
Sassoon, Jacob David 183
Sassoon, Philip Gustave 270
Sassoon, Reuben 181, 182
Sassoon, Shaykh Sassoon ben Saleh 180
Sassoon, Siegfried 181
Saul, King 19, 371–2

Sawt al-Haqq (*The Voice of Truth*) 231
Schechter, Solomon 64
Schwartz, Hillel 319, 325
Sebastian I, King of Portugal 145
Second World War (1939–45) 5, 6, 8, 9, 177, 192, 193–248, 305, 307, 309–10, 316, 329, 359
Secrets of Rabbi Shimon Bar Yochai, The 26
Seidenberg, Avraham 320
Selaniki, Mustafa Efendi 127–8
Selim I, Sultan of the Ottoman Empire 120, 134–5
Selim II, Sultan of the Ottoman Empire 115
Sémach, Yomtov 177
Sephardic Jews 8, 87, 373
  Algeria and 160, 171, 305
  Berlin and 246–7
  Egypt and 158, 165, 184–6, 222, 316, 318
  France and 362, 363
  Khazar kingdom and 73
  London and 150–52, 166, 167
  Morocco and 108, 147, 346
  Ottoman Empire and 6, 113–17, 119–20, 122, 126, 132
  Palestine and 252, 253–5, 262, 264, 283, 289, 381
  Sarajevo and 218–20
  Turkish Republic and 233
Serfaty, Abraham: *Souffles* 315
Serfaty, Judah 174
Sertel, Dönme Sabiha 238
Sétif, Algeria 307; massacre (1945) 212
Seville, Spain 27, 74, 77, 97–8, 103
Sfez, Batto 163–4
Shabbat 22, 57, 58, 64, 65, 116, 136–9, 151, 181, 337, 341, 368
Shalmanaser, King of Neo-Assyrian Empire 62
Shalom Achshav (Peace Now) 297
Shalom, Rabbi Joseph 114
Shalom, Saleh 339

Index

Shalom-Salem 366
Shalom, Yossef Abraham 264
shamanism 64–5, 341
Shanghai, China 181–2, 187–8
Shaprut, Hasdai ibn (Abu Yusuf) 53, 63–4, 76–7
sharia law 39, 128, 300
Sharon, Ariel 295, 296
Shas (*Shomrei Sepharad*, the Guardians of the Sephardim) 289
Shas, Chief Rabbi Ovadia Yosef 289
Shaul, Anwar 330–31
Shlaim, Avi: *Memoirs of an Arab-Jew* 348
shofar (ram's horn blown on the Jewish High Holy Days) 17, 288
Shohat, Ella 347, 348
Shriqui, Mordechai 147
Sidi Mohammed, Bey of Tunis 163, 175
Sidi Mohamed ben Abdallah, Sultan of Morocco 144, 147, 149
Sidi Mohammed ben Youssef, Sultan of Morocco 214, 311–12
Siete partidas (law code) 99–100
Sijilmassa 30
Silahdar 142
Simchat Torah 368
Simhun, Matiah: *Qasida di Hitler* 214
Sinwar, Yahya 372
sipahi (cavalry troops) 128, 129, 194
Siyavush Pasha 218
Slat al Fassiyine 359
slavery 32, 58, 58, 61, 65, 69–71, 101, 106, 135, 157, 171, 219, 243, 260
Smith, George Adam 270
Socialist Federation of Algeria (SFIO) 307
Sokolov, Nahum 273–4
Solidarité 325
Song of Songs 88
SOS Racisme 365
Soviet Union 197, 239, 281, 282, 283, 316, 322, 329–31, 333

Spain 6, 11, 31, 44, 50, 52, 53, 58, 72, 73, 74–111, 112, 167, 315
 Al-Andalus *see* Al-Andalus
 Arab conquest of 28, 74–5, 112, 383
 Bayezid II sends ships to pick up expelled Jews, myth of 119, 126
 Christian kingdoms' treatment of Jews and Muslims after fall of Al-Andalus 99–116, 119, 121–2, 132, 137, 142, 150, 299, 355, 356
 Conversos (New Christians) (converted Jews) *see* Conversos
 Inquisition 6, 103, 105, 109, 356
 Jews expelled from (1492) 6, 103–7, 117, 119, 121, 122, 125, 126, 137, 145, 233, 247, 249
 judezmo (Jewish Spanish) 113
 Moriscos (converted Muslims) 105–7, 109–10, 115
 Morocco and 174–5
 Republicans in 203
 synagogues outside Spain, Spanish 150, 151–2, 292, 378
Spark 227
SS 194, 195, 197, 200, 209, 218, 239, 242–4
Star of David 216–17, 219, 373, 380
Steinke, Ronen 200
Stora, Benjamin 208, 363
Stora, Élie 307
Story of Zionist Espionage in Egypt 321
Strait of Gibraltar 74, 81, 107
Struma 238
Sudan 27, 145
Suez Canal 164, 312, 321–2, 324, 325
Sufism 38, 39, 44, 93–7, 110, 124, 135, 136, 142, 144, 163, 220
Suleiman I, Sultan of the Ottoman Empire 115, 116, 120, 121, 254
sultanate of women 133, 139
Sumbal, Samuel 147
Sunullah Efendi, Shaykh al-Islam 128
Supreme Arab Committee in Palestine 332

Supreme Masonic Council of France 171
Susannah, Operation (1954) 320–21
Suwaidi, Tawfiq al- 337
Svyatoslav of Kyiv 70
symbiosis, Judeo-Islamic 1–2, 36–45, 46
   Al-Andalus and, eighth-seventeenth centuries *see* Al-Andalus
   antagonistic view of Jewish-Muslim relations myth and 5, 7–8, 10, 12, 25, 271, 300, 321, 331, 339, 346–9, 362, 370
   collapse of, modern 366–75, 382
   Jewish adoption of Arabic as main factor in 50–51
   promoting today 362–7
   religious symbiosis, seventh-thirteenth centuries 15–45
   secular symbiosis 4, 45, 46–73, 334–5, 363–8, 374
   severed (1789–1914) 157–92
   tolerance, golden ages and interfaith utopias, myth of and 4–5, 6–7, 10, 12, 25, 33, 75, 76, 86 118–19, 232, 260, 291, 300, 305, 353, 354
synagogue 10, 65, 68, 98
   Ahrida synagogue, Istanbul 119
   Al-Andalus 78, 81, 88, 94, 95
   Al-Hakim bi-Amr Allah destroys 54
   Almohad dynasty destroy 75
   Beirut 316
   Ben Ezra synagogue/synagogue of the Palestinians or Levantines, Cairo 58–9, 352
   Beth-Aaron synagogue, Shanghai 188
   Bevis Marks synagogue, London 150–52, 166–7, 183
   Byzantine desecration of 61
   Christian Spain and 99–100, 102, 105, 111
   Danan synagogue, Fez 358–9
   Dar al-Babunaj synagogue, Derbend 69
   El Ghriba synagogue, Djerba 380, 381
   Eliyahu Ha-Navi synagogue, Alexandria 352
   Etz ha-Haim synagogue, Bursa 11, 112
   France, attacks on 292, 365, 367–8
   Fustat 58–9
   geniza 59, 64, 180, 181, 351, 352
   Great Synagogue of Algiers 306–7
   Great Synagogue of the Exilarch, Baghdad 47
   Heaton Park, Manchester 374
   Hebron 11
   Iraq 338, 339
   Jerusalem 159, 254–5, 289, 380
   la-Azama (Synagogue of the Deportees), Marrakesh 145
   London 150–52, 166–7, 182, 183
   Magen David synagogue, Mumbai 183–4
   Masuda Shemtov synagogue, Baghdad 338, 343
   Morocco 144–5, 174, 357–9
   Moses ben Maimon synagogue, Abu Dhabi 379
   Ohel David synagogue, Pune 184
   Ohr Torah Jewish school, Toulouse 367
   Ottoman Empire 112–16, 119–20, 137, 218
   Pina, Christians and Muslims attack (1285) 102
   PLO/PFLP attacks on 292
   Sarajevo 218–19
   service 37, 78, 81, 88, 94, 95, 383
   Turkey 234, 239, 241, 246, 353, 354
   UK, attacks on 373–4
   Zakho 342, 343
Syria 16, 22, 41, 51, 53, 57, 74, 96, 159, 165, 196, 270, 273, 277, 283, 303, 332, 336
   Arab-Israeli war (1948) and 285–7
   Arab-Israeli war (1967) and 288, 296
   Homs, Jews aide Muslim armies against Byzantines in 11
   Muhammad's armies conquer 25–7, 31
   Nuri Said's plan of creating a Greater Syria 327
   United Arab Republic and 324

Index

Vichy and 224, 228

T

Tadjer, Yehouda 338–40
tahrif (distortion, alteration) 41
Tali, Ibrahim 235–6
Talmud 38, 39, 47, 48, 50, 53, 77, 91
Tamghrut 27, 30
Tan (Dawn) 238
Tangier, Morocco 108, 145, 147, 148, 152, 153, 170, 174, 178, 205, 309–10, 358
taqiyya (dissimulating one's true beliefs to avoid persecution) 93
Tardieu, Michel 205
Tarih-i Naima or Ravdat-ül-Hüseyn fi Hülâsâ-I Ahbâr-il-Hâfikayn (Garden of al-Huseyin, or, Choicest News of East and West; c.1697–1704) (Ottoman chronicle) 133–4
Tawfiq Pasha, Khedive (viceroy) of Egypt 164
Tebal (Abitbol), Abi 169
Tel Aviv, Israel 265, 266, 277, 278, 283, 285
Tell MAMA 374
Ten Commandments 93, 234
terrorism/terrorist attacks 9, 208, 290, 294, 299, 306, 307, 318, 324, 339
  France, attacks in (2000–20) 367–8
  Morocco, attacks in (2003) 359–60
  Munich Olympics attacks (1972) 290, 365
  9/11 (2001) 8
  October 7 Hamas attacks on Israel (2023) 296, 368–9, 370, 373, 375
  PLO/PFLP murderous rampage in Europe (1980–86) 292–3, 367
Tétouan, Morocco 106, 107, 110, 144, 145, 146, 148, 175, 178
Tevfik, Ebüzziya: *Millet-i Isra'iliye (The Jewish Nation)* 189–90, 191
Tevfik, Riza 268
Theresienstadt concentration camp 243
Thousand and One Nights 48
Thrace 233, 235–6, 354
Three Kings, Battle of (1578) 145
Tibbon, Yehudah ibn 50–51, 96
Tiberias, Palestine/Israel 116, 125, 167, 263, 264, 265, 282, 285
Tiglath-Pileser III, King of Neo-Assyrian Empire 62
Tishri 17
Tlemcen, Algeria 104, 151, 169, 173, 205
Toledano, Raphael 313
Toledo, Spain 74, 90, 116
tolerance 9, 34, 50, 54, 103, 197, 209, 218, 309, 366, 379, 380
  Islamic law, system of tolerance developed in 30–33
  Morocco, Jews in and 356–60
  myth of 4–7, 10, 12, 21, 25, 33, 75–6, 86–7, 118–19, 232, 260, 291, 300, 305, 353, 354
  Ottomans and 117–18, 125, 168, 258
  Qur'an, Jews allowed to criticise 79
  Palestinian Arabs and 291
  Turkey and 352, 353
  Zionism and 309
Torah 83, 297, 306, 367–9, 379
  Abraham and 37
  Arab Jews in seventh-century Arabia and Yemen and 16–18
  Arabic and 29, 42, 51–4, 56, 60
  Jewish nostalgia for Egypt and 350
  Jewish philosophers and 88, 91, 102
  Judaism based on written law of 38
  Khazars and 64, 69
  October 7 attacks (2023) and 368, 371–2
  Shabbatai Tzevi and 137–8
  Sudan, Jews in and 27
  synagogue and 59, 102, 306, 379
Touat (Morocco) 27
Trabelsi, René 379–80
Trabzon, Turkey 134–5
trade 29, 35, 45, 113, 115, 160, 172–4, 226, 253, 310, 324, 339, 383
  Abbasid Iraq and 49

483

economic relations of trust between Muslims and Jews, medieval period 55–9 Khazars and 61, 68, 70, 71
Morocco and 107–9, 141–53, 166, 383
slave trade 157–8
Sassoon family and 179–85
Second World War and 214
Transjordan 278, 281, 283
Trench, Battle of (627) 22
Tripoli, Libya 11
Trotskyists 363–6
Truman, Harry 281
tujjar sultan (sultan's merchants) 149
Tunisia 55–8, 104, 106, 147, 160, 307, 308, 309, 312, 323–4, 357, 360–62, 368, 380–81
French colonial 177–9, 188–9
Jewish population (2021) 303
Maghrebi Judaism emerges in 27–9
Pact of Security in 163–4
Second World War and 201, 203–4, 206, 224
Turhan, Hatice 132, 133
Türk Pasaportu (*Turkish Passport*) (film) 353
Turkey 6, 11, 104, 190, 200, 222, 230, 232–48, 299, 300, 304, 309, 347, 352–6, 372–3
Turks
Khazar kingdom and 60–76, 112, 245, 283, 382–3
Oghuz 72, 112
Ottoman Empire and 104, 114, 117, 118, 119, 122, 134, 135, 189, 190, 256, 257, 260, 266–7, 268, 272
Sunni Mamluks and 56
Turtushi, Abu Bakr Muhammad al- 31
Tweig, Sha'ul 332
Twentieth Reserve Corps 238
Tzarfati, Itzhak 118–20, 260
Tzevi, Shabbatai 136–9, 151

U

UGSM (General Association of Confederated Trade Unions of Morocco) 310
Uhud, Battle of (625) 22
Ülkümen, Selahattin 246
Umar I, Caliph/Pact of Umar 30–33, 99, 100
Umayyad dynasty 28, 40, 63, 74–6, 97
ummah, or community 20–21, 34
Union of French Jewish Students 366
United Arab Republic (UAR) 324
United Nations (UN) 317, 323, 336
Arafat invited to address General Assembly (1974) 290
Attlee announces decision to hand Palestine to (1947) 281–3
Resolution 181 (partition of Palestine) (1947) 282, 294, 310, 316, 328
Resolution 242 (recognition of Israel as member state) (1949) 286–7, 294
Resolution 247 (calls for Israeli withdrawal from territories it occupied) (1968) 293–4
Resolution 3379 (declares Zionism 'a form of racism and racial discrimination') (1975) 291–3
United States of America (USA) 8, 147, 148, 153, 161, 174, 200, 217, 270, 281, 282, 283, 296, 315, 321, 322, 359
University of Rabat 314
Urabi revolt (1882) 165, 255
Usque, Samuel: *Consolação ás tribulações de Israel* (*The Consolation of the Tribulations of Israel*) 121
Ustaše 218–19
usury 35, 101
Uzunköprü, Turkey 235

V

Vatan (*Fatherland*) 238
Vatandaş! Türkçe Konuş! (*Citizen, Speak Turkish!*) 234

Index

Veil, Simone 206
Veseli, Hamid 220–21
Veseli, Refik 220–21
Veseli, Xhemal 220–21
Victoria, Queen 167, 182
Vikings 63, 65, 69–71
Visigoths 74, 112

W

Wafd (The Delegation) 223, 226
Waffen-SS units 239
Warsaw Uprising (1944) 197, 239
Weinstein, Carmen 351
Weinstein, Esther 351
Weissberg, Jean-Louis 364
Weizmann, Chaim 222–3, 269, 270, 274
Welby, Archbishop of Canterbury, Justin 375
West Bank 278, 282, 286, 287, 288, 293, 296, 297
women
    AIU teachers/directors as first Jewish professional women in Middle East 176
    Believers and 17, 19
    British army in Egypt and 225
    Cairo, Jewish women in 350–51
    Christian Spain and 100–102, 104, 105
    Holocaust and 242, 243
    Nisa-Nashim (Jewish Muslim women's network) 379
    Ottoman Empire and 117, 118, 123–4, 126–8, 133–4, 136, 137, 139, 140, 141
    pro-Palestine marches in London and 373
World Jewish Congress 224
World Organisation of Jews from Arab Countries 347
World Zionist Organisation 271

Y

Yad Vashem 195–6, 219
    'Righteous Among the Nations', Yad Vashem 200, 201, 221
Yalman, Dönme Ahmet Emin 238
Yassin, Shaykh Ahmed 370
Yathrib, Arabia 19, 21
Yellin, Shlomo (Suleiman Effendi) 267
Yemen 15–16, 22, 24–5, 36, 42–3, 58, 92–3, 165, 177, 252, 291, 298, 303, 382
yeshivot (Talmudic academies) 47–8, 50, 53, 188, 381
Yishuv 194, 329
Yom Kippur 17, 40, 314, 371, 374
Young Egypt 196, 222, 225
Yugoslavia 218, 282

Z

Zahal. *See* Israel Defense Forces
Zakho, Kurdistan 340–43
Zamiro, Abraham ben 107–8
Zaragoza, Spain 96, 101, 102
Zarçamodonia 105–6
Zénata 27–8
Zerbib, Itzhak 171
Zermati, David 307
Zermati, Salomon 168
Zilkha, Yusuf Harun: *Zionism: The Enemy of the Arabs and the Jews* 332
Zionism (Jewish nationalism) 5
    Al-Husseini and 194
    Algeria and 213–14, 308
    Arab-Israeli war (1948) and 280, 283, 285–8
    Arafat distinguishes between Zionists and Jews (1975) 291–3
    blamed for ruining relations between Muslims and Jews 7, 8, 9
    Egypt and 221–7, 260, 270, 279, 283, 302, 316–19, 321, 323, 324, 350
    emergence of 72, 227, 255, 256–84
    Erdoğan on 299

Fifth Zionist Congress, Basel (1901) 258
First Zionist Congress, Basel (1897) 252, 256
interfaith utopia myth and 5, 8, 7
Iraq and 229, 231, 232, 302, 327–8
Judah Halevi promoted as proto-Zionist 80
Marxism and 300
Morocco and 309–11, 315, 359
Ninth World Zionist Congress, Hamburg (1909) 260
Palestine and 194, 222, 223, 224–8, 231, 251, 252, 255–84, 290, 327–38, 339, 341, 342

Twentieth Zionist Congress, Zurich 278
UN General Assembly passes resolution (3379) declaring Zionism 'a form of racism and racial discrimination (1975) 291–3
Ziryab (blackbird or lark) (Abu al-Hasan Ali ibn Nafi) 81
Zirid dynasty 77, 84
Ziyad, General Tariq ibn 74
Zoroastrians 7, 27, 131
Zureiq, Constantine 287

PICTURE CREDITS

Masjid al-Qiblatayn, Medina. Photo: © Esra Hacioglu/Anadolu via Getty Images; Qur'an in Judeo-Arabic text, twelfth or thirteenth century, from the Cairo Geniza. Photo: reproduced by kind permission of the Syndics of Cambridge University Library; Édouard Moyse, 'École juive à Miliana, Algérie', 1861. Musée d'art et d'histoire du judaïsme, Paris. Photo: © mahJ/Christophe Fouin; Théodore Chassereriau, 'Intérieur d'école arabe à Constantine', 1846. Musée du Louvre, Paris. Photo: © Scala, Florence, 2026; Ninth-century Moses coin from the Turkish Jewish Khazar kingdom. Photo: Wikimedia Commons; Statue of Musa ibn Maimun, Córdoba, Spain. Photo: © Getty Images; Alhambra's fourteenth-century Palace of the Lions, Granada, Spain. Photo: © Getty Images; Miniature of a Jewish lady from Enderunlu Fazıl's Zenan-name (Book of Women), 1793. Photo: © The Trustees of the British Museum; 'Man in Oriental Costume', Rembrandt van Rijn, 1635. National Gallery of Art, Washington, DC. Photo: Alamy; 'Portrait de Salomon Zermati', Salomon Assus, 1876. Musée d'art et d'histoire du judaïsme, Paris. Photo: © mahJ/Christophe Fouin; Portrait of David Sassoon and sons, c. 1850. Photo: © Alamy; 'Adolphe Crémieux', Jean-Jules-Antoine Lecomte du Noüy, 1878. Musée d'art et d'histoire du judaïsme. Paris. Photo: © mahJ/Christophe Fouin; Mufti Al-Hajj Amin al-Husseini meeting with Adolf Hitler in 1941. Photo: © Getty Images; Portrait of Rector of Paris Mosque Si Kaddour Benghabrit. Photo: © Bibliothèque nationale de France; The establishment of the State of Israel, 14 May 1948. Photo: © Getty Images; Tents at Pardes Hanna, 1950s. Photo: © Getty Images; André Azoulay paying homage to Moroccan King Hassan II. Photo: © Cecile TREAL/Gamma-Rapho via Getty Images

ACKNOWLEDGEMENTS

As relations between Jews and Muslims worsened in the UK since the latest war between Israel and Hamas began in 2023, I wanted to put my knowledge and experience at the service of fostering conversations that go beyond today's polarized extremes. The result is this book. I wrote it based on research and conversations conducted the past three years in Bosnia–Herzegovina, Cyprus, France, Spain, Tunisia, Morocco, Portugal and the United Kingdom, and the past twenty-five years in Austria, Egypt, Germany, Greece, Israel and Palestine, Switzerland, and Turkey.

I was first introduced to the history of Jewish–Muslim relations as an undergraduate when I took Professor Jacob Lassner's 'Medieval Jewry in the Orbit of Islam' in the Department of Religious Studies at Northwestern University in 1991. Since then, I have pursued the topic in my teaching, publications, and research. Relocating to the UK over a dozen years ago and teaching at the London School of Economics and Political Science has crystalized my ideas. A conversation with Avi Shlaim proved eye-opening.

I first presented this book as a Mosse Lecture at the Humboldt University in Berlin, and I thank the organizers, Ulrike Freitag, and the audience for their insightful questions and comments. My writing was improved by the Silk Road Slippers writing workshop team – Alexandra Pringle, Alex von Tunzelmann and Faiza Khan – and my dozen fellow writers who shared their writing in Marrakesh. I am grateful to Theresa Truax who helped me see the forest for the trees. Thanks to James Nightingale for cutting the text down to size without sacrificing its meaning. Robert Davies made the text even more clear and tolerated my endless revisions. Aaqil Ahmed, Mirjam Brusius, Brian Catlos, Moez Khalfaoui, Louis Fishman, David Motadel, Daniel Schroeter, Adam Sutcliffe, and James Walters offered important corrections and valuable suggestions for revisions. I also thank my agent Adam Gauntlett who again connected me to the best publisher, and Nick Humphrey, Georgina Difford, and the entire team at Profile Books who guided the book from idea to words on the page.